Just Practice

A Social Justice Approach to Social Work

Janet L. Finn, Ph.D.
Department of Social Work
University of Montana
and
Maxine Jacobson, Ph.D.
Department of Social Work
University of Montana

Exclusive marketing and distributor rights for U.K., Eire, and Continental Europe held by:

Gazelle Book Services Limited
Falcon House
Queen Square
Lancaster
LA1 1RN
U.K.

eddie bowers publishing co., inc.
P.O. Box 130
Peosta, Iowa 52068-0130 USA

www.eddiebowerspublishing.com

ISBN 1-57879-046-8

Printed in the United States of America.

9 8 7 6 5 4 3

In memory of my father, Tom Finn, and in gratitude to the many women and men, young and old, in Chile and the U.S. who have taught me so much about the meaning and power of social justice work.

To my cousins Gilbert and Lillian Garber (Gillian) who taught me the meaning of family and helped me to appreciate the importance of history. L'shalom v'da'at.

Contents

Introduction

Chapter 1
Imagining Social Work and Social Justice

Chapter 2
Looking Back

Chapter 3
Values, Ethics, and Visions

Chapter 4
Just Thinking: Theoretical Perspectives on Social Justice-Oriented Practice

Chapter 5
Just Get Started: Engagement

Chapter 6
Just Understanding: Teaching-Learning

Chapter 7
Action and Accompaniment

Chapter 8
Evaluating, Reflecting on, and Celebrating Our Efforts

Chapter 9
Just Futures

Reflections and Actions

Chapter One

Chapter Two

Chapter Three

Chapter Four:

Chapter Five

Chapter Six

Chapter Seven

Chapter Eight

Chapter Nine

List of Figures

Acknowledgements

Just Practice has been shaped by so many people and experiences. The references and bibliography offer only one perspective on thinking that has influenced this book. *Just Practice* is also the product of ongoing reflection, action, and dialogue with students, community members, "clients," colleagues, and friends. We would like to thank social work students at The University of Montana and the University of Michigan who have engaged in the theory and practice of social justice work and utilized and critiqued the action/reflection moments used in the text. Their critiques and suggestions have been invaluable in shaping the book. We also express our gratitude to colleagues Jennifer Stucker, Eastern Washington University, Ryan Tolleson Knee, University of Montana, Lynn Nybell, Eastern Michigan University, and Linwood Cousins, University of North Carolina-Charlotte for their thoughtful conversations, critiques, and reviews that have strengthened *Just Practice*. Our thinking and practice have been challenged and transformed through ongoing relationships and conversations with mentors and friends. We would like to thank Norm and Connie Waterman, whose long-term commitment to just practice made a difference in state-based social services in Montana; Rosemary Sarri, whose indefatigable dedication to social justice has influenced two generations of social work practitioners, educators, policy makers, and researchers; Michael Reisch, whose important work on the history, politics, and future of social work has helped shape the framework of *Just Practice* and continues to challenge and inspire; Paul Miller for his important contributions to social justice work in Montana; and Judy Smith, Kate Kahan, and the women of WORD (Women's Opportunity and Resource Development) and WEEL (Working for Equality and Economic Liberation) who live Just Practice every day.

Preface

Social work in the 21st century faces profound challenges. While advances in information and communication technologies have shrunk distances of time and space, the expansion of the global market has contributed to a widening gap between rich and poor. We are experiencing both global aging and increasing rates of child poverty. The displacement and migration of human populations in response to war, economic dislocation, and environmental disasters pose challenges to states and notions of state-based welfare. More than fifty years have passed since the signing of the Universal Declaration of Human Rights, yet violations of those rights continue worldwide. "Terrorism" has become a subject of everyday conversation as the U.S. has come to confront its vulnerability in the world. On the U.S. front, the state-based social safety net continues to erode as welfare responsibilities devolve to local communities and charities and systems of care and control are increasingly privatized. Political leaders espouse family values at the same time that increasing numbers of children are placed in out-of-home care. Social work in the 21st century calls for new ways of thinking and acting in order to address these challenges and realize our professional commitment to social justice. *Just Practice* responds in a critical and integrated way to these concerns and offers new possibilities for theory and practice.

Just Practice introduces a new framework for social work that builds upon five key themes: *meaning*, *context*, *power*, *history*, and *possibility*. How do we give meaning to the experiences and conditions that shape our lives? What are the contexts in which those experiences and conditions occur? How do structures and relations of power shape people's lives and the practice of social work? How might a historical perspective help us grasp the ways in which struggles over meaning and power have played out and better appreciate the human consequences of those struggles? We argue here that meaning, power, and history are key components to understanding the "person-in-context." It is from that culturally, politically, and historically located vantage point that we appreciate constraints and imagine possibilities for justice-oriented practice. *Just Practice* prepares social workers to engage in new forms of collaborative assessment, planning, intervention, and institution building that 21st century practice demands.

Just Practice is based on a pedagogy of popular education that envisions knowledge development as a collaborative teaching-learning process. We argue that a participatory process, grounded in dialogue and critically attuned to questions of power and inequality, is fundamental to social justice work. The text is designed to facilitate participatory learning in the classroom and to prepare students for participatory approaches to *engagement, teaching/learning, action, accompaniment, evaluation, critical reflection* and *celebration,* the seven core processes of the Just Practice Framework. Linkages among practice, research, and policy are integrated throughout the text. We pay particular attention to the diversity of social work practice and to the possibilities of transforming spaces of inequality, oppression, and marginality into spaces of hope, places of connection, and bases for action.

Just Practice is written with an audience of students in U.S. schools of social work in mind. However, we believe that meaningful engagement with questions of social justice demands a global perspective. We draw on the history of social justice in U.S. social work and beyond U.S. borders to expand our thinking. In this age of transnational movements of people, power, and information, social work practice needs to embrace a commitment to social justice that crosses national, geographic, cultural, and disciplinary boundaries. *Just Practice* provides possibilities and tools for thinking globally even when we are engaged in the most "micro" and "local" levels of practice.

Just Practice is the product of a three-year process of collaboration, dialogue, and reflection on our own experiences as social work practitioners and educators. It reflects our ongoing efforts to grapple with the tensions and contradictions of the profession and our place within it. We are both U.S.-born white women with ties to working-class communities and rural places. Both of us have lengthy histories of employment in human services (child welfare, juvenile justice, chemical dependency treatment, sexual abuse investigation and treatment, and foster care). We both decided at particular points in our careers to leave direct social work practice and pursue doctoral education. We needed to reflect on our practice, challenge the limits of our understanding, and explore alternative theoretical and practice possibilities. As our paths crossed through these journeys, we began to talk and work together. Through our many conversations, a vision of *Just Practice* took shape. With the help of students and colleagues, we translated that vision into words. We look forward to expanding the vision in dialogue with our readers.

Introduction

> "Social work as we know it to-day was born of a sense of responsibility to society. So ran the report of the Committee on Education for Social Work at a recent National Conference of Charities. But that statement does not bring us very far on the road to knowing what social work really is. Is it charity? Is it social reform? Is it professional doing good and earning one's living by it? Is it doing for people what they cannot do for themselves? Is it 'an effort to perfect social relationships?' If you applied for membership in a Social Workers' Club and gave any or all of these qualifications, would you be accepted? Nobody knows."
>
> Arthur James Todd (1920) - *The Scientific Spirit and Social Work*

An Invitation and Challenge to our Readers

Welcome to the complex and dynamic terrain of social work. Some of you will be reading this book because you are planning to pursue a career in social work. Perhaps your image of social work is still fuzzy, waiting to be developed in the coming weeks and months. Others may encounter this book after years of experience in the social work profession. Perhaps your own life and work experiences, political commitments, or concerns about people's everyday struggles for survival, rights, and dignity have brought you to these pages. You may have a clear image of social work practice in mind. Depending on your experience, it may be one you wish to emulate, or it may be one you wish to change.

We invite you to accompany us on this journey into social work and social justice. This is not a guided tour where the reader is the passive recipient of the guides' wisdom. Rather, this is a journey that we take together, teaching, learning, and creating knowledge as we go. *Just Practice* is a different kind of book. It is not a collection of "facts" about the practice of social work. It does not offer much in terms of cookbook "solutions" to various human problems. *Just Practice* is a foundation and starting point for ongoing dialogue and critical inquiry, which, in turn, can serve as a base for your own critical and creative practice of social work.

We invite you to be more than a reader of the text. We challenge you to be an active participant in crafting the possibilities for bridging social work and social justice. We pose more questions than answers. We offer learnings from our experience and that of others, and we invite you to do the same. We challenge our readers and ourselves to walk the talk of social justice in our daily practice of social work. So, unbuckle your seatbelts and prepare for the journey. Social justice-oriented social work practice is neither spectator sport nor sedentary activity.

Why Just Practice?

Many textbooks have been written about the practice of social work. Why do we need another one? What does *Just Practice* offer that is different from the books that have come before it? *Just Practice* puts social work's expressed commitment to social justice at center stage. We offer a framework for thinking about and practicing social work that embraces and engages with the visions, hopes, and challenges of building and living in a more just world. It is one thing to say that social workers are "against" injustice or "for" social justice. It is another to translate that claim into an integrated model for practice.

We draw knowledge and inspiration from many committed social work practitioners, scholars, and activists who have come before us. We explore the contradictions in the field of social work where rhetoric of social justice was often inconsistent with practices of containment and control (Abramovitz, 1998). We seek insight from those who have lived the consequences of unjust social arrangements and from those who have posed challenges to injustice only to find their voices silenced and their contributions neglected in the history of social work practice (see Reisch and Andrews, 2001). They have pushed us to challenge our own certainties about the world and to open ourselves to transformative possibilities. We grapple with the tensions and contradictions that have shaped the history of the social work profession, and we challenge readers to do the same. The writing and reading of textbooks are not only intellectual exercises;

they are also forms of political practice. What stories are told and which ones are omitted? How are the stories told interpreted and put to use? We invite you to question, talk back, and challenge us throughout this journey.

To meet these ends, *Just Practice* is interactive in design, structured to engage readers in an action-reflection dialogue about the challenges and possibilities of what we term "social justice work." *Just Practice* examines the interplay of social work and social justice in historical and cross-national contexts, explores shifts in the profession's orientation and value base over time, and compares diverse approaches to social work across a range of social and political contexts. This examination sets the stage for exploring the processes and developing the skills of justice-oriented social work.

Just Practice is informed by contemporary directions in social and cultural theory (e.g., feminist, social constructionist, practice, and critical race theories), which attend to questions of meaning, context, power, history, and possibility in understanding and shaping processes of individual and social change. We encourage readers to examine the social construction of human problems and their solutions and the ways in which the language and labels of helping professions map onto practices of caring, containment, and control. Questions of gender, class, race, and sexual identity are explored not as "issues" of "populations at risk" but as key axes around which practices of and beliefs about inequality and difference are structured, reinforced, and contested. We challenge readers to examine the classism, heterosexism, and racism embedded in social life, and in social work itself, before turning attention to "target populations." We argue that ongoing critical questioning of one's own certainties is a central component of social justice work, and we create opportunities for self-reflection throughout the text. Likewise, readers are asked to explore alternative ways of thinking and acting in the world that are informed by these diverse perspectives.

A Story of Social Work Practice

What is Social Work and How Do We Tell its Story?

There are many ways to tell the story of social work practice. Some stories offer a chronology of social work's emergence as a profession. Others have analyzed social work's preoccupation with profession-building activities, arguing that it has strayed from its commitment to the poor and concern for social justice in the process (Specht & Courtney, 1994; Wenocur & Reisch, 1989). Some recount the tensions and debates that shape the field, with particular attention to social work's vacillation between providing social service and promoting social change (Withorn, 1984). Some describe the diverse arenas in which social workers practice, such as child welfare, mental health, and gerontology, and the knowledge base and skills needed for each. Most U.S. texts refer only to domestic influences on social work thought and practice. A few seek to illuminate the contributions of both insiders and outsiders who challenge the profession's priorities, practices, and very reason to be. Each account offers a partial view, shaped by the beliefs, values, and perspective of the narrator.

We have made the claim that *Just Practice* tells a different sort of story about the practice of social work. You may be asking: "Different from what?" As an entry point to the Just Practice approach, let us tell *one* story of social work practice. We draw from a range of historical and contemporary social work literature in telling a story of the emergence of the practice of social work and its evolution, shifts, and debates over the course of the 20th century. This story provides readers with a common frame of reference, a rough sketch of the profession, if you will. We invite you to return to this sketch as you make your way through the text. What would you erase? What would you elaborate? What would you challenge? How would you write the story of social work practice to mark the starting point of a journey into social justice work?

According to the *Social Work Dictionary* (Barker, 1995) social work constitutes "the professional activity of helping individuals, families, groups, or communities to enhance or restore their capacity for social functioning and for creating societal conditions favorable to that goal" (p. 4). Miley, O'Melia, and DuBois (1998) describe social work as a practice that involves enhancing people's problem solving and coping capacities, linking people to resources and services, promoting humane and just social services systems, participating in the development of social policy, engaging in research, and changing adverse social conditions. Both of these statements encompass the dual focus on individual needs and social conditions that has long been a source of tension in the profession. Further, given the breadth and generality of these definitions of professional social work practice, it seems that contemporary social workers, like their foremothers and forefathers, still struggle to define what they do. It seems as if social workers face an ongoing quandary as the opening quotation to this introduction suggests: Am I in the social work club? Is it a club I want to belong to? Let's take a look at the formation of the club and the struggles over what constitutes membership.

How Social Work Came To Be

The practice of social work in the U.S. emerged alongside and in response to the contradictions and crises of late 19th and early 20th century industrial capitalism. It began as an outgrowth of the charities and corrections movement in the 1890s. Industrialization, immigration, and urbanization challenged the social order of things. Widespread poverty, the growth of urban slums, and the challenges of "assimilating" culturally different groups posed social, economic, and political problems for the young nation. Two fundamentally different modes of intervention, the Charity Organization Societies and the Settlement House Movement, emerged in response to these conditions. The Charity Organization Societies saw social problems to be the result of individual deficits, such as lack of moral character, training, discipline, or personal capacity. They sought to intervene through "scientific philanthropy," that is, a systematic and painstaking effort to identify personal shortcomings and provide proper support and guidance. The Settlement House Movement, in contrast, focused on the social environment and lack of understanding that contributed to poverty and personal strife. They sought change through education and social action. Thus, the emergent forms of social work practice were in tension with one another from the start, with one emphasizing person-changing interventions and the other focusing on the social environment and the need to change social conditions. Both, however, sought a systematic, scientific approach to their work, variably influenced by the emerging disciplines of psychology, sociology, and psychiatry. These organizations also became vehicles for the entry of women into the newly forming helping professions and into social welfare policy arenas.

The Professionalization of Social Work

By the turn of the 20th century social workers were staking claims to their body of knowledge and systematizing their methods of diagnosis and technologies of intervention. The community-based education and action orientation of the Settlement House Movement did not fit well with the emerging image of professional practice. Social workers shifted their energies toward person-changing approaches and the expanding array of tests, measurements, and technologies that informed those approaches. The work of Sigmund Freud, the father of psychiatry, was influential in shaping thought about psychodynamic processes and furthering the individual treatment approach. Social casework, modeled after the medical approach to diagnosis and treatment, became the hallmark of the social work profession. Mary Richmond's classic text *Social Diagnosis* (1917) became the foundation for social casework. Importantly, Richmond both embraced the scientific approach to investigation and diagnosis and advocated for attention to the social context of individual experience. Richmond saw the need to appreciate a person's history in order to get to the root cause of the problem. She envisioned social diagnosis as an interpretive as well as investigative process. Her work contributed to an understanding of the "person-in-environment" perspective, which continues to be a fundamental premise in social work practice.

In the early 1900s, social work practitioners were working hard to build the profession. They were forming organizations, staking claims to a base of knowledge and skills, establishing programs of professional study, and defining casework as their primary professional commodity. Despite these efforts, the professional status of social work practice remained in doubt. In a 1915 speech to the National Conference of Charities and Corrections, Dr. Abraham Flexner posed the question, "Is social work a profession?" His answer cast doubt on social work's professional status, given its propensity for low-paid, altruistic practice. He claimed that social work lacked both a systematic body of knowledge and theory and societal sanction to act in a particular sphere, characteristics he saw as fundamental to a profession (NASW, 1977, p. 485; Specht and Courtney, 1994, p. 87). Flexner's pessimistic view fueled efforts to establish social work's credibility as a profession.

Following World War I, social work embraced a psychoanalytic approach. Throughout the 1920s, social workers sought to legitimize their practice through close affiliation with psychiatry and medicine, two burgeoning professions closely aligned with the rhetoric and practice of the scientific method. Psychoanalytic casework became a predominant mode of practice as social workers crafted specializations in mental health and in psychiatric and medical social work. Between 1923 and 1929 the Milford Conference, a group representing social casework agencies, convened to create a model for social work intervention across various fields of practice. They claimed social casework as the purpose and method of social work practice. The casework approach placed emphasis on individual experience, the worker-client relationship, and helping the client properly adjust to prevailing social standards (Johnson, 1998, p. 23). In 1929 Porter Lee, the president of the National Conference on Social Work and Dean of the New York School of Philanthropy, proclaimed that social work was no longer about cause (social activism) but about function (service) (Lee, 1930). Specht and Courtney (1994) write:

> Porter Lee… announced the end of social work as a social movement. The 'service,' he said (by which he meant the function of professional social work), would henceforth have top priority. The 'movement' (by which he meant the cause of social reform and betterment) would have to take a back seat. (p. 88)

These factors combined to enhance social work's status and credibility as a profession and to simultaneously move the developing profession away from work with the poor.

The Professional Domain and Debates

By the 1930s schools of social work were expanding, and professional organizations were well established. With the passage of a range of new social legislation in the wake of the Depression, social workers began to expand their professional domain into planning, management, and service delivery in public bureaucracies as well as in private charities. While there was a growing interest in group work, an individualist ideology continued to dominate practice. Within the practice of social casework itself, differing perspectives emerged. Proponents of the Freudian-influenced "diagnostic" school were challenged by the rise of what became known as the functional school.

The "functional" approach to social casework began to be developed in the 1930s. Influenced by the work of Otto Rank, the approach embraced a more optimistic and growth-oriented view of human nature than that expressed in the more determinist Freudian model. The functional approach was characterized by a view of clients as self-determining and of the social work relationship as a helping process that releases the client's power for choice (NASW, 1977, p. 1554). Functionalists challenged the "diagnosis" school of social casework. They differentiated helping from "treatment" and argued that the practice of social work is a helping process that involves giving focus, direction, and content in the context of relationship. According to proponents of the functional school of social work practice, the purpose of social work is:

> …the release of human power in individuals, groups, and communities for personal fulfillment and social good and the release of social power for the

> creation of the kind of society, social policy, and social institutions that make self realization most possible for all men. (NASW, 1977, p. 1281)

The functionalists emphasized the importance of process, respect for human dignity, and concern that every individual have the chance to reach his or her potential.

The functionalists' view was at odds with social work practitioners of the diagnostic school who constituted the majority of the profession at the time. One of the foremost thinkers of the diagnostic school was Gordon Hamilton. As a casework practitioner and educator, she was an influential voice in social casework theory. Hamilton recognized Freud's contributions to casework and the power of psychodynamic processes. At the same time, she argued for social workers to retain a commitment to poor families and to the ways in which social and economic factors contribute to personal distress (NASW, 1977, p. 518). Hamilton was a strong advocate for linking social casework, social welfare policy, and social action. Her diagnostic approach called for appreciation of both the objective situation and the client's subjective interpretation of the situation. She describes the helping process as the interplay of study, diagnosis, and treatment. Her 1940 text, *Theory and Practice of Social Casework,* became a definitive text in articulating the diagnostic approach. The philosophical and theoretical differences between the diagnostic and functionalist schools of social casework were the source of ongoing debate throughout the 1940s. Although we can see the influences of both schools in social work thought and practice today, the two views were seen as antithetical at the time. A serious rift occurred in the profession as proponents of the two schools vied for control over the direction of social casework practice.

During this era, social group work and community organization became more broadly recognized as methods of social work practice. Some group workers adhered to the functionalist school and others to the diagnostic school. For example, Hamilton recognized the importance of group theory and process in understanding the dynamics of family. Social workers engaged in the development of theories and methods of group work as a means for effecting individual and interpersonal change. With the growth of human service bureaucracies, the 1940s also saw a growing interest in community organization to tackle larger scale or "macro" issues. The field and practice of social planning became a more recognized component of social work practice (Johnson, 1998, pp. 23-24). The social work profession came to identify itself in terms of three key aspects of practice – casework, group work, and community organization – and to prepare practitioners with expertise in a particular field. However, the bulk of practice efforts continued to be directed toward person-changing interventions.

Steps Toward Synthesis and a Generalist Approach

By the 1950s, social workers were seeking a synthesis between the diagnostic and functional approaches to practice. They explored the underpinnings of the social work-client relationship and the principles, such as acceptance, individualization, promotion of client self-determination, and confidentiality, that would promote growth and change (Biestek, 1957). Their work in articulating principles of social work practice continues to guide practice today. In 1957, Helen Harris Perlman proposed a new conceptualization of social casework that brought together the functional and diagnostic approaches. She articulated casework as a problem-solving process that reframed "diagnosis" as a broader process of assessment and incorporated the functionalists' assumptions about the potential for human growth and competence. Her more encompassing approach had implications not only for social casework. It also provided a theoretical link among the multiple approaches to social work practice from casework to group work and community organization (Perlman, 1957).

Social workers were influenced by developments in sociology, psychology, and communication theory in the post-war years. They began to articulate the practice of social work in terms of five central concepts – assessment, person-in-situation, process, relationship, and intervention (Johnson, 1998, p. 27). They drew on emerging theories of relationship, psychosocial development, group process, and systemic interaction. By 1970, social work practice was conceptualized as a problem-solving process that could be applied at multiple levels – from the individual to the group, organization, and community. Some practitioners challenged the division of social work in terms of casework, group work, and community organization and called for a unified approach to practice that addressed social work's dual focus (Bartlett, 1970). In 1973, Allen Pincus and Anne Minahan published *Social Work Practice: Model and Method*, which incorporated a systems perspective and put forth a model of social work as a process of planned change (See Chapter Four for further discussion of systems theory and its contributions to social work theory and practice). Their work provided a foundation for what has come to be known and widely accepted as a "generalist" approach to social work practice.

Over the past 30 years, social workers have developed and laid claim to a generalist approach as the foundation for social work practice. The generalist approach is, in many ways, an attempt to weave together various threads of influence on the profession. The generalist approach addresses the importance of the interplay of persons and larger systems in the process of assessment and intervention. It recognizes the centrality of relationships in the helping process and sees the process of change as patterned, sequential, and unfolding over time. Miley, O'Melia, and DuBois (1998) describe generalist social work as:

> ...an integrated and multileveled approach for meeting the purposes of social work. Generalist practitioners acknowledge the interplay of personal and collective issues, prompting them to work with a variety of human systems – societies, communities, neighborhoods, complex organizations, formal groups, families, and individuals – to create changes which maximize human system functioning. (p. 9)

The generalist perspective that encompasses individual concerns and social conditions is often highlighted as a unique and defining feature of social work practice. However, as Landon (1999) notes, there is no agreed-upon definition of generalist practice among social workers. In many ways, this late 20th century meeting of the social work minds harkens back to the conundrum of social work expressed 70 years earlier.

For a century, social work practice has struggled to negotiate the tensions of what has been constructed as a dual mission – responding to individual human needs and to the social conditions that contribute to those needs. At the same time, social workers have been concerned with establishing themselves as a legitimate profession with the authority, sanction, and expertise to claim a portion of the helping profession turf. The efforts of professionalization have often worked at cross-purposes to the values of social justice, with social workers distancing themselves from rather than engaging with broader struggles for social, political, and economic justice. As Stanley Witkin (1998) has noted, person-changing interventions continue to dominate the profession, despite expressed professional values of social justice. Witkin challenges social workers to ask why this is so. Today, most social work texts introduce students to a generalist approach to social work practice. It provides a foundation upon which more specialized approaches to practice are developed. (In Chapter Four we develop more recent trends toward strengths- and empowerment-based practice.)

Telling A Different Story

So, what is the moral to this story of social work practice? We contend that the moral of the story lies in both what the story tells and what it omits. This story of social work practice highlights key aspects of the "official story," the one passed down from teacher to student in many social work texts. It is a story that gives largely a "view from above" – social work practice as seen by the makers of theory and method and the builders of the profession. It is a story of social workers talking to and past other social workers as they try to build and legitimize a profession of helping. It is a story that leaves out the political, historical, and cultural context of social work practice. It is a story that silences many voices of critics inside and outside of the profession who have challenged the direction of practice and posed alternatives. It is a story devoid of the politics of practice, and of the political consequences for those who engaged in radical forms of practice and claims for social justice (Reisch & Andrews, 2001). And it is a story with no "view from below," that is, from the perspectives of those affected by adverse social conditions. We argue that by passing down this story from teacher to student, we reproduce and promote a partial view of social work, one that emphasizes person-changing interventions and adaptation to social conditions.

Just Practice tells a different sort of story, one that looks to and beyond the leading men and women in building the profession. It is in part a reclamation project, recovering the histories, stories, and the sense of urgency and possibility that sparked the imagination and fueled the commitment of those engaged in social justice work. We argue that justice-oriented social work practice is informed by critical dialogue with both noted molders and shapers of the profession and with those whose stories have been silenced and excluded from the official history. We need to ask what is at stake in the telling of a story. How might a different sort of story inform a different sort of vision for social work practice in the present and future? *Just Practice* tells a story of the meanings, contexts, power, histories, and possibilities of social work and its awkward embrace of social justice. The *Just Practice* story informs a new way of imagining and practicing what we call "social justice work."

Plan of the Text and Overview of the Chapters

Just Practice presents an innovative and needed intervention in theory and skills for social work practice. Its central theme, a social justice-oriented approach to social work, reflects the mandates of the Council on Social Work Education to better integrate themes of social justice and diversity, concerns of marginalized and vulnerable populations, and social science knowledge into the theory and practice of social work. *Just Practice* responds in a critical and integrated way to each of these concerns. It provides a new framework for social work that articulates the linkage of epistemology, theory, values, and skills of practice.

Just Practice is divided into nine chapters in which the five key themes of meaning, context, power, history, and possibility and the seven core processes of engagement, teaching-learning, action, accompaniment, evaluation, critical reflection and celebration are developed. The text itself is designed to be interactive and to provide a model for integrating theory and practice. Each chapter contains numerous action and reflection exercises in which substantive material is accompanied by hands-on opportunities for individual or group action, skill development, and critical reflection. Each chapter begins with an introduction and overview of the central themes to be addressed. At the end of each chapter is a story, a case study, resource, or a set of examples that exemplify the integration of social work and social justice, or provide an opportunity for synthesizing material presented in the chapter. These are designed to engage readers as partners in dialogue in the teaching-learning process, develop critical thinking skills, and promote practice competence. Discussion questions and suggested readings are included at the end of each chapter to stimulate further critical inquiry.

Chapter One begins the process of imagining social work within a social justice context and examining the challenges and possibilities this poses for the social work profession. Readers are introduced to ways of conceptualizing social work and social justice, the linkage between them, and the implications for practice. International meanings of social work are presented that further explore the cultural, historical, and political context of practice. The five key concepts of the Just Practice Framework - meaning, context, power, history, and possibility - are introduced, developed, and illustrated through exercises and examples.

Chapter Two examines the practices, actors, institutions, and contexts involved in the emergence of social work as a profession. The chapter examines the significance of history and a historical perspective on social work practice. Readers are invited to explore the silences, shifts, and omissions in the history of social work and to consider the implications for contemporary social work. Special attention is paid to the contributions of advocates and activists whose histories have been largely ignored or erased from the social work canon. The chapter foregrounds the economic and political contexts that shaped the profession and practice of social work in the 20th century. Readers are presented with a long view of social work history and the tensions therein. The chapter highlights the Rank and File movement, the Great Depression, and McCarthyism as aspects of historical knowledge that are essential to understanding the course of contemporary social work practice.

Chapter Three examines the concept of values, the practice of valuing, and the relationship of values to social work practice. Readers are introduced to the core values of the profession as articulated by the NASW Code of Ethics. We explore values and ethics in context, look at the historical evolution of the Code of Ethics, and examine alternative conceptualizations of social work ethics. A comparison of ethical principles developed in diverse national and international contexts illustrates the interplay of politics, history, and values. The discussion moves from a broad perspective on values and valuing to the personal level and engages the reader in the work of self-assessment regarding personal and professional values. The chapter presents The Universal Declaration of Human Rights as a foundation for ethical practice and introduces the concept of an "ethics of participation" as a starting point for social justice work.

Chapter Four addresses the concept of theory and the practice of theorizing. We challenge perspectives that confine theory to the world of "experts." Instead, we explore theorizing as part of our human capacity and concern for "making sense" of the world and our experience in it. Examples are used to illustrate a step-wise process of theory development and the need to be informed makers and users of theory. The relationship of theory to the standpoint and values of the theorist is examined. The chapter reviews the dominant theories shaping contemporary social work practice and critiques each approach in terms of its strengths and limitations. We introduce a range of critical social theory, including feminist, critical race, and practice theories, and consider their implications for social justice work. The core processes of the Just Practice Framework – engagement, teaching-learning, action, accompaniment, critical reflection, evaluation, and celebration - are presented and defined. We conclude the chapter with a matrix of queries that link the core processes to the five key concepts of *Just Practice*.

Chapter Five develops the skills, activities, and issues involved in the process of engagement. Readers are encouraged to explore the meaning of engagement as both a process and a commitment. Engagement provides the entrée to social justice work in community, organizational, and interpersonal contexts. We develop the concept of anticipatory empathy as a time for self-reflection and preparation for engagement with the context of and participants in the change process. We explore a range of listening and communication skills central to the process of engagement. These include observation; attending to issues concerning trust, power, and difference; exploring meanings and interpretations; and respecting resistance. We pay particular attention to engaging groups, given the importance of collaboration in social justice work.

Chapter Six introduces and defines the core process of teaching-learning and the importance of teamwork for justice-oriented social work practice. Readers are introduced to the processes of mutual aid that contribute to effective teamwork. We reframe the assessment process as one of co-learning and examine issues of power and positionality in the teaching-learning process. Readers are introduced to alternative conceptualizations of power and to the skills and techniques of conducting a power analysis. The chapter provides guides and tools for systematic inquiry into communities and a community context of practice. We present several traditional and alternative methods for teaching and learning about people in familial, communal, and historical contexts. We create opportunities for readers to reflect on their cultural meaning systems and learn through difference.

Chapter Seven introduces and defines the core concepts of action and accompaniment. Readers explore the thinking and skills of action and are introduced to the roles of social justice work. We develop strategies for participatory planning and decision-making and for animating and activating the change process. Readers are introduced to skills and strategies for negotiating difference, addressing anger, building coalitions, and engaging in policy practice. We consider the possibilities of popular education for engaging people in the daily issues that affect their lives. The thinking and skills of accompaniment are explored as well as the learning potential inherent in the accompaniment process.

Chapter Eight presents the final three core processes of evaluation, critical reflection, and celebration. We explore diverse approaches to and assumptions about evaluation and questions of reliability and validity therein. We discuss the role of the researcher as *bricoleur* and consider the possibilities of participatory approaches to evaluation that include the voices of people in the issues that concern their lives. Several examples of participatory research illustrate the wisdom of citizen involvement in the formation, planning, and implementation of community projects. The chapter looks at why evaluation is important, what processes and players should be assessed, and how to go about conducting evaluations. Various methods of participatory evaluation are described, providing a wide array of options for evaluation design and the dissemination of results. Cautions, considerations, and challenges of the work are discussed. We address the process of critical reflection, explore its linkage to social justice work, and consider ways to develop reflective capacity. The core process of celebration is presented and developed as an integral component of justice-oriented practice. We introduce readers to a variety of ways in which to think about and celebrate the joy and beauty of the work.

Chapter Nine begins by looking at predictions concerning the future of social work and ways in which social workers can prepare themselves to address these concerns. Readers revisit the Just Practice Framework and are asked to consider its usefulness as a flexible structure to address the fundamental issues that shape contemporary social work practice. Lastly, fifteen principles of social justice work synthesized from the Just Practice approach are presented and discussed. The chapter ends with a case study of a Missoula, Montana-based organization whose processes and practice exemplify social justice work for the 21st century.

Chapter 1

Imagining Social Work and Social Justice

"Social justice is the end that social work seeks, and social justice is the chance for peace."

Former Attorney General Ramsey Clark, 1988[1]

Chapter Overview

In Chapter One we locate social work within a social justice context. We introduce the idea of social "justice" work and its importance for rethinking social work practice. We examine broadly accepted contemporary definitions of social work in the U.S. and in an international context, and we ask you the reader to think about the implications of these diverse meanings for social work practice. This sets the stage for locating concepts of social work in cultural, political, and historical contexts. Likewise, we discuss meanings of social justice and pose the following questions: What is the relationship between social work and social justice? What are the common goals? How do their definitions and context shape the form and content of social work practice? How are both social work and social justice tied to questions of difference, inequality, and oppression? We introduce the Just Practice Framework and its five key concepts – meaning, context, power, history, and possibility. The Just Practice Framework will provide the foundation for integrating theory and practice. Key concepts are developed and illustrated through examples and reflection and action exercises. They push us to explore taken-for-granted assumptions about reality – those ideas, principles, and patterns of perception, behavior, and social relating we accept without question. As learners, this moves us beyond the bounds of familiar and comfortable contexts to challenge old beliefs and ways of thinking. We consider the power of language and image in shaping understandings of social problems and social work. We bring a critical lens to the social work profession itself as a site of struggle and seek to open up challenges and possibilities of that struggle.

Social "Justice" Work

The Idea of Social Work

Each of us has an idea or an image of social work that we carry around in our heads. For some of us this image comes from our experiences as paid or volunteer workers in a community service organization. Others of us may have known social work from the other side, as a "consumer" of services, perhaps as a child in the foster care system or a single parent receiving welfare benefits. Some of us may have little or no experience with the practicalities of social work. Perhaps we have taken a course or two, or we have known social work mainly through its representations in the media. Nonetheless, we have an impression, a mental image if you will, of social work and what we envision ourselves doing as social workers. Accordingly, each of us has an idea or an image of social justice. For some of us, social justice relates to notions of equality, tolerance, and human rights. Others of us know social justice through its absence, for example, through personal experiences of injustice, degradation, and violence.

Meanings of Social Work and Social Justice

Take a minute to consider what social work and social justice mean to you. Most of us take these constructs for granted. We assume we know their meaning. At the same time, we believe others hold these same meanings. What is social work? What is social justice? Now think about the interrelationship between the two. Might some meanings of social work and the ways in which it is practiced neglect considerations of social justice? What images come to mind? Or might these meanings be inextricably linked, making it difficult to tell them apart? What examples of social work practice illustrate the interrelationship of social work and social justice?

Linking Social Work and Social Justice

The reflection exercise above asks you to think about the meanings of social work and social justice, to explore their dynamic relationship, tensions, and harmonies, and to make concrete applications to the world of practice. Our bias is that social work should have a middle name – social "justice" work. Thinking about social work as social justice work accomplishes several important goals:

- Social justice work highlights that which is unique to social work among the helping professions (Wakefield, 1988a,1988b). Few other professions have identified challenging social injustice as their primary mission (NASW, 1996).
- Social justice work implies that we take seriously the social justice principles of our profession and use these to guide and evaluate our work and ourselves as social workers. In subsequent chapters, we will introduce you to early justice-oriented social workers such as Jane Addams and Bertha Capen Reynolds, who have already paved the way.
- Social justice work reminds us of the need for a global perspective on social work as the crisis of late capitalism leaves its mark on our own and distant economies, creating greater gaps between the rich and the poor and transgressing the boundaries of nations and national sovereignty (Giddens, 1991; Keigher & Lowery, 1998; Korten, 1995; Ramanathan & Link, 1999).

Some might say that giving social work "justice" as a middle name is hardly necessary. After all, women and minorities in the U.S. struggled long and hard and finally won the right to vote, and there is some evidence of increased equality between men and women. The United Nations Universal Declaration of Human Rights (see Appendix, p. 397) celebrated its 50th anniversary in 1998. But much injustice persists. Violations of human rights and struggles to retain, recognize, and realize these rights continue on many fronts. Those struggles force us to ask: What conditions of humanity are necessary for people to claim the most basic of human rights – the right to have rights (Arendt, 1973, p. 296 cited in Jelin, 1996, p. 104)?

The Challenge of Social Justice Work

Struggles for women's rights continue around the world in the face of persistent gender inequality. Loss of rights have contributed to increased rates of depression

FIGURE 1.1

Global Distributions of Income. Source: UNDP Human Development Report, 1992

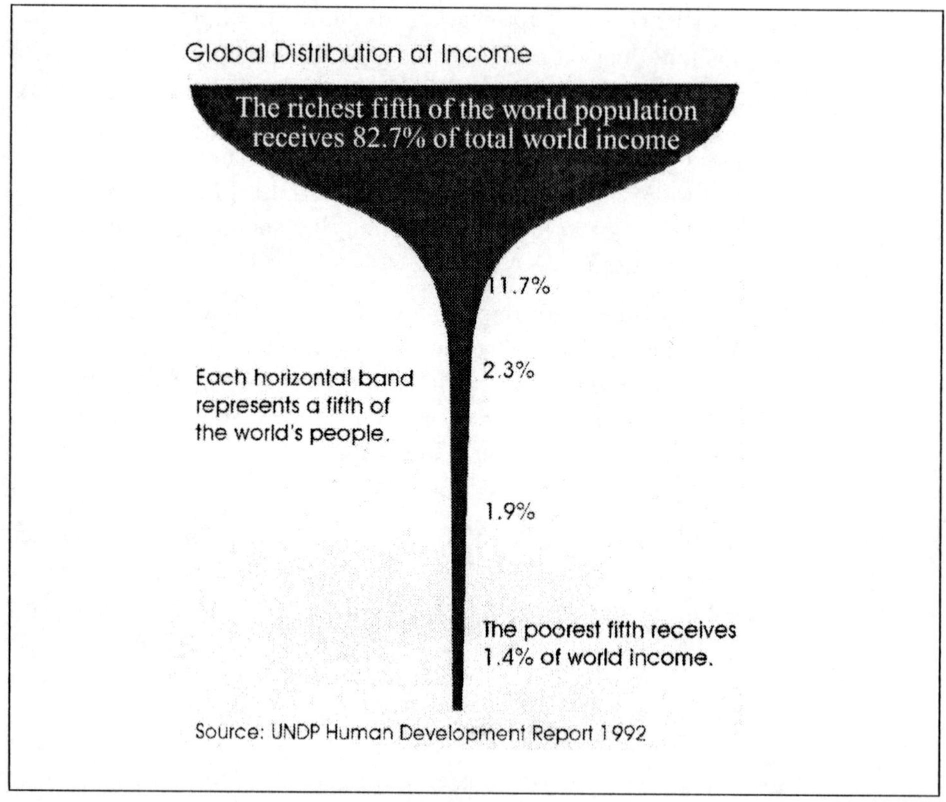

and suicide among women (Goodman, 1998). In 1999, lawmakers in the state of Michigan decided that prisoners no longer count as "persons" under state law, thus limiting their protection under the Civil Rights and Americans with Disabilities Act. Prisoners have been denied a basic aspect of humanity. The rights associated with citizenship and "home" are denied to 23 million refugees displaced from their homelands by war and its social, political, and economic devastation (Lyons, 1999, p. 110). How can we speak of universal human rights when more than one billion people earn less than one dollar per day, when nearly one billion adults are illiterate and when more than one billion people lack access to safe water (ILO, 1998; Reisch, 1998a)? These are some of the challenging questions we face when we take social justice work seriously.

Taking a Global Perspective

Ideological precepts written into the U.S. Constitution over 200 years ago speak of "equality and justice for all." These same precepts fuel and continue to feed the fires of revolutionary claims and movements around the world. Yet as Figure 1.1 indicates, the contemporary world is characterized by brutal inequalities of wealth and poverty. Like the tipsy champagne glass image it suggests, it is an unstable world with no solid foundation. We argue that the foundation must be built from the bottom up with the help of social justice work. We believe that meaningful engagement with questions of social justice demands a global perspective. We will be reflecting on the history of social justice in U.S. social work, and we will draw from knowledge and practice beyond U.S. borders to challenge and expand our thinking. In this age of transnational movements of people, power, and information, we need an approach to social justice work that crosses national, geographic, cultural, and disciplinary boundaries and expands our thinking along the way.

We find inspiration in the work of international social work and social welfare organizations for framing a global understanding of social work. For example, the International Federation of Social Workers (IFSW), in trying to develop a global definition of social work, has identified three concepts that are key to justice-oriented social work: *peace, environment,* and *citizenship* (IFSW, 1997). Oxfam, a non-governmental international aid and development organization, argues that we have to attend to the basic rights of subsistence and security before we can address other human rights (Lyons, 1999, p. 9). Karen Lyons, a social work educator at the University of East London, argues that if we are to think of social work and social justice on a global scale for the 21st century, we need to think about poverty, migration, disasters, and their global impacts (1999, p. 14). Clearly, these challenging issues are interrelated, and we will return to them to explore patterns that connect throughout the book.

Challenging Our Thinking

The challenge of social justice work calls for challenging ways of thinking. That is, we have to challenge ways we have been taught to think and critically engage with perspectives that disrupt our certainties about the world, our assumptions about what is "right," "true," and "good." Our (the authors') own perspectives have been shaped by diverse influences ranging from African American and Italian social theorists and activists (W.E.B. Dubois and Antonio Gramsci) to French philosophers (Michel Foucault), Brazilian and U.S. popular educators (Paulo Freire and Myles Horton), "first" and "third" world feminists (bell hooks, Patricia Hill Collins, Chandra Mohanty), critical cultural theorists in Europe and North America (Anthony Giddens, Pierre Bourdieu, Sherry Ortner, Dorothy Smith) and indigenous scholar-activists (Linda Tuhiwai Smith). We include a selected bibliography of these works at the end of this chapter.

There are common threads among these diverse influences on our thinking. They have challenged us to examine the social construction of reality, that is, the ways we as human beings use our cultural capacities to give meaning to social experience. They pose questions about the relations of power, domination, and inequality that shape the way knowledge of the world is produced and whose view counts. Moreover, they call on us not only to question the order of things in the world but also to be active participants in social transformation toward a more just world. To understand social justice work and to engage in justice-oriented practice, we must first think critically about its component parts by looking at meanings of social work and social justice.

Meanings of Social Work

Struggles Over Definition

Perhaps there are as many meanings of social work as there are social workers. When adding movement across time and place to the mix, the meaning of social work becomes a kaleidoscope of interpretations. As noted in the Introduction, there have been struggles for control of social work's definition since its inception. Partially, this struggle is attributable to what some believe is social work's dualistic nature and location, wedged between addressing individual need and engaging in broad-scale societal change (Abramovitz, 1998). A justice-oriented definition of social work challenges the boundaries between the individual and the social. Instead, it considers how society and the individual are mutually constituting – we individually and collectively make our social world and, in turn, through our participation in the society and its institutions, systems, beliefs, and patterns of practice, we shape ourselves and are shaped as social beings. The progressive U.S. social worker, educator, and activist Bertha Capen Reynolds (1942) called this "seeing it whole." Historically, forces both within and outside social work have influenced its dominant definition. In Chapter Two we follow the course of these tensions and strains as we explore the history of social work in the U.S.

First, we start with some commonly held contemporary definitions of social work in the U.S. and then move to alternative and international definitions. We ask you to consider this question: How is it that a profession that calls itself by one name – social work – can have such diverse meanings and interpretations? Also, think about the different contexts that shape these meanings and how these translate into different ways of conceptualizing social work practice. How do countries with different dominant value systems from the U.S. practice social work? How do these practices differ from our own? Do other countries understand the meaning of social justice differently than we do in the U.S.? How do you explain this difference?

Official Meanings

Council on Social Work Education. Professions have formalized organizations that oversee their functioning, determine standards, and monitor practice. The Council on Social Work Education (CSWE), for example, is the accrediting body for schools of social work education in the U.S. CSWE's primary role is to ensure the consistency of knowledge, values, and skills disseminated through social work education. CSWE describes the purpose of the social work profession as the "enhancement of human well-being and the alleviation of poverty and oppression" (1994, p. 135). This purpose is realized through the following activities:

1. The promotion, restoration, maintenance, and enhancement of the functioning of individuals, families, groups, organizations, and communities by helping them to accomplish tasks, prevent and alleviate distress, and use resources.
2. The planning, formulation, and implementation of social policies, services, resources, and programs needed to meet basic human needs and support the development of human capacities.
3. The pursuit of policies, services, resources, and programs through organizational or administrative advocacy and social and political action, so as to empower groups at risk and promote social and economic justice.
4. The development and testing of professional knowledge and skills related to these purposes. (CSWE, 1994, p. 135)

National Association of Social Workers. The National Association of Social Workers (NASW) is the largest organization of professional social workers in the U.S. It works to enhance the professional growth and development of its members, both bachelor of social work (BSW) and master of social work (MSW) practitioners. NASW also helps to create and maintain professional standards and to advance social policies. The Preamble to the Code of Ethics (1996) contains NASW's definition of social work:

> The primary mission of the social work profession is to enhance human well-being and help meet the basic human needs of all people, with particular attention to the needs and empowerment of people who are vulnerable, oppressed, and living in poverty. A historic and defining feature of social work is the profession's focus on individual well-being in a social context and the well-being of society. Fundamental to social work is attention to the environmental forces that create, contribute to, and address problems in living. (NASW, 1996)

Comparing the Two. What do the CSWE and the NASW definitions of social work mean to you? How do these definitions compare to your own definition? Like other definitions of a profession, these embody the value systems of their creators and their supporters. These organizations have the power to officially sanction not only how we define social work but also how we outline the parameters of its practice and articulate the values believed to be central to the work. This official sanction refers not only to words and to the language we use to describe what we do but also to the actions we take that exemplify our practice.

Shifting Meanings

What meanings are communicated by CSWE and the NASW in their definitions of social work? How might these meanings guide practice? For example, think of yourself working with children and families or in a health care or community center. Given these definitions, how might you relate to the people, the neighborhoods and the communities with whom you will work? Would your relationships be top/down, bottom/up, or side-by-side? How do social workers promote, restore, maintain, and enhance human functioning? Who defines groups at risk? Now let's shift our vision from "inside" the profession and look at meanings of social work from the "outside," through the eyes of those whom social work is meant to serve. For example, imagine yourself to be:

- a homeless person turned away from a full shelter for the third night in a row;
- a nine-year-old child in a county receiving home awaiting temporary placement in a foster home;
- a school principal making a referral of child neglect to the local child protection services office;
- a welfare recipient whose monthly benefit has been reduced for failure to provide proper documentation of a part-time day care arrangement.

How would you define social work through these eyes? As you look at the meaning of social work from an outsider point of view, does this change your conceptions of social work?

CSWE and NASW are powerful meaning-makers in defining the nature of social work. More often than not, social work texts include these definitions of social work in their introductory chapters (for example, see Dubois & Miley, 1999; Morales & Sheafor, 1998; Sheafor, Horejsi, & Horejsi, 2000). Although these definitions are certainly the most dominant, they are not the only ones. Next, we will look at some alternative meanings, those that go against the official grain, or, at the very least, critique social work's dominant definitions. These meanings of social work support its inescapable political nature and ask us to consider issues of power as they concern social workers' relationships to those with whom they work. As you read the following definitions, write down what you think might be factors that shape different meanings of social work and definitions of the helping relationship.

Other Meanings to Consider

Social Work as a Transformative Process. Paulo Freire (1974,1990), a Brazilian educator, argues that social work is a transformative process in which both social conditions and participants, including the social worker, are changed in the pursuit of a more just world. Paulo Freire is noted for his contributions to popular education, a social-change strategy through which critical literacy opens liberatory possibilities (We address popular education further in Chapter 7.). Freire taught literacy to Brazilian peasants through group discussions that prompted critical reflection on their life conditions. Weiler (1988) writes that Freire:

> . . . is committed to a belief in the power of individuals to come to a critical consciousness of their own being in the world. Central to his pedagogical work is the understanding that both teachers and students are agents, both engaged in the process of constructing and reconstructing meaning. (p. 17)

In Freire's view, social work involves critical curiosity and a life-long, committed search for one's own competence; congruence between words and actions; tolerance; the ability to exercise impatient patience; and a grasp of what is historically possible. Similarly, Stanley Witkin (1998) asks us to consider the qualities of social work in its adjective form: ". . .pertaining to a human service activity (social work practice) or form of social inquiry (social work research) that is focused on individual and social change from a contextual perspective informed by human rights, social justice, and respect for people" (p. 486).

Social Work as a Political Process. David Gil (1998, pp.104-108) defines social work by outlining what he sees as its principles. Similar to other scholars of social work (Barber, 1995; Fisher, 1995; Reisch, 1997, 1998b), he asks us to affirm the undeniable political nature of social work and its value system. He believes social work should confront the root causes of social problems by moving beyond mere technical skills. Like Freire, Gil asserts that social work must promote critical consciousness, that is, an awareness of the interconnected nature of individuals, families, and communities, and a society's political, economic, and social arrangements. To achieve these ends, Gil contends that social workers must strive to understand their own and others' oppression and consider alternative possibilities for human relations. He, too, argues that there is need for fundamental social change.

Five Simple Principles. These ideas about social work resonate with Bertha Capen Reynolds' (1934, 1942, 1963) contributions to the social work profession. Reynolds was a social worker and social work educator in the U.S. whose life and work modeled a commitment to progressive, justice-oriented social work. Reynolds' work bridged the individual and social. Like many social workers of her time, she was trained in psychoanalytic techniques, but she never lost sight of the contextual nature of individual problems. Reynolds set forth "five simple principles" she believed necessary to the practice of social work:

1) Social work exists to serve people in need. If it serves other classes, it becomes too dishonest.
2) Social work exists to help people help themselves. . . we should not be alarmed when they do so by organized means, such as client or tenant or labor groups.
3) The underlying nature of social work is that it operates by communication, listening, and sharing experience.
4) Social work has to find its place among other social movements for human betterment.
5) Social workers as citizens cannot consider themselves superior to their clients as they do not have the same problems (Reynolds, 1963, pp. 173-175).

Reynolds' understanding of social work continues to inspire individuals interested in social change as attested to by the progressive social work organization founded in her name – formerly the Bertha Capen Reynolds Society, now the Social Welfare Action Alliance.

International Meanings of Social Work

International Federation of Social Workers' Definition. Much can be learned about social work when we step outside U.S. soil and learn about its meaning on different social, political, and cultural terrain. Professional organizations other than CSWE and NASW have set forth definitions of social work. For example, the International Federation of Social Workers (IFSW) is a global organization founded on the principles of social justice, human rights, and social development. IFSW achieves these aims through the development of international cooperation between social workers and their professional organizations. In 2000, IFSW developed a new definition of social work. It replaces a definition adopted in 1982 and reflects the organization's effort to address the evolving nature of social work. It reads as follows:

> The social work profession promotes social change, problem solving in human relationships and the empowerment and liberation of people to enhance well-being. Utilising theories of human behaviour and social systems, social work intervenes at the points where people interact with their environment. Principles of human rights and social justice are fundamental to social work.[2]

Global Interdependence. In keeping with international concerns and connections, other social workers continue to forge new definitions of social work that capture global concerns and ideals. For example, Link, Ramanathan, and Asamoah (1999) contend that a global approach to social work must view the world as a system of interdependent parts, account for the structures that shape human interactions, and challenge culture-bound assumptions about human behavior. For instance, they point out the culture-bound nature of concepts such as "independence," "self-esteem," and "motivation" that have been predicated on particular modern Western concepts of personhood and the self. They call on social workers to reach for constructs that can relate to many differing cultures "such as interdependence of self (with family, village, and community life), social well-being, empowerment, resilience, reverence for nature, artistic expression, and peace" (p. 30).

Social Work in Nicaragua

Let's consider how social work has been conceptualized in Nicaragua, where the field's own history is inseparable from the country's struggles for democracy. During the 1980s under the Sandinista government, spaces opened for experimentation in participatory approaches to community and social development. Social work, however, was originally viewed by the Sandinistas as a tool of the old regime, serving to mediate class struggle rather than support the revolutionary process. With the revolution, they argued, social work would no longer be necessary (Wilson & Whitmore, 1995, p. 66). In 1980 the country's only social work school was closed to new admissions. Wilson and Whitmore write that social workers began to mobilize in order to implement the national call for participation. In 1984, social work was redefined as "service to the process of social transformation" (Wilson & Whitmore, 1995, p. 67). The social work program reopened at this time at the Universidad Centroamericana with the stated mission to prepare its graduates to "facilitate the democratic process of popular participation in the structural changes required to achieve a more just and egalitarian society" (p. 67). The mission further states that intervention at the microsocial level must serve the interests of the popular sectors, involving: "the sensitization and organization of these popular sectors [which] allows them to make themselves subjects of their own transformation" (ETS, 1984). The overriding mission of social workers, then, is to enhance "the organized participation of people in the development of the society . . .as the practice of popular democracy" (ETS, 1984, cited in Wilson & Whitmore, 1995, p. 67). What does this story teach us of the meaning of social work? Can we understand the meaning of social work outside of the social, political, or cultural context in which it is practiced? How might stepping outside our usual frame of reference inform us of the tightly woven connections between social work, politics, economics, and social arrangements?

Defining Social Work in Diverse National Contexts. We have chosen several examples to illustrate the meaning of social work in diverse national contexts. We hope these will spark your interest to investigate other countries on your own. Here are some clues about social work. See if you can guess the country. (Answers in endnotes for this chapter.)

- Social work in this country bears some resemblance to social work in the U.S. because these countries share a common border. Social work started here at approximately the same time as it did in the U.S. This country exported practice methods and philosophies from the U.S. and Great Britain. In fact, the country's longest serving prime minister was employed at Hull House in Chicago as a caseworker when it was under Jane Addams' leadership. In part, this explains the commonality of social services and policies adopted in this country during the 1940s when compared to the U.S. (e.g., income security programs, minimum wage legislation, old age security, family allowances, and unemployment insurance). There are also some startling differences. For example, this country created a universal medical care program and a comprehensive and integrated social assistance program in the 1960s (Hopmeyer, Kimberly, & Hawkins, 1995). What factors might account for the different meanings of social work in this country and the United States?
- Social work in this country is barely ten years old. Imagine a country where it was believed there was no need for social workers. Better yet, imagine a country where, due to the social, political, and economic structure, there "should be no need" for social workers. Only recently has this country begun to consider social work a part of its agenda because of a major shift from socialism to a market

economy (Driedger, 1995). How will social work configure itself against this newly forming landscape?

- As part of this country's historic ideology, for hundreds of years a good society was a society where the masters at different levels were just and took good care of their subordinates (Frick, 1995). Beginning in the 1930s, this country evolved away from the concept of the state as the benevolent caretaker toward a new ideology based on solidarity, democracy, equality, and brotherhood. "Individual rights as citizens were stressed together with the belief in collective solutions to social problems and a preparedness to use the state as an instrument for such solutions" (Frick, 1995, p. 146). What is the meaning of social work in a country that bridges individual rights and collective solutions?
- During the Allied occupation of this country after World War II, social work and a system of social welfare were introduced based on models developed in the U.S. This is a good example of a powerful meaning-maker spreading its ideas of social work to another country. While it may be efficient to buy something ready-made, often a good fit to new surroundings is sacrificed. However, in this country's case there was no other choice. With conquest and domination came the power to impose meanings on a culture and its people. Old meanings were replaced with new ones and in the process, the importance of cultural congruence was ignored. While this country continues to forge an indigenous system of social welfare, social casework is still the dominant model of practice (Matsubara, 1992).
- This was the first country in South America where social work emerged, beginning in 1925. Influenced initially by European models of practice, the profession underwent a transformation during the mid-to-late 1960s. The theories of Paulo Freire, the noted Brazilian popular educator mentioned earlier, who was living in exile in this country, had a transformative influence on both the practice and the teaching of social work. Consciousness-raising and rethinking the power dynamics inherent in the social worker/client relationship became points of reflection that changed the nature of practice. Social workers in this country contested the individualistic, apolitical emphasis of social work in other countries, especially the imperialistic, colonizing model evident in the U.S. (Jimenez & Aylwin, 1992).[3]

Meanings of Social Justice

Understanding Social Justice in Context

Notions of justice have been debated since the days of Socrates, Plato, and Aristotle. Like social work, the meaning of justice is contextually bound and historically driven. The ideas we have about social justice in U.S. social work are largely derived from Western philosophy and political theory and Judeo-Christian religious tradition. The Social Work Dictionary defines social justice as "an ideal condition in which all members of a society have the same rights, protection, opportunities, obligations and social benefits" (Barker, 1995, p. 354). Our conceptions of justice are generally abstract ideals that overlap with our beliefs about what is right, good, desirable, and moral (Horejsi, 1999). Notions of social justice generally embrace values such as the equal worth of all citizens, their equal right to meet their basic needs, the need to spread opportunity and life chances as widely as possible, and finally, the requirement that we reduce and where possible, eliminate unjustified inequalities.

Perspective of U.S. Catholic Bishops' Conference

Some students of social justice consider its meaning in terms of the tensions between individual liberty and common social good, arguing that social justice is promoted to the degree that we can promote positive, individual freedom. Others argue that social justice reflects a concept of fairness in the assignment of fundamental rights and duties, economic opportunities, and social conditions (Miller, 1976, p. 22, cited in Reisch, 1998a). For example, in their 1986 pastoral letter, the U.S. Catholic Bishops' Conference outlined three concepts of social justice[4]:

- **Commutative justice** calls for fundamental fairness in all agreements and exchanges between individuals or private social groups (U.S. Catholic Bishops, 1986, #69).
- **Distributive justice** requires that the allocation of income, wealth, and power in society be evaluated in light of its effects on persons whose basic material needs are unmet (#70).
- **Social justice** implies that persons have an obligation to be active and productive participants in the life of society and that society has

> a duty to enable them to participate in this way (#71). The meaning of social justice also includes a duty to organize economic and social institutions so that people can contribute to society in ways that respect their freedom and the dignity of their labor (#72).

Rawls' Theory of Justice

A number of social workers and social theorists concerned about questions of social justice have turned to the work of philosopher John Rawls (1971) and his theory of justice. For example, Wakefield (1988a) argues that Rawls' notion of distributive justice is the organizing value of social work. For Rawls, distributive justice denotes "the value of each person getting a fair share of the benefits and burdens resulting from social cooperation" both in terms of material goods and services and also in terms of nonmaterial social goods, such as opportunity and power (Wakefield, 1988a, p. 193).[5]

Albee (1986) turns to Rawls' work on the characteristics of a just society to inform his thinking about the relationship between social injustice and psychopathology. According to Albee, Rawls recognizes that most people are quite able to say what they see to be "unjust." However, it is more difficult to talk about what a just society would look like. Rawls (1971) asks, what would be the characteristics of a just society in which basic human needs are met, unnecessary stress is reduced, the competence of each person is maximized, and threats to well-being are minimized? Rawls tries to imagine whether a small group of people, unmotivated by selfish interests, could reach consensus regarding the characteristics of a just society. In his book *A Theory of Justice* (1995), Rawls imagines such a small group, selected at random, sitting around a table. He places an important limit on this vision: no one at the table knows whether he or she is rich or poor; black, brown, or white; young or old. He assumes that, without knowledge of their own immediate identities, they will not be motivated by selfish considerations. Rawls concludes that the group will arrive at two basic principles:

1. Justice as Fairness: "According to this principle, each person has an equal right to the most extensive basic liberty compatible with a similar liberty for others" (Albee, 1986, p. 897).
2. Just Arrangements: "Social and economic inequalities are arranged so that they are both to the greatest benefit of the least advantaged

> and attached to offices and positions open to all under conditions of fair and equal opportunity" (Albee, 1986, p. 897).

From this perspective, society must make every attempt to redress all those social and economic inequalities that have led to disadvantage in order to provide real equality of opportunity. This demands a redistribution of power; the rejection of racism, sexism, colonialism, and exploitation; and the search for ways to redistribute social power toward the end of social justice (Albee, 1986, p. 897).

Social Workers Conceptualize Social Justice

Reisch (1998a) draws on Rawls' principle of "redress," that is, to compensate for inequalities and to shift the balance of contingencies in the direction of equality, in articulating the relationship between social work and social justice. He argues that a social justice framework for social work and social welfare policy would "hold the most vulnerable populations harmless in the distribution of societal resources, particularly when those resources are finite. Unequal distribution of resources would be justified only if it served to advance the least advantaged groups in the community" (Reisch, 1998a, p. 20; Rawls, 1995).

Similarly, Saleebey (1990, p. 37) has detailed what social justice means to social work:

> a). Social resources are distributed on the principle of need with the clear understanding that such resources underlie the development of personal resources, with the proviso that entitlement to such resources is one of the gifts of citizenship.
>
> b). Opportunity for personal and social development are open to all with the understanding that those who have been unfairly hampered through no fault of their own will be appropriately compensated.
>
> c). The establishment, at all levels of a society, of agendas and policies that have human development and the enriching of human experience as their essential goal and are understood to take precedence over other agendas and policies is essential.
>
> d). The arbitrary exercise of social and political power is forsaken.
>
> e). Oppression as a means for establishing priorities, for developing social and natural resources and distributing them, and resolving social problems is forsworn.

Summary

These important efforts help us to conceptualize the meaning of social justice and its relation to social work and to begin to map the challenging territory ahead. Even as these writers spell out principles of social justice, they reveal how complex the concept becomes as we try to translate it into policies and practices. And if we look closely at these brief discussions above, we see that they, too, are filled with certainties grounded in particular world views that value particular understandings of individual personhood, rights, equality, and fairness. However, as Lyons (1999) reminds us, these certainties may not fit with other culturally grounded conceptualizations of social relations or selfhood. How do notions of cultural rights, which are of critical importance to indigenous people, fit into these depictions of social justice? How should group or collective rights be recognized and addressed?

Similarly, there are particular understandings of resources, development, and compensation assumed in discussion of rights and justice that also may hold very different meanings to different groups. For example, the notion of monetary compensation for harm done to people or a group is a very historically, culturally, and socially particular idea. For many people, it is inconceivable, even offensive, to negotiate a material compensation for personal or social harm. These conceptualizations of justice also speak to broad societal responsibilities. These responsibilities cannot be readily confined to the concerns and obligations of particular states or nations. These are issues that cross borders. If we limit our focus on the situation of justice within a given nation-state, we miss the questions of fundamental inequalities among countries and the transnational policies and practices that maintain and justify them. Can one make meaningful claims for social justice in the U.S. if those claims are premised on the exploitation of people outside U.S. borders? As Lyons (1999) notes, citizenship as it is conceptualized and practiced at the national level is inherently exclusionary when we consider the differences in power and access to resources among states. If we take the principles of distributive justice, social justice, and environmental sustainability seriously then we have to develop an international or transnational perspective on what we mean by the obligations of citizenship. This is a big challenge, and one that we will keep with us as we build our road to social justice by walking it.

Thus far, we have been probing the multiple meanings of social work and social justice and the dynamic relationship between them. We have encountered differing perspectives about the nature of the profession, the meaning and power of social justice therein, and the implications for practice. In order to effectively engage with these diverse meanings and explore the interplay of social work and social justice, we need to examine questions of difference and the relationship of difference to forms and practices of inequality and oppression.

Thinking about Difference, Inequality, and Oppression

Beyond Diversity

The practice of social justice work and the complexities inherent in meanings of social justice call on us to examine questions of difference, inequality, and oppression. We will do so throughout the book, and we encourage all of us to do so in our everyday lives. It is not enough to talk about and celebrate human diversity. We need to go further and challenge ourselves to address the historical, political, and cultural processes through which differences and our ideas about difference are produced (Hill Collins, 1990; Dirks, Eley & Ortner, 1994). As Reed, Newman, Suarez and Lewis (1997, p. 46) argue, "recognizing and building on people's differences is important and necessary, but not sufficient for a practice that has social justice as a primary goal." For social justice work, "both *difference* and *dominance* dimensions must be recognized and addressed. Developing and using individual and collective critical consciousness are primary tools for understanding differences, recognizing injustice, and beginning to envision a more just society" (Reed et al., 1997, p. 46). We have to look not only at differences, but also at the ways in which differences are produced and given meaning. We are challenged to recognize and respect difference at the same time that we question how certain differences are given meaning and value. We need to work collectively to understand and challenge connections among forms of difference, relations of power, and practices of devaluation.

Difference

Let's think for a moment about the concept of difference. How do we categorize human difference? What are the "differences that make a difference," so to speak?

What meanings do we give to particular forms of difference in particular contexts? What meanings do we give to the categories through which social differences are named and marked? How do we construct images of and assumptions about the "other" – a person or group different from ourselves? Too often, the marking of difference also involves a devaluing of difference, as we have witnessed historically and continue to see today, for example, in the social construction of race, gender, or sexual orientation. Author H.G. Wells (1911) presents a classic example of difference and devaluation in his short story, "The Country of the Blind." Nuñez, an explorer and the story's protagonist, falls into an isolated mountain valley and is rescued by the valley's curious inhabitants. Once Nuñez realizes that all of the residents are blind and have no conception of "sight," he muses, "in the country of the blind the one-eyed man is king." He assumes that, by virtue of his sight, he is superior to the valley's residents. The residents, in turn, find Nuñez unable to respond to the most basic rhythms and rules of their society. They see him as slow and childlike, and they interpret his nonsensical ramblings about this thing called "sight" as another sign of his unsound mind (Wells, 1911). Wells skillfully illustrates the ways in which our constructions and (mis)understandings of difference are linked to assumptions about worth, superiority and inferiority, and ways in which they inform relations of domination and subordination. We will revisit these themes as we elaborate the foundations and possibilities of social justice work in the following chapters.

Meanings of "Race" and the Making of Difference

One of the most powerful social categories for making and marking human difference is that of "race." As social scientists have acknowledged, "race" is a social, not biological, concept. It is a complex social construction with profound human consequences. Read the American Anthropological Association's statement on race at the end of this chapter beginning on page 40 and consider the following question: Does this discussion of "race" inform or challenge your thinking? How so? Why is history important in understanding the concept of "race?" What questions does this raise about other categories of difference and the social meanings given to forms of human diversity? Where else do we see human difference constructed in terms of "rigid hierarchies of socially exclusive categories?" Is it possible to think of human difference outside of hierarchies and categories? How might a critical examination of the concept of "race" inform social justice work? Are there challenges you would pose to the crafters of this statement?

Positionality

We construct human difference in terms of cultural practices, gender, racial/ethnic identification, social class, citizenship, sexual orientation, etc. Our "*positionality*," or location in the social world, is shaped in terms of these multiple identifications. Our positionality configures the angle from which we gain our partial view of the world. For some, that is a position of relative privilege and for others a position of subordination and oppression. As Bertha Capen Reynolds reminds us, it is the mission of social justice workers to align themselves with those who have experienced the world from positions of oppression and work to challenge the language, practices, and conditions that reproduce and justify inequality and oppression. To do so we must recognize and learn from our own positionality, consider how we see and experience the world from our positioning in it, and open ourselves to learning about the world from the perspectives of those differently positioned. As Reed et al. (1997) contend:

> Although some people suffer a great deal more than others, positionality implies that each and every one of us, in our varied positions and identities as privileged and oppressed, are both implicated in and negatively affected by racism, sexism, heterosexism, homophobia, classism, and other oppressive dynamics. The recognition of positionality, and of one's partial and distorted knowledge, is crucial for individuals of both dominant and subordinate groups, or we all contribute to perpetuating oppression. (p. 59)

Interlocking Systems of Oppression

Patricia Hill Collins (1990), writing from her positionality as a black feminist woman, argues that we can not think of difference and domination in "additive" terms. Instead, she challenges us to critically examine interlocking systems of oppression, such as those of racism, classism, and sexism, their systematic silencing of "other" voices and ways of knowing the world, and their power in determining and (de)valuing difference. She asks us to examine our locations within these matrices of domination, recognize the critical perspectives of those who have experienced the world from positions of oppression, and engage in critical dialogue and action to challenge and change relations of power and domination that reproduce social injustice. Thus, in order to meaningfully engage in social justice work, we must start by both honoring difference and critically examining its production. We need to recognize our own positionalities in the social world and the fact that our worldviews are always partial and open to change. We have to "learn how to learn" about other people, groups, and their experiences (Reed et al, 1997, p. 66). We turn now to an overview of the Just Practice Framework, which will be our guide to that process.

The Social Justice Scrapbook

Each class member brings into class newspaper and magazine articles that illustrate value dilemmas and social justice challenges. Take time as a class each week to review and discuss one another's contributions to the scrapbook. As a class, build a collective archive of social justice over the course of the semester. One member of the class could take on the job of archivist, or the class as a whole might revisit the collection at the end of the term and decide how to organize and present the material gathered. Another option is to take time outside of class to review the scrapbook and reflect on the issues raised. What value dilemmas do you see? What "isms" play out in these accounts? What "isms" have you internalized? Where do you find your values most challenged? How would you address the challenge?

Just Practice Framework: Meaning, Context, Power, History, and Possibility

As we mentioned in the Introduction, the Just Practice Framework emerged from our own practice, reflection, and long-term dialogue regarding the meaning of social justice work and the challenges of linking thought and action. The process of integrating social work and social justice to build a coherent understanding of social justice work revolves around five key concepts and their interconnections: *meaning, context, power, history,* and *possibility*. These key concepts are the foundation of the Just Practice Framework. This framework brings together a set of interrelated concepts that help to explain social justice work and guide the development and implementation of just practice principles and skills.

Take a minute to consider the following questions: How do we give *meaning* to the experiences and conditions that shape our lives? What are the *contexts* in which those experiences and conditions occur? Who has the *power* to have their interpretations of those experiences and conditions valued as "true?" How might *history* and a historical perspective provide us with additional contextual clues and help us grasp the ways in which struggles over meaning and power have played out and better appreciate the human consequences of those struggles? And how do we claim a sense of *possibility* as an impetus for just practice? We will expand on these key concepts through this book. We begin with a brief introduction to each concept in this chapter to provide a foundation for future reflection.

Meaning

Meaning is often defined as the purpose or significance of something. All human beings are meaning-makers. We make sense of the world and our experiences in it through the personal lenses of culture, race, place, gender, class, and sexual orientation. We come to new experiences with a history that influences our ways of making sense of our circumstances. Sometimes we share meaning with others based on commonalities of social experience and life circumstances. Often, however, we differ from others in how we come to understand ourselves, others, and the events and circumstances surrounding our lives. Think for a moment about the partiality of our knowledge, the difficulty we have in fully understanding another person's experience or what sense this person makes of happenings and circumstances. For this very reason, in social work practice it is essential that we attempt to understand how others make sense of their world and the commonalities, tensions, and contradictions this creates as we compare their meanings to our own. At the same time we need to stay mindful of the partiality of our own understanding. Just practice means grappling with the ways in which we individually and collectively make sense of our worlds. Meanings can constrain us, keep us stuck, or create new possibilities for ourselves and the people with whom we work.

Searching for meaning requires reflexivity. This is the act of reflection, a process of self-reference and examination. It is a foundational skill upon which to build the knowledge base and skills of just practice. Although it may not appear to be the case, reflection takes practice. It requires going beyond surface content to contemplate meanings; to submerge oneself in thoughtful reverie; to question taken-for-granted assumptions about reality; to consider the significance of situations and circumstances; and to share these thoughts with others through critical dialogue and critical question posing. Critical dialogue "is the encounter between men [sic], mediated by the world, in order to name the world" (Freire, 1974, p. 76). It is a process of engagement with others to develop, recreate, challenge, and affirm meaning. Critical question posing differs from ordinary question posing. Critical questioning asks learners to make connections among seemingly disparate issues or events or to discover the underlying themes that resonate or have a pervasive influence for an individual, group, organization, or community.

Context

Context is the second key concept. Context is the background and set of circumstances and conditions that surround and influence particular events and situations. Social work's legacy, and what distinguishes it from other helping professions, is its fundamental view of individuals, groups, organizations, and communities within a larger framework of interactions. These considerations include cultural beliefs and assumptions about reality, and social, political, and economic relationships. Context shapes meaning and helps us make sense of people, events, and circumstances. We know this only too well when we take something (person or life event) out of context and attempt to understand it devoid of its surroundings. If we ignore context, our interpretation of a situation is myopic. We see only that which fits on the slide but nothing beyond the microscope. We miss the intricate connections, patterns, and dynamic relationships.

We often think of social work practice in terms of interpersonal, organizational, community, and socio-political contexts. While, for analytic purposes, we may focus on one at a time, our practice plays out in these multiple and mutually influencing contexts. Consider for a moment the context of agency-based social work practice. Social workers work in organizations situated in communities and neighborhoods. The characteristics of communities and neighborhoods differ. Some have an abundance of resources and helping networks and others have to make do with little but their own ingenuity. Communities and organizations have distinct cultures that include spoken and unspoken rules and established patterns of commonly shared values and beliefs. Organizations, for example, are generally funded by state, federal, or private sources, each of which mandates funding allocations, types of services, who can be served, and the rules and regulations for receiving services. As we expand our contextual horizons, we discover that state and federal policies are linked to services, and these also are embedded with assumptions about what constitutes a social problem and how it should be addressed. Policies are, in effect, cultural snapshots framed by particular assumptions and philosophies of what is true, right, and good. Think for a moment about how these various contexts influence and shape both the social worker and the work.

Rural Context of Practice

Imagine yourself in western rural U.S. You are a child protective service worker working in a two-person agency. The town you practice in has a population of barely 2,000 inhabitants, and the locals are quick to say there are more cattle than people. As the crow flies, the nearest metropolis is a full day's drive away. The community has few social service resources, and those that exist are staffed much like your own agency, mostly solo operations that are understaffed and overworked. Although policies that govern your work are decided in the halls of justice hundreds of miles down the road, they shape your daily existence from the supplies you are allocated to the procedures that structure your work. This ranching community takes pride in its rugged individualism. Families survive and thrive by sheer grit and stubborn determination during long winters where the wind-chill factor can reach 60 below. Take a few minutes to think about the various ways in which your child protection work might be affected in this situation by context. What comes to mind?

Power

Power is the third key concept. Numerous scholars have investigated its meaning and proposed interpretations ranging from the abstract to the practical. Some contend that the idea of power embodies purpose or intent. Dennis Wrong (1995, p. 2) defines power as the "capacity of some persons to produce intended and foreseen effects on others." Some have viewed power from a standpoint of exclusion, domination, and repression. However, Homan (1999, p. 136) argues that: "Power is not dominance. Dominance is the way some people *use* {emphasis added} power. Collaboration is the way other people use power." Power can be manipulative but it does not have to be. Foucault (1979) describes power as follows:

> What gives power its hold, what makes it accepted, is quite simply the fact that it does not simply weigh like a force that says no, but that it runs through, and it produces things, it induces pleasure, it forms knowledge, it produces discourse; it must be considered as a productive network which runs through the entire social body much more than as a negative instance whose function is repression. (p. 36)

There are many ways to conceptualize power. French sociologist Pierre Bourdieu (1984) writes about the importance of symbolic power. He describes symbolic power as the power to impose the principles of the construction of reality on others. He argues that this is a key aspect of political power. Others have pointed to the power of language and rhetoric, the power of emotion, and the power of collective memory as sources for resistance and motive forces for action on the part of people in less powerful positions (Freire, 1990; Gramsci, 1987, Kelly & Sewell, 1988; Tonn, 1996). Through a workshop they conducted in Tapalehui, Mexico, Janet Townsend and her colleagues learned that poor, rural Mexican women had something to say about power (Townsend, Zapata, Rowlands, Alberti & Mercado, 1999). The women, activists in grassroots organizations, joined academic women to discuss women's power, roads to activism, and possibilities for transformative social practice. Drawing from the women's on-the-ground experience, the authors identified four forms of power: 1) power over, 2) power from within, 3) power with, and 4) power to do. They describe *power over* as institutional and personal forms and practices of oppression that often serve as poor women's first reference point in discussion of empowerment. As women get out of their houses and come together to share their struggles and hopes with other women, they begin to discover the *power from within*. They discover *power with* others as they organize to address the conditions that affect their lives. They articulate the *power to do* in concrete, material terms, such as making money, designing projects, and getting funding. Through close attention to accounts of lived experience, the authors are able to present a nuanced view of the ways in which poor rural women give meaning to and negotiate the relations of power that affect their lives.

What meaning does power have for you? Who or what has the power to affect your own or another's behavior? How is power created, produced, and legitimized, and what are the varied ways in which it can be used? How might power influence the nature of the relationships you form in social work practice with those with whom you work and those for whom you work?

Meanings of Power

As a class, take turns bringing in images of what power means to you. The images may be of your own creation, photos or texts from magazines, a collage, etc. Describe these images in class, place them in a container with other classmates' contributions, and pass the container on to a classmate. The classmate has the responsibility of carrying the container home, adding his or her own image, and bringing the image and container back to the next class meeting. At the end of the term, as a class, engage in a collective decision-making process regarding what you wish to do with the images. For example, you could design a collage incorporating all of the images and hang it in a public place where it may evoke further dialogue. The exercise creates an opportunity to reflect on both individual and collective representations of power. It demands responsibility on the part of the participants, and it opens discussion regarding many forms of power.

Take a moment to think about how these understandings of power might translate into your work as a social worker. What does power mean to the social worker? Is it about control or being in charge? Does it connote expert knowledge or knowing what is right for others? To what forms and sources of power might you have access as a social worker? What sorts of cautions and challenges does power evoke in practice? Can you think of examples from social work that illustrate Townsend et al's notions of power over, power from within, power with, and power to do?

History

History is the fourth key concept. The dictionary defines history as "a chronological record of significant events (as affecting a nation, institution) including an explanation of their causes" (Merriam-Webster's Collegiate Dictionary, 1971, p. 395). Jenkins (1995, p. 20-21) describes history as being composed of individual discrete facts that paint a "picture of the past" made up of the impressions of the historian. History is also defined as a story or a tale, hinting that it might fall somewhat short on truth-value. This latter definition gets at the socially constructed, mutually constituted nature of knowledge (Gergen, 1999), which suggests that to understand history, it is important to know the storyteller. Clearly these definitions indicate that history is much more than an objective reporting of the facts.

Zinn (1995, pp. 7-9) illustrates well the inescapable ideological presence of the historian in *A People's History of the United States*. For example, he recounts the European invasion of the Indian settlements in the Americas and the heroizing of Christopher Columbus in the stories of history read by school children. Forgotten in most historical reports is an alternative story of America's "discovery, one less inclined to see the genocide of Indian people and their culture as a reasonable price to pay for progress" (p. 9). Zinn (1995) suggests that the closest we can come to objectively reporting the past is to consider all the various subjectivities in a situation. These subjectivities include the opinions, beliefs, and perceptions of the historian. Carr (1961) also reminds us of the importance of the historian and the historian's social and historical background when he tells us, ". . . the facts of history never come to us 'pure,' since they do not and cannot exist in a pure form; they are always refracted through the mind of the recorder" (p. 16). Innumerable factors affect perceptions. These include gender, race, class, religion, sexual orientation, and political ideology, to name a few. Whereas the historian may be able to accurately report chronology, that is when a specific event occurred, where it occurred, and the player involved, the event is storied through the layered nuance of the historian's perspective. History, then, is at best a partial perspective.

Paulo Freire (1990, p. 9) adds yet another dimension to the meaning of history and understands it as a critical factor in shaping the work of justice-oriented social workers. He envisions ordinary people as active players in its creation. Freire contends that we are historical beings, meaning that, unlike animals, we are conscious of time and our location in time. History is a human creation and we are continually making history and being shaped by history:

> As I perceive history, it is not something that happens necessarily, but something that will be made, can be made, that one can make or refrain form making. I recognize, therefore, the importance of the role of the subjective in the process of making history or of being made by history. And this, then, gives me a critical optimism that has nothing to do with history marching on without men, without women, that considers history outside. No, history is not this. History is made by us, and as we make it, we are made and remade by it. (Freire,1974, pp. 3-4)

This idea that we are all makers of history opens up spaces of possibility and hope as people engage with life to create history and be created by history. With these definitions in mind, let us consider why history is important to our work as social workers. The following reflection exercise offers an opportunity to reflect on why history matters.

Connecting with History

Take a moment to think about the life experiences that have shaped your decision to become a social worker. Share your story with fellow students in pairs or in small groups. When did you decide to become a social worker? What social, political, economic, familial, or cultural circumstances, situations, or events shaped your decision? What other careers had you considered? What made you change your mind? Or perhaps you are still undecided about your career goal. As you share your story with other classmates, do you discover similar influences that affected your decisions to become social workers? What do you notice about the histories of other students that differ from your own? How might history influence the way in which social work is practiced? Now take a moment to think of an important historical event occurring at the time of your birth, or during your formative years, for example, threat of nuclear war, the fall of the Berlin Wall, the Vietnam War, President Kennedy's assassination, the Challenger explosion, the passage of Roe v. Wade, or the September 11th attack on the World Trade Center. What historical events stand out, and how have they affected your way of perceiving or acting in the world? How might a historical perspective be helpful to your work as a social worker? Take a moment to write down a few reasons and discuss them with others.

Possibility

Possibility is the fifth key concept. This concept asks us to consider what is historically possible and to move beyond the past and the present to contemplate alternatives for the future. A sense of possibility enables us to look at what has been done, what can be done, and what can exist. It engages us in reflection, and helps us formulate a vision of something different. It is a way to get unstuck from deterministic, fatalistic thinking where "that which has been will always be." As historian E. P. Thompson reminds us, it is possible for people to make something of themselves other than what history has made of them (Thompson, 1966).

Possibility challenges us to think differently about practices, people, and programs. It draws attention to human *agency*, or the capacity to act in the world as intentional, meaning-making beings, whose actions are shaped and constrained, but never fully determined by life circumstances. Australian social work educators Anthony Kelly and Sandra Sewell (1988) write about "a trialectic logic," or a logic of possibility, as a key part of community building. They write: "the task of a trialectic logic is to grasp a sense of wholeness which emerges from at least three sets of possible relationships among factors... it is out of the context of their interdependent relationships that new insights into social realities can emerge, and hence new ways to solve problems" (pp. 22-23). As we expand our possibilities for thinking, we may change the way a problem is perceived and envision new possibilities for action. Kelly and Sewell exemplify the logic of possibility with the title of their book, *With Head, Heart and Hand.* They write:

> Knowing, feeling and doing describe three human capacities, each one important in itself. No one of these, by itself and without addition of the other two is enough. Even taken in pairs, no two are sufficient without the third:
>
> - **head and hand** (without **heart)** is a familiar combination in public life – the politician or public administrator whose feelings are blocked, or considered irrelevant;
> - **heart and hand** (without **head**) leads to impulsive and undisciplined action;
> - **head and heart** (without **hand)** leaves us stuck with knowledge and good intentions, but with no action direction to pursue.
>
> To bring all three together, in a piece of work or in a relationship or to an understanding of our context, is to expand a social reality to at least three factors. **Head, heart** and **hand** points to a quality of wholeness – even if an attempt at wholeness – in life and work. (pp. 23-24)

It is this spirit of hope and sense of possibility that we wish to infuse in the thinking and practice of social justice work. Throughout the text we will share the stories of courage and inspiration from people who have confronted contradictions and worked to transform oppressive life circumstances into spaces of hope, places of possibility, and bases for critical and creative action.

Probing the Possibilities

Take a close look at the figure on the following page. How many squares do you see? Now get together with a classmate. Compare numbers and the ways you counted the squares. Working together, can you expand the possibilities and find more squares? What are some other concrete examples of expanding the possibilities once you are able to see things from another perspective?

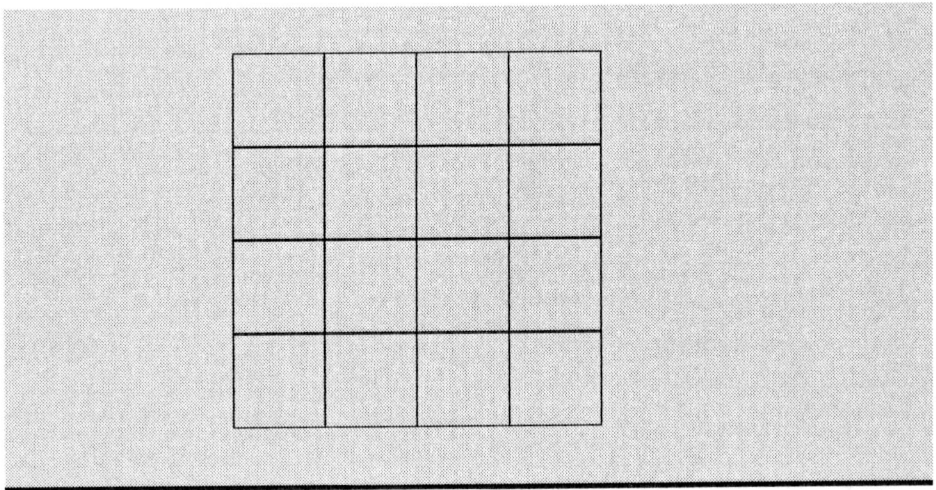

Putting It All Together

Meaning, context, power, history, and possibility and the ways in which they interrelate provide a framework for critical analysis (see Figure 1.2). They provoke us to question our assumptions about reality and make us look at how certain assumptions gain currency at certain moments in time. As a foundation for social-justice oriented social work practice these key concepts invite us to question received truths. We use them as a point of departure and a framework for reflection. How are certain ideas accepted as true? How have those ideas changed over time? What evidence is brought to bear to support their truth claims? What goes without saying in our assumptions and actions? How do rather arbitrary ideas about what constituted "correct" social relationships and behaviors, values, and concepts come to be seen as "natural" and "true"?

Think for a moment about some of the arbitrary concepts that shape the way we think and act in the world. For example, concepts of time and money, the side of the road on which one drives, or the people one considers to be family. Over time, these arbitrary and variable concepts have become structured, institutionalized, and rule-bound in differing sociocultural contexts. They have become infused with meaning. We have been learning about and absorbing those meanings just like the air we breathe since infancy. We have learned some of these rules so well that they seem natural, given, and absolutely true. They are so much a part

FIGURE 1.2

Key Concepts of Just Practice

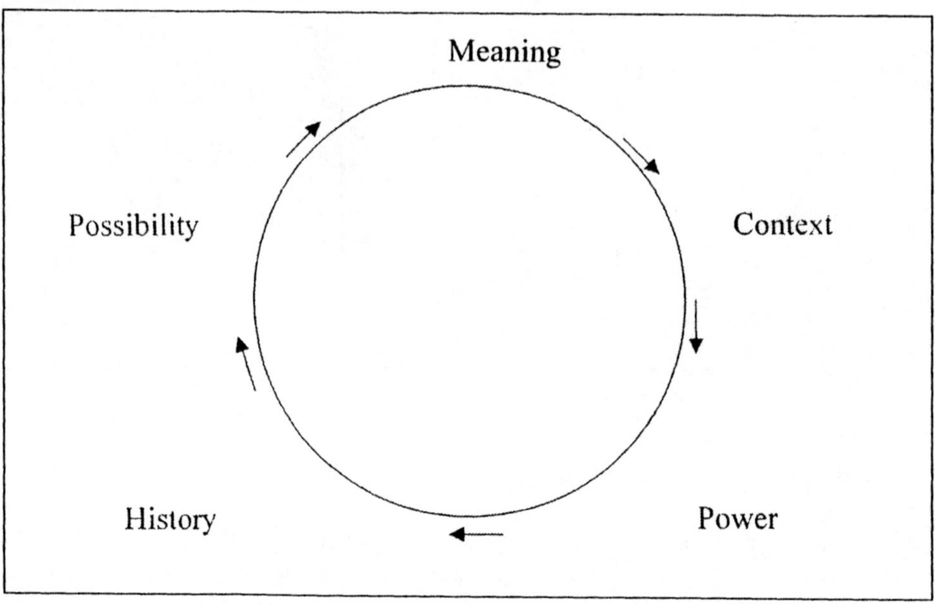

of our experience that they go without saying. If we encounter someone who lives by a different set of rules, our response is often to think that her rules are wrong while ours are right. In other words, the deep meanings of these taken-for-granted certainties have become intertwined with our power of judgment and our valuing of good and bad or right and wrong.

Social justice work challenges us to examine the social construction of reality, that is, the ways we use our cultural capacities to give *meaning* to social experience. It guides us to look at the *context* of social problems and question the relations of *power*, domination, and inequality that shape the way knowledge of the world is produced and whose view counts. It forces us to recognize the importance of *history* and a historical perspective to provide a window into how definitions of social problems and the structuring and shaping of institutions and individuals are time specific and contextually embedded. Finally, social justice work opens up the *possibility* for new ways of looking at and thinking about programs, policies, and practices, and to envision the people with whom we work and ourselves as active participants in social transformation toward a more just world.

The Five Key Concepts

Take a minute to reflect on something that is very meaningful to you. Perhaps it is a photo or letter that brings to mind a special person or event. Maybe it is a small daily ritual practiced with people you love, such as kissing your children goodnight. Or it might be a family or religious celebration in which you participate or a routine that is practically a part of who you are. Think about the meaning you give to and take from this object or action. How has that meaning been shaped? What are the contexts or the events and circumstances surrounding this object or action? Have these changed over time? Imagine the loss of this meaningful part of your life. Who or what might have the power to take it from you? How might you respond? These are questions about meaning, context, power, history, and possibility. We ask that you hold on to the images from this exercise as one way of staying personally connected to the key concepts of social justice work.

Chapter Summary

In this chapter we have examined the meanings of social work and social justice and the relationship between them. We have attempted to expand our thinking on the meaning of social work by looking beyond U.S. borders. We have argued that social justice works demands that we take questions of difference, inequality, and oppression seriously. In so doing, we are challenged to probe the ways in which differences are produced and how they map on to values. We have introduced five key concepts that constitute the Just Practice Framework, and we have offered opportunities for both action and reflection. We close this chapter with a powerful essay by John Brown Childs that provides an opportunity to reflect on the themes of meaning, context, power, history, and possibility. In Chapter Two we turn to questions of history.

Teaching-Learning Resource: Themes of Just Practice

The following essay poignantly addresses the themes of meaning, context, power, history, and possibility that are at the heart of social justice work. Take a moment to read and reflect on John Brown Childs' story. What feelings does the story evoke? How does he challenge dominant views of "race" and "difference"? What lessons for social justice work can be learned?[6]

Red Clay, Blue Hills: In Honor of My Ancestors

John Brown Childs

> In every place visited among the Sakalava we found events and names recalled by tradition still living in memory... we have heard the Sakalava invoke these names in all important activities of their social life and recall with pride these events...
>
> Charles Guillain (1845), cited in Raymond K. Kent, *Early Kingdoms in Madagascar, 1500-1700*

I must speak about my ancestors. It is from them that I have received the desire to contribute to the best of my ability to what I hope is constructive cooperation leading to justice, equality, and peace in the world. I owe it to them to make these comments. What I say in these pages flows from two great currents, the African and the Native American, whose conflux runs through my family and infuses my spirit today. In the 1990s, when I went to visit my family in Marion, Alabama, my cousin Arthur Childs, who had served as a lieutenant in World War II in Burma, and who was the family storyteller, took me immediately to the cemetery, where in the midst of red clay dust he told me the histories of those who had passed on.

The African-Malayo grandmother of my grandmother of my grandmother of my grandmother, known as The Princess to her captors, was born in Madagascar, an island peopled by populations from the Pacific and Africa. In 1749, the Princess was a member of a Madagascan delegation on board a French ship bound for France, where she apparently was to go to convent school. Their ship was captured by English privateers. All the Madagascans on board were captured and sold into slavery in the English colonies. My ancestress found herself in chains being sold as property to a Thomas Burke, a leading figure in North Carolina government, to be given as a wedding present for his new wife at a wedding ceremony in Norfolk, Virginia (Bond, 1972, 22).

The story handed down within both the Burke family and my relations is that when "the Princess" was brought first to the Virginia plantation where she began her career as a slave, the other enslaved Africans acknowledged her royal origin and gave her the respect due to one of her background" (Bond, 1972, 23).

The descendants of The Princess established their families in the red clay country of Marion, where they (as property of whites) had been transferred through the infamous network of the slave trade. Marion, in Perry County, Alabama, has for a long time been a dynamic wellspring in southern African-American life. Marion is where my father's forebears, Stephen Childs and family, created the Childs Bakers and Confectioners, Growers, and Shippers store on Main Street. This store was an economic bulwark of the African American community there. My father, born in the heart of what had been the slave-holding region of the southern United States, was named after John Brown, the revolutionary fighter who gave his life in the battle against slavery.

Marion is where James Childs and nine other African-Americans, newly liberated from slavery after the Civil War, established the first African American school, The Lincoln Normal School, in the late 1860's...

The school's teachers were housed in a building that had been taken away from the Ku Klux Klan, whose aim was to keep people of African descent in subordination and indignity...

Lincoln Normal School went on to become an influential African-American educational institution. Dr. Horace Mann Bond noted the broad community significance of the Perry Country Lincoln Normal School in his study of Black American Scholars, which analyzes the roots of southern African-Americans holding Ph.Ds after the Civil War...

Among my relatives influenced by Lincoln Normal was William Hastie, a civil rights legal advocate and the first African-American federal circuit court of appeals judge, as well as an important participant in President Franklin Delano Roosevelt's "Black Cabinet." In 1943 Hastie resigned a government position as assistant to the U.S. Secretary of War to protest over racial segregation of the African-Americans in the U.S. military.

My Childs family relations, along with other African Americans in Marion, worked in the midst of Ku Klux Klan country, to create Lincoln Normal School as a sustaining community in the midst of a dangerous, often lethal environment of racial oppression. They sought to use their roots in the rural and small-town Deep South as a basis for construction of a bastion of justice and dignity.

I was born in 1942 in the Roxbury ghetto of Boston, Massachusetts. As a small child I lived in a housing project called Bataan Court. My birthplace is only a few miles north of a state recreational park; there, in the Blue Hills is a body of water called by its Native American name *Punkapoag*, which means "the Place of the Fresh Water Pond." Punkapoag is where some of my mother's Native-American ancestors once lived. My relations were members of the Algonkian confederacy known as the Massachusetts – or to be more precise, *Massachuseuck*, which means "The Place of the Big Hills." The Massachusetts nation, like many Native-American nations, was an egalitarian confederacy comprising several communities such as the Punkapoag, the Nipmuck, and Neponset, and the Wesaguset.[7]

Closely related neighbors of the Wampanoag ("The People of the Dawn"), who, as with the Nipmuck ("The People of the Fresh Water Place") today are vibrant communities in Massachusetts, these ancestors of mine encountered Europeans under the command of Giovanni de Verrazano in 1524. Verrazano described the Massachusett as a "most beautiful" people who were "sweet and gentle, very like the manner of the ancients." They were, he observed, expert sailors who can, "go to sea without any danger" in boats made "with admirable skill" (Brasser, 1978:78). Almost one hundred years later, in 1614, Captain John Smith, while "visiting" the Massachusett, described their land as " the paradice [sic] of all these parts" (Salwen, 1978: 170). This paradise was soon decimated by the wave of epidemics that ravaged much of new England as larger ships carrying more Europeans brought diseases such as smallpox, to which native peoples had no immunity...

The Massachusetts people were particularly hard hit this way. Their population plummeted from an estimated thirty thousand to a few hundred by the mid 1650s. By that time, the surviving members of those nations that had been undermined were forcibly concentrated into small villages called "Praying Towns" where they were supposed to adapt to and adopt Christianity. One of these towns was Punkapoag, originally the main home of the Massachusetts, but later turned into a mix of concentration camp/refugee center...

Many of the Praying Town inhabitants, the so called Praying Indians, although they provided men to serve in colonial militias (against the French) were attacked, dispersed and killed. For those who survived, and for their descendants, such atrocities clearly drew the final bloody message that their ancient homelands were no longer the richly textured environments of deeply rooted free-life, but had to a large degree become the places of tears. Many Narragansett, Pequod, Mohegan, Massachusett, and other natives were now exiles "in the land of the free" (Lyons, 1992). As a coherent cultural entity, the Punkapoag community of the Massachusett confederacy, with it members forced into exile and finding intermarriage with other peoples the only means of survival, ceased to exist as a social whole.

Responding to the long decades of cultural erosion and terrorism directed against them, a gathering of Christian native peoples, including some of my ancestors, under the leadership of Rev. Samson Occom – a Mohegan man and a Presbyterian minister who had struggled against great odds to attain his "calling" – sought and were generously given land by the Oneida nation in what is now New York State. It was there, in a 1774 ceremony, that they were adopted as "the younger brothers and sisters" of the Oneida.

My Native-American ancestors, whose family name had become Burr, intermarried with the Oneida. Eventually, in the early 1800s, they moved back to their ancestral homeland of Massachusetts (see Doughton, 1998). Eli and Saloma Burr, my great, great, great grandfather and grandmother, settled in the western part of Massachusetts near Springfield. Eli and Saloma, and their children Vianna, Fidelia, Alonzo, and Albert, are listed in the 1868 Massachusetts State "Indian" census as Oneida people. Eli's grandfather has been an "Oneida chief" according to these state records. Eli and Saloma's children married African-Americans, including Zebadee Carl Talbott, a sharpshooter and "one of the best pistol shots in the country" according to a *Springfield Republican* report. One of the grandchildren, James Burr, became well known as an African-American inventor.

A 1915 obituary in the Massachusetts *Springfield Republican* newspaper noting the death of one of their grandsons, John Burr, contains information that could have only come from the Burrs, namely, that his ancestors were originally from "Ponkapog" Massachusetts, and that they had been adopted by the Oneida in the 1700s. So, well over 100 years after their ancestors had left New England for the Oneida sanctuary of Brothertown, the Burrs still carried the memories both of their Massachusetts origins and of the importance of their adoptive Oneida homeland.

From these currents of Massachusueck/Brothertown-Oneida, and Africa came my mother Dorothy Pettyjohn, who was born in Amherst, Massachusetts.

She became a teacher who, as a young woman, went to "Cotton Valley" in Alabama of the 1930's to teach in a school for impoverished rural African-American children not far from Marion and its Lincoln Normal School. It was there that she met and married my father. So, the waves of oppression, crashing over many peoples, driven from their land, forged many of them into complex syntheses of memory and belonging that link Africa and Native America for me.

In 1835, Alexis de Tocqueville's soon to be famous, vast overview of the young United States, entitled, *Democracy in America*, was published. Among his otherwise astute descriptions based on his travels in "America," Tocqueville inaccurately pictures what he calls "the three races of the United States." These are, he says, "the white or European, the Negro, and the Indian" which he claims are always distinctly separate populations. Concerning "the Negro" and "the Indian" he writes that these "two unhappy races have nothing in common, neither birth, nor features, nor language, nor habits" (1954, 343; for an epic depiction of the cross-currents created by oppression in the Americas, see Galeano, 1985).

If this assertion by Tocqueville were true, then I could not exist, given my African and Native American currents that have flowed together for more than two hundred years. My family relations cannot be compartmentalized into these rigid sealed-off categories such as those suggested by Tocqueville. Nor can the depths of their courage be plumbed by his superficial description of the "unhappy races," no matter how terrible their tribulations as they have flowed through so many valleys of oppression. Today I recognize that from Punkapoag in Massachusetts, and Brothertown in New York State, to Lincoln Normal School in Alabama, my relations were among those establishing roots in what they hoped would be sustaining communities that could buffer people against the forces of hatred while offering solid ground for justice and dignity. I know that my connection to my ancestors is not only genealogical, as important as that is. My connection to them is also that of the spirit. I have for many years worked alongside those trying to create places of freedom from injustice. I continue to do so today. I now understand, after years of my own internal development, with guidance from elders and friends, that this work of mine is propelled by those currents flowing from the springing hopes of my ancestors.

I do not feel like one of those "crossing border hybrids," now so much discussed by scholars who examine post-modernity. Nor does the older Latin

American term "Zambo" for "half Black/ half Indian," describe how I know myself. It is not in such a divided fashion that I recognize my existence. To the contrary, in the language of my Algonkian ancestors, *Noteshem* – I am a man – who stands at *newichewannock*. "the place between two strong currents." Without these two distinct streams there can be no such "in-between place" to be named as such. But, at the same time, this place is real and complete unto itself. In the same way, I emerge a full man, not a simple bifurcated halfling, from the two strong currents of Africa and native America. It is this *newichewannock* that marks the place of my spirit, and that propels me today.

References

Bond, Horace Mann. *Black American Scholars: A Study of their Origins.* 1972, Detroit, Mich: Balamp.

Brasser, T.J. "Early Indian-European Contacts," In *Handbook of North American Indians*, 1978, ed. Bruce Trigger, et al. Washington D.C., Smithsonian Press.

Doughton, Thomas, L. "Unseen Neighbors: Native Americans of Central Massachusetts: A People Who had 'Vanished.'" In *After King Philip's War: Presence and Persistence in Indian New England*, 1998, ed. Colin G. Calloway. Hanover, N.H.: University Presses of New England.

Galeano, Eduardo. *Memory of Fire* (3 volumes), 1985. New York: Pantheon.

Kent, Raymond K. *Early Kingdoms in Madagascar, 1500-1700*, 1970. New York: Holt, Rinehart and Winston.

Lyons, Oren. "The American Indian in the Past." In *Exiled in the Land of the Free: Democracy, Indian Nations, and the U.S. Constitution*, 1992, ed. Oren Lyons et al. Santa Fe: Clear Light.

Salwen, Bert. "Indians of Southern New England and Long Island, Early Period." In *Handbook of North American Indians*, 1978, ed. Bruce Trigger et al. Washington, D.C.: Smithsonian Institution.

Tocqueville Alexis de. *Democracy in America.* 1960, New York: Vintage.

American Anthropological Association (AAA) Statement on "Race"[8]

As a result of public confusion about the meaning of "race," claims as to major biological differences among "races" continue to be advanced. Stemming from past AAA actions designed to address public misconceptions on race and intelligence, the need was apparent for a clear AAA statement on the biology and politics of race that would be educational and informational.

The following statement was adopted by the Executive Board of the American Anthropological Association in May 1998, based on a draft prepared by a committee of representative anthropologists. The Association believes that this statement represents the thinking and scholarly positions of most anthropologists.

In the United States both scholars and the general public have been conditioned to viewing human races as natural and separate divisions within the human species based on visible physical differences. With the vast expansion of scientific knowledge in this century, however, it has become clear that human populations are not unambiguous, clearly demarcated, biologically distinct groups. Evidence from the analysis of genetics (e.g., DNA) indicates that most physical variation, about 94%, lies within so-called racial groups. Conventional geographic "racial" groupings differ from one another only in about 6% of their genes. This means that there is greater variation within "racial" groups than between them. In neighboring populations there is much overlapping of genes and their phenotypic (physical) expressions. Throughout history whenever different groups have come into contact, they have interbred. The continued sharing of genetic materials has maintained all of humankind as a single species.

Physical variations in any given trait tend to occur gradually rather than abruptly over geographic areas. And because physical traits are inherited independently of one another, knowing the range of one trait does not predict the presence of others. For example, skin color varies largely from light in temperate areas in the north to dark in tropical areas in the south; its intensity is not related to nose shape or hair texture. Dark skin may be associated with frizzy or kinky hair or curly or wavy or straight hair, all of which are found among different indigenous peoples in tropical regions. These facts render any attempt to establish lines of division among biological populations both arbitrary and subjective.

Historical research has shown that the idea of "race" has always carried more meanings than mere physical differences; indeed, physical variations in the human species have no meaning except the social ones that humans put on them. Today scholars in many fields argue that "race" as it is understood in the United States of America was a social mechanism invented during the 18th century to refer to those populations brought together in colonial America: the English and other European settlers, the conquered Indian peoples, and those peoples of Africa brought to provide slave labor.

From its inception, the modern concept of "race" was modeled after an ancient theorem of the Great Chain of Being, which posited natural categories on a hierarchy established by God or nature. Thus "race" was a mode of classification linked specifically to peoples in the colonial situation. It subsumed a growing ideology of inequality devised to rationalize European attitudes and treatment of the conquered and enslaved peoples. Proponents of slavery in particular during the 19th century used "race" to justify the retention of slavery. The ideology magnified the differences among Europeans, Africans, and Indians, established a rigid hierarchy of socially exclusive categories, underscored and bolstered unequal rank and status differences, and provided the rationalization that the inequality was natural or God-given. The different physical traits of African-Americans and Indians became markers or symbols of their status differences.

As they were constructing US society, leaders among European-Americans fabricated the cultural/behavioral characteristics associated with each "race." Linking superior traits with Europeans and negative and inferior ones to blacks and Indians. Numerous arbitrary and fictitious beliefs about the different peoples were institutionalized and deeply embedded in American thought.

Early in the 19th century the growing fields of science began to reflect the public consciousness about human differences. Differences among the "racial" categories were projected to their greatest extreme when the argument was posed that Africans, Indians, and Europeans were separate species, with Africans the least human and closer taxonomically to apes.

Ultimately "race" as an ideology about human differences was subsequently spread to other areas of the world. It became a strategy for dividing, ranking, and controlling colonized people used by colonial powers everywhere. But it was not limited to the colonial situation. In the latter part of the 19th century it was employed by Europeans to rank one another and to justify social, economic, and political inequalities among their peoples. During World War II, the Nazis under Adolf Hitler enjoined the expanded ideology of "race" and "racial" differences and took them to a logical end: the exterminations of 11 million people of "inferior races" (e.g. Jews, Gypsies, Africans, homosexuals, and so forth) and other unspeakable brutalities of the Holocaust.

"Race" thus evolved as a world view, a body of prejudgments about human differences and group behavior. Racial beliefs constitute myths about the diversity in the human species and about the abilities and behavior of people homogenized into "racial" categories. The myths fused behavior and physical features together in the public mind, impeding our comprehension of both biological variations and cultural behavior, implying that both are genetically determined. Racial myths bear no relationship to the reality of human capabilities or behavior. Scientists today find that reliance on such folk beliefs about human differences in research has led to countless errors.

At the end of the 20th century, we now understand that human cultural behavior is learned, conditioned into infants beginning at birth, and always subject to modification. No human is born with built-in culture or language. Our temperaments, dispositions, and personalities, regardless of genetic propensities, are developed within sets of meanings and values that we call "culture." Studies of infant and early childhood learning and behavior attest to the reality of our cultures in forming who we are.

It is a basic tenet of anthropological knowledge that all normal human beings have the capacity to learn any cultural behavior. The American experiences with immigrants from hundreds of different language and cultural backgrounds who have acquired some version of American culture traits and behavior is the clearest evidence of this fact. Moreover, people of all physical variations have learned different cultural behaviors and continue to do so as modern transportation moves millions of immigrants around the world.

How people have been accepted and treated within the context of a given society or culture has a direct impact on how they perform in that society. The "racial" world view was invented to assign some groups to perpetual low status, while others were permitted access to privilege, power, and wealth. The tragedy in the United States has been that the policies and practices stemming from this world view succeeded all too well in constructing unequal populations among Europeans, native Americans, and peoples of African descent. Given what we know about the capacity of normal humans to achieve and function

> within any culture, we concluded that present-day inequalities between so-called "racial" groups are not consequences of their biological inheritance but products of historical and contemporary social, economic, educational, and political circumstances.
>
> American Anthropological Association, Washington, DC, 1998

Questions for Discussion

1. Based on your reflections on social work and social justice, how would you define the practice of social justice work?
2. What are some factors that contribute to different meanings of social work locally and globally?
3. What are some social justice issues affecting residents of your community? What understandings of social justice stem from these issues?
4. In what ways have you experienced the valuing and devaluing of difference?
5. How do you make sense of the key concepts of meaning, context, power, history, and possibility through your reading of John Brown Childs' story, "Red Clay, Blue Hills: In Honor of My Ancestors?"

Suggested Readings

Bourdieu, P. (1977). *Outline of a theory of practice.* (Trans. R. Nice). Cambridge: Cambridge University Press.

Hill Collins, P. (1990). *Black feminist thought: Knowledge, consciousness, and the politics of empowerment.* Boston: Unwin Hyman.

DuBois, W.E.B. (1989) *The souls of black folks.* New York: Bantam. (Original work published 1903)

Foucault, M. (1980). *Power/knowledge: Selected interviews and other writings, 1972-1980.* (Ed. and Trans. C. Gordon). New York: Pantheon.

Freire, P. (1974). *Pedagogy of the oppressed.* New York: Seabury Press/Continuum.

Giddens, A. (1979). *Central problems in social theory: Action, structure, and contradiction in social analysis.* Berkeley: University of California Press.

Gramsci, A. (1971). *Selections from the prison notebooks.* New York: International Publishers.

hooks, b. (1994). *Feminist theory from margin to center.* Boston: South End Press.

Horton, M. (1998). *The long haul: An autobiography* (with Judith Kohl and Herbert Kohl). New York: Teachers College Press.

Mohanty, C. (1991). "Under western eyes: Feminist scholarship and colonialist discourses." In C. Mohanty, A. Russo, L. Torres (Eds.), *Third world women and the politics of feminism.* (pp. 51-80. Bloomington, IN: Indiana University Press.

Ortner, S. (1989) *High religion: A cultural and political history of Sherpa Buddhism.* Princeton: Princeton University Press.

Smith, D. (1987). *The everyday world as problematic.* Toronto: University of Toronto Press.

Tuhiwai Smith, L. (1999). *Decolonizing methodologies: Research and indigenous peoples.* London: Zed Books.

Chapter 2

Looking Back

"You can't cut off the top of a tree and stick it in the ground somewhere and expect it to grow – you have to know the roots."

Myles Horton (1998), *The Long Haul*[1]

Chapter Overview

In Chapter Two we examine the practices, actors, institutions, and contexts in the emergence of social work as a profession. We claim a historical perspective for social justice work and illustrate how this perspective helps us become critical actors in our profession. We explore the development of social work alongside industrial capitalism and consider the significant tensions, struggles, and contradictions that shifts in the political economy created for social work. We invite readers to explore the silences, shifts, and omissions in the history of social work practice. We organize our representation of social work's history thematically instead of linearly in order to highlight dimensions that help us understand social work today. We call attention to the contributions of advocates and activists whose histories have been largely ignored or erased from the social work canon. Our examples highlight people both inside and outside the boundaries of social work whose work reflects social justice-oriented practice. We link social work history to struggles for human rights, peace, and citizenship, and we explore marginalized or long-forgotten models and strategies of practice.

Why Does History Matter?

Why look back? Why scrutinize our personal or familial history, revisit yesterday's trials and triumphs of the social work profession, or map out the evolution of a social problem and its ever-changing political, economic, and cultural context? What can history teach us about today? And what lessons can it offer to guide us to a more just tomorrow? In this section, we present some reasons why a historical perspective is important to justice-oriented social work practice. We invite you to expand on our list:

1. *History serves as a warning device and thus compels us to scrutinize the present.* Discovering our biases today is easier if we seek to critique the past (Zinn, 1970). When we look back we can more clearly see the whole of a situation and its mitigating factors. Here the old saying, "Hindsight is 20/20" makes perfect sense. For example, "the Great Depression of the 1930s demonstrated that social and economic forces rather than individual fault created poverty, hitting both the wealthy and the poor laboring classes" (Day, 1997, p. 270). Contemporary federal welfare reform policy defines poverty as an individual failing. Today's mantra of welfare reform is about self-sufficiency and getting mothers into the work force regardless of whether the wages earned will raise a family out of poverty. How did the Great Depression challenge existing definitions of poverty in that moment? What makes definitions of poverty so different in this moment?
2. *History helps us create linkages and connect themes across time.* For example, taking a historical perspective on women and work teaches us about women's history of inequality. We discover that women earned one-half of what men earned for similar labor at the turn of the 20th century (Van Kleeck, 1917). Learning that women still earn less than three-quarters of what men earn for equal work today (Albelda & Tilly, 1997, p. 5) teaches us a powerful lesson regarding the persistent discrimination women have experienced over the past one hundred years. Knowing this slow rate of progress makes it harder to convince ourselves that the fight for women's equality has been won.
3. *History helps us understand how power works.* History provides a window into how definitions of social problems and the structuring

and shaping of institutions and individuals are time-specific and contextually embedded. For example, theories explaining the nature of child abuse were nonexistent until the late 1800s. They evolved based on shifting definitions of children and childhood throughout the last century and increased faith in the power of science and medicine to cure societal ills. History teaches us how those with the power to shape new meanings come to have their definition of a social problem accepted as truth.

4. *History inspires us to act.* History reminds us of possibilities for change created by ordinary people at times when it seemed as if all hope were lost. Think for a moment of Rosa Parks, an African American woman who played a part in the Civil Rights movement in Montgomery, Alabama during the 1950s. As a trained activist, she took a monumental step and created possibilities of gaining power and access to ordinary ways of life for herself and other African Americans by taking a seat at the front of the bus, a place reserved at the time only for whites. Zinn (1970, pp. 282-284) would describe her behavior as acting "as if" she were free: "Acting as if we are free is a way of resolving the paradox of determinism and freedom, of overcoming the tension between past and future" (p. 283). Zinn claims that assuming one is free is far less risky than assuming one is not free. Adherents to this assumption have moved us toward a more just world. Martin Luther King Jr. and Gandhi are examples of individuals who acted as if they could make a difference. They faced overwhelming odds yet mobilized the possibilities of freedom. Their compassion and conviction inspire us today to have hope and take action for a more just tomorrow.

Claiming a Historical Perspective for Social Work

Marginalization of History in Social Work

Now that we have made claims for the importance of a historical perspective for social work education and practice, let us take a brief look at why a perspective that makes such critical and intuitive sense seems to carry little weight in social work. Think what this omission means for social work and the implicit ways in which this omission shapes practices, programs, and policies. Reisch (1988) claims we are an ahistorical culture. He says that we have become accustomed to fragments of information, sound bytes, if you will (i.e., from the O.J. Simpson trial—"If the glove doesn't fit, we must acquit."), instead of what he calls the "connective tissue," that is, themes that span time and integrate information across decades, centuries, and millenniums. Sound bytes (and text bytes too!) are the stock and trade of the mass media. They influence and shape the very ways we think about and process information. Too often, we fail to question these bytes of information as morsels. Instead, we accept them as the whole story. Context falls out along with history.

The Presidential Election of 2000

Think for a moment about the presidential election of 2000 and the complicated process of tallying the votes in Florida. Remember all of the problems created by misshapen, half-punched, and pregnant "chads;" outmoded voting equipment and ballots; accusations of election tampering; and the early closing of polls in highly-populated Democratic districts represented by large numbers of African American registered voters. Once the Supreme Court determined the tallying was over, news that had once completely overshadowed all other news on television and the front pages of newspapers across the country virtually disappeared. Bush won the election, ostensibly because the Supreme Court thought it wise to move on. Their decision signaled that Americans should have a president, even though popular opinion polls reported the public was interested in, not alarmed by, this unfolding of events. U.S. citizens just wanted it done right. Contestations to the elections faded almost entirely out of sight the day following the Supreme Court decision. What were we to think? Yet reports that a group of 450 African Americans believed their constitutional rights were violated by the election and were prepared to stand their ground was news relegated to the not-so-important newspaper sections hidden near the classifieds.[2] How is it that the conflicts and tensions surrounding Election 2000 faded so quickly from public view? Who decides, for example, that we should devote two years of media attention to the O.J. Simpson trial yet only two months to an issue challenging democracy and citizen participation so vital to us all? In effect, whose history is erased, and who has the power to erase it?

Contributions of the Social Welfare History Group

In general, history has been marginalized in social work education. However, there have been brief periods where the contributions of historical knowledge and method were valued. For example, Fisher (1999) investigated the emergence of the Social Welfare History Group (SWHG) in the mid-1950s. This collection of social welfare historians and social workers met to share their interest in teaching social welfare history and to encourage the use of historical research methods. DeSchweinitz, a social work scholar and administrator at the University of California, School of Social Work, spearheaded the formation of the SWHG. He had this to say about social work education and history:

> I wonder how far we are going to get in education for leadership unless we do more, than I suspect is now being done, to give social workers historical perspective. I covet for our students more philosophic sweep and a wider knowledge of past experience as background for developing the ability to plan and to conceive social programs and social legislation. We are behind other professions in the attention we pay to history (as cited in Fisher, 1999, pp.192-193).[3]

Fisher notes that in social work's history, a push toward understanding the past generally occurs when conservative political forces exert a repressive influence on the profession. A return to history re-ignites the fires of progressive values and practices. At these times, social workers use history as a "shoulder to stand on" (p. 210). Fisher also speculates that the opposite is true. Liberal political forces dampen reflective tendencies and steer social workers toward planning. In his critique of social work's neglect of history, Reisch (1988) observes how the theoretical perspectives that guide social work practice rarely consider time as an essential factor. These include the person-in-environment and the eco-systems perspectives, two approaches to social work practice that we discuss in Chapter Four. Take a moment to think about the social work texts you have read. Which ones paid attention to history? Of the possible actors and institutions, what history did the text most represent and whose stories did it leave out?

History as Method

Reisch (1988) claims that history is also a method, an essential tool of inquiry. He stresses how historical inquiry helps us compare fact and interpretation and contextually ground social research, policy analysis, program evaluation, and individual or community assessment. Historical inquiry guides social workers to the implicit and explicit meanings of individual or family case histories. Germain's (1994, pp. 260-261) work on families provides an example of history as a tool of inquiry. Germain conceptualizes time in historical, social, and individual layers. *Historical time* refers to the effects of historic forces on groups of people born at particular points in time. *Individual time* reflects how people experience these circumstances, expressed through life stories. *Social time* merges the individual with the collective and intertwines development from one generation to the next. Social time supports the notion that parents and children develop simultaneously, each affecting the growth of the other. These three conceptions of time help us think about history in terms of synergistic processes rather than in terms of linear, cause-and-effect patterns.

A Historical Perspective Informs the Questions We Ask

What would it mean to claim a historical perspective for social work? How might this perspective transform our modes and methods of practice? What questions would a historical perspective compel us to pose regarding practices, problems, and policies; our personal histories; and the histories of our neighborhoods, organizations, and communities? Here is a list of questions that a historical perspective prompts us to ask:

1. What does it mean to leave history out? (for an individual, a family, a community, ourselves, or our profession?)
2. Who serves to benefit from these omissions?
3. Who and how might these omissions harm?
4. How has the nature, definition, and context of a particular problem, people, or situation changed over the course of time?
5. When did this particular problem, or situation emerge?
6. What contextual clues can you think of that enrich your understanding of this problem, people, or situation?
7. What role does power play in the unfolding of this historical event, theme, or situation?
8. What possibilities do you see for alternative scenarios?
9. What legends or scripts from the past have worn out their usefulness?

10. How does this history shape the meanings we give to notions of race, class, gender, ability, and sexual orientation?
11. What lessons do we learn from this history to guide our practice?

What questions might you add to this list to claim a historical perspective for social justice work? How might posing these questions help you as a social worker and those you work with?

The History of Intelligence

One theme that has shaped areas of social work practice is intelligence. If we examine the concept of intelligence from a historical perspective we discover that in the early 1900s terms such as "idiot," "imbecile," and "moron" were used as descriptors in the classification scheme for the Stanford-Binet intelligence test (Gould, 1981). A shift in terminology occurred between 1950 and 1970 when the term "mentally retarded" came into use to describe an intelligence "deficiency." Today we note yet another shift: "Developmentally disabled" or "developmentally challenged" gradually replaced mentally retarded. These shifts in the languaging of intelligence give us a potent message about the historical context of meaning, language, and power. Now take a moment to consider what these terms imply and how they might influence your practice as a social worker. What do these words mean to you? What actions might you take or what services might you develop or recommend based on your interpretations of these shifts in the languaging of human intelligence? What issues of power play through these practices?

Let us continue with this snapshot of history. H. H. Goddard, one of the leading pioneers of hereditarianism in the U.S, brought the Stanford-Binet intelligence scale to America from France in the early 1920s. Whereas Binet's vision of the intelligence scale was to use it to identify and assist individuals in their intellectual development, Goddard had a radically different vision in mind. By continuing to develop the scale, he "wished to identify [intelligence] in order to recognize limits, segregate, and curtail breeding to prevent further deterioration of an endangered American stock, threatened by immigration from without and by prolific reproduction of its feebleminded within" (in Gould, 1981, p. 159). While Goddard's plan may assault our present-day sensibilities, it formed an ideological base (theory) that guided action. Around the turn of the 20th century, many newly-landed immigrants to Ellis Island in New York were tested and denied admission to the U.S. based on intelligence scores alone. Ironically, test administrators conducted the test in the English language, a language most immigrants did not speak. Test scores also legitimized the adoption of forced sterilization laws in a number of states. In effect, these laws stripped many people of color and individuals of minority status, deemed intellectually deficient, of their right to bear children. The sterilization of over 7,500 women and men occurred in Virginia alone between 1924 and 1972 (Gould, 1981, p. 335).

Similar examples from more recent history suggest a larger pattern of discrimination and oppression of women and minorities. For example, "public health" campaigns were organized to promote sterilization of Native American and Puerto Rican women during the 1960s and 1970s (Garcia, 1982; Karsten-Larson, 1977).[4] Sterilization occurred at times against women's will or without informed consent. These campaigns and their consequences graphically demonstrate the ways in which language masks racist agendas and shapes beliefs about human capacity and public policies that target vulnerable groups. Where do you encounter similar examples of racist, sexist, or heterosexist beliefs shaping understandings of difference and public policies toward "other" groups today? How does language play into these differences? What examples might you find in your local newspaper over the course of the next week?

Connecting Historical, Political, Cultural, and Practice Contexts: The Social Construction of Child Sexual Abuse

Feminist theory forged what has become a basic principle of critical practice, that is, recognizing the linkage between the personal and the political. This principle reminds social workers to look for fundamental connections between seemingly personal problems and their genesis in hidden and overt, powerful political structures and patterns of practice that exert influence on peoples' lives. Social justice work also foregrounds considerations of history and culture as essential components of critical analysis. Attending to history and culture brings power into focus and how relations of power, inequality, and injustice shape the context of lived experience and the discursive terrain of problem construction. For example, what counts as a problem and for whom? What historical events and cultural surrounds, social relations, and political processes shape problem definition? How do these elements connect on a practice-level and how do they play out in our work?

One way to make these connections is to start with history, investigate the chronology of a social problem from its inception, and study its meanderings through time as it intersects with the development of theory, policy, and practice to address the problem. Social problem definitions change over time.

Maxine Jacobson shares an example of a time line she constructed to better understand the social construction of child sexual abuse and its influence on the shaping of multidisciplinary team practice. The time line illustrates historical markers, the emergence of theory explaining the etiology of child sexual abuse, the development of policy, and finally, how history, theory, and policy converge in particular responses and practices.

As you move through the timeline (in order of the numbered dots), think about a social problem that captures your attention. What particular problem comes to mind? Where might you begin your investigation? How might you use this method to ground your investigation in a historical perspective that considers the evolution of theory, policy, and practice to address this problem? How does the information you collect inform you of practices, strategies, and methods for addressing this concern? How have these evolved over time? What lessons do you learn from this history that inform practice today?

FIGURE 2.1

The Social Construction of Child Abuse Timeline

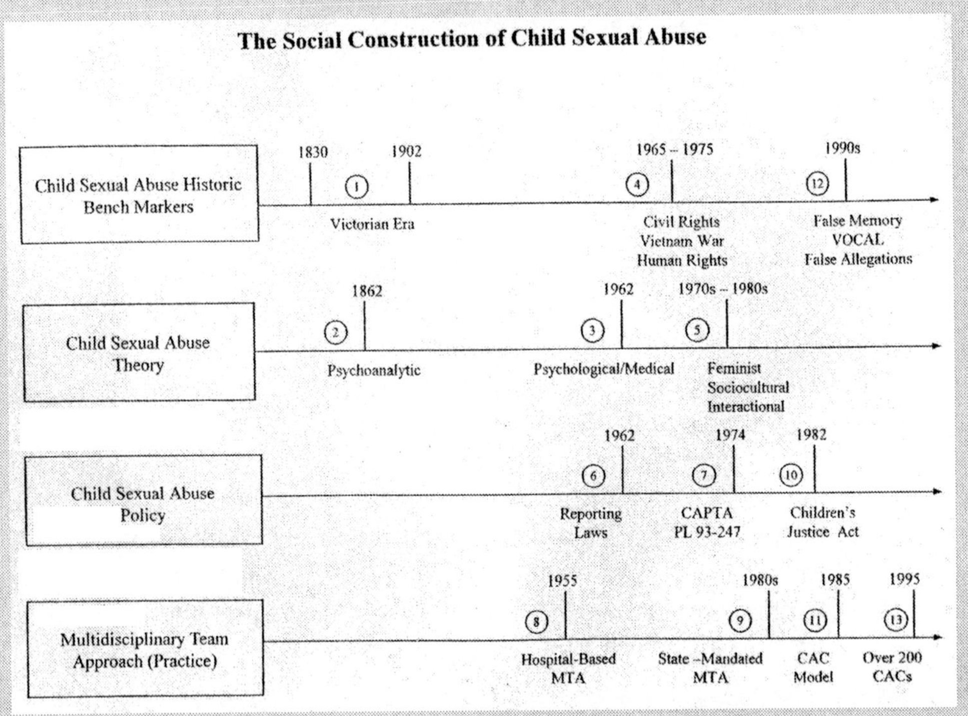

Follow the dots:

1. Historically speaking, child sexual abuse had barely been defined before the turn of the 20th century. Certainly, child sexual abuse existed during the Victorian Era but it was not a "talkable" issue. No treatment existed for child victims or those who sexually abused them. Children were viewed as property.
2. Beginning with Freud and the development of psychoanalytic theory, child sexual abuse became a "talkable" subject. Freud initially believed child sexual abuse was a significant factor shaping the etiology of hysteria. His adult middle- to upper-class women clients told him of incidents of early childhood sexual abuse. When he discussed his findings with other male colleagues, they disputed his claims. The stories he had been witness to implicated middle- and upper-class males as potential perpetrators of abuse. This was unthinkable and unspeakable. The cultural climate was not at all ready to support Freud's initial claim. Freud went back to the drawing board, revamped his theory, and set forth the claim that the stories he had heard existed entirely in the fantasy worlds of his women clients (Herman, 1992. pp. 16-20).
3. The late 1950s and early 1960s are often referred to as the period of the "rediscovery" of child abuse. Doctors in hospital emergency wards recognized the "unthinkable:" that children were vulnerable to physical and sexual abuse at the hands of adults. Child sexual abuse was radically transformed and socially constructed as a manifestation of characteristics rooted firmly within the individual abuser. The psychological/medical interpretation of the child sexual abuse problem continues to shape policy and practice today (Pfohl, 1977).
4. The 1960s can be described as an intersection of cataclysmic change that would have reverberating effects on the U.S. for decades to follow. Women and people of color formed social movements to protest inequalities of gender and race. People organized and protested violations of human rights and the Vietnam War. This change rippled through the culture, forging new constructions of reality that exposed the inherent racist and sexist nature of society's long-standing institutions.

5. On the tails of change, new theory developed that subverted long-held assumptions about the nature of reality. Feminist theory highlighted inequality and injustice particularly as these applied to the lives of women and children, those with the least power in society to voice their concerns. This body of theory viewed child sexual abuse as inherent within powerful structures and institutions that demean, negate, and marginalize the experiences of women and children. From a feminist perspective, child sexual abuse is about power. Sociocultural theory paints a picture of a culture that accepts overt and covert violence against women and children. Interactional models integrate and explain individual, social, and cultural factors that coalesce in the sexual abuse of women and children.
6. Beginning with the "rediscovery" of child sexual abuse in the 1950s, the U.S. was witness to the expeditious passage of child abuse reporting laws. Reporting laws are often described as the most rapid enactment of legislation in history (Nelson, 1984). Within a few years, every state in the U.S. had child abuse reporting laws.
7. The Child Abuse Prevention and Treatment Act (1974) defined child abuse in individualist terms. With the finger pointed at individuals as the root cause of the problem, the social, political, and economic contributors to the child sexual abuse problem went unattended and ignored.
8. The multidisciplinary team approach to child sexual abuse was developed by hospital physicians who wanted to ensure children's safety once they left acute care and reentered the community and their homes. Because child sexual abuse is defined as a medical, psychological, and legal problem, professionals representing these areas of concern became team representatives.
9. Beginning in the 1980s, many states across the U.S. formalized the use of multidisciplinary teams by passing legislation sanctioning their use.
10. The Children's Justice Act of 1985 further legitimated the use of a multidisciplinary effort to combat the problem of child sexual abuse by recommending that to receive government funding for programs, communities must develop and implement multidisciplinary teams to investigate and process cases of child abuse.

11. Beginning in the 1980s, new approaches to multidisciplinary teams developed. The Children's Advocacy Center (CAC) is one example. CACs provide a home-like, "child-friendly" atmosphere for the investigation and interviewing of child victims. Research literature indicates that children are often retraumatized by repeated interviewing, which occurs when child protection efforts are poorly coordinated. CACs strive to interview a child only once.
12. The 1990s were witness to considerable fallout concerning the issue of child abuse. Many felt that the pendulum had swung too far and that courts and child protection agencies were overzealous in their efforts to address the problem. Issues surfaced regarded false memory syndrome and false allegations of abuse. Professionals also began to question the popular theory that "children never lie about abuse." Investigators were criticized for asking leading questions and being biased in favor of all allegations being true. Victims of Child Abuse Laws (VOCAL), an organization that contested many cases of child abuse, surfaced and forged a place for itself as an advocate of those falsely accused of perpetrating child abuse.
13. As of the late 1990s, over 200 Child Advocacy Centers were operating in the U.S.

Social Work in the 20th Century

Introduction

In this section we summarize social work's history from its emergence around the turn of the 20th century through present time. Our presentation is brief, partial, and focused. We color in social work's background and, in so doing, call attention to the factors that influenced how the profession took shape. We respond here to the following questions: Why did social work emerge when it did in U.S. history? What factors influenced its development? Specifically, what has been the ongoing role of the economy in this development? Historically, what has social work's relationship been to social justice-oriented practice? What erasures and omissions does this historical perspective bring to the forefront? What key lessons can history teach us about social work's legacy of justice-oriented practice and people? As you read this section think of the relevance of the key practice concepts of meaning, context, power, history, and possibility and how these bear on our representation of social work's history.

Setting the Stage

Context of Social Turbulence. To understand social work and its emergence as a profession, it is important to understand its *context*, or the conditions that helped to influence and shape its development. Social work in the U.S. grew out of social turbulence around the turn of the 20th century when the country entered a period of tremendous change brought on by high unemployment, rapid industrialization, and increased urbanization and immigration (Axinn & Levin, 1997; Day, 1997; Ehrenreich, 1985; Reisch & Wenocur, 1986). Ehrenreich (1985, pp. 20-24) emphasizes the profundity of these changes. Imagine this:

- From the end of the Civil War through 1914, approximately 27 million people immigrated to the United States.
- The Civil War marked the beginning of mass emigration from rural areas and small towns as individuals and families searched for employment in urban areas.
- By 1914, almost 70% of the work force was involved in nonagricultural employment.
- Infant mortality rates were high because of rampant epidemics caused by poor living conditions.
- One percent of the population owned 47% of the country's assets creating a concentration of economic and political power in the hands of monopolistic corporations.
- Cultural clashes and competition for sustainable employment created increased tension between American-born residents and those from other countries seeking a new way of life.

Factors Contributing to Social Crisis. Scholars of social work history (Day, 1997; Ehrenreich, 1985; Reisch & Wenocur, 1986; Wenocur & Reisch, 1989) describe the confluence of factors that created a social crisis at the turn of the 20th century:

1. *Industrialization*: The fifty-year period following the Civil War was one of massive industrialization in the U.S. Not only did this change the face of the economy, the nature of work, and how and what we produced, bought, and consumed, but it also changed the ways in which people lived and how they defined themselves and their relationships to one another. (We will dig further into the issue of capitalism in the following section on Social Work and the Economy.) To understand the changes we are talking about here, imagine if you will, the shift from horse-drawn carriages to the automobile—each mode of transportation embedded in its own culture. Using horses for travel entails ranching, training, feeding, breeding, carriage building, and the teamsters. Now contrast this with the automobile, and its culture of gas stations, auto repair, metal smelting, assembly-line production of parts, road building, and massive changes in time and space, and gas and oil exploration. Think for a moment how these shifts influence the intricacies and intimacies of people's lives – how long it takes to get from here to there, the types of jobs created, and why a Muncie, Indiana judge referred to the car as a "house of prostitution on wheels" (Allen, 1975, p. 100 as cited in Ehrenreich, 1985, p. 50). How might the automobile have changed the face of intimate relationships, increased the number of children born, or prompted marriage? Think for a moment of other industrial/technological creations. What comes to mind? How do these define and structure our very existence?
2. *Immigration*: America was literally built on the backs of immigrants. In the industrializing U.S. when we needed railroad track laid or coal mined, immigration was encouraged. When foreign-born workers were perceived as taking away the jobs of the native born, or during times of labor glut, the government enacted quotas to limit immigration. Immigration caused social problems as well. Not only were immigrants poor, they were different. They spoke other languages and practiced different religions. They were viewed as "altogether a threat to 'decent' values and the structure of the American community" (Ehrenreich, 1985, p. 22).
3. *Mass emigration and urbanization*: In search of employment, large numbers of people emigrated from rural America to urban industrial centers. Whereas just before the Civil War approximately 60 percent of the labor force worked in agricultural employment, by 1914, almost 70 percent of the labor force had nonagricultural jobs. Here

again, think of how this shift created enormous change in people's lifestyles, their roles as men and women, and their conceptions of work. Factory work was based on a new set of principles, those promoting scientific management, and the belief that increased efficiency leads to increased profits.[5] Routine and regimentation structured the factory workers' day. Work was accomplished in bits and pieces with no one worker connected to the whole. This was the beginning of the assembly line.

4. *Concentration of power in the hands of a few*: At the turn of the century, the U.S. had large numbers of people living in wrenching poverty and a growing middle-class. Power was concentrated in the hands of monopolistic corporations owned by one percent of the population, the wealthy elites. Money commands political influence. Graft and corruption were common concerns of the general population. For example, Ehrenreich (1985, p. 23) points out that prior to the Civil War the U.S. claimed only a handful of millionaires. However, by the turn of the 20th century, hundreds to thousands of U.S. citizens had sufficient assets to call themselves millionaires. Ehrenreich estimates that at least twenty of these individuals were U.S. senators.

Documenting Desperate Times. Jacob Riis (1890) was a photographer, police reporter, and author of "*How the Other Half Lives.*" His work chronicling tenement-house life in New York City at the turn of the 20th century provides a picture of the human fallout of these changes. Riis used photographs and anecdotal material to illustrate how the "lower half" lived. He put a face on poverty for middle- and upper-class Americans and gave them indirect, and therefore safe, access to crowded housing conditions, disease, hunger, and the desperation of poor immigrants. Riis's work showed that many who came seeking the American dream found instead a political and economic nightmare:

> To-day three-fourths of its [New York City's] people live in the tenements, and the nineteenth century drift of the population to the cities is sending ever-increasing multitudes to crowd them. The fifteen thousand tenant-houses that were the despair of the sanitarian in the past generation swelled into thirty-seven thousand, and more than twelve hundred thousand persons call them home . . . We know now that there is no way out; that the "system" that was the evil offspring of public neglect and private greed has come to stay, a storm-centre forever of our civilization. Nothing is left but to make the best of a bad bargain. (p. 60)

At the time, Riis' work did much to expose the underbelly of poverty in the tenements of New York. The middle and upper classes took notice. On the other hand, his work also sensationalized poverty and created images of "otherness." He speaks, for example, of poor men, women, and children in language that evokes images of wild and hungry animals or swarms of angry bees poised for attack. These images effectively separate "us" from "them," the humans from the beasts and the bugs. They mapped out difference and played on the fears of a middle class uncertain of its own social footing and anxious about slipping into poverty's abyss.

Charles Loring Brace (1872, p. 29), author of *The Dangerous Classes of New York and My Twenty Years Work Among Them,* spoke of impending doom as social, economic, and political factors coalesced in a city of one million near the turn of the 20th century. Like Riis, Brace describes the poor in animalistic terms and makes a case for addressing the problems of the "dangerous classes." In recalling the street riots in 1863, Brace begs his readers not to forget how quickly the "desperate multitude" rose up like "creatures who seemed to have crept from their burrows and dens to join in the plunder of the city. . .who look with envy and greed at the signs of wealth and luxury all around them, while they themselves have nothing but hardship, penury, and unceasing drudgery" (pp. 30-31). As you can see, these contradictory images of the poor illustrate a moment in the growth of industrial capitalism and concomitant poverty. They also illustrate how constructions of difference intermingled with and helped to shape discourses of helping and concern.

Social Work and the Economy

Social Work and Industrial Capitalism. Social work emerged as a means of bringing equilibrium to an industrializing society in crisis. Therefore, to understand social work we must situate ourselves at its emergence with industrial capitalism. Day (1997, pp. 31-33) contends that the polity – the exercise of power in a society - and the economy – the production, distribution, and consumption of goods and services - are the most influential social institutions shaping our actions, values, and relationships. According to Day, "In the United States, the polity and the economy are so closely tied that it is difficult to see them as separate, for laws and regulations are based on the ideals of capitalism and the free market and much of the economy is politically supported" (p. 33). Others (Harvey,

1989; Wenocur and Reisch, 1989) emphasize the power of the polity and the economy to influence and shape not only who we are, but also what we value. (We expand on this idea in Chapter 3.) Capitalism influences and shapes people's lives, and it is more of a process than a thing. Harvey (1989) sums it up in these words:

> [Capitalism] is a process of reproduction of social life through commodity production, in which all of us in the advanced capitalist world are heavily implicated. Its internalizing rules of operation are such as to ensure that it is a dynamic and revolutionary mode of social organization, restlessly and ceaselessly transforming the society within which it is embedded. The process masks and fetishizes, achieves growth through creative destruction, creates new wants and needs, exploits the capacity for human labour and desire, transforms spaces, and speeds up the pace of life. It produces problems of overaccumulation for which there are but a limited number of possible solutions. (p. 343)

Redressing the Failings of Capitalism. One way to view the emergence of social work is as an attempt to redress the failings of capitalism. Given this interpretation, social work easily falls prey to the trap of being construed as the handmaiden of the political economy. That is, social work serves to mitigate the consequences of capitalism and care for its causalities. Let us go on to examine this viewpoint while keeping in mind that there have always been spaces of resistance carved out by social workers throughout its history. These spaces create a sense of hope and optimism and challenge deterministic and pessimistic views of social work practice.

Shortly before social work emerged in the U.S., the economy had experienced a series of severe depressions. Ehrenreich (1985, pp. 26-27) recounts how a number of observers believed American markets had more goods than they could sell. They felt the only solution was to look to other countries as potential markets for U.S. goods. These countries could also be resources for less expensive raw materials needed for production, including an even cheaper labor force (Sound familiar?). Only when the working class fought against these conditions by organizing and striking did the middle and upper classes take notice. Ehrenreich (1985) cites the concerns of Teddy Roosevelt, who, like others at the time, believed the rich had to take some responsibility for the current state of affairs. His words capture a climate ripe for resistance and revolt as he critiques a privileged point of view:

> I do not at all like the social conditions at present. The dull, purblind folly of the very rich men, their greed and arrogance, and the ways in which they have unduly prospered by the help of the ablest lawyers, and too often through the weakness of shortsightedness of the judges. . . ; These facts, and the corruption in business and politics, have tended to produce a very unhealthy condition of excitement and irritation in the popular mind, which shows itself in part in the enormous increase in the socialistic propaganda. (p. 27)

Political Economy and Professionalism. Wenocur and Reisch (1989) suggest that, in a capitalist system, the political economy helps to shape a profession's goals, structure, ideology, and the dominant forms of practice. Reisch (1998, p. 161) poses a cogent argument for "...why social workers in the United States maintained a focus on clients' needs even as their counterparts in other industrializing nations created policies and practices that emphasized clients' rights." According to Reisch, with the advent of industrialization, business or market methods and values penetrated family life, the nature of philanthropy, and social work practice itself. The logic of capitalism transformed family life by fragmenting traditional support systems. It created new kinds of workers, made it necessary for more women to enter the workforce to sustain family incomes, and produced and reproduced consumers for the goods and services needed to fuel the economy. The first order of business in a capitalist economy is to continue and sustain growth. In fact, lack of growth signals a crisis of capitalism. Think for a minute about the ways in which capitalism penetrates the very fabric of social life. In what ways do the mentality of markets and the purchasing of goods and services influence social work?

The Emergence of Social Work: Dichotomies in Practice

Contradictions. Life is full of contradictions, and social work and its practice are no exception. Kelly and Sewell (1988) contend that binary logic, or a logic of contradiction, is the dominant mode of thinking in the U.S. The tendency in binary logic is to divide things into mutually exclusive or dichotomous groups – for example, black or white, or good or bad. In dichotomous thinking, there are no shades of gray. Social work practice mirrors the dichotomous ways in which we view the problems of the poor. Historically, society has grouped poor people into dichotomous categories of worthy or unworthy based on criteria that have persisted over the years. Dating back to the 1600s, the Protestant ethic believed in the godly inheritance of wealth, the wisdom of members of the "ruling class," and the genetic deficiencies of the poor, thus sealing their fate at birth. This belief persists and bumps up against a newly forming conception of the poor as victims of circumstances and specifically as victims of a capitalist system. Beginning around the turn of the 20th century, additional factors shaped shifting perceptions of the poor. For example, a new middle class of professional-managers emerged, many of whom were educated women who contested traditional roles ascribed to women. They were less inclined to separate themselves from their newly acquired knowledge to marry and raise a family. They brought to social work the ideals they learned through formal and religious education.

Mediating Containment and Change. As members of the newly forming profession of social work, they became the mediators between the forces of change and the ever-present human need for stability. Abramovitz (1998, p. 512) refers to these forces as the "twin pressures of containment and change." From its inception, the profession of social work developed methods to forge both change and stability. These tensions have persisted for more than one hundred years.

The Charity Organization Society (COS) and the Settlement House Movement (SHM) were the early forerunners of social work. Administrated primarily by middle- and upper-class women, both the COS and the SHM worked toward stabilizing the crisis of capitalism. However, each operated with quite distinct philosophies and methodologies. Figure 2.2 illustrates these points of comparison.

FIGURE 2.2

Contrasting Modes of Practice: Charity Organization Society and the Settlement House Movement

Characteristics	Charity Organization Society	Settlement House Movement
Key Figures	Mary Richmond; Edward Devine	Jane Addams; Lillian Wald
Language of Helping	Clients	Neighbors
Method of Practice	Casework; Friendly Visiting	Group Work; Education; Advocacy
Philosophy	Scientific; Expert	Participatory Democracy
Power in Relationship	Hierarchical	Toward Equal and Shared
Definition of Poverty	Result of Individual Failings	Result of Sociopolitical, Economic Conditions
Focus of Change Effort	Individual/Familial	Sociopolitical, Economic, Individual
Professionalization	Primary Concern	Not a Concern – A Distraction
Practice Theory	Personal Deficits	Political Economy

Charity Organization Societies. The COSs were based on principles of scientific charity, which sought to find a balance between giving handouts to those in need and providing assistance in the form of moral uplift. Agencies distinguished the "worthy" from the "unworthy" poor: the worthy poor were poor through no fault of their own, for example, widows, orphans, and the elderly. The unworthy poor were those individuals whom the agency believed would rather live off charity than earn a decent living on their own (drunks, "fallen women," malcontents). The primary goal of charity was to "fix" the poor and make them independent, responsible, and self-reliant. These ends were to be achieved through contacts with "friendly visitors." The visitors provided "not alms but a friend." Their activities included teaching the importance of regular mealtimes and educating about proper nutrition. It was believed that through example, visitors would strengthen their clients' moral fiber. An anecdote that gets to the heart of the irony of COS goals and the realities of those living in poverty is quoted by Ehrenreich (1985) from a short story entitled "My Own People" by Anzia Yeziersha. The story's heroine, Hannah Breineh, cries out:

> [The friendly visitor] learns us how to cook oatmeal. By pictures and lectures she shows us how the poor people should live without meat, without milk, without butter, and without eggs. Always it's on the tip of my tongue to ask her, 'You learned us to do without so much, why can't you yet learn us how to eat without eating?'"(p. 39)

Gordon (1988, pp. 61-64) describes how the COS defined pauperism as hereditary poverty "caused by loss of will, work ethic, thrift, responsibility, and honesty." The COS workers' scientific approach was based on principles that were later solidified by Mary Richmond in her text *Social Diagnosis* (1917). The scientific approach to social diagnosis consisted of documenting contacts with clients, collecting voluminous client and family histories, categorizing and assessing areas of concern, and providing each family with an individualized approach. Mary Richmond's vision of social casework differs from the predominant vision today. Richmond viewed the case file as a way to keep a record of clients' development for the following purposes: to guide future actions; to provide training material for other caseworkers; to document the numerous ways in which problematic social conditions impact people's lives; and to be used as a basis for statistical and other forms of inquiry (Richmond, 1922, pp. 22-28). These early intentions have been lost or overshadowed by the present day practice of using case files almost strictly to inform the client's or family's next caseworker.

Gordon (1988), however, makes the point that although reform-minded workers identified the environmental factors contributing to poverty, the persistent undercurrent was one of preventing the undeserving from receiving charitable relief. Tice (1998) describes a variety of ways through which the COS tried to disseminate their message regarding the problems inherent in alms giving. For instance, the Russell Sage Foundation funded and published a three-act play in 1915 entitled "A Bundle or a Boost?" Tice states:

> The performance was designed as a visualization of how to give advice over material aid, a preferred charity organization society practice. The case included the villainous "Father Springfield," whose primary task was to hand out bundles of provisions. In contrast, "Mr. Better Way, " the charity organization hero, had no bundles to distribute but "more to give," so ultimately the poor would receive "help so that they won't need relief." The play ended with Mr. Better Way surrounded by a cheerful throng of deserving poor who had been referred to the society by a teacher and truant officer. (pp. 34-35)

In summary, the Charity Organization Society remained true to its class-based origins. Workers adhered to a definition of poverty that viewed individual failings as the root cause. They sought to produce change in the lives of immigrant poor families by "passing on" the values of the middle-class. Through the efforts of Mary Richmond, the COS sought to align itself with the newly emerging scientific movement in an effort to gain increased credibility for the profession of social work.

Settlement House Movement. The Settlement House Movement emerged in reaction to the moralistic paternalism of the COS and was less stingy in its attitude toward the poor. While still steeped in the middle-class values of the Progressive Era, and believing that the presence of someone of higher caliber would enlighten the lives of those in poverty, the SHM carved out a different location for itself among the poor. Settlement workers believed poverty stemmed from a confluence of social, political, and economic conditions. They moved to poor, immigrant neighborhoods and opened the doors of their houses for cultural gatherings, classes, youth activities, and other community events. Settlements supported labor unions and conducted research that addressed issues such as child labor, unsafe working conditions, and wage inequality for women. In her descriptions of the settlement house, Jane Addams (1910), founder of Hull House, a Chicago settlement stated:

> It aims in a measure, to develop whatever of social life its neighborhood may afford, to focus and give form to that life, to bring to bear upon it the results of cultivation and training; but it receives in exchange for the music of isolated voices the volume and strength of the chorus... (p. 125)

The group work tradition in social work emerged from the Settlement House Movement. Small groups were a context for action, a site for learning and practicing democracy, and an expression of the connection between the individual and the social (Schwartz, 1986). For this very reason Catheryne Cooke Gilman of the Northeast Neighborhood Settlement House in Minneapolis suggested that the motto of the settlements should be: "Keep your fingers on the near things and eyes on the far things" (Chambers, 1963, p. 150). This motto expresses the twin emphases of group work, to pay attention simultaneously to individual need and social reform through the themes of shared control, shared power, and shared agenda. These egalitarian notions alone give us ample indication of settlement house practice principles. Although settlement houses continued throughout social work's history, beginning in the 1920s they gradually moved away from reform efforts and toward the provision of client services.

At the height of the Settlement House Movement, there were 413 settlements located in 32 states. Settlement houses weathered many political storms, and today there are still over 300 settlements in 80 U.S. cities. Karger (1987, p.105) discusses the evolution of the settlement houses and their practice beginning in the 1920s. Following World War I and the Russian revolution, dominant middle-class American society became less tolerant of foreign ideas and cultures, and consequently demanded an uncompromising allegiance to Americanism. Practice within the settlement houses reflected this shift in cultural attitudes and beliefs. Influenced by xenophobic and nativistic tendencies, settlement house workers pressured immigrant neighbors to enter the melting pot of Americanization. Many settlements evolved into neighborhood service centers by the 1930s. While funding for settlements shifted from dependence on philanthropic support to competing for governmental grant funding, they continue to hold sacred their historic mission of treating poor people as citizens, not clients (Husock, 1993).

Tensions of Social Service and Social Change[6]

A confluence of events created a deepening divide within social work between the casework focus of the COS and its emphasis on personal maladjustment, and the social change focus of the SHM. A number of factors were at play here. In this section, we look at some distinct moments of tension between social service and social change. We highlight the Rank and File Movement and the Great Depression, the McCarthy era, and the civil unrest of the 1960s.

End of the Progressive Era. Following World War I, many of the advances made by labor during the Progressive Era beat a speedy retreat. Increasingly under corporate attack, union membership decreased. Industry and labor regulations fell prey to efforts on the part of business and government to meet their own needs for control, power, and wealth. Social achievements rolled back to restore class relations wherein capital had ultimate control (Ehrenreich, 1985, p. 45). This period witnessed the first "red scare," (fear of socialism and communist political ideology) wherein "twenty-four states passed 'red flag laws'" (Ehrenreich, 1985, p. 47), which made it illegal to use a red flag in public gatherings, parades, or general assemblies. While this sounds unbelievable or even ridiculous today, courts of law across the country jailed over 350 people for this offense. Methods of repression such as this cooled the fires of reform and activism that had distinguished the Progressive Era. Repression also helped to shape the nature of social work practice. Think for a moment what it might be like if you believed government was responsible for and to, at least in part, its citizenry. Moreover, what if this way of thinking branded you a communist? Ehrenreich (1985, p. 48) tells the story of how the American Medical Association favored national health insurance until 1916. With a change of leadership, the Association challenged this idea as one step on the road toward full-blown communism. If the "red scare" had such a powerful restraining influence on the medical profession, how might its force restrain and energize the social work profession?

Rank and File Movement. Some social workers resisted this regressive trend. For example, the Rank and File Movement started in the midst of the Great Depression with the Social Work Discussion Group of New York in 1930, a group of relief agency employees. They pooled their resources to confront poor working conditions within their agencies such as low wages, primitive working conditions and lack of job security. These workers were mostly from outside the social work profession or those bachelor-level social workers excluded from joining the American Association of Social Workers (ASSW). The ASSW, founded in 1921, was the first professional social work organization. From its inception, it allowed membership only to those workers who had an advanced degree (Fisher, 1936/1990).

Rank and Filers were acutely sensitive to the plight of the poor because they shared many of the same concerns. Garnering mutual support from others in the same boat and raising their consciousness about economic and political concerns empowered this group to speak out against oppressive work environments and the social work profession itself. They believed many social workers were content to "adjust" to the economic and social crisis brought on by the depression instead of taking action (Fisher, 1936/1990).

Bertha Capen Reynolds (1932/1992) was a member of the Rank and File movement and an educator in the social work program at Smith College. In the 1930s she wrote about the Great Depression and how quickly sentiment toward the poor had changed. In the early years of the Depression people were asked to donate money to relieve the suffering of the poor; in later years, she noted, the tune changed and played off people's fear: "Give to protect your homes from the public enemies of poverty, disease, and crime" (p. 74).

Contrary to most social workers' beliefs in the U.S. as a functioning democracy, Reynolds saw the political economic system in the U.S. as an oligarchy of wealth. Individuals with money had the power to influence government and, in fact, individuals with power to influence *are* the government. According to Reynolds, this oligarchy controlled the media and the press and as a result, exerted sufficient power to influence the middle class to be critical of the poor. Reynolds called the poor "victims of economic disaster." Her view reframed beliefs about the causes of poverty from individual failings to structural deficits. In a telling quote, Reynolds speculated on what hindsight might reveal about the "true" nature of this period: "Was the meager provision for relief to be seen, in the long perspective of history, as just enough to keep alive without giving life – in reality as a preventive of really fundamental solutions?" (p. 77).

Members of the Rank and File movement formed discussion groups, and within two years these spread to other large cities in the U.S. Rank and Filers disseminated critical knowledge on the labor movement, social welfare policy, social conditions, and world affairs by publishing their own journal, *Social Work Today* (Ehrenreich, 1985). Rank and File numbers grew to exceed the membership of AASW by 1935. More traditional social workers criticized Rank and Filers for being too involved with their clients, lacking professionalism, and being guided more by economic theories than those of personal maladjustment. On the other hand, Rank and Filers criticized mainstream social work for focusing more on professionalization to gain status and prestige than on attention to the concerns of the poor.

Professionalization. By the end of the 1930s, even though Fisher (1936/1990) predicted the Rank and File Movement was "here to stay," it dissolved, and its members reentered the mainstream of social work (Ehrenreich, 1985, p.120). Many attribute the decline in the Rank and File Movement and the Settlement House Movement to the increased professionalization of social work beginning in the 1930s. Husock (1993) addresses how " the settlement style, with it's use of volunteers and emphasis on group activities and recreation, would pale in contrast to a paid, credentialed, apparently scientific helping profession [casework]" (p.19). Settlements began to lose their community focus and eventually, those that survived were a hybrid, offering programs simultaneously to combat problems, and clubs and group meetings to bring together neighbors with common interests. Professionalization was a double-edged sword for social work. On one hand, it provided social work with status, a sense of expertise, and professional privilege. On the other hand, many believed social work had sold out to the status quo.

Reisch and Wenocur (1986) define what it means to be a profession and in so doing, explore the power base a group must build and maintain to make such a claim. They believe the compulsion to professionalize rose out of the Industrial Revolution and mirrors the colonizing activities of corporations as they capture new territory and set up the necessary structures, policies, and mandates to ensure their survival. Although Rank and File workers preferred to unionize, social work's predominant middle- and upper-class membership aligned more with the ideology of establishing a privileged position for itself. Before the 1920s, social activism and reform work made up approximately one half of social workers activities. Workers were involved in such diverse areas of practice as child labor reform, women's suffrage, civil rights, peace, social insurance, industrial safety, and labor organizing. By the 1930s, funding streams and dominant discourses on the definitions of social problems supported casework as the preferred method of social work practice. These alterations in social, economic, and political conditions compromised the reformist momentum in social work.

McCarthyism. McCarthyism also had an incredible impact on shutting down the social action stream of social work. Andrews and Reisch (1997) recount how the most oppressive political climate in the U.S. stretched from 1945 to 1960. During this period, "thousands of workers lost their jobs and millions of others curtailed their political activities out of fear of being labeled a communist or a communist sympathizer" (p. 31). Andrews and Reisch make an important point that U.S.

policy makers, backed by the concerns of big business, do not tolerate beliefs that challenge property rights and free enterprise. They also stress how McCarthyism was not a grassroots movement but rather "artificially stimulated at the national and local level by competing political elites, and fanned in turn by mass media motivated both by panic and opportunism (Caute, 1973, p. 320, as cited in Andrews and Reisch, 1997, p. 31).

Andrews and Reisch (1997, pp. 32-33) discuss a book published in the mid-1940s by the Department of the Army entitled "How to Spot a Communist." It warns that a communist is someone critical of the FBI, the American Legion, and the Daughters of the American Revolution. The book outlines a list of words commonly used by communists and sympathizers such as "progressive," "colonialism," "exploitation," "civil rights," "discrimination," and "unions," to name a few. Many federal- and state-funded institutions and programs required their employees to sign a loyalty oath. Liberals fearful of losing their jobs often went to great extremes to prove their loyalty by introducing legislation that would further curtail the activities of the Communist Party or by informing on coworkers who were involved in organizations that addressed issues such as peace or labor rights.

Many social workers were fearful of taking a stand on controversial issues during the McCarthy era (Andrews & Reisch, 1997; Reisch & Andrews, 2001; Schreiber, 1995). Social activists in the 1930s and 1940s were reluctant to continue their activities openly. At a professional meeting, Bertha Capen Reynolds argued that McCarthyism could be defeated, "if plain folks like ourselves" would just demand democracy of the people, by the people, for the people (as cited in Andrews & Reisch, 1997, p. 36). Increasingly marginalized, to the point where she was "let go" from her position at Smith College, Reynolds gradually receded from the social work's mainstream. It is interesting to note that although she made incredible contributions to social work practice through the bridging of social action and individual change, social work texts make little or no reference to her enormous contributions to the profession.

Jacob Fisher, a colleague of Reynolds in the Rank and File movement of the 1930s, also found himself abandoned by co-workers and colleagues. In 1954, his employers at the Social Security Administration charged him with being a security risk based on his activities and memberships. "While some social workers publicly supported him most did not. Unable to find social work employment and alienated from his former colleagues, Fisher left the field of social work. Years later, through the Freedom of Information Act, he learned that some of his social work friends and colleagues had informed on him" (Andrews & Reisch, 1997,

p. 36). The McCarthy senate committee investigated Verne Weed, another Marxist member of the Rank and File movement and a lifelong activist. Many social workers attacked her for her involvement in the peace movement (Andrews & Reisch, 1997).

After passage of the New Deal legislation in the 1930s and through the period shortly following World War II, the welfare state expanded from the pressures caused by economic conditions and global war. Reisch (1998) contends that the improved economy and prosperity of post-WWII influenced the nature and development of social work practice for the remainder of the century. The end of WWII signaled the beginning of multinational corporations, the spread of consumerism, increased government intervention in the economy, the expansion of the military industrial complex, and the post-industrial shift toward an information-based and service-based economy. These conditions, combined with the repressive politics of McCarthyism, put a major damper on social workers' social activism.

Questions from History. This snapshot of history brings a number of questions to mind: How is it that some social workers' stories are legitimized through history and given voice, while others are ignored? Who decides whose stories are included and which ones are left out of the "official" history? What would be the point of omitting the stories of Bertha Reynolds, Jacob Fisher, and Verne Weed? What might be gained by these omissions and what might be lost? What positions or stances might a social worker in the U.S take today that would result in blacklisting? What might be the limits of a social worker's freedom of expression in another political context? Think for a moment beyond U.S. borders to the practice of social work elsewhere. How might the rise to power of a dictator and the involvement of social workers in peoples' resistance efforts affect the practice of social work? How do situations such as these provide cause to rethink our notions of the social work profession and its location in a political context?

"What's Love Got to Do With It?"[7]

As you can see from our presentation of social work's history, it is a history filled with contradiction and tension between social service (providing care and control) and social change (Withorn, 1984). David Wagner (2000, p. 4) grapples with the contradictions built into social work, especially those that surface around the issue of care and control. Wagner argues that assumptions about caring or, at the very least, going through the motions of caring, mask the need to make structural changes in society's institutions that would eliminate poverty, inequality, and discrimination based on race, class, gender, and sexual orientation. Wagner tries to make sense of this contradiction by pointing out the U.S. irony of calling ourselves a caring, altruistic society at the same time that we have one of the highest rates of poverty and inequality and one of the poorest social welfare systems among industrialized western societies. He argues that we tend to ignore the realities that challenge our views of ourselves as good and caring.

Think of the ways in which you might ignore the social problems you see in your city, town, or neighborhood. Do you make eye contact with people who beg for food or money on the street corner? Do you skip elections that only have "local issues" on the ballot? Are there ways in which you deny the reality that the U.S. dollar has lost its buying power and more and more of our real incomes go to put a roof over our heads? What do you tell yourself about the tremendous growth in prisons in the U.S. and the overrepresentation of people of color among their inhabitants? Think for a moment of contradictions in your everyday life. Perhaps you can think of examples where your words said one thing and your behavior was quite the opposite. How did you make sense of the contradiction? Now reflect back to our previous discussion about the contradictions in social work between social service and social change, what we referred to earlier as the twin pressures of containment and change (Abramovitz, 1998, p. 521). What sense do you make of these contradictions in light of social work practice?

Social Work's Struggles for Human Rights, Peace, and Citizenship

Jane Addams' Legacy

Struggles for human rights, peace, and citizenship have intertwined with the practice of social work since its inception. Jane Addams (1910), in her early description of the Settlement House Movement, viewed the movement as:

> . . . an experimental effort to aid in the solution of the social and industrial problems which are engendered by the modern conditions of life in a great city.

> It is an attempt to relieve, at the same time, the over-accumulation at one end of society and the destitution at the other; but it assumes that this over-accumulation and destitution is most sorely felt in the things that pertain to social and educational advantage. (pp. 125-126)

Addams understood the advantage of privilege and, along with other settlement house residents and neighbors, worked to combat social inequality and injustice. Settlement house workers understood through lived experience that, in order to achieve equality and social justice, their concerns and actions must be directed toward gaining human rights over industrialization. They strove to achieve these ends and, through organized social reform efforts, they sought to rectify the conditions that depleted the human spirit.

As the President of the Women's Peace Party, Addams argued against war for its cruelty and inhumanity and because it reversed the function of human relationships, something she saw as the essence of human need (Lee, 1992). In speaking of the ludicrousness of the human sacrifice of war, Addams (1930) stated,

> It took the human race thousands of years to rid itself of human sacrifice; during many centuries it relapsed again and again in periods of national despair. So have we fallen back to warfare, and perhaps will fall back again and again, until in self-pity, in self-defense, in self-assertion of the right of life, not as hitherto a few, but the whole people of the world, will brook this thing no longer. (p. 121)

Mary Church Terrell and Ida B. Wells-Barnett

A similar history is evidenced in the work of early African American women social workers and their struggles to achieve reform. For example, Mary Church Terrell and Ida B. Wells-Barnett made significant contributions in struggles for human rights. Both fought for the equality of African American people and committed their careers to forge international peace. Peebles-Wilkins and Francis (1990) resurrect these women's histories from marginalized status in social work and emphasize the significant contributions these women made at a time when black women bore the brunt of "double discrimination," due to both their womanhood and the color of their skin. Mary Church Terrell promoted gender and race equality in her unfailing advocacy attempts to gain women's vote and racial integration. Ida B. Wells-Barnett, only one generation removed from the horrors of enslavement, was mobilized by family history of slavery and turned tragedy into action through her involvement with anti-lynching campaigns. She viewed the lynching of blacks as a direct consequence of persistent struggles for equality and freedom and the relentless, uncompromising pursuit of social justice.

Jeannette Rankin

Jeannette Rankin is another example of an early human rights activist who devoted her life to struggles for peace and equality. She was educated at the New York School of Philanthropy where she studied social work. In 1916, she was the first woman elected to the U.S. Congress. Her slogan was "Peace is a woman's job." In accordance with this belief, she voted against U.S. entry into World War I. Shortly after, in 1918, she lost the Congressional election but was re-elected in 1940. She was the lone vote against U.S. involvement in World War II. Jeannette Rankin was a world-renowned pacifist and peace activist. She moved to Georgia in the 1930s and organized the Georgia Peace Society. Jeannette Rankin's legacy continues in her hometown of Missoula, Montana where the building that houses the Department of Social Work at The University of Montana bears her name and the Jeannette Rankin Peace Center carries on the work she started almost one hundred years ago (O'Brien, 1995).

Bertha Capen Reynolds

Bertha Capen Reynolds was a teacher, a caseworker, and an activist. She organized with other Rank and Filers during the Depression years to form unions and to question the status quo in social work. Her work provides us with an excellent example of bridge building in social work practice. She connects the need for social service and social change and does so through an intermingling of Freudian theory and Marxist analysis. Reynolds (1963, p. 174) believed:

> [S]ocial work has to find it's place among other movements for human betterment, to be concerned with civil rights, equality of opportunity, decent housing, public health, and community sharing of common hazards like unemployment, sickness and old age through social insurance—all needful things which cannot be secured without the whole community taking some responsibility for their being available to everyone. If social work is a remedial service only, it cannot be remedial for the ills beyond its scope, like mass unemployment, but neither can it ignore the existence of such ills as make impossible a sane administration even of "tinkering" services. Social work must look to the setting as well as to the minutiae of its professional practice.

Ongoing Efforts

Abramovitz (1998) reminds us that efforts to forge equality, social justice, and an enduring peace have persisted throughout social work's history, albeit influenced and shaped by the political, social, and economic tenor of the times. Wars and their aftermath of economic revitalization have caused a waxing and waning of these struggles, as many social workers "settled in" and focused inward on establishing credibility for themselves and the profession. Abramovitz states that: " It took the massive disorders of the 1960s, however, to rekindle the profession's social action spirit fully. Finding social work far behind the social-change curve, critics from within and outside the field accused it of having its head in the sand" (p. 517). According to Abramovitz, social work students carried the banner of social change during this era:

> Students charged that organizational maintenance interests overrode addressing clients' needs in agencies. They also lambasted rigid welfare bureaucracies, condemned school curricula as parochial and outdated, reproached social work's view of social problems as rooted in individual development or family dynamics, and protested social work's lack of response to the black revolution. (p. 517)

This period bore similarities to the Rank and File Movement of the 1930s. In the 1970s, posing challenges to social work's intensified move toward professionalization, social workers joined labor unions and formed groups composed of individuals historically excluded from social work's prestigious professional organizations. They founded organizations of their own such as the Association of Black Social Workers, the Association of Women and Social Work, the Bertha Capen Reynolds Society and the Radical Alliance of Social Service Workers (Abramovitz, 1998). Even social work's more staid organizations (the National Association of Social Workers and the Council of Social Work Education), called attention to the need for social policy change and mandated curriculum changes in social work education to address questions of peace and justice. These efforts continue today, letting us know that the fires of social change keep burning at the heart of the social work profession.

History's Challenge to Contemporary Social Work

This snapshot of history reveals that struggles for human rights, social justice, and equality have played out through the organized and concerted efforts of social work movements for change. These efforts call on the participation of social workers and citizens alike, to ban together and form a solid, powerful base for change. Wagner (2000, p. 4) makes the point that major positive changes for poor people have come not from philanthropy but from social movements. He speculates about what might happen if all the effort and time spent in volunteering and in supporting the work of nonprofit service organizations were channeled into a movement of people to change society for the better. He asks us to imagine what today might be like for us all if Mother Jones or Martin Luther King Jr. had handed out meals at a soup kitchen, or if they had become therapists or program administrators instead of being leaders of social movements. Wagner also pushes us to consider why we view only the Mother Teresas as a symbol of love, and fear or pass over as "cranks" those individuals who organize against, write about, or protest social injustice. He gives us much food for thought as the social work profession moves into the 21st century.

Chapter Summary

In this chapter we have explored the reasons why history and a historical perspective are important to social justice work. We have presented a brief history of social work beginning with its emergence around the turn of the 20th century. We have emphasized the interrelationship between social work and the economy and explored polarities in the philosophies and practice of social work. We have highlighted the contributions of advocates and activists who have been marginalized in many accounts of social work's history. And we have provided biographical sketches of activists inside and outside of social work who have inspired us to question the status quo and pushed us to strive toward increased congruence among our words, values, and actions. In the next chapter we address questions of values and ethics and their relationship to the possibilities of social work practice.

Teaching-Learning Resource: Exploring the Contributions

Stories and Scripts from a Century of Activism

A number of individuals have made significant contributions to social work's history of activism and have "consistently kept the voice of change alive" (Abramovitz, 1998 p. 524). It is important to (re)claim these people we hear so little about but whose histories shed light on possibilities for justice-oriented practice today. As Abramovitz (1998) notes:

> Their ongoing fights against the conflicts stemming from the profession's structural location in society, the narrowing forces of professionalization, and the rise of conservative political climates ensured social work remained an arena of struggle throughout the 20th century. Without such political struggles neither social work nor society would have changed for the better. (p. 524)

The following section presents an example of Reader's Theater and brief histories of people in and outside social work who believed they could make a difference. These are individuals with a deep sense of purpose and an abiding commitment to social justice. As you read these vignettes think of the lessons to be learned from their histories. Are there commonalities you see in the actions they took, what they valued, or the issues upon which they took a stand? What set of justice-oriented practice principles emerge and how would you apply these to social work practice today? You may also want to draw on these vignettes in the creation of your own Reader's Theater.

Reader's Theater

The following "Reader's Theater" scripts were prepared by Janet Finn and Sally Brown, drawing from the life, work, and words of two of social work's "founding mothers." A reader's theater is a brief dramatization where readers take on the roles of people in the scripts. Janet and Sally performed these scripts for a number of social work audiences, wearing period hats and dresses to bring their characters to life. What other scripts would you add to expand a reader's theater production of the history of social justice work?

Jane Addams and Bertha Reynolds: "The Jane and Bertha Show"

Jane: Let me tell you a bit about myself. I was born in Cedarville, Illinois, in 1860, the same year Abe Lincoln was elected President. I was only 4 when Lincoln died, but he looms large in my memory. He was a man of conscience and integrity, like my father. My mother died when I was only two. My father was the most important influence in my life. He was a Quaker, mill owner, banker, and for 16 years, an Illinois State Senator. I adored him and tried hard to live up to his example. My father taught me "to be honest with myself inside, whatever happened." I still remember his words of wisdom: "No matter what your role is in the great drama of life, act well your part."

My father encouraged me to pursue my education and a career. He never saw my gender as a limitation. So I went to Rockford Seminary, a boarding school near my home, and planned to study medicine at Women's Medical College in Philadelphia. My dear father died right after I graduated from boarding school, and I felt like my whole life was crumbling around me. I lost all my incentive. I became ill and had to drop out of school. I felt like such a failure. For several years, I was adrift. I was "weary of myself and sick of asking what I am and what I ought to be."

I traveled to Europe with my stepmother. In my day, that was how one cultivated the graces of womanhood. But that was not for me. I made a second trip to Europe in 1887. This time I did not visit cathedrals and galleries but factories and slums. I had seen poverty among rural farmers in the Midwest, but now I came face to face with the suffering and struggles of the urban poor. I attended meetings of the London match girls who were on strike. I saw the hunger and need in the faces of tenement dwellers in London's East End. And, finally, in 1888, I made a visit to a place called Toynbee Hall, the first Settlement House, established in East London. It was an experiment in Christian socialism dedicated to meeting the needs of the poor. It was then and there that I realized that to be true to myself I would have to cast my own lot with the poor.

And so, in the fall of 1889, I moved to an industrial district of Chicago. My school friend Ellen Starr and I found a decaying old mansion on Halsted Street. On September 18, 1889, we opened its doors to all who cared to enter. I remember how my father had never locked his doors, and I decided from the start that the doors of Hull House would always be open to the world. Halsted Street was teeming with immigrants, and with bars and brothels and pawnshops. It was here we began our experiment in social work.

At Hull House, we learned about immigration and community life from immigrants. These were the people making the clothing that Americans wore, growing the food and working in the stockyards to feed Americans. They lived under conditions of oppression, both in the countries they left behind and in their new home in the United States. Yet they also lived with music and art, with joy and laughter. Hull House became a center of community life, struggling with their challenges and celebrating their successes. It became a university, concert hall, gymnasium, library, and clubhouse of the neighborhood. We took pride in the fact that our first new building was an art gallery. Over time at Hull House we established a working girls' home, a day nursery, a labor museum, boys' club, and theater. We were always seeking funding, but we turned down any money with strings attached that would compromise our mission.

We approached our work at Hull House with the enthusiasm of an artist, trying to translate a vision into reality. It was a place where those who have a passion for human joy, justice, and opportunity came together. We were painfully aware of the confusions and struggles all around us, but we also believed that struggle itself might be a source of strength. The Settlement was, above all, a place of tolerance and openness. We had to let go of our preconceptions and open ourselves to learning from and in the neighborhood.

We soon learned that so-called "simple" people are interested in large and vital subjects. Residents and community members became involved in policy and legislative issues, such as child labor laws, and together we conducted investigations of the area's living and working conditions. The investigations carried out at Hull House arose from the problems of peoples' everyday lives. For example, our investigation of sanitary conditions was prompted by the fact that neighborhood residents lived alongside garbage dumps. Our children played in and around huge wooden garbage boxes overflowing in the streets. We initiated an effort to get the boxes removed and began a systematic investigation of the city's system of garbage collection. Members of the Hull House Women's Club came together to discuss the high death rate in our ward. They began to investigate the conditions of alleys in the ward and document violations of health regulations. Because of our dogged efforts, the mayor appointed me garbage inspector for the ward with a salary of $1,000 a year!

Narrator: After the outbreak of World War I, Jane Addams dedicated herself to world peace. She was a founding member of the Women's Peace Party in 1915. She came under severe public criticism for her pacifist position during World War I. She headed the U.S. delegation to the 2nd Women's Peace Conference in 1919. She was elected the first president of the Women's International League for Peace and Freedom. She dedicated herself extensively to international peace issues in the 1920s.

Addams: "I believe that peace is not merely the absence of war but the nurture of human life and that in time this nurture would do away with war as a natural process."

Narrator: In 1931 Jane Addams was awarded the Nobel Peace Prize. Jane Addams was both activist and intellectual, theorist and organizer. She spoke of concern over class division of society and over the incompatibility of industrialism and humanity. She offered a strong critique of society over the years even as she maintained an optimism for the empowering possibilities of a true social democracy. She died in Chicago on May 21, 1935.

In one of her last public appearances, at the 20th anniversary celebration of the Women's International League, three weeks before her death, Addams spoke these words:

Addams: People must come to realize how futile war is. It is so disastrous, not only in poison gas used to destroy lives, but in the poison injected into the public mind. We are suffering still from the war psychology. We can find many things which are the result of war, and one war is really the result of past wars... If it became fixed in the human mind that killing was not justified, it would be done away with...

Bertha: My name is Bertha Reynolds. I was born in rural Massachusetts in 1885, about the same time Jane was in Europe learning how to be a lady. I come from a family of very modest means. My father and two of my siblings died when I was quite young. I was raised by my mother, a high school teacher, and her family. I was home-schooled until I was twelve, and graduated Phi Beta Kappa from Smith College in Psychology.

My first job was as a teacher in an all-black high school in Atlanta. It was an important learning experience for me. I was only able to stay barely a year and had to leave the post due to emotional and physical illness. I returned to Boston and after recovering my strength, I entered a one-year certificate program in social work offered by the Boston School of Social Work and Simmons College.

I found my studies fascinating, and I ended up entering the first class for psychiatric social workers at Smith College. I worked for the Boston Children's Aid Society for five years, then went on to receive my MSW. Eventually I was offered the position of Associate Director of the Smith College School of Social Work.

I left the position at Smith over a widening chasm between my approach to social work and that of the prevailing theory and practice at the time. I took a very practical approach, looking at the connections between social work and social living, and thinking about the ways in which social work respected or denied people their full adult status. I looked at problems from an environmental perspective and was concerned about the ways social work was integrated with social change. I didn't fit too well with the Diagnostic School, the more popular social work approach at the time, which focused on individual problems and treatment.

In the 1930s I became an active member of the political left, joined the Communist and later the Socialist party, and got involved in labor organizations. My colleagues and I started the Rank and File Movement, a broad-based organization made up largely of public sector workers without professional credentials. We published the journal *Social Work Today*, a magazine for and about the work of activist social workers. I learned a great deal working with merchant seamen at the National Maritime Union, not your typical social work clients, as we set up social services for the union members. The work helped me develop new theories about what social work should and should not be.

For me, social work must stay the course with a focus on humanitarian concerns and social reform. We, as social workers, need to work as advocates and activists for structural change. I have tried to sum up what social work means to me in five simple principles: 1) Social work exists to serve people in need. 2) Social work exists to help people help themselves. 3) Social work operates by communication, listening, and sharing experiences. 4) Social work has to find a place among other movements for human betterment. And 5) social workers as citizens cannot consider themselves superior to their clients. We too, have the same problems.

Narrator: Reynolds professed and practiced social work based on four key values: belonging, keeping full adult status, mutuality, and no strings attached. Her practice wisdom serves us well today. Reynolds died in 1978. The legacy of her work continues through the Social Welfare Action Alliance (formerly the Bertha Capen Reynolds Society), an organization of activist social workers dedicated to progressive social change.[8]

Reclaiming Histories, Voices, and Possibilities

In this section we present brief autobiographies of five inspirational people in the history of social justice work: Mary Abby Van Kleeck, Jeannette Rankin, Myles Horton, Mary Harris "Mother" Jones, and W. E. B. DuBois. We invite you to draw on these vignettes to create your own performance. For example, class members could participate "in character" in discussions and debates about social justice issues. Perhaps you could put together a panel of speakers presenting different times in the history of social work or orchestrate a debate among historical figures on a specific topic such as poverty, discrimination, or war. What dialogue can you imagine occurring between Jane Addams and Mother Jones? Between W. E. B. DuBois and Myles Horton? How might these key figures view social work today? What might they recommend for a justice-oriented approach to social work? We encourage readers to learn about other inspirational people who have shaped the history of social justice work. Create and perform your own scripts. It is a great way to inspire others.

Mary Abby Van Kleeck (1883-1972)

I was born in upstate New York, and my father was a minister. By the age of 21, I had completed my bachelor's degree from Smith's College. This is when I joined the College Settlements Association, and I began my career as an economist, social researcher, and social reformer. From the very beginning of my research career, I studied issues that concerned labor. For example, I completed a study on children's home labor and three on women's labor as factory workers, milliners, and artificial flower makers. I enjoyed researching these topics because it fit so well with my interest in economics and was such a good way to publicize the plight of working class people in the U.S. at the turn of the century. I was well organized and had a knack for getting people to collaborate on a research project.

For several decades, I served as the director of Russell Sage Foundation's Department of Industrial Studies. I like to think that my work helped bring about legislative reform by shedding light on exploitive work conditions (i.e., long hours, poor equipment, and miserly wages) in various trade occupations. My devotion to the rights of labor, especially women's work, led me to help set the War Labor Policies Board standards during World War I. This really needed to happen so big business would not continue to exploit women working in the war industry. I was appointed head of the Women in Industrial Service agency established within the Department of Labor. This later became the United States Women's Bureau.

After the war, I returned to Russell Sage Foundation where I took on more research to investigate the underlying causes of job insecurity and labor unrest. With the stock market crash in 1929 and the advent of the Great Depression, my philosophical beliefs and my critical analysis of government, corporate interests, and labor found a home in socialism. A turning point in my life happened in 1933 when I resigned from a new position I had taken with the Federal Advisory Council of the United States Employment Service after only one day on the job. While other social workers and reformers were singing the accolades of the New Deal policies, I had an entirely different way of looking at what I believed was a "three-cornered conflict of interest." This triangle of interests was among those who own and control the economic system; the workers, who were claiming their right to a livelihood in an age of plentiful production; and the government, which has always more closely identified itself with property rights. To attain human rights there must be struggle.

I firmly believed that most people, including social workers, have illusions regarding government and unless we break through this fog, social workers will continue to play down elements of power so essential to maintaining property rights over human rights. I warned other social workers against cooptation by the New Deal and other government reforms. My conviction in these principles shaped my actions as a social reformer. Social workers should have a closer association with workers' groups than with boards of directors and governmental officials. Only then will the practice of social work have the vitality of social purpose that comes out of the genuine experience of life of the underprivileged. I presented some of my ideas at a National Conference of Social Work in 1934 where I received an award for my social activism work. I based my analysis on two theories of government:

> That government stands above conflicting interests in a democracy and can be brought, by majority vote, to decide between those conflicts and compel standards and policies which are in the best public interest. . . Another theory . . . is that government essentially is dominated by the strongest economic power and becomes the instrument to serve the purposes of the groups possessing that power. (Van Kleeck, 1934/1991, p. 79)

I believed communities were composed of groups with conflicting interests rather than common interests and that "(t)he government will then represent the strongest power and will develop instruments of defense of that power—army, navy, militia, and police." While the audience responded to my words with both uproar and exultation, social work went on to accept the New Deal as an interim measure, never fully coming to grips with their illusions of government. Throughout my life I continued to contend that relief programs such as the New Deal were ploys to suppress the possibility of grassroots revolt. They were a way to avoid making fundamental structural change in our social institutions.

In 1948, following World War II, I retired from the Russell Sage Foundation. Shortly thereafter, I ran unsuccessfully for the New York State Senate on the American Labor Party ticket. Through my organizational affiliations with the Episcopal League for Social Action and the Church League for Industrial Democracy, I pursued postwar interests such as disarmament and the peacetime uses of nuclear energy.[9]

Jeannette Rankin – (1880 –1973)

I was the first woman elected to the U.S. House of Representatives and the only member of Congress to vote against entry of the United States into both world wars. I was born on Grant Creek Ranch, six miles from Missoula in Montana Territory, to Olive and John Rankin. I attended grade school in Missoula and was a member of the first University of Montana graduating class in 1902 with a B.S. degree in Biology. In 1908, I left Montana to study at the New York School of Philanthropy (now known as the Columbia University School of Social Work) and, subsequently, practiced as a social worker in Montana and Washington.

I joined the suffragist ranks and helped win women's right to vote in state elections in California, Washington, and Montana. In 1916, I ran for Congress from Montana. I campaigned successfully on a progressive Republican platform calling for women suffrage, protective legislation for children, tariff revision, prohibition, and "preparedness that will make for peace." On April 6, 1917, I voted against the United States' entry into World War I. This act publicly identified me as a pacifist for the first time.

From 1920 until 1939, I worked for various peace and public interest groups. Growing increasingly impatient with the foreign policy of F.D.R., I ran again in 1940 for Congress as a Republican pacifist and was elected. On

December 8, 1941, the day after Pearl Harbor, I cast the single vote against the American entry into the Second World War. That vote cost me my Congressional seat. After my term was over, I went back to social work and progressive political activities. Simultaneously, I settled into a dirt floor homestead in Georgia where I tended my garden and taught children what I called, "peace habits." I wanted to prove that people could live more simply.

Throughout the 1950s, I quietly opposed all manifestation of the cold war, including the United States' involvement in Korea. The war in Vietnam revitalized my public career. I had been out of the public limelight for two decades when the Jeannette Rankin Brigade was organized in 1967. The brigade demonstrated against the war in Washington, D.C. on January 15, 1968.

Jeannette Rankin died of a heart attack in Carmel, California in 1973. Her life epitomizes the experience of a western woman among a generation of female pacifists who believe in a global society of peace. [10]

Myles Horton (1905-1990)

I was born in Savannah, Tennessee on July 9, 1905. My parents were both school teachers before the time when it was necessary to have a formal teaching degree. When that changed, they took odd jobs, but we never thought of ourselves as working class or poor—just regular people who didn't have any money. I got some early training from my grandfather that set the course of my life. He was an illiterate mountain man who thought rich people were evil and were going to hell. I took this for granted and didn't understand the meaning of this belief until I started working myself and saw how unfair the wage system really was. Why should one person work so hard and get so little while another hardly works at all and benefits from the other's labor? This question planted the seeds that would later grow into my work as an educator, labor organizer, civil rights activist, and in 1932, one of the founders of Highlander Folk School.

I loved schooling and learning. I saw learning as a life-long process, and I combined this with a good sense of what was right and what was wrong. I believe I got this from my mother and I took it to another level—it's the principle of trying to serve others and build a loving world. I attended college and Union Theological Seminary. I learned about unionism, communism, socialism, and pacifism but I tried not to let any of these "isms" become a dogma in my life. I went to the University of Chicago in 1930 to learn about sociology and how to help people solve social conflicts and change society. I was really looking for a model for how to work in Appalachia, my home. One day I went with a group of students to visit Hull House. Jane Addams was there and so was Alice Hamilton, the mother of industrial medicine. When asked why each of us had come to visit, all the others talked about their interest in social work. When it was my turn, I came straight out and said I had no interest in what Hull House had become, but I was interested in what it used to be. I wanted to know about the early struggles, how they dealt with being labeled Communist and being put in jail, and about their involvements in the early labor movement. Jane Addams personally asked to speak to me after that day. She helped me get some of my ideas together about the meaning of democracy that led to the next leg of my journey.

In 1927, I spent the summer teaching Bible classes back home in Tennessee. From working with the poor mountain people, I began to formulate my plan to start a school different from other schools. I wanted to help people transform their oppressive life situations into action. I left Chicago a year later and headed for Denmark. I had discussed my ideas about a school with two Danish-born ministers I had met. They thought the Danish folk schools came really close to my descriptions of a democratic education model. This model had originated out of social ferment in Denmark in the mid-nineteenth century. Back in the U.S. a year later, I pulled together a group of like-minded friends and we started Highlander Folk School in Monteagle, Tennessee. Highlander was known as a hotbed of radicalism. We taught leadership skills to blacks and whites in the same classroom, something unheard of and down right illegal at the time, given segregation laws. We stayed true to our convictions. We lived democracy as we tried to change the so-called democratic social, political and economic structures of government and the institutions of power in the U.S. We worked with labor unions, anti-poverty organizations, and civil rights leaders. Highlander got a name for itself as the spark that ignited the civil rights movement.

In 1960, right in the midst of the civil rights movement, the Tennessee courts closed Highlander. They said it violated its charter by permitting integration of blacks and whites. We opened it right up again and called it Highlander Research and Education Center in Knoxville. In 1971 we moved to a 100-acre, mountainside farm in New Market, Tennessee. I'd have to say that one of the biggest learnings of my life was the realization that if we think we have the answers to other peoples' problems then we close the door to the answers they have for themselves. If, on the other hand, we realize we don't have the expert answers, we open up the door to the possibilities for change. I've always believed that people are experts on their own lives.[11]

Mary Harris "Mother" Jones (1830-1930)

I was born in Cork, Ireland in 1830. My family was poor and had been fighting for Ireland's freedom for generations. My father, Richard Harris, came to America in 1835, and as soon as he became an American citizen, he sent for his family. His work as a laborer in railway construction brought my family to Toronto, Canada. (Although I was raised in Canada, I have always been proud of my American citizenship.) After school, I returned to America to become a teacher. In 1861, I met my husband while teaching in Memphis, Tennessee. He was an iron moulder and an active member of the Iron Moulder's Union. In 1867, a yellow fever epidemic swept Memphis. Its victims were mainly among the poor and the workers. One by one, my four children and my husband sickened and died.

After the union buried my family, I nursed the remaining sufferers until the plague was stamped out. Afterward, I went to Chicago into the dressmaking business. I worked for the aristocrats of the city and as a result, had ample opportunity to observe the luxury and extravagance of their lives. Often while sewing for the rich who lived in magnificent houses on Lake Shore Drive, I would look out the windows and see the poor, shivering wretches, jobless and hungry, walking alone along the frozen lakefront. The contrast of their condition with that of the people for whom I worked was painful to me.

In October 1871, the great Chicago fire burned up my business and everything that I had. The fire made thousands homeless. Along with many other refugees, I stayed at Old St. Mary's church. Nearby in an old fire scorched building the Knights of Labor held meetings. During this time, I spent my evenings at their meetings, listening to the splendid speakers. I became more and more engrossed in the labor struggle and decided to take an active part in the efforts of the working people to better the conditions under which they worked and lived.

From 1880 on, I became wholly engrossed in the labor movement as a labor organizer. I went to Ohio and Baltimore to organize railroad laborers, to Chicago to organize lake seamen and dock laborers and to Virginia to organize coal miners. In 1899, I was asked to help the United Mine Workers organize the coalfields of Arnot, Pennsylvania. After five months of striking, the men had become despondent. So I told the men to stay home with the children and urged their wives to take their dishpans, brooms and hammers to the fields. I instructed them to hammer and howl and chase the scabs and mules away when they approached. And it worked, because no scabs went to work that day or any other. The union was victorious.

In 1903 I went to Kensington, Pennsylvania to strike with textile workers who wanted more pay and shorter hours. At least 10,000 of the 75,000 laborers were little children. I helped to assemble a number of the children who were striking one morning in Independence Park. After a large crowd had gathered, I held up the children's mutilated hands and told the people that Philadelphia's mansions were built on the broken bones, quivering hearts and drooping heads of the children who worked in the textile mills. When things began to calm down in Kensington, I decided to stir them up again. At the time the Liberty Bell was traveling around the country and drawing large crowds. This gave me an idea. I decided to take the little children from the textile mills on a tour.

We went all over Pennsylvania, New Jersey and New York, drawing in great crowds and educating people about the horrors of child labor. Not long afterward, the Pennsylvania legislature passed a child labor law that sent thousands of children home from the mills to get an education and kept thousands of other children from entering the factory until their were fourteen years of age.

When Mother Jones died in 1930, she was the single most beloved individual in the whole history of the U.S. labor movement. She devoted her life to enhancing the power of working class people. [12]

W.E.B. DuBois (1868-1963)

I was born in Berkshire County, Western Massachusetts, five years after the Emancipation Proclamation began freeing American Negro slaves. I learned my patterns of living in Great Barrington, Massachusetts in the town schools, churches, and general social life. As a child, although my schoolmates were invariably white, I had almost no experience of segregation or color discrimination. I joined quite naturally in and excelled at all games and excursions, I was in and out of nearly all the homes of my mates and ate and played with them. I understood nevertheless that I was different, that I was exceptional in appearance and that most of the other colored persons I saw, including my own folk, were poorer than the well-to-do whites, lived in humbler houses and did not own stores.

Early in life I understood that the secret of loosing the color bar rest in excellence and in accomplishment, that the only way colored people could gain equality was to get an education, work hard and excel. If visitors to school remarked on my brown face, I waited in quiet confidence. When my turn came, I recited persuasively and correctly and then sat back complacently.

In the summer of 1885 I began college at Fisk University, a college for Negroes in Nashville, Tennessee. The excellent and earnest teaching, the small college classes and the absence of distractions enabled me to arrange and build my program for the freedom and progress of Negroes. I spent my summers traveling and teaching summer school in the country districts of the South. I wanted to know the real seat of slavery. The net result of my experiences at Fisk was to broaden the scope of my program of life, not essentially to change it; to center it in a group of educated Negroes, who from their knowledge and experience would lead the masses.

It was a piece of unusual luck, much more than my own determination, that admitted me to Harvard. There had been arising in Harvard in the 1880's a feeling that the institution was becoming too ingrown. I saw advertisements of scholarships and submitted applications. I was immediately accepted. In 1888, I went to Harvard as a Negro, not simply by birth, but by recognizing myself as a member of a caste whose situation I accepted but was determined to work from within that caste to find my way out. I pursued philosophy as my life career, with teaching for support at Harvard from 1888 to 1890.

It wasn't until I went to Germany, to attend the University of Berlin, that I began to start seeing the race problem in America, the problems of peoples of Africa and Asia, and the political development of Europe as one. At this time I began to feel that dichotomy which all my life characterized my thought: how far can love for my oppressed race accord with love for the oppressing country? And when these loyalties diverge, where shall my soul find refuge?

From the autumn of 1884 to the spring of 1910, for 16 years, I was a teacher and a student of social science. For two years I remained at Wilberforce, for a year and a half at the University of Pennsylvania, and for 13 years at Atlanta University in Georgia. I sought in these years to know my world and to teach youth the meaning and way of the world. The main significance of my work at Atlanta University during the years 1897 to 1910, was the development of a program of study on the problems affecting the American Negroes. This program produced an encyclopedia on the American Negro that was widely distributed and used by other scholars. Between 1896 and 1920 there was no study made of the race problem in America that did not depend in some degree upon the investigations made at Atlanta University.

In 1905, I organized a conference, later known as the Niagara Movement, in response to the growing philosophical divisions among American Negroes. The Niagara Movement's objectives were to advocate for freedom of speech and criticism, an unfettered press, manhood suffrage, the abolition of all caste distinctions based on race and a belief in the dignity of labor. In 1909 I was invited to join a conference sponsored by white liberals for scientists, philanthropists, social workers and Negroes interested in the race problem. The National Association for the Advancement of Colored People or NAACP formed as a result and I was asked to join the organization as Director of Publications and Research.

The span of DuBois' life from 1910 to 1934 is chiefly the story of "The Crisis," the NAACP newspaper. He dedicated the rest of his life to working for peace on Earth and to Pan-Africanism or the organized protection of the Negro world led by American Negroes. DuBois died at the age of 95, a member of the communist party and a citizen of Ghana.[13]

Questions for Discussion

1. Given the reasons cited in the chapter regarding the importance of a historical perspective for social-justice oriented social work, what reasons of your own might you add and why?
2. What examples of the history of a particular social problem or construct could you use to illustrate the importance of a historical perspective to social work practice?
3. In reflecting upon the history of social work in the U.S., how can the key themes of meaning, context, power, history, and possibility help bring understanding to this history?
4. What are some historic or contemporary examples that illustrate the intertwining nature of social work and the economy?

5. What factors account for the differences between the Charity Organization Society and the Settlement House Movement?
6. What factors contributed to the decline of social justice-oriented practice in social work's history beginning in the 1920s?

Suggested Readings

Addams, J. (1910). *Twenty years at Hull House.* New York: Macmillan.

Ehrenreich, J. H. (1985). *The altruistic imagination: A history of social work and social policy in the United States.* Ithaca, NY: Cornell University Press.

Fisher, R. (1999). "Speaking for the contribution of history: Context and the origins of the Social Welfare History Group." *Social Service Review*, 73(2), 191-217.

Gould, S. (1981). *The mismeasure of man.* New York: W.W. Norton and Co.

Reisch, M. & Andrews, J. (2001). *The road not taken: A history of radical social work in the United States.* New York: Brunner/Routledge.

Reynolds, B.C. (1987). *Social work and social living.* Silver Spring, MD: National Association of Social Workers.

Wagner, D. (2000). *What's love got to do with it: A critical look at American Charity.* New York: The New Press.

Wenocur, S. & Reisch, M. (1989). *From charity to enterprise: The development of American social work in a market economy.* Chicago: University of Illinois Press.

Chapter 3

Values, Ethics, and Visions

"The philosophy of social work cannot be separated from the prevailing philosophy of a nation, as to how it values people and what importance it sets up for their welfare... Practice is always shaped by the needs of the times, the problems they present, the fears they generate, the solutions that appeal, and the knowledge and skills available."

Bertha Capen Reynolds (1951), *Social Work and Social Living*

Chapter Overview

In Chapter Three we explore the concept of values, their formation, and their place in our everyday lives. How are values and the practices of valuing shaped and challenged over time? How are values entwined in our most basic assumptions about the world and how we relate with others? How are values translated into standards for ethical practice? We examine the value base of social work and introduce readers to the core values of the social work profession as described in the Code of Ethics of the National Association of Social Workers in the U.S. We then turn to a consideration of ethics and values in context, looking at changes in the code over time and examining the guidelines for ethical practice developed in other organizational and national contexts. We conclude with a consideration of the relationship among values, human rights, and social justice work. What are the values that guide social justice work and inform a framework for Just Practice?

What Do We Mean by Values?

Defining Values

Webster's dictionary (1983) defines value as "that which is desirable or worthy of esteem for its own sake; a thing or quality having intrinsic worth" (p. 2018). Interestingly, the first five definitions of "value" refer to monetary worth, which may tell us something about what is valued in contemporary society. Values are often described as guides to individual and collective action. Values are not provable "truths." Rather, they can be summarized as guides to behavior that grow out of personal experience, change with experience, and are evolving in nature (Johnson, 1998, p. 49). Some social work writers describe values as principles about that which we ultimately hold as worthy and good; about desired ends; and about the means of achieving those ends. Values are the principles upon which we base critical reflection and action. Frederic Reamer (1995) describes the attributes and functions of values as follows: "they are generalized, emotionally charged conceptions of what is desirable; historically created and derived from experience; shared by a population or group within it; and they provide the means for organizing and structuring patterns of behavior" (p. 11). Attention to the emotional component is important. People feel deeply about that which they value, and value conflicts can provoke strong emotional responses.

Our values are not random (Miley, O'Melia, & DuBois, 1998, p.65); they have histories. They are learned through our experiences in families, communities, and other social groups. Values are emergent and dynamic, both shaping and shaped by our beliefs about and experience in the world. We learn, internalize, and question our values in historical, political, and cultural contexts. We learn powerful lessons in values through participation in schooling, religious institutions, work, the market place, and from the media. However, the value lessons being learned may be very different from the value lessons purportedly being taught.

Values in Context

Values and moral authority have been the subject of study and debate by philosophers, religious and political leaders, and everyday people struggling to make their way in the world. Plato sought to identify moral values, or "virtues" as he called them, that guided both individuals and societies. He described a fundamental virtue to be acting wisely and courageously with temperance and justice (Dobelstein, 1999, p. 27). In a similar vein, Confucius wrote, "wisdom, compassion and courage... are the three universally recognized moral qualities of men" (Confucius, *The Doctrine of Mean, Ch. XX, 8)*.[1] French philosopher Denis Diderot saw the capacity for valuing and judgement to be fundamental to humanity. He wrote,

> Descartes said, "I think therefore I am." Helvetius (French philosopher and contemporary of Diderot) wants to say, "I feel therefore I want to feel pleasantly." I prefer Hobbes who claims that in order to draw a conclusion which takes us somewhere we must say, "I feel, I think, I judge, therefore, a part of organized matter like me is capable of feeling, thinking and judging." (Diderot, "On Man," 1774, in Seldes, 1985, p. 108)

Echoing Diderot, German-born American political philosopher Hannah Arendt wrote: "Thinking, willing and judging are the three basic fundamental activities. They cannot be derived from each other, and although they have certain common characteristics, they cannot be reduced to a common denominator" (*Life of the Mind,* unfinished trilogy in Seldes, p. 16). German philosopher Friedrich Nietzsche wrote: "Revaluation of all values: that is my formula for an act of ultimate self-examination by mankind in which he has become flesh and genius" (*Ecce Homo*, 1908 in Seldes, p. 311). Albert Einstein (1934) held that "the true value of a human being is determined by the measure and the sense in which he has attained liberation from the self"(in Seldes, p. 119). And physician and philosopher Albert Schweitzer contended that "a man is truly ethical only when he obeys the compulsion to help all life which he is able to assist, and shirks from injuring anything that lives" (1923, in Seldes, 1985, p. 376). How would you define values? Do you agree that there are universally recognized moral qualities of human beings? How would you describe your personal philosophy of human values? Where does your philosophy agree with or differ from those mentioned above?

Many writers have sought to describe "universal" human values that remain constant through time and across human groups. However, the very concept of "value" is socially constructed, imbued with multiple and contested meanings.

One of the challenges of social justice work is to both appreciate diverse constructions of values and question the modes of power at work in the process of valuing. As Dobelstein (1999) describes, in the U.S. context values:

> have gradually become associated with nouns rather than verbs or adverbs, as if values were things rather than action. When objects are valued over actions, then much of the moral authority of the value is lost...(T)urning values into things without concern for how the things are achieved empties them of much of their authority to guide morally relevant behaviors. (p. 26)

Thus, value has come to have a different meaning as it has become more closely associated with the goal-driven nature of economic rationality and less with a notion of virtue that guides individual and social actions (pp. 26-27).

Dobelstein (1999) writes that values are based on ideologies, that is, our beliefs about what is "true." As we saw in Chapter Two, values are deeply embedded in our political, social, and economic institutions, creating an ideological foundation for institutional structures and practices that often goes largely unquestioned. For example, in the U.S. the value of "freedom" is broadly invoked as a fundamental value with the force of moral authority. The dominant concept of freedom in the U.S. is one grounded in liberalism, capitalism, and positivism, and constructed in terms of individualism and individual rights (p. 24). Discourses of individual rights often serve to limit reflection on another value, that of social responsibility. We frequently hear claims for rights to privacy, to bear arms, to choose. These seem to drown out discussion of responsibility to the common good. Some social workers have challenged the silencing of social responsibility and have called on us to recognize the intimate connection between rights and responsibilities. For example, in 1910, in the heyday of industrial capitalism, Jane Addams wrote: "The good we secure for ourselves is precarious and uncertain... until it is secured for all of us and incorporated in our common life" (Addams, 1910, cited in Ramanathan & Link, 1999, p. 229).

Personal Core Values

It does not take long to see the complex nature of values and valuing and the tensions in play as competing values are espoused, practiced, and challenged. Similarly, we encounter tensions and contradictions in our efforts to formulate and practice our own core values. Take a few minutes to reflect on your own core values. Try to identify **six core values**, ways of being and doing that you hold to be good and desirable. Think about what these values mean to you. Would you describe these as personal values? Social values? Both? Have you experienced a time when two or more of these values were in conflict with one another? What were the circumstances? Were you able to resolve the conflict? What values guided your actions? Now think about a time when your own everyday action in the world has contradicted one of these values. What was the context? How did you negotiate that predicament? What sorts of feelings did it provoke? How did you justify your actions to yourself or to others? As meaning-making beings with the capacity to evaluate and reflect on our actions in the world, we often find ourselves up against conflicts and contradictions. We are, as the country music singers tell us, "walking contradictions."

American Values?

We often hear talk about "American values," "societal" values, or "middle-class" values. Such sweeping notions of values suggest that these values are broadly shared and uncontested. They also assume that "America," "society," and the "middle class" are homogeneous groups who would readily agree on a set of shared values. Such value claims are often held up to be both correct and normative, that is, the norm by which "other" values held by "other" groups are to be judged. Such a view of values denies the complexities and conflicts of interests, beliefs, values, and practices within contemporary U.S. society. It creates boundaries between "us" and "them" and contributes to particular assumptions about difference and similarity. These all-encompassing notions of values may reflect the particular interests of dominant groups who wish to maintain the status quo; they neglect the possibility that "others" may share similar values but are denied the resources and opportunities to realize them. Further, individuals and groups may give very different meanings to the same expressed value. Consider, for example, the many possible meanings of "success." For some it may be measured in terms of individual achievement and monetary gain, while for those with a collectivist, non-capitalist orientation, such a measure would be antithetical to their values.

Consider for a moment some of the values we commonly hear described as "American" values. We list some of those values: freedom, opportunity, individualism, enterprise, pragmatism, efficiency, equality, progress, democracy.

What else would you add to the list? These values are deeply embedded in our social, political, and economic institutions and practices. As Johnson (1998, p.50) describes, "(t)hese values have had their origin in a combination of sources including (1) the capitalistic-Puritan ethic; (2) the Judeo-Christian heritage; and (3) humanistic, positivistic, utopian thinking." They have evocative force. They are often paired with the value of patriotism and touted as values that "others" should embrace. And yet, as we look at our list, we can point to values that may be in conflict with one another. Moreover, we can identify other values and virtues that are not part of our list, but we could readily argue as desirable in guiding human action. And we can describe a litany of examples that demonstrate the ways in which individual and institutional practices contradict these values. What are some contradictions that come to mind as you reflect on your list of "American" values? As you compare your list to your experiences of everyday life in the U.S.? Where are the contradictions most salient for you?

Now, imagine for a moment a first-time visitor coming to the U.S. with little prior knowledge of popularly expressed American values. She has an opportunity to travel, to visit cities and towns, to read newspapers, to watch television, and to participate in other activities of contemporary social life. Based on these experiences, how might she describe "American values?" Perhaps she would describe Americans as placing a high value on size, where bigger always seems to be better. After a trip around the country she may note an American value for mobility, given the impressive amounts of pavement, cars, and trucks. A trip to a few supermarkets may leave her with the impression that Americans highly value choice, packaging, pets, and hygiene. A pass through the checkout stand would confirm suspicions about the valuing of sports heroes, diets, gluttony, political scandal, celebrities, greed, horoscopes, and pop psychology experts. She may be perplexed by reading a headline that says a high court has upheld the fundamental separation of church and state, then paying for her groceries with money that claims, "In God We Trust." A trip to a suburban housing tract may suggest that conformity is more highly valued than individualism. What other impressions of "American values" might our first-time visitor gain? What sorts of contradictions might she encounter? If you were to take a visitor on an "American value tour" where would you go?

Values are also shaped in relationship to social class. For example, how a person gives meaning to "success" or comes to value certain kinds of knowledge and forms of labor may be powerfully shaped by class-based experience. Those who have been involved in working-class struggles for the right to organize may value solidarity and mutual support over autonomy and assistance. Too often, helping professionals have taken a particular set of "middle-class" values to be the norm and have made faulty assumptions about other persons and groups based on those values. People in different class positions may express values in common, such as the desire for a healthy environment, a comfortable home, and a good job. They may, however, give very different meanings to those values. And their differing access to resources profoundly shapes their possibilities for translating the visions of what they value into reality.

The Social Class Questionnaire

Take a few moments to reflect on your own social class background and the values associated with your class-based experience. Turn to the "Social Class Questionnaire" at the end of this chapter (p. 130). First, take time to respond individually to the questions posed. Then get together with a classmate and discuss your responses. What did you learn about the intersection of values and social class through this exercise?

Family Values?

The concept of "family values" is another case in point. While many people might share a valuing of "family," they may strongly disagree on the definition. Family means different things to different people, and kinship is constructed in a remarkable variety of ways. The concept of family promoted in the "family values" discourse of recent years is based on one very particular family form – the nuclear family - made up of two parents and their children, with the father as the authority figure and mother as nurturer. This model is one that serves to justify and maintain gender and generational inequality (Day, 2000, p.10; Finn, 1998b, pp. 205-217). The question of what constitutes family values depends on who counts as family. Rather than assuming the nuclear family as the norm, we can learn more about both family and values by appreciating the different ways in which we imagine and create families and practice family relations.

The Meaning of Family

What does family mean to you? Take a minute and write down your definition of family. Get together with a small group of your classmates and share your definitions. See if you can come to agreement on a definition of family. Have one member of each small group write the group's collective definition(s) on the board. Take time to read the definitions. What do the definitions have in common? How do they differ? Is it possible to reach consensus as a class on a definition of family? Do the definitions reflect values about what a family *should* be? Do the definitions reflect your own *experience* of family? How do values shape our understandings of family? How do our experiences in family shape values?

It is hard to define family in a way that captures its many and complex meanings. Nicholson (1986) defines family as a historically and culturally variable concept that connects positions within a kinship system and household. DiLeonardo (1984, 1987) points to the problems of equating family and household. Baber and Allen (1992) describe families as powerful socializing institutions, arenas of affection and support and tension and domination between genders and across generations. Hartmann (1981) keeps her definition simple: "Any two or more individuals who define themselves as family" (p. 8). Perhaps we can best think of family as a culturally and historically located ideology and practice of more or less enduring forms of relationship. It is an arena of struggle where power and intimacy, conflict and support play out in shaping gendered and generational relationships (Baber & Allen, 1992; di Leonardo, 1984, 1987; Ferree, 1990; Thompson, 1992; Thorne & Yalom, 1982).

Our differing experiences in families shape the meanings we give to family, which, in turn, shape our understanding of "family values."[2] Take a few moments to reflect on your own experiences of family life. What were some of the messages you received while growing up that indicated what attributes and actions were or were not valued? For example, what and how did you learn about the value of family, work, education, religion, achievement, money, relationships, or helping? From whom did you receive those messages? The expressions we pass down through families often serve as vehicles for inculcating values. Consider the following common expressions: "A penny saved is a penny earned;" "time is money;" "children should be seen and not heard."[3] What values are expressed here? Think for a moment about the expressions you heard while growing up. What did they teach you about values?

Family and Values

Families are powerful crucibles in forging values regarding, gender, race, class, sexuality, and other forms of difference. Think back to your own childhood experiences. What messages did you receive about what it meant to be male or female in your family? What messages did you receive about race and racism? About social class? About the valuing of "whiteness"? About heterosexuality and sexual difference? From whom? Can you identify some values that you have incorporated? Values that you have resisted? Can you identify changes in your values over time? What forces or experiences prompted those changes?[4]

The Practice of Valuing

Let's begin to think about "valuing" as a verb that describes the process by which we make judgements about what is desirable and preferred. As cultural beings constantly interpreting and making sense of the world, we are also engaged in an ongoing practice of valuing. Learning to value is part of our broader experience of acquisition of cultural knowledge. Through our everyday interactions in the world, in families, schools, neighborhoods, communities, and cultural groups, we are subjects of, witnesses to, and participants in practices of valuing. Those practices are shaped by the political, economic, social, and historical circumstances of our lives. The lessons in valuing learned by a white boy growing up in an upper-middle class Chicago suburb may be very different from those learned by a Chippewa-Cree boy growing up amidst poverty and unemployment on the Rocky Boys Reservation in Montana, or those learned by a boy surviving on the streets of Sao Paulo or Seattle.

When we shift our attention to valuing as a verb it helps us to think about the many ways that we learn which qualities and behaviors are considered desirable and by whom. Families are powerful arenas for learning to value. From our earliest social experiences we are enmeshed in the practices of valuing. Some of these practices, such as the ways in which resources of time and space are organized and managed in the context of family, are so deeply ingrained in our experience that they go without saying (Germain, 1994b, p. 261). For example, values of individualism and privacy are structured into the design of living space in the U.S. and are expressed in the middle-class expectation that children have "their own rooms." No matter how small the overall living space, it is divided into units that break up the social group. In other social and cultural contexts, such use of space would be inconceivable both in terms of use of material resources and in terms of the social isolation it would impose on family members who have learned to value the collective rather than the individual. Values shape and are shaped by the social structuring of our lives as well. As Germain (1994b, p. 261) describes, "family paradigms" – members' shared, implicit beliefs about themselves and their social world - profoundly shape one's orientation to and patterns of action in the world. Through the everyday routines, the messages and silences, and the crises of family life many of us learn powerful lessons in valuing.

Learning to Value Beyond the Family

The Power of Schooling. Families are powerful, but not the only, sources for lessons in valuing. We learn about the differential valuing of people and place through the structures of our everyday lives – the homes we live in; the food we eat and water we drink; the hours and conditions in which we work and rest; our access to jobs, recreation, transportation, education, and health care; and our opportunities for social, cultural, and political participation. Schools are particularly powerful sites of valuing. Public schools have played a key role in the inculcation of "middle-class" values and in the organization of working-class life (Apple, 1982; Ehrenreich, 1985; Willis, 1981). A number of critical education theorists have argued that public schooling plays a key role in socializing children for their class position in capitalist society at the same time that it promotes the myth of classlessness and equality of opportunity to "get ahead" (Apple, 1982; Aronowitz & Giroux, 1985; Shor, 1980). They argue that, in theory, public schools are democratic places of equal opportunity. In practice, they are places where class differences play out and get reproduced, whether in the form of unequal funding for "rich" and "poor" school districts or in the everyday indignities and exclusions experienced by poor and working class children. A closer look at the history of education in the U.S. reveals that, while schooling has created opportunities for some groups, it has served as a powerful form of discipline, containment, and social control for others. In the following section we address the place of boarding schools in the history of Native American education in the U.S. as a case in point. Boarding schools offer a provocative site for reflecting on questions of values, power, and difference.

Education and American Indians. For nearly a century (1870-1968) federal government-run boarding schools played a powerful role in the "education" of American Indian children in the United States. In the mid-1800s many American

Indian groups were forcibly relocated to reservations to make way for economic development of the Western U.S. Not long afterward, developers saw that reservation lands themselves had value for logging, mining, and cattle interests, and tribal organization was an impediment to that development. A new thrust in federal Indian policy (through the General Allotment Act) emerged calling for the "assimilation" of American Indians through "reduction to citizenship," establishment of individual property rights, and education into mainstream white culture (Smith, 1985; Takaki, 1979, 1993). Boarding schools played a key role in this federal effort. By 1890 there were 140 federal boarding schools with an enrollment of nearly 10,000 students (Morgan, 1890, in Washburn, 1973, p.44). Below are two quotes from Commissioners of Indian Affairs regarding American Indians and the value of education. What values are reflected in these quotes? What is the meaning of Indian education to the Commissioners? What might the educational experience have meant to an Indian child enrolled in boarding school in 1890? What questions do these passages raise regarding the relationship between values and social policy? What lessons might we draw as social workers?

> He (the Indian) should be educated to labor. He does not need the learning of William and Mary, but he does need the virtue of industry and the ability of the skillful hand… And the Indian should not only be taught how to work, but also that it is his duty to work; for the degrading communism of the tribal reservation system gives to the individual no incentive to labor, but puts a premium on idleness and makes it fashionable. Under this system, the laziest man owns as much as the most industrious man, and neither can say of all the acres occupied by the tribe, "This is mine." The Indian must, therefore, be taught how to labor; and, that labor may be made necessary to his well being, he must be taken out of the reservation through the door of the General Allotment Act. And he must be imbued with the exalting egotism of American civilization, so that he will say "I" instead of "We," and "this is mine" instead of "This is ours."
>
> Commissioner of Indian Affairs John H. Oberly, 1888[5]

****

> It is of prime importance that a fervent patriotism should be awakened in their minds. The stars and stripes should be a familiar object in every Indian school, national hymns should be sung, and patriotic selections be read and recited. They should be taught to look upon America as their home and upon the United States Government as their friend and benefactor. They should be made familiar with the lives of great and good men and women in American history, and be taught to feel a pride in all their great achievements. They should hear little or

> nothing of the 'wrongs of the Indians' and the injustice of the white race. If their unhappy history is alluded to it should be to contrast it with the better future that is within their grasp. The new era that has come to the red men through the munificent scheme of education, devised for and offered to them, should be the means of awakening loyalty to the Government, gratitude to the nation, and hopefulness for themselves.
>
> Commissioner of Indian Affairs T.J. Morgan, 1889.[6]

These words of the Commissioners of Indian Affairs and the values they reflect may provoke and disturb us. Some may argue that these accounts are more than a century old and things have changed. Yes, many things have changed. But we continue to see the differential valuing of children by class, race, and gender in our educational systems. As Jonathan Kozol (1991) has shown in his powerful book *Savage Inequalities,* poor children of color in the U.S. attempt to learn in underfunded, unsafe schools, where there are often not enough books, materials, or teachers to go around. Meanwhile, children of the majority, white middle and upper classes enjoy the safety of suburban schools equipped with the latest technologies and resources. Every day, children learn lessons in values informed by their differing school experiences. In reflecting on your own school experiences, what are some of the values you were expressly taught? What did you learn through your daily observations and experiences of valuing? Did you face any contradictions between the values taught and the values practiced?

Values of Education

Attend a school board meeting in your community with a classmate. Each of you take detailed notes on the discussion and proceedings. After the meeting, review your notes individually. Make a list of the values that informed the discussion. Were there values that were directly discussed? Were there unspoken values that informed stated assumptions? Were there values that were contested among members of the board and audience? Compare your list with that of your classmate. Where do your observations and interpretations coincide and where do they differ? What, would you argue, are the values that inform the board's decision-making? How do these values fit with your own core values?

Power, Inequality, and Valuing

Much can be learned about the practices and contradictions of dominant values and valuing from the perspectives of less powerful people and groups. Single mothers raising children in poverty live the contradictions of the "family values" discourse. Children of color who suffer the highest rates of poverty in the U.S. must wonder what political leaders have in mind when they claim, "our children are our future." Young black men in the U.S. see that they are more valued as prisoners than scholars, given that their chances of incarceration are better than their chances of going to college. Millions of the world's poor live (and die) the daily reality of human devaluation and disposability in the "new world order." They have been denied the very basic value of their humanity.

The work of W.E.B. DuBois (1985, 1989) is important in thinking about the contexts of inequality and the questions of meaning and power through which our lessons in values are filtered. (See Chapter Two Resource for biographical sketch). DuBois writes about his experiences with racism in the U.S. and the ever-present but rarely asked question: How does it feel to be a problem? He goes on to describe the "strange experience" of "being a problem" through a story from his childhood school days:

> *In a wee wooden schoolhouse, something put it into the boys' and girls' heads to buy gorgeous visiting-cards – ten cents a package – and exchange. The exchange was merry, till one girl, a tall newcomer, refused my card,- refused it peremptorily, with a glance. Then it dawned on me with a certain suddenness that I was different from the others; or like, mayhap, in heart and life and longing, but shut out from their world by a vast veil...*

He continues:

> *...the negro is a sort of seventh son, born with a veil, and gifted with second-sight in this American world, — a world which yields him no true self-consciousness, but only lets him see himself through the revelation of the other world. It is a peculiar sensation, this double-consciousness, this sense of always looking at one's self through the eyes of others, of measuring one's soul by the tape of a world that looks on in amused contempt and pity. One ever feels his twoness, - an American, a Negro, two souls, two thoughts, two unreconciled strivings; two warring ideals in one dark body, whose dogged strength alone keeps it from being torn asunder.* (1989, pp. 1-3)

What lessons in valuing can we draw from Du Bois' reflections?

Valuing as a Dialectical Process

In summary, valuing is a complex and contested process. We incorporate, resist, reproduce, and change values over time through the dynamics of our life experiences. The process of valuing cannot be separated from the contexts of power and inequality in which it plays out. We grapple with value contradictions in our everyday lives even as we practice and resist the (de)valuing of others and ourselves. We are social beings with interests, desires, and relations at stake. Valuing is a dialectical process. Our actions in the world are shaped in part by our valuing of the world. Our experiences in the world, in turn, shape our values. It is important to critically reflect on our values and the processes through which they have been formed and challenged.

We continually bring our values and valuing to bear in the practice of social work. A commitment to social justice work demands a constant search for competence; an honest examination of our personal as well as professional values; and a commitment to making our actions fit our words (Freire, 1990). Are our actions consistent with our expressed values? Do our values form the basis for justice-oriented action? Our values can be thought of as screens through which we interpret actions and give meaning to experience. They are shaped by our power and positioning and by the history of our experience. But our values are never fully determined or determining. There is always the possibility of new understandings and relations and thus alternative values and approaches to valuing.

Values, Ethics, and Social Work

> *"Human service workers are walking value systems, and ... they must become aware of those values, evaluate them rationally, and change the irrational ones."*
>
> Naomi Brill, 1976[7]

Social Work as a Value-Based Practice

Social work is a value-based practice. According to Reamer (1995, p. 12), social work values shape the mission of the profession; relations with clients, colleagues, and members of the broader society; decisions about intervention methods; and the resolution of ethical dilemmas. Writers in the field frequently describe social work's value base as a defining feature of the profession's uniqueness. Miley, O'Melia, and DuBois (1998) see human dignity and worth and social justice as the overarching values of social work. Similarly, speaking of social work in an international perspective, Ramanathan and Link (1999) contend that human dignity, worth of the individual, and sanctity of life are transcendent values. Miley, O'Melia, and DuBois (1998) describe values that shape the everyday practice of social work. "They include acceptance, individualization, nonjudgmentalism, objectivity, self-determination, access to resources, confidentiality, and accountability" (p. 55). The Council on Social Work Education embraces these values as guides to professional practice. The Council also addresses values of mutual participation, peoples' right to make independent decisions, and respect for diversity. It calls on social workers to build more just social institutions. Social workers have developed ethical codes that translate expressed values into standards for professional practice. As Johnson (1998) notes, "codes of ethics flow from values; they are values in action" (p. 51).

Core Values: An Overview

The Preamble to the National Association of Social Workers Code of Ethics states in part:

> The mission of the social work profession is rooted in a set of core values. These core values, embraced by social workers throughout the profession's history, are the foundation of social work's unique purpose and perspective.
>
> - Service
> - Social justice
> - Dignity and worth of the person
> - Importance of human relationships
> - Integrity
> - Competence
>
> This constellation of core values reflects what is unique to the social work profession. Core values, and the principles that flow from them, must be balanced within the context and complexity of human experience. (NASW, 1996)[8]

We refer you to the National Association of Social Workers (NASW) website for a complete version of the Code of Ethics (www.naswdc.org/pubs/code). Virtually every contemporary U.S. social work practice text spells out the core values of the profession as articulated by the NASW. Writers often praise the uniqueness and righteousness of a profession founded on these core values and implore budding social workers to embrace them wholeheartedly and put them into practice. Less attention is given to critical reflection on these values, their meanings, their relationship to the history of social work, the challenge of practicing them within a context of unequal power, and the tensions among them and between this core set of values and one's personal values. Discussion generally sidesteps the practices of valuing within the field of social work. By providing a definitive list of core values and locating "social justice" as one among several values to be embraced we unnecessarily constrain a discussion of *possible* values that could illuminate a vision of a just world. Take a close look at these six core values. It seems that they could have different meanings for different people in different situations. What do they mean to you? Are they meaningful outside of a context in which they are applied? Do they define a core of social justice work? Are there values you would add, delete, or question?

Examining Social Work's Core Values

In this section we critically reflect on the core values of social work and we consider their incorporation into standards for practice. Just as we explored earlier the tensions and contradictions among our personal "core values," so will we probe the tensions and contradictions in social work values. The NASW preamble states that these values have been embraced by social workers throughout the profession's history. However, as we learned in Chapter Two, social work has a complicated history fraught with tensions. We believe it is important to grapple with those tensions rather than gloss over them if we are to truly face the challenges of social justice work. Rather than assume the essential goodness of social work we need to ask, "What is the good in social work and how can it be made to appear" (Epstein, 1999, p. 15)?

Value Tensions. Phyllis Day (2000, p. 4) contends that two basic characteristics of human society are *mutual aid* and *protection from others and otherness.* She sees social work as a profession situated at the nexus of these social tensions between belonging and difference, a fundamentally contradictory position. Social work is thus enmeshed in the meaning making processes and relations of power through which belonging and difference are negotiated. As Laura Epstein (1999) describes, "dissonance is intrinsic to the nature of social work, to its essence" (p. 9). Social justice work demands the ongoing acknowledgement of this tension, recognition of the partiality of our knowledge, and critical reflection on our values and actions.

Day (2000, p. 4-12) develops an important discussion of the basic "social values" that shape human services in the U.S. She points to the tensions among values and the inconsistencies between values and practices. She identifies the most basic values as: 1) Judeo-Christian charity values; 2) Democratic egalitarianism and individualism; 3) The Protestant work ethic and capitalism; 4) Social Darwinism; 5) The New Puritanism; 6) Patriarchy; 7) Marriage and the nuclear family; and 8) the "American Ideal." Day argues that Judaic and Christian teachings historically promoted a concept of charity as social justice – the belief that persons in need have a right to receive help and that society has an obligation to help them. She argues that this conception of charity has been lost over time, and while social work codes of ethics express Judeo-Christian values, social work practice tends to favor individualism.

According to the principles of democratic egalitarianism, all citizens are equal before the law. However, we have only to look to the unfinished history of civil rights struggles in the U.S. to see that our practices do not match expressed values. In line with this, Day points out that egalitarianism is closely tied to individualism in the U.S. context. This individualist perspective is expressed in the popular mythology that everyone can "get ahead" and that "any child can grow up to be President." The same sort of popular mythology bolsters "blame the victim" thinking wherein poverty is conceived of as a personal problem, a lack of ability or effort, rather than a consequence of structured conditions of inequality.

Closely in line with expressed values of egalitarianism and individualis[illegible] are the Protestant work ethic, capitalism, and Social Darwini[illegible] scribes, the Protestant work ethic blends the valuing [illegible] ment, and work for economic gain as measures of "s[illegible] to one's paid work, and those who don't work don't [illegible] Darwinist terms, "economically unfit" and thus "unw[illegible] this value complex has a long and powerful history w[illegible] practices of social welfare in the U.S., it has been reinvented and sanctified through what Day calls the "New Puritanism." The New Puritanism is expressed in the political discourse of the Religious Right, which has gained a dominant position in the U.S. political arena and in both popular and professional discourse. Day argues that the New Puritanism blends reactionary values of the past with post-modern technologies to deliver messages about the "proper" behavior of women (subservience to the patriarchal order), the criminality of difference, abstinence from "vice" in its many forms, condemnation of homosexuality, and a militaristic vigilance concerning the order of things.

A cornerstone of the New Puritanism is patriarchy, "a system in which power and authority are vested in men, whereas women and other powerless groups, such as children, workers, and slaves, are oppressed and often owned... In patriarchal society, male authority permeates every institution" (Day, 2000, p. 9). Challenging fervent claims of equal opportunity and the bridging of the gender gap, Day exposes the fundamental power of the value of patriarchy in our social institutions. The power of patriarchy is articulated in the 1996 welfare reform legislation that produced "Temporary Assistance for Needy Families (TANF)," which explicitly argues that (heterosexual) marriage is the better alternative to public assistance for poor, single women. Heterosexual marriage and the nuclear family are deeply embedded in the "American value" system. While the status of "married with children" is romanticized, alternative family forms and singlehood are conversely devalued in our social welfare institutions, policies, practices, and discourses. Taken together, these "American values" reinforce the underlying "correctness" of a white, heterosexual, middle-class, Anglo-Saxon Protestant ideal. Social work has historically privileged these values and adopted them as the standard against which "others" are judged and (de)valued.[9]

Value Conflicts in Historical Context. Day challenges us to move beyond righteous claims about the goodness of the profession and the "correctness" of our interventions. Instead, she prompts us to honestly and critically reflect on social work's past, present, and future and the value conflicts therein. Social work practiced by late 19th century charity workers was informed by a powerful moral discourse, as we saw in Chapter Two. For example, friendly visitors directed their energies toward the inculcation of "proper" habits and morals among the growing immigrant classes. "Child savers" promulgated fear of the "dangerous classes" of immigrant youth and called for the "moral disinfection" of cities through the "placing out" of youth with "proper" rural families in the West (Brace, 1872; Finn, 2001a). Social work emerged as a normalizing profession concerned with policing the poor and managing the marginal (Epstein, 1999, p. 9). Jane Addams and other women of the Settlement House Movement learned, with time, to appreciate the cultural knowledge, values, capacities, and practices of immigrant individuals and groups. However, as Addam's biographical sketch in Chapter Two conveys, they had to critically question the values they had come to embrace as part of their own positionalities as educated, middle-class white women and open themselves to new ways of experiencing and interpreting the world in order to appreciate differing ways of knowing and valuing.

Thus, social work's history reveals a rather awkward "embrace" of the profession's core values. As John Ehrenreich (1985) describes, and as we saw in Chapter Two, social work emerged in conjunction with the growth of industrial capitalism. Industrial capitalism was premised not only on mass production but also on mass consumption. It demanded new kinds of workers, consumers, and citizens and required new forms of labor discipline that extended from the factory floor to the regulation of the habits and intimacies of family life (Ehrenreich, 1985; Finn, 2001a; Harvey, 1989). Twentieth century capitalism forged the re-organization of working- class life and fueled the emergence of a professional middle class (Ehrenreich, 1985, p. 28-30). Social workers played key roles in monitoring working-class life and instructing working-class immigrants in the values conducive to capitalist production and consumption. For example, Ford Motor Company was on the cutting edge of the making of new kinds of workers, and Henry Ford hired social workers to help. According to David Harvey (1989):

> Ford sent an army of social workers into the homes of his 'privileged' (and largely immigrant) workers to ensure that the 'new man' of mass production had the right kind of moral probity, family life, and capacity for prudent (i.e. non-alcoholic) and 'rational' consumption to live up to corporate needs and expectations. (p. 126)

Ehrenreich (1985) offers a more vivid description:

> When Ford Motor Company introduced its celebrated $5-a-day wages…it set up a Sociology (social services) Department, whose thirty investigators were to screen applicants and monitor the behavior of employees. Gambling, drinking, and, of course, radicalism, and unionism were forbidden; "proper" (i.e. middle-class) diet, recreational habits, living arrangements, family budgets, and

> morality were taught and encouraged. For the foreign-born, English classes were mandatory, with the text used beginning with the lesson "I am a good American." Symbolizing the school's function was the "graduation" ceremony: walking on stage in the costumes of their native lands, graduates disappeared behind a giant cutout of a "melting pot." After their teachers had stirred the "pot" with long ladles, the graduates appeared on the opposite side of the pot dressed in proper American attire and waving American flags. (p. 31)

The molding and monitoring of poor, working-class, and immigrant family life is another part of social work's history. What values would you say underlie these practices? Rather than brushing this history under the rug, we contend that social workers need to learn from it and consider the inconsistencies between our expressed values and our actual practices. We need to examine the values reflected in these practices and ask how it was that these practices were promoted and justified. What other possible courses of action might social work and social workers have taken that would have been consistent with the profession's core values? What lessons can we draw from this history to help our actions match our words today?

The History of Social Work Ethics

Social Work Values and Emerging Professionalism. By the 1920s, social work in the U.S. was coming to value itself as a profession. Social workers were focusing on tests and measurements, diagnosis and treatment, and the casework approach (Richmond, 1917). Practitioners were turning away from environmental models and urban community work in favor of psychological models that emphasized the individual as the locus of concern and intervention (Day, 2000). Schools of social work were growing in number as was concern with professional training, credentials, and ethical standards of practice. As early as 1919 there were attempts to draft professional codes of ethics for social work (Reamer, 1995, p. 6). The Depression prompted a new wave of social action and advocacy in social work that disrupted the dominance of the individual pathology model for a time. As described in Chapter 2, some social workers sought to build alliances with labor and working-class movements, organize social workers in trade unions, and take part in human rights struggles. They were deeply critical of the professionalization of social work, its lack of political commitment to social justice, and the inequalities of power inherent in it. These values-based divisions prompted a crisis in social work centered on the question of professionalization and the theories informing it (Ehrenreich, 1985, pp. 104-138).

Profession Building. By the mid-1940s concern for professionalism and expertise, based on a "client" model, had solidified its dominance over advocacy and social action as the direction for social work practice. During the 1940s and 1950s professional ethics became a subject of study in its own right in social work, and in 1947 the Delegate Conference of the American Association of Social Workers adopted a code of ethics, thereby formally translating a values base into principles of practice and standards of professional conduct (Reamer, 1995, p. 6). The move toward professionalism was a move away from positioned advocacy and political critique. In a 1957 article in *Social Work,* University of California professor Ernest Greenwood argues that social workers "might have to scuttle their social action heritage as a price of achieving the public acceptance accorded a profession" (Greenwood, 1957 cited in Ehrenreich, 1985, p. 59). Let's take a minute to think about the implications here. What does it mean to say that activism "undermines professionalism?" What values are being embraced here? Does a negation of activism suggest a political commitment to the status quo? Professionalism, defined by unequal relations of power, control of expert knowledge and technologies of intervention, objectivity, and distance, seems to be fundamentally at odds with a value of social justice based on participation and committed to challenging social inequality. Is activism antithetical to professionalism, or do we perhaps need to explore other possibilities for understanding and acting as professionals and as activists?

Social Justice, Professionalism, and Radical Challenge. Many social workers in the 1960s took up these questions as they claimed that struggles for social justice, equality, and human rights were part of their professional obligations. The National Association of Social Workers adopted its first Code of Ethics in 1960 (Reamer 1994, p. 197). The historic events of the decade forced practitioners to reflect on constructions of ethical practice in the face of the civil rights struggles and the War on Poverty. By 1970 there was also a growing interest in the study of applied and professional ethics and an increase in litigation regarding violations of ethical principles. Some social workers promoted a radical approach to practice in the 1970s, much like Bertha Reynolds, Mary Van Kleeck, and others had done a generation earlier. In the U.S., community action workers in the War on Poverty and community organizers sought to change social conditions by building grassroots organizations through which poor and disenfranchised people could have a say in the decisions that affected their lives (Naples, 1998).

In England radical social workers founded Case Con, a critical action organization that sought to "give an answer to the contradictions that we face" (Bailey & Brake, 1976, p. 144). In the organization's "Manifesto" they critiqued the social control role of social work and the profession's failure to meet the real needs of the people it purports to help. They challenged the specialized and exclusive nature of professionalism and a casework model that blames individuals for conditions of poverty. They argued that: "Professionalism is a particularly dangerous development specifically because social workers look to it for an answer to many of the problems and contradictions of the job itself – i.e. being unable to solve the basic inadequacy of society through social work" (Bailey & Brake, 1976, p. 146). And, echoing the demands of their radical predecessors, they called on social workers to organize independently of the state and promote rank-and-file trade union organization. Once again, value conflicts rocked the foundation of social work.

Case Con Manifesto

The following is the opening statement of the Case Con Manifesto. This statement was written in the early 1970s. As you read the statement, think about how the document might have been informed by historical and political contexts. What values underlie this statement? How does it fit with contemporary social work? What challenges does it pose?

No Easy Answers

Every day of the week, every week of the year, social workers (including probations officers, educational social workers, hospital social workers, community workers, and local authority social workers) see the utter failure of social work to meet the real needs of the people it purports to help. Faced with this failure, some social workers despair and leave to do other jobs, some hide behind the façade of professionalism and scramble up the social work ladder regardless; and some grit their teeth and just get on with the job, remaining helplessly aware of the dismal reality. Of course, some do not see anything wrong in the first place.

CASE CON is an organization of social work (in the broadest sense), attempting to give an answer to the contradictions that we face. Case Con offers no magic solutions, no way in which you can go to work tomorrow and practice some miraculous new form of social work which does meet the needs of your 'clients.' It would be nice if there were such an easy answer, but we believe that the problems and frustrations we face daily are inextricably linked to the society we live in, and that we can only understand what needs to be done if we understand how the welfare state, of which social services are a part, has developed, and what pressures it is subjected to. It is the purpose of this manifesto to trace briefly this development, to see how it affects us and our relationships to the rest of society, and above all to start working out what we can do about it.[10]

Conceptualization of a Professional Value Base. The service-oriented model of social work continued to largely dominate the change-oriented approach, and the development of ethical standards reflected this dominance. In 1976 C. S. Levy published *Social Work Ethics*, a foundational text that sought to articulate the philosophical and conceptual basis for social work ethics. Levy (1973) also classified social work professional values in three categories: preferred conceptions of people; preferred outcomes for people; and preferred instrumentalities for dealing with people. Levy's classification of social work values is summarized in Figure 3.1[11].

FIGURE 3.1

Levy's Classification of Social Work Values

Preferred Conceptions of People	**Preferred Outcomes for People**	**Preferred Instrumentalities for Dealing with People**
Belief in:	*Belief in society's obligation to:*	*Belief that people should:*
• Inherent dignity and worth • Capacity for change • Mutual responsibility • Need to belong • Uniqueness • Common human needs	• Provide opportunity for individual growth and development • Provide resources and services for people to meet basic needs • Provide equal opportunity for social participation	• Be treated with dignity and respect • Have right to self-determination • Be encouraged to participate in social change • Be recognized as unique individuals

Levy's conceptualization is frequently cited in social work texts as the classic formulation of social work values. Levy's schema brings together humanitarian values and a sense of societal obligation to create conditions in which these values can be expressed. He recognizes and articulates the fundamental linkage of the personal and the social, or, "person-in-environment" perspective as it is commonly called, that has been central to dominant depictions of social work's professional uniqueness (we elaborate on this in Chapter Four). Levy implies that society has an obligation to the poor and that people should participate in the decisions that affect their lives. However, he does not develop a political and ethical critique of the *conditions* of poverty, inequality, and exploitation, and of the arrangements and relations of *power* that create and maintain those conditions. Nor does Levy address the discourses of pathology and difference that mask those conditions and justify individualist, deficit-oriented, "professional" approaches to social work intervention. Levy speaks of common human needs, but does not address basic human rights. He speaks to opportunities for social participation but not of struggles for social justice. In contrast to the Case Con Manifesto, whose authors directly confront these contradictions, Levy's schema stops short. How is it that Levy's formulation has become central to values discussions in social work while the principles articulated by two generations of social justice workers have been erased from or relegated to the footnotes of social work history?

Values and Survival of the Profession. By the 1980s, with the retrenchment of federal support for social welfare under the Reagan administration, the growing anti-welfare movement, and the massive privatization of social services, social work seemed to value professional survival more than anything. The profession was preoccupied with professional licensure and credentialing for private practice (Specht & Courtney, 1994; Reisch & Wenocur, 1986). Graduate school enrollments expanded as the job market contracted. Many social workers were carving a niche in the clinical practice market and valuing the knowledge, skills, and professional accreditation that would secure their positions. The NASW professional Code of Ethics, revised in 1979, detailed attention to professional-client relations, confidentiality, access to records, payments for services, and responsibilities to professional colleagues. The revised Code reflected the "medical model" of social worker, that is, social worker as professional expert engaged in client treatment focused on change at the personal and interpersonal level. Social workers were not ethically obliged to combat conditions of violence, inequality, and exploitation, nor were they obligated to make the concerns of people living in poverty their priority. It was not until 1983, as the U.S. social context grew bleaker, that the Council on Social Work Education (CSWE), the profession's academic accrediting body, called for the study of oppression and injustice as part of the social work curriculum (Gil, 1994, p. 258).

Tearing the Social Safety Net: A Challenge to Professional Values. By 1990, "ending welfare as we know it" became the mantra of U.S. social policy regarding the poor. The social safety net continued to contract with cuts in federal spending and the "devolution" of social costs to state and local governments and private charities. Organized labor suffered tremendous losses. "Managed care" became a household word as individuals were forced to bear ever-increasing burdens of the costs of health care. As oppression and injustice increased in the U.S., some groups within social work began to mobilize in response. As welfare "reform" legislation moved toward passage, some social workers joined with welfare rights groups to challenge punitive social policy. Some worked within social work organizations to focus attention on the value of social justice. In 1992, CSWE put forth a curriculum policy statement that made it the responsibility of schools of social work to teach about social justice and approaches to overcoming oppression more explicit. However, as Gil (1994) notes, "the 1992 revision reflects the fallacious assumption that discrimination, oppression, and injustice affecting women, minorities, and other discrete social groups can be overcome without eradicating their sources in the occupational and social class divisions of contemporary capitalism" (p. 259).

Responding to the Challenges: Claiming Social Justice

Revising the Code of Ethics. In August 1996, the NASW Delegate Assembly adopted a revised code of ethics that went into effect in January 1997 (NASW, 1996). In contrast to the earlier code, which summarized social work values to include: "the worth, dignity, and uniqueness of all persons as well as their rights and opportunities" (NASW 1979 rev. 1990, 1993), the 1996 code specifically spells out the mission of social work:

> *The primary mission of the social work profession is to enhance human well-being and help meet the basic human needs of all people, with particular attention to the needs and empowerment of people who are vulnerable, oppressed,*

> *and living in poverty. A historic and defining feature of social work is the profession's focus on individual well-being in a social context and the well-being of society. Fundamental to social work is attention to the environmental forces that create, contribute to, and address problems in living.*
>
> *Social workers promote social justice and social change with and on behalf of clients. "Clients" is used inclusively to refer to individuals, families, groups, organizations, and communities. Social workers are sensitive to cultural and ethnic diversity and strive to end discrimination, oppression, poverty, and other forms of social injustice. These activities may be in the form of direct practice, community organizing, supervision, consultation, administration, advocacy, social and political action, policy development implementation, education, and research and evaluation. Social workers seek to enhance the capacity of people to address their own needs. Social workers also seek to enhance the responsiveness of organizations, communities, and other social institutions to individual needs and social problems.*

Naming Poverty, Oppression, and Injustice. The 1996 code provides a pronounced shift in attention to questions of poverty, oppression, and injustice. It calls on social workers to take social justice seriously. The ethical standards now spell out social workers' responsibilities to the broader society. Examples of these responsibilities include:

- Social workers should promote the general welfare of society, from local to global levels, and the development of people, their communities, and their environments. Social workers should advocate for living conditions conducive to the fulfillment of basic human needs and should promote social, economic, political, and cultural values and institutions that are compatible with the realization of social justice.
- Social workers should promote the conditions that encourage respect for cultural and social diversity within the United States and globally. Social workers should promote policies and practices that demonstrate respect for difference, support the expansion of cultural knowledge and resources, advocate for programs and institutions that demonstrate cultural competence, and promote policies that safeguard the rights of and confirm equity and social justice for all people.

- Social workers should act to prevent and eliminate domination of, exploitation of, and discrimination against any person, group, or class on the basis of race, ethnicity, national origin, color, sex, sexual orientation, age, marital status, political belief, religion, or mental or physical disability. (NASW, 1996)

The Challenges Ahead. These are daunting standards. They pose challenges and opportunities as social workers make the commitment to translate them to practice. However, as Gil (1994) notes with regard to the CSWE curriculum standards, we cannot overcome the oppression, exploitation, and discrimination experienced by discreet groups without confronting the underlying systemic inequalities. Here we must return to the beginning of this section and ask ourselves, are social work's stated core values a sufficient guide for the task at hand? We cannot merely claim a revisionist history of social work. We need to confront the clear and present challenges of enacting these standards in social work practice. Might our key concepts for just practice – meaning, context, power, history, and possibility - also be thought of as guides for "valuing?" What values might you add to, take from, or question in social work's core? What values would you draw on in realizing your vision of social justice work? How would you translate them into standards of ethical practice?

Social Work Values: Alternative Conceptualizations

Thus far, we have focused mainly on the values articulated by the National Association of Social Workers, the predominant professional association in the United States. There are, however, alternative conceptualizations articulated in the definitions and codes of practice developed by other social work groups both within and outside of the U.S. In this section we will take a look at some alternative conceptualizations and the questions they raise. We will return to the question of social work and human rights that we raised in Chapter One and consider the relationship between social work and the Universal Declaration of Human Rights. We ask you to consider this question: Are we able to talk about the ethical base of social work without talking about the political base of social work?

National Association of Black Social Workers

Several other social work organizations in the U.S. have developed their own Codes of Ethics. For example, introduction to the National Association of Black Social Workers states the following:

> In America today, no Black person, except the selfish or irrational, can claim neutrality in the quest for Black liberation nor fail to consider the implications of the events taking place in our society. Given the necessity for committing ourselves to the struggle for freedom, we as Black Americans practicing in the field of social welfare set forth this statement of ideals and guiding principles.
>
> If a sense of community awareness is a precondition to humanitarian acts, then we as Black social workers must use our knowledge of the Black community, our commitments to its self-determination and our helping skills for the benefit of Black people as we marshal our expertise to improve the quality of life of Black people. Our activities will be guided by our Black consciousness, our determination to protect the security of the Black community and to serve as advocates to relieve suffering of Black people by any means necessary. (National Association of Black Social Workers, 1971).[12]

The code calls for workers to commit to the welfare of black individuals, families, and communities as the primary obligation and to make no distinction "between their destiny and my own." Black social workers are expected to serve the Black community, work as instruments for social change, and promote the development of Black institutions. The code challenges the value of "professional distance" between worker and "client." It rejects notions of social worker neutrality. It calls on workers to make the community's struggles their own and to dedicate themselves to advocacy in, for, and with the Black community. The impassioned tone of the code also sets it apart from that of NASW. What other points of comparison or contrast do you see? How do the values articulated here fit with your values?

Code of Ethics for Radical Social Service

Now let's turn to the Code of Ethics for Radical Social Service, prepared by Jeffrey Galper (1975). This code developed from the work of radical social workers in the U.S. who, like their counterparts in Case Con in England, were confronting the contradictions of social work and questioning the logic of capitalism in which U.S. social work had emerged. It reads:

As an effort to contribute to the development of radical ideology and commitment capable of informing radical practice, we close by returning to the Code of Ethics of the professional social work association, the National Association of Social Workers. This Code contains a conservative bias that serves the best interests of neither client, workers, nor social well-being in general. As the existing Code encapsulates the analysis and goals of conventional practice, so our modifications encapsulate the analysis and goals of the radical social worker. Our code will have 14 planks.

1. *I regard as my primary obligation the welfare of all human kind.*
2. *I will work toward the development of a society that is committed to the dictum, "From each according to his or her ability, to each according to his or her need."*
3. *I will struggle for the realization of a society in which my personal interests and my personal actions are consistent with my interests and actions as a worker.*
4. *I will consider myself accountable to all who join in the struggle for social change and will consider them accountable to me for the quality and extent of work we perform and the society we create.*
5. *I will work to achieve the kind of world in which all people can be free and open with one another in all matters.*
6. *I will use information gained from my work to facilitate humanistic, revolutionary change in society.*
7. *I will treat the findings, views and actions of colleagues with the respect due them. This respect is conditioned by their demonstrated concern for revolutionary values and radical social change.*
8. *I will use all the knowledge and skill available to me in bringing about a radically transformed society.*
9. *I recognize my responsibility to add my ideas and findings to our society's knowledge and practice.*
10. *I accept my responsibility to help protect the community against unethical practice by any individuals or organizations in the society.*
11. *I commit myself fully in the struggle for revolutionary change.*
12. *I support the principle that all persons can and must contribute to the realization of a humanized society.*
13. *I accept personal responsibility for working toward creation and maintenance of conditions in society that enable all people to live by this Code.*
14. *I contribute my knowledge and skill and support to the accomplishment of a humanistic, democratic, communal socialist society.* (Galper, 1975, pp. 224-227*)*

This code posed its own set of challenges to mainstream social work values and ethics.

What points of comparison and contrast do you see? How do the values articulated here fit with your own values? How do they differ?

Looking Beyond the U.S.

We encounter a range of value positions expressed among social work organizations outside of the U.S. as well. Many social work organizations in diverse parts of the world have adopted standards of ethical practice regarding professional obligations, competence, and responsibilities to "clients," the profession, and social change that closely resemble those of NASW. Others address the importance of ethical, responsible behavior by social workers but do not standardize those value expectations in a code of ethics. We find interesting and important variations in the ways values and expectations are expressed. For example, the Canadian Association of Social Workers (1994) recognizes a commitment to the values of acceptance, self-determination, respect of individuality, and belief in the intrinsic worth and integrity of every human being. It also acknowledges the obligation of all people to provide resources, services, and opportunities for the overall benefit of humanity and calls for the respect without prejudice of individuals, families, groups, communities, and nations.[13] In contrast, social workers in India have "questioned the relevance of clinically-oriented Western codes for Indian community development and prefer the term 'declaration' of ethics for people-centered work" (Desai, 1987, cited in Link, 1999).

The Danish Association of Social Workers describes itself as a professional organization and trade union with an interest in both working conditions and working methods. Their model is reminiscent of that of the Rank and File Movement in the U.S., discussed in Chapter Two. The Association practices a strong commitment to international cooperation. It is committed to promoting social development in impoverished countries and backing colleagues in these countries in their struggles to organize groups of social workers and develop local social services. For example, the association's solidarity funds have supported exchange programs with Chilean colleagues, a center for victims of torture in Chile, a seminar on human rights and social work in the Philippines, and the development of the Nicaraguan Association of Social Workers. Similarly, social workers in Norway and Finland are organized in trade unions and professional associations and maintain a strong international focus.

International Federation of Social Workers Declaration of Ethical Principles. Many of these national social work associations are affiliated with the International Federation of Social Workers (IFSW). They variably voice their support for the IFSW statement of ethical principles and standards and the United Nations Universal Declaration of Human Rights and challenge the culture- and time-bound limits of these documents. They recognize their diverse positionings in a global context and the value of a critical global perspective to inform thought and practice. Let's take a look at the declaration of ethical principles and standards to which member associations of the IFSW and their constituent members are expected to adhere. What assumptions inform this statement? What values are reflected? How does the declaration compare with the values and principles articulated by NASW?

FIGURE 3.2

International Declaration of Ethical Principles

The International Declaration of Ethical Principles

Social workers serve the development of human beings through adherence to the following basic principles:

1. Every human being has a unique value, which justifies moral consideration for that person.
2. Each individual has the right to self-fulfillment to the extent that it does not encroach upon the same right of others, and has an obligation to contribute to the well-being of society.
3. Each society, regardless of its form, should function to provide the maximum benefits for all of its members.
4. Social workers have a commitment to principles of social justice.
5. Social workers have the responsibility to devote objective and disciplined knowledge and skill to aid individuals, groups, communities, and societies in their development and resolution of personal-societal conflicts and their consequences.
6. Social workers are expected to provide the best possible assistance to anybody seeking their help and advice, without unfair discrimination on the basis of gender, age, disability, language, political beliefs, or sexual orientation.

7. Social workers respect the basic human rights of individuals and groups as expressed in the United Nations Declaration of Human Rights and other international conventions derived from the Declaration.
8. Social workers pay regard to the principles of privacy, confidentiality, and responsible use of information in their professional work. Social workers respect justified confidentiality even when their country's legislation is in conflict with this demand.
9. Social workers are expected to work in full collaboration with their clients working for the best interest of the clients but paying due regard to the interest of others involved. Clients are encouraged to participate as much as possible, and should be informed of the risks and likely benefits of proposed courses of action.
10. Social workers generally expect clients to take responsibility, in collaboration with them, for determining courses of action affecting their lives. Compulsion which might be necessary to solve one party's problems at the expense of the interests of others involved should only take place after careful explicit evaluation of the claims of the conflicting parties. Social workers should minimise the use of legal compulsion.
11. Social work is inconsistent with direct or indirect support of individuals, groups, political forces or power-structures suppressing their fellow human beings by employing terrorism, torture, or similar brutal means.
12. Social workers make ethically justified decisions, and stand by them, pay due regard to the IFSW International Declaration of Ethical Principles and to the International Ethical Standards for Social Workers adopted by their national professional association.[14]

We can point to many areas of common concern between the International Declaration of Ethical Principles and the values and principles articulated by NASW. Both honor human uniqueness, the right to self-determination, and the commitment to social justice. Both speak to professional competence, client participation, and the interplay of personal and societal obligations. The international principles, however, explicitly embrace the United Nations Universal Declaration of Human Rights (see Appendix p. 397 for full text) and recognize the acts of violence through which those rights are violated. They also suggest the complexity of making ethically justified decisions in differing cultural and political contexts. Based on this declaration, what would you describe as the core values of IFSW? How do those values fit with your own?

A View from the Latin American Southern Cone. The IFSW Declaration of Ethical Principles and the understanding of social work upon which it is premised have come under criticism in some quarters.[15] Critics argue that the declaration accepts the role of social worker as professional and assumes a "client-oriented" model of practice. This contrasts with the critiques of professionalism put forth by radical and progressive social workers. It contrasts as well with participatory empowerment models committed to transformation of social conditions through participatory democracy. For example, the Latin American Southern Cone Committee of Professional Social Work and Social Service Organizations have voiced their criticism.[16] They argue that the understanding of social work embraced by IFSW is disconnected from the social realities and pressing concerns of people in different countries and regions of the world. Members of the Southern Cone organizations have developed their own statement of ethical and political principles to guide social work practice. Their statement recognizes their differing social realities and their common concerns regarding social exclusion, the violation of human rights, and conditions of widespread poverty. They directly voice concern over globalization and its impacts on cultural identity in Latin America. The members criticize the neoliberal economic model of late capitalism; the concentration of economic and political power in the hands of the elites; and the barriers to democratization throughout the region. These forces, they argue, have severely limited social work's historic commitment to social justice. They point to the urgent need for social workers to assume a *political-ethical* position in the face of these forces and engage in the struggle for social transformation.[17]

In sum, these alternative conceptualizations of social work values reflect the intimate linkage between ethics and politics. They suggest the importance of understanding values in context. And they remind us of the dynamic nature of codes of ethics. Perhaps we can best think of codes of ethics as living, evolving documents, shaping and shaped by the historical, political, social, and cultural context of practice.

Social Work and Human Rights

Human Rights as a Foundation for Ethical Practice

Let's return for a moment to the question of social work and human rights. A number of organizations and people mentioned above call on social work to use the United Nations Universal Declaration of Human Rights as a foundation for ethical practice. The Declaration is a remarkable document crafted in response to the horrors of World War II and the Nazi Holocaust. It was endorsed by member states of the newly formed United Nations in 1948, who explicitly recognized its principles as the "common standard of decency." Its fundamental implicit principle was that less powerful people and groups needed protection against those with more power, especially the state (Nagenast and Turner, 1997, p. 269).

The document is a product of the historical and political moment in which it was crafted and ratified. It has been criticized for its privileging of Western conceptions of personhood, individual rights, and citizenship (Jelin, 1996; Link, 1999; Lyons, 1999,Turner, 1997). However, as Stanley Witkin (1998) notes, the declaration is significant for articulating the idea of universal rights that cannot be separated from political, social, and economic arrangements (p.197). It embraces a philosophy that all human beings are equal in dignity and rights, and it incorporates economic, social, and cultural rights. It addresses positive rights, such as freedom of thought and religion and the right to recognition as a person before the law, and negative rights, such as protection from arbitrary arrest and detention. Its very existence provides a basis for grappling with complex questions of national sovereignty, cultural relativity, collective rights, the nature and extent of rights, the very right to have rights, and the myriad tensions therein.

Witkin (1998) points out that the values articulated in the declaration are central to social work. He contends, however, that a true commitment to human rights is neither visible in social work practice nor integrated into social work education in the U.S. Witkin argues that U.S. social work's continued emphasis on individual change and psychological explanations for complex human concerns and non-critical acceptance of capitalism and Western individualism obscure the view of broader human rights issues (pp. 199-200). He calls on social workers to challenge individualist, medicalized explanations of peoples' pain and troubles and to make human rights a part of all aspects of practice, from assessment to intervention and evaluation criteria (p. 201).

Rights, Values, and Social Justice Work

Take some time to read and reflect on the Universal Declaration of Human Rights (see Appendix p. 397). What do you see as its strengths? As its limitations? How do the values encoded in the Declaration fit with the core values of social work? With your own core values? Now, turn to Chapter Seven,

p. 316, and read the case example of the "Lost Boys." Try making an assessment of the situation from a human rights perspective. What might be some of the criteria for your assessment? How might your assessment differ from what Witkin describes as an "individualist" or "medicalized" approach? How might you use the Declaration in establishing goals for practice? How might your goals differ from those put forth in a more "traditional" approach to social work in the U.S.? Has your engagement with the Declaration prompted you to think differently about yourself as a social worker or the possibilities for social work practice? If so, how? How would you describe the relationship between human rights and social justice work?

Incorporating Human Rights in Practice

It is easier to talk about human rights than to actively incorporate them in our practice and struggle with the tensions and contradictions therein. As Janet George (1999) notes, "[h]uman rights are rather like motherhood" (p. 15). Everyone agrees they are a "good thing." But translating them into practice is another story. Can notions of values and right and wrong be extracted from their cultural, historical, and political context? How do we address the dilemmas inherent in a notion of universal rights and a notion of cultural relativity? How do we support less powerful people's claims to individual or group rights? Who counts as a "citizen" and who decides what the role of the state should be in protecting and enforcing rights? How do we respect cultural difference and stay critically aware of our own values and assumptions? How do we recognize the historical struggles against structured inequalities within cultural groups? George argues that social workers are not well prepared in the conceptual and practical issues of human rights. Further, social workers seldom have working knowledge of other United Nations Conventions, such as those addressing the rights of the child and social development.[18] She notes that concepts such as human rights imply a value judgment, and thus make it logically impossible to come to full agreement. The process of naming and claiming rights is always emergent and negotiated – a work in progress.

Manuel Garretón (1998, p. 39), writing on human rights in the Southern Cone of Latin America, argues that human rights are basically historical and cultural concepts centering on the right to life. They are constructed hand-in-hand with our ideas of citizenship and the state. He asks how human rights get addressed in situations where the state is responsible for their massive violation. How do we come to terms with massive violations of human rights? What are the tensions and contradictions in trying to translate human rights reparations into remunerative compensation? These are difficult questions that may seem to be beyond the bounds of social work. However, as George (1999) argues: "If social work as a profession espouses a commitment to social justice, then a role in the promotion of human rights is implicit. Developing that role involves considerations that are conceptual, cultural, and political" (pp. 21-22). One of the implications for social work in the U.S. is that we must move beyond the safety of local and national boundaries and consider the potential political and ethical ramifications of our privileged positioning in the "Global North" and the action generated from that positioning. It means that we must embrace what Rosemary Link (1999, p. 85) calls an "ethics of participation."

Toward an Ethics of Participation

We will explore the politics and ethics of practice and processes of an ethics of participation in more detail in Chapters Six to Eight. We close this chapter with a starting point for an ethics of participation. An ethics of participation demands, most fundamentally, that the people affected by particular issues or circumstances and events need to be present in the process of decision-making. Discussions need to take place in people's first language. And people need to have a legitimate voice in all decisions that affect them (Link, 1999, pp. 85-86). Link puts forth a number of universal principles for social workers who seek social and economic justice. She organizes the principles into three broad categories:

1. **Widest perspective for assessment**
    - Before acting, review personal values, history, and cultural bias; ask the question, "How am I influenced personally and professionally by this question or problem?"
    - Review the value base, history, and culture of the other(s) concerned with the ethical question.
    - Question geocentrism and the impact of location of people involved; what would be different if this dialogue were happening elsewhere in the world and why?

2. Inclusion of the service user in dialogue and decisions

- Discuss the "right to reality" of the service user and their family or community; spend time defining this reality.
- Acknowledge the "power" of the professional.
- Attend to the use of clear language.
- Consider the question of "conscientization": To what extent is the immediate ethical tension reflective and part of wider societal and global issues?

3. Joint Evaluation

- Was the outcome lasting in its resolution of the ethical questions in the workers', service users', and community view?
- Which actions by the workers worked best?
- Which actions by the service user(s) worked best?
- Did all members feel included and respected?
- What would be different in a future instance of this ethical decision?

(Link, 1999, p. 90)

Take a moment to consider these principles. Do they provide a starting point for guiding the politics and ethics of social justice work? How might you modify these principles? What would you add, delete, or change? Using these questions and guidelines, take time to reflect on an ethical dilemma you or others have faced as you have engaged in social work practice. Do you see alternative possibilities for understanding the problem, building relationships, and developing courses of action? We will return to specific questions of values, ethics, and participation as we explore the core processes of social justice work in the following chapters.

Chapter Summary

In this chapter we have examined the concept of values, their place in our everyday lives, and their role in shaping social work thought and practice. We have considered values in political, historical, and familial contexts, and we have addressed the practice of valuing. We have considered the core values of social work, the relationship between values and ethics, and the contradictions therein. We have challenged the ethical boundaries of social work in the U.S. by examining alternative constructions of values and standards of ethical and political practice in diverse organizational and national contexts. Finally, we considered the relationship of social work and human rights and put forth ethical and political principles that may guide us in the pursuit of social justice work. In Chapter Four, we turn our attention to theory, the dialectics of understanding and action, and the Just Practice Framework and processes.

Teaching-Learning Resource: The Social Class Questionnaire

This questionnaire was used in an introductory undergraduate course at Brown University taught by Professor Susan Smulyan entitled "Basic Issues in American Culture." The questionnaire was reprinted in *Readings for Diversity and Social Justice* (Adams, Blumenfeld, Castañeda, Peters, & Zuñiga, 2000, pp. 432-434) with an editorial note suggesting that teachers duplicate and use this questionnaire in class. We find this questionnaire helpful in exploring the intersection of values and social class.[19]

Please respond to the following questions:

1. How would you characterize your family's socioeconomic background? (For example: poor, working class, lower-middle class, middle class, upper-middle class, upper class, ruling class).

   What tells you this?

2. What was/is your father's occupation (if applicable)?

   What was/is your mother's occupation (if applicable)?

3. How would you characterize the socioeconomic nature of the neighborhood(s) you grew up in?

   Of the larger community you grew up in?

4. Select, from the list below, five values/expectations/orientations that seem to be most valued in your family. Then select five that seem to be least valued or important. Do these most valued or least valued lists characterize class values?

   Getting by

   Making a moderate living

   Making a very good living

   Open communication among family members

   Going to a place of worship

   Keeping up with the neighbors

   Being physically fit or athletic

   Working out psychological issues through therapy

   Helping others

   Getting married and having children

   Respecting law and order

   Defending one's country

   Staying out of trouble with the law

   Being politically or socially aware

   Recognition

   Community service

   Saving money

   Making your money work for you

   Enjoying your money

   Getting a high school degree

   Getting a college degree

   Getting an advanced or professional degree

   Learning a trade

   Helping to advance the cause of one's racial, religious-cultural group

   Physical appearance

Being a professional

Being an entrepreneur

Owning a home

Being patriotic

Going to private school

Not being wasteful

Having good etiquette

Others: __________

5. Think of one or two people who you perceive to be from a different social class from you (someone from high school, from a job, from your university). What class would you say they belong to? What tells you this?

   Besides money, what do you see as distinguishing them from you (or your family from their family)?

   How would you characterize their values or their family's values?

   How are their values the same as or different from yours?
6. What do you appreciate/have you gained from your class background experience?
7. What has been hard for you being from your class background?
8. What would you like never to hear said about people from your class background?
9. What impact does your class background have on your current attitudes, behaviors, and feelings (about money, work, relationships with people from the same class/from a different class, your sense of self, expectations about life, your politics, etc.)?

Questions for Discussion

1. What set of values are expressed in the construction of housing projects in inner city urban areas, the development of city parks and playgrounds, or the gated communities of suburbia U.S.A.?
2. Imagine taking a visitor on a "value tour" of your community. Where would you go? What impressions might your visitor take away from the tour?
3. Phyllis Day describes the dominance of the "New Puritanism" in shaping contemporary social welfare policy. What would a social welfare policy informed by the values of social justice look like?
4. Reflecting on your own values, what life experiences have posed the greatest challenges to your values? What institutions beyond the family have shaped your values? How have your values evolved or changed as a result?
5. How do social work codes of ethics vary across contexts, and what does this say about the contextual nature of valuing?
6. Based on your review of a number of codes of ethics, what would you include if you were to write a code of ethics for 21st century social justice work?
7. How are the concepts of social justice and human rights connected?
8. How do the five key concepts of meaning, context, power, history, and possibility suggest a framework for valuing?
9. Using the Internet as an investigative tool, what other codes of social work ethics can you find internationally? How do these differ from those presented in this chapter?

Suggested Readings

Adams, M., Blumenfeld, W. Castañeda, R. Hackman, H., Peters, M. & Zuñiga, X. (2000). *Readings for diversity and social justice.* New York: Routledge.

Epstein, L. (1999). "The culture of social work." In A. Chambon, A. Irving, and L. Epstein (Eds.), *Reading Foucault for social work* (pp. 3-26). New York: Columbia University Press.

Kozol, J. (1991). *Savage inequalities: Children in America's schools.* New York: Crown Publishers.

Naples, N. (1998). *Grassroots warriors: Activist mothering, community work, and the war on poverty.* New York: Routledge.

Ramanathan, C. & Link, R. (1999). *All our futures: Social work practice in a global era.* Belmont, CA: Wadsworth.

Rawls, J. (1995). *A theory of justice* (2nd ed.). Cambridge, MA: Harvard University Press.

Reamer, F. (1995). *Social work values and ethics.* New York: Columbia University Press.

Sklar, H. (1995). *Chaos or community? Seeking solutions, not scapegoats for bad economics.* Boston: South End Press.

Takaki, R. (1993). *A different mirror: A history of multicultural America.* Boston: Little, Brown.

Chapter 4

Just Thinking: Theoretical Perspectives on Social Justice-Oriented Practice

Theory, n.: [Fr. theorie, from L. theoria, a theory, from Gr. theoria, a looking at, contemplation, speculation, theory.]

1. Originally, a mental viewing; contemplation.
2. An idea or mental plan of the way to do something.
3. A systematic statement of principles involved; as the "theory" of equations in mathematics.
4. A formulation of apparent relationships or underlying principles of certain observed phenomena which has been verified to some degree: distinguished from hypothesis.
5. That branch of an art or science consisting in a knowledge of its principles and methods rather than its practice; pure, as opposed to applied, science, etc.

Webster's Unabridged Dictionary (1983)

"I came to theory because I was hurting—the pain within me was so intense that I could not go on living. I came to theory desperate, wanting to comprehend—to grasp what was happening around and within me. Most importantly, I wanted to make the hurt go away. I saw in theory a location for healing."

bell hooks (1994), *Teaching to Transgress* [1]

Chapter Overview

In Chapter Four we define and discuss theory and the practice of theorizing in social science inquiry and everyday life. We consider theorizing as a fundamental human capacity and activity through which we work to make sense of our worlds, experiences, and relations. We examine theory in the context of social work and present a brief overview and critique of several approaches to social work theory and practice – **medical, ecosystems, structural, strengths,** and **empowerment.** We then introduce readers to a range of critical theoretical contributions that have been developed by people outside of social work who are concerned with questions of social justice and social change. They address questions about the *politics of knowledge development,* the workings of *nonviolent domination* ("hegemony"), and the *positivist assumptions of objectivity.* They explore the *intersectionality* of race, class, gender, sexuality, citizenship, and age in systems of oppression, and the centrality of language, meaning, and narrative in the crafting of human experience. In Chapter One we introduced you to some of the critical theorists who have influenced our approach to social justice work. In this chapter, we reflect on their contributions and the ways they have informed our thinking about the Just Practice Framework. We return to our key concepts – *meaning, context, power, history,* and *possibility* – and argue their relevance for social justice work. We then introduce the *seven core processes – engagement, teaching/ learning, action, accompaniment, evaluation, critical reflection,* and *celebration* – through which the concepts are translated into practice.

What is Theory?

Challenge of Defining Theory

Explicitly and implicitly, formally or informally, theory is ever present in our practice. It is an important foundation of our work as social workers. If social work practice is a house we build, then theory is its blueprint. Nevertheless, say the word "theory" to many social work practitioners and be prepared to hear of its irrelevance outside the classroom. The dialogue goes much like this: "Theory is what they teach you in school. This is the real world and theory has no meaning here. We need skills, tools, and methods to guide our practice." Does theory seem too abstract and disconnected from the "real" world of the practicing social worker? Perhaps its devaluation lies in the fragmented way in which we teach theory within social work programs. It is often separated and removed from the whole. Theory is seen as intangible, ultimately academic, and entirely intellectual (read boring). In school we learn theory without "doing" theory and we learn theory without recognizing that we have been doing theory all of our lives. The irony here is that theory is *always* in play in our work, whether we take the time to reflect upon it or not. It underscores every action we take as social workers. It informs our behavior, the choices we make, and the interventions we plan and carry out. Now let us define theory, explore the many ways in which it works, and consider its contributions to social work practice.

A Child's Eye View. We opened this chapter with some contrasting definitions of theory. Webster's dictionary offers definitions of theory as a systematic statement of principles about a phenomenon and as a "contemplation" or "mental view." The former has the tone of scientific formality while the latter speaks more to our human sense of wonder and curiosity. Now think of that favorite phrase of toddlers: "But why?" With those two words, children enter into theorizing about the world and their experience in it. They are seeking explanations and trying to grasp cause and effect. They are trying to understand the rules, the way things work. Remember for a moment a childhood experience – perhaps lying down outside and contemplating the clouds. What did you wonder about clouds, their shape, and movements? What might have been your theory of clouds? What was your mental view?

Think for a moment of the theories you created as a child. This calls for visualizing yourself in certain situations, remembering your thinking patterns, and recalling how you approached the world as you attempted to discover and make sense it. Some of these theories continue to hold explanatory power for you today. You may have revamped others according to changing contexts in your life, personal development, and the addition of new experiences. For example, what made a car move down the highway? Why did music come out of a radio? Why did boys and girls line up separately to go to the lunchroom at school? What theories did you have about where babies came from? How did this theory change during the course of your childhood? What theories did you construct about different expressions you noticed on your parent(s)' face and what they meant? What are other examples of theorizing from everyday experience?

Children Making Theory

Holly Peters-Golden, a medical anthropologist, teaches us about theory and theorizing from the experiences of everyday life. Several years ago, Holly was home caring for her preschool-age daughter, who had a bad case of the flu. As she stroked her daughter's feverish forehead, she said, "Honey, you just feel miserable, don't you?" Her little girl looked up at her and asked: "Mommy, what makes mizzuhble happen?" Her daughter's question is about theory, about trying to understand her pain and give meaning to her experience. She is trying to construct a theory of health and illness. Reflect on a moment in your own early life experience that you struggled to understand. How did you give meaning to the experience? What information did you draw on to come to your understanding? Did you share your theory with others? Did they share your interpretation of the experience or did they have a different understanding? Did your theory change over time as you gathered more information? What might reflection on your own experience suggest about theory and theorizing more broadly?[2]

The Urgency of Theory. bell hooks, whose quote begins this chapter, speaks to the urgency, emotionality, and, most fundamentally, the necessity of making sense of our life experiences and conditions. Her sense of desperation to grasp and give meaning to the power and pain of her experience contrasts sharply with a sterile notion of theory as separate and separable from "practice." Her understanding of theory parallels that of Antonio Gramsci, the Italian Marxist philosopher who theorized about culture, power, history, and Fascism from his prison cell. Gramsci spent the last eleven years of his life – 1926-1937 – in prison for his participation in working-class movements and his promotion of the dangerous idea that poor and working-class people were capable of critically understanding and collectively changing the conditions of their lives (Forgacs, 1988; Gramsci, 1987). Like hooks, Gramsci wrote about theory with a sense of urgency, filling notebooks from his prison cell. He lived the inseparability of theory and practice and wrote: "so the unity of theory and practice is also not a given mechanical fact but an historical process of becoming…" (Gramsci, 1987, p. 67). He argued the importance of grasping the:

> . . . passage from knowing to understanding and to feeling and vice versa from feeling to understanding and to knowing. The popular element 'feels' but does not always know or understand; the intellectual element 'knows' but does not

> always understand and in particular does not feel... the intellectual's error consists in believing that one can know without understanding and even more without feeling and being impassioned. (Gramsci in Forgacs, 1988, p. 349)

Theory and Oppression. Writing from an indigenous vantage point, Linda Tuhiwai Smith (1999) notes that the word "theory" is a word that can provoke a whole array of feelings, values, and attitudes. She points out that, in many ways, indigenous peoples have been oppressed by theory. Outsider understandings and assumptions have guided the probing into "the way our origins have been examined, our histories recounted, our arts analysed, our cultures dissected, measured and torn apart..." (p. 38). Tuhiwai Smith recognizes the power of theory in crafting social reality and making claims about that reality. She reminds us that theory is not made in a vacuum but in the context of cultural understanding and social and political relations. She calls on indigenous people to participate in the theory making that shapes understanding of their histories and experiences. Tuhiwai Smith writes:

> I am arguing that theory at its most simple level is important for indigenous peoples. At the very least it helps make sense of reality. It enables us to make assumptions and predictions about the world in which we live. It contains within it a method or methods for selecting and arranging, for prioritising and legitimating what we see and do. Theory enables us to deal with contradictions and uncertainties. Perhaps more significantly, it gives us space to plan, to strategize, to take greater control over our resistances. The language of a theory can also be a way of organizing and determining action. It helps us interpret what is being told to us, and to predict the consequences of what is being promised. Theory can also protect us because it contains within it a way of putting reality into perspective. If it is a good theory, it also allows for new ideas and ways of looking at things to be incorporated constantly without the need to search constantly for new theories. (p. 38)

Theory as Explanation and Prediction. In their most positivist (scientific) sense, theories explain or predict certain behaviors or particular social phenomenon (Payne, 1997; Robbins, Chatterjee, & Canda, 1998, 1999; Schriver, 1998). Positivism refers to an ideology, or set of beliefs, that assumes there is a stable, "knowable" world, governed by natural laws, that can be discovered through controlled, objective, value-free, systematic inquiry. Theories are thus "based on cognitive abstractions that develop over time and are both a description and generalization from our experiences" (Robbins, Chatterjee, & Canda, 1999, p. 375). In their social work practice text, Sheafor, Horejsi and Horejsi (2000) write that a theory "offers both an explanation of certain behaviors or situations and guidelines on how they can be changed" (p. 51). Lengermann and Niebrugge-Brantley (1998, p. 2) describe theory as a "lens that directs the eye towards a given reality so that one focuses on some of its features while filtering out others."

Theory as Survival Skill. Lemert (1999, p.1) describes theory as a basic survival skill. In so doing, he moves theory from its privileged academic location as "a special activity of experts" and demystifies it by illustrating how ordinary people create theory and do it quite well. He uses an example from Alex Kotlowitz's book, *There Are No Children Here* (1991), where the author relays the story of a young boy trying to survive in Chicago's most dangerous public housing project (contemporary tenement houses). This ten-year old child says, "If I grow up, I want to be a bus driver." Think for a moment of what the word "if" means in this case. Contrast this with the common phrase of the privileged child: "When I grow up. . ." In the story, the boy's mother adds increased depth and richness to social theory through her comments, "But you know, there are no children here. They've seen too much to be children." Lemert (1999) tells us this is social theory: "The boy and his mother both put into plain words the social world of the uncounted thousands of urban children whose lullaby is gunfire" (pp. 1-2). What theories of children and childhood do this boy and his mother express? How do they test out these theories everyday? Are there other places in the world where this theory might apply? What might be the circumstances and how in these circumstances is theory a basic survival skill as bell hooks recounts in this chapter's beginning quotation?

The Social Construction of Theory

Theory and Values. Robbins et al. (1998, 1999) remind us that theory is socially constructed. This means that we are all born into a preexisting society and its cultural context of norms and patterns of acceptable behavior. From generation to generation, we socially transmit our notions of reality and internalize these through socialization processes. This socially and culturally transmitted knowledge that we acquire from infancy equips us with systems of language, screens of meaning, patterns of practice and shared assumptions through which we engage in the world and from which we come to question, explore, and theorize about the world. Our theories about human behavior and processes of change are intimately linked to these broader systems of values, meanings, assumptions, and practices that shape our worldviews. Rarely do we question this taken-for-granted knowledge. Remembering that all knowledge is socially constituted allows us to understand theory as an expression of values and as such, representative of different ideological systems of thought (Berger & Luckman, 1966).

The Case of Psychosocial Development and Moral Reasoning – Erikson and Gilligan. Keeping this in mind let us see how values not only shape the development of theory but also how they influence practice. Erik Erikson's (1963) theory of psychosocial development is an excellent example. Perhaps you learned of this theory in an introductory psychology course or in a social work course in human behavior in the social environment (HBSE). Erikson postulated that human development occurs in sequential stages, predetermined steps if you will. He called these the "eight ages of man" and wrote about them in his seminal work published in 1950, *Childhood and Society*. Erikson based his theory on research conducted on white, heterosexual, middle-class males. The theory made an important contribution to the linkage of psychological processes and social experience, and it challenged us to think about human development as a process that continues through the life course.

Thirty years later, Carol Gilligan (1982), informed by a growing body of feminist theory, criticized Erikson's work for portraying male development and experience as the norm. She asserted that Erikson's theory ignores differences among people in the developmental process, and represents and privileges a white, middle-class, male notion of the meaning of development. She showed how a partial view of the world, based on a privileged masculine "positionality" shared by Western white male theorists, researchers, and subjects, was assumed the norm and presented as a universal model of human psychosocial development. In short, she pointed out that Erikson was not theorizing from an objective and omniscient position but rather from a particular *standpoint*, informed and limited by his social location and experience.

Regardless, Erikson's theory continues to set the standard for how others assess psychosocial development. Women's experience was not seen as an issue and was subsumed under the male model of experience articulated by Erikson. It is important here to consider how the values, history, and context (positionality) of the theorist (Erik Erikson), influenced and continue to influence notions of normalcy and deviance in present day society. Given these considerations, how do you think power bears on theory? If we base our practice on this theory, how might we inadvertently set a standard of human development that is inherently classist, sexist, and racist? What other examples come to mind of ways in which theories of human behavior "normalize" and "universalize" the experience of particular, privileged groups? Whose experiences count and whose are discounted? What might be some practical consequences of such universalizing theories?

The Case of Loss and Grief. Theorizing about loss and grief provides yet another example of the intertwining nature of theory and practice. Many of us may be familiar with the theory of loss and grieving developed by Elisabeth Kubler-Ross. Based on her work with and observation of people in the process of bereavement, she developed a model for understanding the stages of loss and the tasks of grieving.

Stages of grief. Kubler-Ross describes the initial reaction as one of shock and denial, followed by a series of emotional stages, moving from anger to sadness and depression, and finally to a place of acceptance of the reality of the loss (Kubler-Ross, 1970). Her model has been broadly applied in processes of healing and support, not only for people who have lost loved ones to death, but also for understanding and addressing other losses such as divorce, loss of a job, and loss of capacity due to illness or injury. However, as Mark Marion (1996) argues in his important work on AIDS and loss, Kubler-Ross's model is not sufficient for understanding the progressive, multiple loss and trauma experienced by gay men in the face of the AIDS epidemic. Marion explores the trauma associated with losses that continue and accumulate over time. He argues that the experience of multiple loss can shatter one's assumptions about self worth, the meaning of life and a just world. He writes that, for multiple loss survivors, "(l)ike a tiny boat in a pounding surf struggling to find its moorings, more trauma and loss keeps pounding away at the sense of self-worth, sense of safety in the world, and sense of meaning" (Marion,1996, p. 65).

The global loss model. Drawing on the experiences of gay men in the last decade of AIDS, Marion developed the concept of "global loss" to comprehend their experiences that could not be contained even within the concept of "multiple loss." With the experience of global loss, "no aspect of life or identity is unaffected…there is a loss of community," and "there is no safe haven" (1996, pp. 65-66). Gay men and gay communities have been experiencing "losses too big to grieve." Marion describes four symptoms of coping he has witnessed among gay men struggling with global loss: psychological fatigue, depression, survivor guilt, and shame (p. 68). He argues that we need to develop a new language to describe global loss that encompasses its profound grief and trauma. He proposes a circular model of denial, anxiety, anger, depression, and adaptation to begin to articulate the experience of global loss that has no defined beginning or end. Marion stresses that this is a model about living and writes: "In fact, gay men surviving and thriving in the global loss of AIDS are doing just that: living in a community where traumatic loss is ongoing and creating ways to live passionate and meaningful lives in the midst of it" (p. 80). Take a minute to think about the practice of theorizing here. Marion is constructing new ways of thinking about the social reality he confronts. He is trying to give meaning to human pain and struggle. And he is engaged with theorizing as a survival skill. His concept of Global Loss is profound. What thoughts and feelings does the concept provoke for you? In what other contexts might a theory of Global Loss be applied? How might practice guided by a concept of global loss differ from practice guided by Kubler-Ross's more linear model of loss and grieving?

In summary, theories are not facts. As tools of inquiry, theories aid in the study of human behavior, provide us with ways in which to explain how the world works, and help us build frameworks, models, and guidelines for practice. Theories, however, are this and much more. They are value-laden social constructs, the process and products of our search for meaning, and part of our human repertoire of survival skills. They emerge at particular points in history, are molded and shaped by that history, and serve to transmit values and ideology. Thinking of theory in these ways reminds us that we must search for the meanings others create and make no assumptions about how others construct their world views. It also compels us to look critically at our own thinking and practice.

Making Theory

Making theory is something we all engage in every day of our lives as we act in and reflect on the world. In our work, play, and relationships we use theories to interpret our experiences. We "gather data" from the trial and error experiences of everyday life, sometimes changing our practices and sometimes changing our thinking along the way. We apply our "folk theories" about the body, health, and illness as we take our family cures for hiccups or the common cold or as we adopt and invent new remedies. Parents apply and develop theories of child rearing as they put personal and cultural knowledge into practice each day. Likewise, children develop their own theories about the meaning of adulthood and the practice of parenting based on their experiences. Their respective theories of childhood and adulthood may be sharply contrasting, given their very different "positionalities."

Developing Alternative Perspectives

The making of new theory is often rooted in both the appreciation and critique of existing theoretical perspectives. As we addressed earlier in this chapter, Carol Gilligan used Erik Erikson's theory as a springboard into alternative theory development. She both appreciated Erikson's work articulating the linkage of psychological, social, and development processes and critiqued the gender-bound limits of his approach. Her theory added a different voice to human development theory as she stretched the boundaries of traditional approaches to include and reflect the unique experiences of females. In her research, she uncovered two different modes of thought, not necessarily gender-based but reflective of individualization and rights on one hand, and connectedness and responsibility on the other. She criticized traditional developmental approaches for their depiction of females as inferior rather than stressing the limitations of the theory. Gilligan made new theory from critical engagement with previously existing theory.

Carol Stack – Rethinking Moral Development. Anthropologist Carol Stack (1990) crafted new theoretical insights as she critiqued the limitations of Gilligan's theory in explaining moral reasoning among working class African-American adolescents and adults.[3] While Gilligan paid attention to gender, Stack showed how Gilligan failed to attend to the intersectionality of gender, race, and class. Stack's work talks back to feminist theories that take gender as a serious issue but fail to question their own assumptions about the universality of white, middle-class experience. For five years, Carol Stack lived and worked with African-American return migrants - men, women, and children moving back to their homeplaces in the rural southern U.S. She was especially interested in children's movements back and forth between family ties in the urban North and rural South and the real-life moral dilemmas they faced regarding where to reside, with whom, and the responsibilities therein. Her findings paid particular attention to differences of class and race as well as gender in the practice of moral reasoning. She found that both men and women, adults and adolescents alike, were equally oriented toward both justice and caretaking. The data from Stack's study suggested that men's and women's shared experience of oppression "informs both self-identity and group-identity among return migrants and these converge in the vocabulary of rights, morality, and the social good" (1990, p. 24). Further, she found that boys and girls alike were aware of the "tyranny of racial and economic injustice" from an early age. She writes:

> Likewise, the interviews with children reveal a collective social conscience and a profound sensitivity among young people to the needs of their families. The children's voices tell a somber story of the fate, circumstances and material conditions of their lives. Their expectations about where they will live in the coming year conform to the changing needs and demands of other family members, old and young, and family labor force participation. (p. 25)

Standpoint Theory and Positionality

Revisiting the Concept of Positionality. Rather than accepting white, middle-class experience as the norm, Stack showed how theory can be broadened, challenged, and enriched by considering social reality and relations from diverse "positionalities." Let's return for a moment to the subject of "standpoint" and "positionality" that we introduced in Chapter One and have been discussing here. As engaged human beings we bring our histories and experiences with us as we act in and make sense of the world. Our positionalities are shaped through ongoing processes of identification. By this we mean that, as social actors, people are at once claiming identities, being labeled by others, and experiencing the world in terms of those multiple identities such as race, gender, age, class, citizenship, ethnicity, and sexual orientation. As Reed, Newman, Suarez and Lewis (1997) note:

> Some of these identities give us, almost automatically, and certainly at times unconsciously, certain privileges and stakes in power; alternatively, some of these identities work to produce us as oppressed. ...Positionality underscores the necessity that each of us locate himself or herself along the various axes of social group identities. We must begin to articulate and take responsibility for our own historical and social identities and interrogate (challenge or questions and work to understand in an ongoing way) how they have helped to shape our particular world views. (p. 58)

Implications for Theory – Theories Reflect Standpoints. So what does this mean in terms of theory? Proponents of various standpoint theories argue that people with different positionalities acquire differing standpoints, positions from which they view and experience reality and from which alternative views may be obscured. Just as people acquire differing standpoints, so do the theories they construct reflect their standpoints (hooks, 1984; Hill Collins, 1990; Swigonski, 1994).[4] According to Patricia Hill Collins (1990), standpoint theory argues that group location within the context of unequal power relations produces common challenges for individuals in those groups. Further, Hill Collins contends, those shared experiences shape similar angles of vision leading to group knowledge or standpoint that is essential for informed political action. Sociologist Dorothy Smith (1974) also addresses the issue of standpoint and argues that:

> Women's standpoint, as I am analyzing it here, discredits sociology's claim to constitute an objective knowledge independent of the sociologist's situation… To begin from direct experience and return to it as a constraint or "test" of systematic knowledge is to begin from where we are located bodily. The actualities of our everyday world are already socially organized. Settings, equipment, environment, schedules, occasions and so forth, as well as our enterprises and routines, are socially produced and concretely and symbolically organized prior to the moment at which we enter and at which inquiry begins. By taking up a standpoint in our original and immediate knowledge of the world, sociologists can make their discipline's socially organized properties first visible and then problematic. (pp. 21-24)

Smith calls on us to recognize and acknowledge our standpoints in the practice of making theory rather than operate from a pretense of objectivity.

According to some standpoint theorists, people in oppressed social positions experience a different reality from those who enjoy positions of privilege. As W.E.B. DuBois (1989) has argued, oppressed people develop a critical consciousness as part of their survival strategy. They must be attuned to the dominant rules and vigilant in their social practice. As a result, people in positions of oppression develop a more critical and complex view of social reality, a "double consciousness," so to speak. As critical race and gender theorists have argued, the crafting of theory from the standpoint of the oppressed is not simply an intellectual exercise but a matter of survival (Hill Collins, 1990; hooks, 1984; Mohanty, 1991; Moraga & Anzaldúa, 1981). For instance, Patricia Hill Collins, addressing black feminist consciousness, calls on black women to claim their standpoints, recognize the power in their positioned knowledge, and make their critical knowledge of the world a base for transformative action (1990, pp. 21-33).

Your Standpoint

Reflect for a moment on the many facets of your own "positionality." What are some of the identities and experiences that shape your positionality? How would you describe the standpoint you have acquired? How has knowledge gained from your standpoint aided you in surviving and negotiating your way in the world? What might be some of your "blind spots?"

Grounded Theory

The kind of theory we have been discussing has been built from the ground up. Qualitative researchers who study cultures, peoples, institutions, and practices to uncover and explore lived experiences and their meanings call this grounded theory (Strauss & Corbin, 1990). Grounded theory is derived inductively instead of deductively through traditional scientific methods. That is, theory is built bottom-up, from the concrete, empirically grounded realities of people's lives, experiences and narratives, rather than top-down from general, abstract principles (Lengerman & Niebrugge-Brantley, 1998, pp. 40-43). Carol Stack (1990), for example, grounded her critique of Gilligan's theory of moral reasoning in concrete knowledge gained from her observations and conversations with people differently positioned than those in Gilligan's study. Now we can also begin to see points of connection between the concept of grounded theory and that of standpoint theory. Both attend to and emphasize the importance of what we might call "local knowledge," or knowledge that is explanatory and particular to certain people at particular points in time. Both validate the importance of *relationship* in the generation of knowledge. Both ask: "How do we build knowledge about the world through concrete engagement with people's experiences in the world?" The making of grounded theory calls for an appreciation of the "positionalities" of the researcher and the subjects of study and a recognition of the limits of one's hands-on knowledge.

Examples from Our Experiences. We offer some examples from our own experiences as researchers to better illuminate the notion of grounded theory. Here is Janet Finn's story:

> In the early 1990s, I spent three years tacking back and forth between two copper mining towns, Butte, Montana and Chuquicamata, Chile. The towns had been the copper-producing hubs for the Anaconda Copper Mining Company for the better part of the 20th century. I wanted to learn how residents imagined and built community with and in resistance to a powerful corporation. Most accounts of mining towns and their histories focus on men's experiences. I was especially interested in learning about community history and practices from the perspectives and experiences of "working-class" women – the wives, mothers and daughters of miners, many of whom were workers themselves. I spent time living in both towns, talking and working with women, and recording their stories of community support, struggles, and survival. Women in Butte told stories about the temporal structuring of their lives around three-year labor contracts as they maintained a vigilance of family and community life during times of employment and mobilized networks of friend- and kinship to hold the "body and soul" of community together during strikes. In contrast, women in Chuquicamata told stories of the spatial structuring of their lives as they got up at dawn to stand in line at the company store every day in order to provide for their family's needs. The lines shaped the social space of women's lives, where they came together, shared their stories, and built solidarity and support. Their critical consciousness of their positionings as women and of the possibilities for collective action was honed through their everyday struggles for family and community survival. Drawing from their stories, I began to develop a theory of gendered social practice grounded in women's experiences of "crafting the everyday." Women crafted a sense of the ordinary to hold family and community together during hard times. They used their material and emotional resources to create community and a sense of the possible. They were craftswomen, using the tools and supplies at hand to create new meanings and purpose. (Finn, 1998a, p.176)

Maxine Jacobson's (1997, 2001) story of grounded theory springs from her research on multidisciplinary teams that investigate child sexual abuse:

> I became interested in multidisciplinary teams because of my experience as a team member on three different teams in Montana in the 1980s and early 1990s. When I began my research, I was interested in how teams from different locations in the state made sense of the causes of child sexual abuse and what connection, if any, these theoretical underpinnings had for how teams practiced. In other words, how did theory and practice intersect and were there differences based on location or context? I discovered that teams made sense of child sexual abuse through a multitude of explanations ranging from individual causes such

as low self-esteem, sexual deviance, and learned family patterns to broader societal causes such as the acceptance of violence against women and children, patriarchy, poverty, and other environmental stressors. Although unarticulated as such, teams operated from dominant theories on the nature of child sexual abuse, but their practice was shaped and constrained by the availability of community service resources, community culture, and beliefs about the efficacy of treatment as a panacea for the child sexual abuse problem. The most rural team in the study, the team I called the "frontier team," stood out in this regard. This team had limited access to services for the treatment of child sexual abuse, but this was business as usual in a remote rural community in Montana. Team members made do with what they had, and ingenuity and creativity highlighted their practice. For example, one team member shared the following story:

> We do some creative sentencing—We had an old man who had to be 80 years old. He had a long history, and every once in a while he would chase little kids and flash. What we did with him—we knew that there were no programs that would touch him so we told him he had to report to the sheriff's office once a week, and we gave him a two year sentence. We never told him when his sentence was over so he reported to the sheriff's office once a week until he died—and I bet it was five or six years—and we never had any trouble with him as long as he had that reminder that he had to go to the sheriff's office. (Jacobson, 1997, p. 209)

The frontier team was situated at least 200 miles away from residential, foster care, and psychological services. Besides having limited access to services, frontier team members expressed concerns regarding the efficacy of a costly 30-day treatment regime as the answer for the child sexual abuse problem. Instead, they questioned dominant professional beliefs about the nature of "treatment," and individuals as "points of intervention." Although connected to other teams across the states through policy mandates and prescribed team structures, local knowledge and local resources shaped team practice:

> I think we just see some things being used that you wouldn't see otherwise. Maybe you've got an adolescent that's getting in a lot of trouble and needs some structure that he's not getting at home with his mother and father—whatever. You happen to know someone whose husband does fencing in the summer and who likes to hire youth to do that. So let's see if we can get this kid hitched up for the summer—do some hard work and get him straightened out—something like that. So that might not seem ethical—

> you know, I'm going to set that kid up with my cousin who does fencing but in a situation like this when there are no other alternatives, it would probably be real helpful—and it could probably work out well. (Jacobson, 1997, p. 209)

Theory and Meaning Systems. Dennis Saleebey (1993, 1994) provides another example of grounded theory. He brings the workings of theory to a generative level, that is, discovering with practitioners through dialogue the theoretical/practice linkages they make. This implies an inductive approach to theory and compels us to start from the ground up to look for understandings in people's lived experiences. Saleebey looks at theory as the meanings we construct to explain our reality. He sees culture as the raw material from which we construct these meanings. Saleebey asks social workers to look for theories in the meaning systems people create such as stories, narratives, and individual and collective versions of myths. This pushes us to look at the meanings conveyed in peoples' words and actions and to see these as the embodiment of theory. Borrowing from Saleebey (1994), and as a case in point, the following story tells us of how two very different people made sense of a particular situation:

> *A first-year social work student, with no previous social work experience, begins work with a young man, a heavy drug user in the past, who is ostensibly in the throes of the last stages of acquired immune deficiency syndrome (AIDS). In the hospital, all but isolated if not morally quarantined by staff, he is, in effect, a pariah. One doctor, answering the student's question about involving the family, suggests that people "like this" typically do not have families who care. (This is the doctor's story, by the way.) Innocent, unnerved, but dedicated, the student does not know what to do—but she does the most human thing; she solicits and really listens to the young man's story. He rallies for a few days, days made passable (maybe even possible) by his storytelling. At a point at which death seems near, he says to the student, "I love you." She, against her learning, replies in kind. Through her encouragement of the story and, thus, the self, she and the young man trafficked in the possible, acknowledged the past, and laid some ghosts to rest. But for the student, there is a political lesson here. Her client's story and others like it must get out, and she will assist in that project.* (p. 355)

What does this story teach us about the power relations inherent in labeling, expert knowledge, and the dehumanizing of those reduced to the status of other through labeling? What theories of practice are at play in this story given the doctor's conceptualization of the patient with AIDS? The student's?

In sum, theorizing is a critical and creative process of making sense of and giving meaning to the world and our experience in it. Theorizing is a survival skill that enables us to bring a sense of coherence to the demands of everyday life. Theorizing is part and parcel of our social practice. We have attempted to bring the process of making theory to light in order to systematically reflect on it and examine the relationship between theory and practice. In the following section we turn to theorizing in social work and the relation of theory to practice.

Theory and Social Work Practice

Historical Snapshot

As we saw in Chapter Two, a historical perspective helps us better understand the relationship of theory to social work practice. It helps us step back for a moment and contemplate the power and importance of theory to guide our practice as social workers. Near the end of the Progressive Era social work practice gravitated toward the "objectivity" of scientific methods. It was a time when science claimed and colonized social work and other professions with its promise of finding the right and true solutions to address the struggles and challenges of the human condition. Mary Richmond (1917) (re)languaged social casework to reflect this scientific allegiance and further the advancement of a professional standard for social work. Richmond spoke of "social diagnosis," instead of "investigation" and forged the marriage of social work and medicine through what she called "medical-social service." Bringing medicine to bear on social work provided it with credibility. This was an act of (re)theorizing social work. Medical theory reconfigured practice. It defined and reflected the familiar power relationships of doctor and patient, expert and the uninformed. This configuration established the basis of the casework relationship. It also guided workers to look for the source of problems within individuals and less so in environmental circumstances and structures. Even settlement house work, once predicated on the principles of participatory democracy, showed signs of theoretical infiltration and alteration as the language of clients, problems, and needs circumvented that of citizen, participation, and rights.

This historical snapshot gives us a space to imagine how theory influences and shapes the very essence of our work as social workers, from deciding the location of our work and its rules and regulations, to defining the very nature of the relationships we establish and how these are predicated on our understandings of the process of change. Theory steers us to develop particular kinds of programs and services or to even think in terms of programs and services as the means through which we conceptualize that which we believe to be helpful. They underlie the strategies we use and our formulations of change. Some of our theories reduce people to needs and problems. Others view them as active participants in shaping their own reality.

The Lobotomy: From Preferred Practice to Cruel and Unusual Punishment. Differing theoretical perspectives can have profound consequences for practice. Between 1930 and 1970, a surgical procedure called the lobotomy was the preferred mode of treatment for a number of debilitating mental health problems such as schizophrenia and chronic depression. The procedure consisted of the following: "After drilling two or more holes in a patient's skull, a surgeon inserted into the brain any of various instruments—some resembling an apple corer, a butter spreader, or an ice pick—and, often without being able to see what he was cutting, destroyed parts of the brain" (Valenstein, 1986, p. 3). A theory legitimizing lobotomies claimed that pathologically fixed thoughts localized in the brain's prefrontal lobe caused the patients' symptomatology. Fixative surgery destroyed these abnormal pathways, thus releasing patients from agonizing mental disorders (Valenstein, 1986, p. 84). Some practitioners contested use of the lobotomy over the course of its forty-year history. Nevertheless, even though the theories it was based on were discredited, many accepted claims of its success. In 1949, the Nobel Prize was awarded for its discovery. In contrast, Nolan Lewis, director of the New York State Psychiatric Institute had this to say about "successful cases:"

> *Is the quieting of the patient a cure? Perhaps all it accomplishes is to make things more convenient for the people who have to nurse them. . . . The patients become rather childlike. . . .They act like they have been hit over the head with a club and are as dull as blazes. . . . It disturbs me to see the number of zombies that these operations turn out. I would guess that lobotomies going on all over the world have caused more mental invalids than they've cured. . . . I think it should be stopped before we dement too large a section of the population.* (as quoted in Valenstein, 1986, p. 255)

While the lobotomy is certainly a dramatic example of a practice that did more harm than good, might we look back from some future vantage point and be appalled at our acceptance of some of our "best" practices today? Might we judge them as inappropriate, insufficient, cruel, and inhumane? What examples come to mind?

Theory and Contemporary Social Work

Now let's shift our attention to theories that guide more contemporary social work practice. In this section we will describe a number of contemporary social work theories and consider both their contributions as well as their limitations. But first, we want to equip you with some tools so that you can engage in your own critique of theory. We present nine questions to guide your critical reflection on theory. We invite you to join us in thinking about the contributions and limitations of the range of theories that inform and guide contemporary social work in the U.S.

Critiquing Theory

Given its inherently ideological, socially constructed nature, it is important to analyze theory in depth. It is equally as important to consider what working theories are at play in particular social work practices and "interventions." Although implicit, these underpinnings are powerful determinants of practice. As you read through the list of questions provided below, think of particular examples of theories that inform social work practices of "intervention," and then subject them to analysis and critique.

1. What contextual aspects or forces does this theory address (individual, relational, familial, communal, political, cultural, economic)?
2. How congruent is this theory with the values and ethics of social work practice?
3. Does this theory support or promote particular values or assumptions about human behavior, human nature, and how the world should be?

4. At what particular point in time is this theory historically situated? When did it develop and what was its contextual surround?
5. Does this theory contribute to preserving and restoring human dignity?
6. What truth claims support this theory? (empirical, heuristic) What is the power of this theory to define, explain, and interpret reality?
7. Does this theory recognize the benefits of and celebrate human diversity?
8. Does this theory assist us in transforming our society and ourselves so that we welcome the voices, the strengths, the ways of knowing, and the energies of us all?
9. Does this theory reflect the participation and experiences of males and females; economically well off and poor; white people and people of color; gay men, lesbians, bisexuals, heterosexuals; old and young; and people with disabilities?

(Adapted from: Robbins et al., 1998 and Schriver, 1998)

Return for a moment to Saleebey's story of the first-year social worker student and the young man dying of AIDS on page 150. Use the questions posed here as a guide to analyze the various theories that you see coming to bear on this situation. What does this reflection teach you about grounded theory?

Systems

Overview. For the past 25 years, social systems or ecological (ecosystems) perspectives have dominated social work theory in the U.S. The systems approach argues that individuals are complex living systems and that human behavior needs to be understood in its broader systemic context. A system is defined as "an organized whole made up of components that interact in a way distinct from their interaction with other entities and which endures over some period of time" (Anderson & Carter, 1990, p. 266-267). Social systems theory argues that human needs must be understood in light of the larger systems in which people function. Systems maintain boundaries that give them their identities, and they tend toward homeostasis, or equilibrium (Hutchinson & Charlesworth, 1998, p. 44), which means they try to maintain a balance between sameness and change. Systems theorists view systems holistically such that "every part of a system is so related to its fellow parts that a change in one part will cause a change in all of them and in the total system (Watzalawick, Bavelas, & Jackson, 1967, p. 123 cited in Miley, O'Melia & Dubois, 1998, p. 44). Proponents contend that the systems perspective provides a means for considering the total social situation and intervening accordingly. Systems theories shifted attention from the past to the present, focusing on possibilities for creating change rather than on "why things happened" (Strom-Gottfried, 1999, p. 7).

Person-in-Environment. Systems theories attracted a following in social work for their fit with a "person-in-environment" perspective (Germain, 1994, p. 104). For example, in their classic 1973 text, *Social Work Practice: Model and Method*, Pincus and Minahan applied systems theory to social work practice. They argued for an integrated approach to problem assessment and planned change that addressed the role of "systems" as well as "people" in the helping process. They put forth a conceptual model for social work practice that identified four systems central to the change process:

- The *change agent system* includes the social worker, the agency, and formal and informal resources they bring to bear.
- The *client system* contracts with the worker to engage in a process of planned change.
- The *target system* includes those individuals, groups, that the client and worker seek to change or influence in order to achieve the client's goals.
- The *action system* includes all those involved in the change effort (Based on Pincus and Minahan, 1973, p. 63).

Systems theories were readily adopted into social work understandings of human behavior in the social environment and practice with families, groups, and communities (see for example Hartman and Laird, 1983).

Toward an Ecosystem Perspective. By the 1980s, systems theorists had begun to incorporate the language of human ecology in order to more specifically conceptualize the dynamics of exchange between people and their social and physical environments (Germain, 1979, 1983; Germain and Gitterman, 1995). In 1980, Germain and Gitterman published *The Life Model of Social Work Practice*. They embraced an ecological approach, promoted the "person-in-environment" language and perspective, and identified both persons and social systems as contributing to the problem-solving process. According to the emerging "ecosystems" perspective "persons and environments are not separate but exist in ongoing transactions with each other" (Germain, 1983; Miley, O'Melia & DuBois, 1998, p.32). According to Miley, O'Melia, and DuBois (1998), the ecosystems perspective "conceptualizes and explains human system functioning. Specifically it:

- Presents a dynamic view of human beings as systems interacting in context.
- Emphasizes the significance of human system transactions.
- Traces how human behavior and interaction develop over time in response to internal and external forces.
- Describes current behavior as a comfortable fit of "persons in situations."
- Conceptualizes all interaction as adaptive or logical in context.
- Reveals multiple options for change within persons, their social groups, and in their social and physical environments" (p. 32).

Key Contributions. The ecosystems perspective constructs human interaction with the social environment in terms of resources, niches, carrying capacity, adaptation, and competition. It emphasizes the integrated nature of human behavior, the interplay of multiple systems, and the "fit" between people and their environments. It takes a "transactional" view of "dysfunction" that might arise as "persons and environments" strive for mutual adaptation (Miley, O'Melia & Du Bois, 1998, p. 36). By 1986, Whitakker, Schinke, and Gilchrist (1986) proclaimed that social work had a new "paradigm" - the ecological paradigm. Paradigms refer to worldviews, ways of thinking, or systems of belief that denote certain methods of practice (Lincoln & Guba 1985, p. 15; Maguire, 1987, p. 11; Patton, 1975, p.9). [5]

Since the 1980s the ecological or "ecosystems" paradigm has powerfully shaped social work thought and practice in the U.S. Let's consider some of the contributions of the various systems, ecological, or ecosystems approaches. These approaches point to the fundamental importance of context and draw attention to the person-environment relationship. They provide a theoretical basis for social work's professional uniqueness, which is predicated upon the grasp of this relationship. Systems and ecological approaches challenge understandings of social problems based on a "medical" or "personal deficiency" model that emphasizes individual problems or deficits. They looked beyond the individual person in crafting solutions. These approaches have pointed to social work's historic concern for environmental conditions, as evidenced in the Settlement House Movement. What do you see as other contributions of an ecosystems approach? Return for a moment to the nine questions for critiquing theory presented above. How would you rate systems theory or an ecosystems perspective? What additional information do you need to respond to the questions?

Critiques. Despite its continued prominence in the field, the ecosystems perspective has also been criticized on a number of fronts. Some critics see the perspective as so vague and general that it can be broadly applied yet gives us very little specific guidance for practice. Its focus on the here-and-now situation and possibilities of intervention has resulted in a neglect of history. Critics also argue that the emphasis on "fit" tends to support the status quo rather than question the dominant order of things. Ecosystems perspectives emphasize strategies for adaptation to, rather than transformation of, existing structural arrangements. Questions of power and conflict, so important to considerations of practice, are not addressed. For example, Amy Rossiter (1996) argues that the ecosystems perspective incorporates an uncomplicated view of both person and environment, assuming that both are stable, knowable and non-problematic concepts. Further, the perspective assumes a fundamental distinction between the person and society rather than seeing the dialectical, mutually constituting relationship between people and society (Rossiter, 1996). In their more recent writing on the ecological or ecosystems perspective, Germain and Gitterman (1995) have responded to some of these concerns and called for consideration of dimensions of power, history, and life course development in the definitions and dynamics of person-environment transactions. Take a minute to think about these critiques. Are these critiques that you agree with? Are these critiques you would challenge? What arguments or evidence would you bring to bear?

Structural Social Work

Overview. The structural approach (also referred to as a political economy or conflict approach) to social work is part of a larger radical social work movement.

Structuralists view the problems that confront social work as a fundamental, inherent part of the present social order wherein social institutions function in ways that systematically work to maintain social inequalities along lines of class, gender, race, sexual orientation, citizenship, etc. (Mullaly, 1997, p. 104). Informed by Marxist theory, structuralists place questions of conflict and exploitation at the center of social work theory. They see personal problems as resulting from structural injustice and the resulting unequal access to means and resources of social and economic production. From the structuralist perspective, clients are viewed as victims of inequality and exploitation. Structuralists raise questions about the historical and material conditions through which inequalities are structured and experienced.

Key Contributions. The structural approach has made significant contributions to social work practice. Structuralists have placed questions of power and inequality at the center of theory and practice. They have challenged social workers to see personal problems as resulting from structural injustice and have advocated for systems changing interventions. Structuralists have engaged in a critique of the relationship between social work and capitalism and have contended that the goal of social work practice is the transformation of the social structure to a new order grounded in social justice, egalitarianism, and humanitarianism (Bailey & Brake, 1976; Coates, 1992; Galper, 1975).

Critiques. While structural social work has long been a prominent voice in Canadian, Australian, and British social work theory and practice, it has largely been marginalized in the U.S. Structural social workers have been criticized for being "too political" in their sympathies for a socialist alternative to the dominant political order and unrealistic about the possibilities of achieving structural change. The structural approach has also been critiqued for its emphasis on persons as "victims" of structural inequalities rather than as actors capable of participation in processes of personal and social change. What do you see as possible strengths and limitations of a structural approach? What evidence would you bring to bear?

Strengths

Overview. In recent years a strengths perspective has gained prominence in social work in the U.S. The strengths perspective emerged as a corrective to social work's problem-focused approach, arguing that, to be true to the value base of the profession, we need to begin by recognizing people's capacities and the potential of their circumstances. The strengths perspective calls for a shift from problem- to solution-focused processes that stem from the "client's values, hopes, and desired goals" (Saleebey, 1997, p. 35). Social workers are encouraged to attend to the resource potential of the environment and appreciate human resiliency, creativity, and capacity for survival in the face of adversity. The basic premises of the strengths perspective are as follows:

- Clients have many strengths
- Client motivation is based on fostering client strengths
- The social worker is a collaborator with the client
- Avoid the victim mindset
- Any environment is full of resources (Saleebey, 1997).

Key Contributions. Working from a strengths perspective, the social worker seeks to identify, facilitate, or create contexts in which people who have been silenced and isolated gain understanding of, a voice in, and influence over the decisions that affect their lives. The perspective promotes belonging, healing, and relationship building through dialogue and collaboration. Rather than asking, "what's wrong?" the social worker operating from a strengths perspective asks, "what's possible?" (Saleebey, 1992; Cowger, 1994).

Critiques. Proponents of the strengths perspective point to its compatibility with an ecosystems approach. Rather than challenging the fundamental tenets of the ecological model, the strengths perspective is generally seen as offering an enhanced lens through which to view the person-environment nexus. The strengths perspective has been praised for recognizing human capacity and agency. It has been criticized for underplaying constraints and the often overwhelming struggles that poor and oppressed people face in their everyday lives (Barber, 1995; Brown, 1996; Coates & McKay, 1995; Fisher, 1995; Gutiérrez & Lewis, 1999; Howe, 1994; Margolin, 1998). What do you see as possible contributions and limitations of a strengths perspective? Take a minute to return to our nine questions about theory and ask them of a strengths perspective.

Empowerment

Overview. The empowerment approach in social work has been gaining prominence over the past decade. The empowerment approach is premised on a recognition and analysis of power, group work practices of consciousness raising and capacity building, and collective efforts to challenge and change oppressive social conditions (see for example, Gutiérrez and Lewis, 1999; Miley, O'Melia & DuBois, 1998). This approach makes linkages between the personal and the political. Empowerment theorists frequently speak of personal, interpersonal, and political levels of empowerment and advocate forms of social work practice that engage all three. Lorraine Gutiérrez and Edith Lewis have developed empowerment approaches to social work with women of color (1999). They write:

> The three types of empowerment (personal, interpersonal, political) are unified by a central belief, namely that social work's primary goal is to help individuals, families, groups and communities develop the capacity to change their situations. The social worker's role is to help people change the situation and prevent its recurrence. The effects of powerlessness occur on many levels, so change must be directed toward both large and small systems; it is insufficient to focus only on developing a sense of personal power or providing skills or working toward social change. Practice at all three levels when combined comprises empowerment practice. (p. 12)

According to Gutiérrez and Lewis (1999, p. 18-20), the key methods for empowering social work practice are education, participation, and capacity building. Following Freire (1970-1974), they see education as a critical process of raising consciousness. To develop critical awareness, one must engage in a power analysis of the situation wherein connections are made between the immediate practice context and the distributions of power in society as a whole.

Key Contributions. Empowerment approaches build on the social work traditions of self-help, mutual support, and collective action. Some empowerment theorists have drawn on both feminist and critical race theories in critiquing the limitations of competing approaches and articulating an alternative direction for social work (cf. Gutiérrez and Lewis, 1999). For example, Gutiérrez and Lewis argue that social work can work toward greater social justice by simultaneously building on individual and social transformation. They recognize the possibilities of human agency and the significance of cultural and political knowledge and histories.

Critiques. Empowerment perspectives have been praised for bringing questions of power to the center of social work theory and practice and for recognizing the mutual constitution of individual and society. Concepts of empowerment have been criticized for being so broadly applied to such diverse practices that the term itself becomes meaningless. More recently, we have seen the appropriation of the term "empowerment" to describe punitive practices. For example, time limits imposed by welfare reform under Temporary Assistance for Needy Families (TANF) Program have been described by proponents as "incentives" that "empower" poor people to "get off welfare." This use of the term masks the power relations in play in the politics of welfare and makes poverty a personal problem that can be ameliorated through "self-help" without structural change. Critics have argued that social workers may be more likely to embrace the language than the practice of empowerment. Leslie Margolin (1998) contends that most empowerment perspectives fail to fully acknowledge social work itself as a type of power, a way of seeing things. He points to the ways in which a language of empowerment may mask practices through which social workers "stabilize middle-class power by creating an observable, discussible, write-aboutable poor" (p.5).

Meanings of Empowerment

Think for a moment about where you have heard the word "empowerment" used. For example, we now have "empowerment zones" in urban areas struggling for economic survival. Welfare reformers talk about "empowering the poor" to help themselves. Women's organizations around the U.S. have mobilized action empowering women to stand collectively against violence and fear and "take back the night." In what other contexts do you hear people talk of "empowerment?" Are there differing meanings of empowerment being used in these differing contexts? What does the idea of empowerment mean to you? What might be an example of a situation in which you were empowered? Disempowered? What are some of the feelings that you associated with those situations? What did you learn from the experiences? How did the experience limit or enhance your sense of possibility?

Comparing Approaches

Review the approaches to social work practice we have presented thus far, then get together with your classmates in a small group and consider the following scenario:

Lynn, a single mother of three, is 27 years old. She and her children live in a small older mobile home located in a trailer park near the edge of Middleton, a community of 40,000. Lynn grew up in Middleton and graduated from high school here. She had her first child, Bobby, at age 16. She married Rob, the baby's father, the following year. Lynn and Rob were together for eight years, and they moved frequently in that time. Lynn had two more children, a boy (Brandon) and girl (Heather), now ages 8 and 5. She and Rob returned to Middleton when Lynn was pregnant with her youngest child. Rob has been both physically and verbally abusive to Lynn during their time together. After a particularly serious assault, Lynn left briefly with the children, and threatened to get a restraining order. Lynn and Rob reconciled for a time, then separated 18 months ago. Rob left town shortly thereafter to take a construction job. He sends an occasional support check.

Lynn's mother died when Lynn was 19, and her father abandoned the family when she was in grade school. Lynn has one older brother who lives in Middleton. He has recently remarried. Between his work and family time, he has seen little of Lynn in the past few years. Lynn has lost touch with many of her high school acquaintances since returning to Middleton three years ago.

Lynn has been working day and evening shifts in a local restaurant. Money is tight, and Lynn is behind on several bills. Lately, she has had to go to the community food pantry for help by the end of the month. Lynn's boys are in school, and Heather attends a Head Start full day program. A neighbor woman in the trailer court watches the children at times when Lynn is at work. Occasionally, Lynn has to rely on Bobby to take care of the younger ones for a few hours in the evenings and on weekends when she has to work. Lynn has been trying to work extra shifts in order to get caught up on bills. The children have missed several days of school this year. Bobby seems listless and distracted. He has been falling behind in his classes, and Lynn has not responded to attempts from the school to set up a meeting with her. You are the school social worker, and you have received a request from Bobby's teacher to follow up on the situation at home. How will you proceed in assessing the situation?

Now chose two of the approaches to compare in assessing the case. For example, you could compare the systems approach with the structural approach or the strengths approach with the systems approach. Respond to the following questions in your comparison:

1. How does each approach differently define the problem?
2. Who is responsible for resolution of the problem? (i.e., the individual, society or both)
3. What is the focus of the intervention?
4. What is the role of the social worker in the assessment plan?
5. What is the role of the client in the assessment plan?
6. How would you describe the nature of the social work relationship?

Take 15-20 minutes to consider the direction your assessment and intervention might take. How do the approaches you chose to compare differ? Where do they differ? How do the theories you chose for understanding human problems shape your approach to assessment and intervention? How do the approaches differ in what you consider important and what you leave out of the process? What do you see as the limits of the approaches you used? Of the two approaches, which one do you see as most compatible with your knowledge and values? Why? If you were to develop a third approach that addresses some of the limitations you encountered in the two approaches you used to complete this exercise, what would it look like? What would you call your approach?

Expanding the Theoretical Possibilities

In contemporary U.S. social work, ecosystems, strengths, and empowerment constitute the field's most widely taught theoretical perspectives. Unfortunately, too much of our practice still seems to be guided by the medical or personal-deficit model that reduces social problems to personal troubles. What are some possibilities for challenging the limits of theory and practice and realizing the possibilities of social justice work? We turn to the diverse and challenging terrain of critical social theory to address this question.

Understanding Critical Social Theory

Social work is not alone in grappling with questions about the production and practice of knowledge. Over the past two decades there has been considerable attention to the "crises" of theory throughout the social sciences (Agger, 1998). Critical social theorists have questioned ideologies of scientific objectivity and have explored the social construction of knowledge. They have challenged notions of determinist, universal social laws and pointed to the possibilities of changing history. A number of these theoretical debates have filtered into social work. We have already introduced you to several theories and theorists that have influenced our thinking about social justice work. It has been through our long-term engagement with the dominant theories of social work, exploration of alternative theoretical possibilities, and reflection on our own practice that we have come to craft a new framework for social justice-oriented social work. In this section we further explore some of these contributions and point out ways in which they have shaped our development of the Just Practice Framework.

The concept of "critical social theory" as used here encompasses a range of perspectives, including feminist, post-structural, postmodern, and critical race theories. The significant differences among these perspectives are beyond the scope of this chapter, and they have been addressed elsewhere (see for example, Agger, 1998; Dirks, Eley, & Ortner, 1994; Figueira-McDonough, Netting & Nichols-Casebolt, 1998; Hill-Collins, 1990; Lemert, 1993; and Weedon, 1987). They have in common a critique of positivism ("a family of philosophies characterized by an extremely positive evaluation of science and scientific method" (Reese, 1980, p. 450, as quoted in Lincoln & Guba, 1985, p. 19)); a concern for questions of power, difference, and domination; attention to the dialectics of structure and human agency; and a commitment to social transformation (Agger, 1998). Critical social theorists address the mutual constitution of forms of knowledge and relations of power (Foucault, 1977, 1980). These common themes form the foundation of our thinking. In the following discussion, we highlight some of these influences and ideas that have shaped our thinking about social justice work. First, we address the concepts of "discourse," "domination," and "globalization" as they relate to our thinking about social justice work. These concepts are essential to understandings of critical social theory. We then turn to the work of feminist, critical race, and practice theorists and discuss their influence on our development of the Just Practice Framework. We find this material both "hard to think" and "good to think." We argue that engagement with ideas that push us out of our comfort zones is part of the process of social justice work.

Discourse. Some critical theorists have focused on questions of language, discourse, and power in the construction of social reality (Derrida, 1976; Weedon, 1987). The concept of *discourse* as used here is about more than language and "talk." It refers to ways of constituting knowledge together with social practices, forms of subjectivity, and relations of power. Chambon (1999, p. 57) writes: "More than ways of naming, discourses are systems of thought and systematic ways of carving out reality. They are structures of knowledge that influence systems of practice." Thus, the concept of social work discourse brings critical attention to the mutual constitution of systems of knowledge- what counts as "truth"- and systems of practice - what count as problems and interventions. For example, Leslie Margolin (1998) writes about the power of social work discourse in constructing both "clients" and their "problems." He writes:

> My point is that social work's original clients, consisting largely of foreigners who swelled American cities at the turn of the twentieth century, were not allowed to read what investigators wrote about them. They were not allowed to offer corrections, or monitor the uses to which their biographies were put. Entering into social workers' language 'for their own good' made clients subordinate objects in it. They were engaged in a mass of records that captured and exposed them. . . . And because written words are more easily controlled than speech, fine distinctions can be drawn between those who should have access and those who should not, between those who can make additions and corrections and those who cannot. Recordkeeping, in other words, is the mechanism that assures the differential distribution of power. (p. 37)

The concept of discourse has helped us think more specifically about the ways in which knowledge is constructed and the relationship of power and inequality therein. It allows us to move from a more abstract level of theoretical, political, and ethical concerns to the concrete realities of the power of language and the ways we carve out terrain of the "talkable" and that which goes without saying. For example, how is it that only certain kinds of social benefits are construed as "welfare"? How did "welfare" come to be thought of as a dirty word, associated with the "dependency" of the poor? And how is it that "dependency" is constructed as a bad thing, pitted against the "correctness" of "independence?"[6] What are the social and political consequences of omitting discussion of interdependence and social as well as personal responsibility from the welfare debates? These are questions of discourse. Michael Moore, in his irreverent book *Downsize This: Random Threats from an Unarmed American* (1996), a provocative critique of corporate and political power and the consequences for working-class people, gets to the heart of the issue of welfare discourse. He writes:

> Each year, freeloading corporations grab nearly $170 billion in tax-funded federal handouts to help them do the things they should be paying for themselves (and that doesn't even count all the corporate welfare they are getting from state and local governments). That's $1,388 from each of us going to provide welfare to the rich! . . . .
>
> By contrast, all of our social programs combined, from Aid to Families with Dependent Children (AFDC) to school lunches to housing assistance, amount to just $50 billion a year. That breaks down to only $1.14 a day from each of us. . . So why is it that when we say the word *welfare* the first image that comes to mind is the single mother with a half-dozen kids living in the inner city? Aside from the fact that it's racist, it isn't true. (pp. 43-44)

Domination. Other critical theorists have pursued the relationship among practices of knowledge production, the making of social subjects, and the logic of capitalism (Harvey, 1989; Rouse, 1995; Thompson, 1966; Williams, 1977). They have returned to the work of Antonio Gramsci (who we introduced at the beginning of the chapter) for guidance. These questions were central to his work. Gramsci asks us to think not only about the structure of capitalism as an economic model based on the production of profit for the few through the extraction of "surplus value" from the many. He asks us to also think about how it is that the many come to accept a logic that seems to serve very particular interests. How is it that those in less powerful positions come to accept as "common sense" and to participate in the systems of domination and exploitation that conflict with their interests? What is the role of economic systems in producing particular kinds of social and cultural subjects and shaping their interests, dispositions, and desires? Through posing and reflecting on these sorts of questions, Gramsci put forth his notion of "hegemony" to describe processes of non-violent domination and the ways in which people become participants in systems that continue to oppress them (Gramsci, 1987; Williams, 1977, 1980). And he explored the ways in which the everyday practices of capitalism worked in shaping people's dispositions and desires as particular kinds of producers, consumers, and citizens. As John Ehrenreich showed us in Chapter Two, many social workers became partners with industrial capitalists in the making of "good workers" during the early 20th century.

We find Gramsci's insights to be provocative for social work theory and practice today for the following reasons:

1. He offers analytical tools for thinking critically about the ways in which the logic and workings of the economy penetrate our everyday lives and sense of self.
2. He provides us with the means for exploring how non-violent forms of domination work and what their human consequences may be.
3. We can draw on his insights to help us see how the social production of social work knowledge and practice – the framing of theories, problems, and interventions; the structuring of "worker-client" identities and relations; and the location of the profession in society – is intimately implicated in the workings and logic of the larger economic system.

We have found Gramsci's work very important in helping us think critically about questions of meaning, power, and history in the making of social problems and interventions. He reminds us that we are never outside of the political, cultural, and economic systems that shape our experiences, interpretations, and actions. He challenges us to question received "common sense" and to pose questions that may help us come to an alternative common sense regarding root causes of social problems and the words and actions that both mask and justify structured inequalities.

Crime and Punishment

Below is the mission statement for "Critical Resistance," an organization dedicated to challenging the "justice" behind the burgeoning prison population in the U.S. Take a moment to read the mission statement and reflect on the questions that follow.

> Prisons and incarceration have become the panacea for all our social ills. Where once the U.S. looked to the welfare state to alleviate social problems, today the U.S. looks to prisons, prisons, and more prisons. Critical Resistance (CR) uses the term Prison Industrial Complex (PIC) to encompass both this phenomenon and the corresponding reality that capitalism flourishes from locking people in cages.
>
> CR recognizes that an integral component of the PIC is the dramatic increase in the incarceration of people of color, women, and the poor, along with the continued imprisonment of political prisoners. CR is strongly committed to challenging the existing structure of "criminal justice" which is based on revenge, punishment, and violence. As part of the emerging international movement for penal abolition, we envision a society where fundamental social problems are no longer "solved" through the mass warehousing (and periodic torture) of human beings, the overwhelming majority of whom are poor people of color and non-violent. CR's mission is to build a national campaign to challenge the Prison Industrial Complex.[7]

Think about the term "prison industrial complex." What images does it bring to mind? What questions might it spark regarding the production of "crime," "criminals," "prisoners," and "justice"? How is it that U.S. prison populations have exploded in recent years? How is it that people of color are vastly over-represented in prisons? What "common sense" is at work here? How does the discourse of crime and punishment work to construct not only a certain "common sense" but also an economic industry of the keepers and the kept? What "alternative common sense" is suggested by the work of Critical Resistance?

Globalization. More recently, the shift in attention to "late capitalism," characterized by the global reorganization of work and the making of new social subjects (such as "flexible" workers, "displaced" workers, "migrant" workers, and refugees) and new strategies of resistance, has raised further critical questions for social work (Harvey, 1989; Rouse, 1995). Critical theorists of late capitalism have drawn attention to globalization as both an *ideology*, or set of beliefs, regarding the "inevitability" of the new world order, and a *political strategy*, a systematic effort to consolidate power, create "flexible" workers, and open borders to the movement of corporate interests (Korten, 1995, Piven & Cloward, 1997). They recognize the transnational penetration of "neoliberal" economic politics and practices as a driving force in the production of new forms of social exclusion and political conflict (Alvarez, Dagnino & Escobar, 1998; Lowe & Lloyd, 1997). Critical understanding of and attention to these processes are essential to social justice work, even in its most "local" and "personal" forms.

David Korten (1995, pp. 11-14), in his book *When Corporations Rule the World,* succinctly addresses the issue of globalization and what is at stake. Over the past two decades we have experienced accelerating social and environmental degradation and rising rates of poverty, unemployment, inequality, and violence on a global scale. This has been accompanied by a five-fold increase in economic output since 1980 that has pushed human demands on ecosystems beyond sustainability. The continued quest for economic growth has intensified the competition between the rich and poor for scarce resources, and the poor have been the losers. Korten further argues that national governments have been incapable of responding. The result is a crisis of governing:

> . . .born of a convergence of ideological, political, and technological forces. . . [that is] shifting power away from governments responsible for the public good and toward a handful of corporations and financial institutions driven by a single imperative - the quest for short-term financial gain. This has concentrated massive economic and political power in the hands of an elite few whose absolute share of the products of a declining pool of natural wealth continues to increase at a substantial rate – thus reassuring them that the system is working perfectly well. (p. 12)

The logic of late capitalism and the forces of globalization have profoundly shaped social conditions, social welfare policies, and social work practice. We are witnessing the shrinking of the social safety net accompanied by the privatizing of social work and the increasing complexity of human problems that transgress national borders. Social justice workers need the theoretical and political capacity to grapple with questions of discourse, domination, and globalization in order to be effective players on this challenging terrain.

Feminism and Critical Race Theories

Feminist perspectives and practices have presented an important challenge and corrective to contemporary social work. And as women entering into our adult professional lives in the midst of what has come to be called the "second wave" women's movement of the 1970s, we (the authors) have been influenced by feminist theory, practice, and politics. Feminist movements have challenged the political, social, and economic marginalization of women and the systems of thought and practice that have informed and justified women's marginality and inequality. Feminist theorists and activists have sought to raise consciousness of the many forms of women's oppression, whether it occurs in the home or workplace, in schools or on the streets.

The accomplishments of the women's movement have been far reaching. Feminists have made gender an issue and have examined the workings of patriarchy in the family and larger society that systematically structure women's subordination (Jaggar, 1983; Ortner & Whitehead, 1981; Rosaldo & Lamphere, 1974; Smith, 1990). They have addressed the connection of the "personal" and "political" and critically examined the politics of family and everyday life that have contributed to women's oppression. In social work, feminist scholars have explored the assumptions about gender, women, marriage, and family that have informed and continue to inform social welfare policies (Abramowitz, 1998; Gordon, 1990). Feminist scholars have questioned the assumptions about motherhood and the "good mother" that underlie child welfare policies and practices (Armstrong, 1995; Finn, 1994, 1998b; Gordon, 1988). In their discussion of the integration of gender and feminist thought into social work practice knowledge, Figueira-McDonough, Netting, and Nichols Casebolt (1998, pp. 19-20) have articulated a set of intellectual and practice guidelines that reflect principles of feminism and critical theory. These principles also undergird our thinking about Just Practice:

1. Recognition that gender is a complex social, historical, and cultural product.
2. Rejection of the study of unique histories and specific social formations as universal.
3. Recognition of institutionalized perceptions and patterns of behavior that are diverse and changeable without falling into polarizations or homogenized categories.

4. Promotion of methodologies that allow for the study of the relative salience of other divisions within gender.
5. Analysis of gender embeddedness so that other forms of patterned inequality can be assessed.
6. Recognition, exploration, and valuation of women's experience as a precondition to understanding the impact of different and unequal contexts on identities.
7. Initiation of a process of integration in knowledge construction guided by praxis.
8. Awareness that the end of subjugation, not difference, is the target of action.

Critical theorists have also challenged "scientific racism," the bodies of knowledge about "race" produced within biological and social sciences and designed to "prove" the inferiority of people of color. They have addressed the social construction of race, ethnicity, and racist ideologies; processes of *racialization* (assignment of racial meaning to a previously neutral event); and practices of everyday racism as well as the social and institutional structures of inequality. They have examined the mutually constituting relationships among race, difference, discourse, and inequalities (see for example, Gates & West, 1996; Gilman, 1985; Marable, 1997, 1999; West, 1993). Important linkages between race and gender theories have been addressed in the work of "third-world" feminists, women of color, and critical race theorists (see for example Hill Collins, 1991; hooks, 1984; Mohanty, Russo, & Torres, 1991). They have challenged the limits of "liberal," "radical," and "socialist" feminisms articulated by white women, have spoken to the super-exploitation of women of color, and have addressed the importance of narrative and experience in voicing the feminist stories of women of color (see for example Jones, 1984; Moraga & Anzaldúa, 1983). The contributions of Black and Latina feminists, for instance, have encouraged us to listen to and respect stories of survival and strength rather than pathology in understanding cultural diversity in the constructions of family and gender (Segura & Pearce, 1993; Zavella, 1994). They have addressed the need to examine the specific historic, economic, and cultural contingencies and the gendered strategies for responding to those circumstances rather than falling back on simple generalizations about ethnicity, class, and gender that may tell us very little.

Theories of "Practice"

A Different Way of Thinking About "Practice." The Just Practice Framework we develop here is grounded in a reconceptualization of "practice" informed by critical social and cultural theory. The term "practice" in contemporary social theory does not have the same meaning as "practice" in the traditional social work sense of a series of planned interventions. Rather, practice refers more broadly to social action carried out in the context of unequal power relations (Dirks, Eley & Ortner, 1994; Ortner, 1984, 1989, 1996).[8] Practice theorists have attempted to place human agency and social action at the center of new social theory. They are responding to what they see as overly deterministic structural approaches that ignore human actors, and overly "actor-oriented" approaches that neglect attention to the structural forces that shape and constrain human action (Giddens, 1979).

The Interplay of Culture, Power, and History. Practice theorists are concerned with the interplay of culture, power, and history in the making of social subjects and in the processes of social reproduction and change (Bourdieu, 1977; Dirks, Eley & Ortner, 1994). A number of practice theorists have drawn on the work of French philosopher Michel Foucault in thinking about the disciplinary practices at work in the shaping of positionality, discourses, and social relations. Foucault paid particular attention to localized, institutional contexts, such as clinics and prisons, where one could witness the power of what he termed "disciplinary practices," those that contributed to the production of particular kinds of social subjects. He was concerned with the power of modern scientific reason, of objectivity, measurement, classification, and evaluation at work in the disciplining of bodies and making of particular kinds of social subjects. Foucault argued that power is not ultimately in the strong arm of the state, but rather it is a productive force exercised through relations between people (Foucault, 1977, 1978, 1980).

Although the language of practice theory may sound unfamiliar to social work, we argue that the issues practice theorists are grappling with go to the theoretical and practical heart of the profession. The practice perspective attends to the mutual constitution of the person and society; points to the irreducible connection of structure and practice; and addresses the power of discourse in the construction of the terrain of the thinkable, talkable, and doable. Working from a practice perspective, we are challenged to consider the cultural and political *processes* and historical *contexts* in which we construct social problems; imagine "clients," "helpers," and their respective "roles" and relationships; and develop social policies and intervention technologies. Importantly, then, a practice perspective makes power, inequality, and transformational possibility foci of concern, thus offering a theoretical bridge between the concept of social justice and the practice of social work.

We have covered considerable conceptual ground in this section. Our abbreviated discussion does not do justice to the richness and complexity of the theoretical terrain. Our journey across this terrain continues. Our purpose in this section has been to point to some of the important influences on our thinking and to offer readers some theoretical benchmarks to guide your own journeys.

Just Practice: Framework and Processes

An Integrated Approach

These significant, critical interventions have posed challenges to dominant modes of social work theory and practice. Concerns over questions of meaning, power, and knowledge in social work have been variably addressed by empowerment, narrative and social constructionist, and "postmodern" approaches. Some of these approaches have emphasized questions of meaning, others have addressed relations of power and inequality, and a few have attended to questions of history (Guitérrez and Lewis, 1999; Laird, 1993; Leonard, 1997, Mullaly, 1993; Parton, 1996; Payne, 1991; Pease and Fook, 1999; Rossiter, 1996; Swingonski, 1994). However, none of these have articulated an *integrated* approach to social work that theoretically and practically links themes of meaning, power, and history to the context and possibilities of justice-oriented practice. As we reflected on these diverse, challenging, and at times problematic theoretical influences we began to build our own critical thinking around the five key themes of Just Practice. What were we pulling from these influences that helped us envision social justice work? Could these five themes be the necessary and sufficient elements for a foundation? As we held these five independent themes in relation and explored their interconnection, what new possibilities for thought and practice might emerge? We began to explore those possibilities.

In crafting the Just Practice Framework we have organized our thinking around five key terms: *meaning, context, power, history,* and *possibility.* In articulating the framework, we attempt to incorporate the critical insights of practice theorists and bring the meaning and power of transformative possibility to the fore in shaping struggles for social justice-oriented social work. As we have argued above, the challenge of social justice work calls for challenging ways of thinking and the disruption of our certainties about the world. We argue that the Just Practice Framework offers not "answers" but a model for critical inquiry that enables us to disrupt assumed truths, explore context, and appreciate ways in which social location may shape interpretation. To recap, the five key themes provide the basis for question-posing to inform and shape the practice of social justice work. How do people give *meaning* to the experiences and conditions that shape their lives? What are the *contexts* in which those experiences and conditions occur? What forms and relations of *power* shape people and processes? How does *history* make people and how do people make history as they engage in struggles over questions of meaning and power? How might an appreciation of those struggles help us imagine and claim a sense of *possibility* in the practice of social justice work? These questions are translated into action through *seven core processes* that link theory and practice: *engagement, teaching/learning, action, accompaniment, evaluation, critical reflection,* and *celebration.* In this section we address each of the core processes and consider how they work with the five key themes of the Just Practice Framework. This foundation provides the theoretical and practical support for the subsequent chapters in which we develop the processes and present concrete skills and exercises that help us think about and engage in social justice work.

The Core Processes

The theory, politics, and ethics of social justice work are translated into practice as participants in the change process engage in the *praxis* of action and reflection for personal and social transformation.[9] It is possible to think of the core processes as a series of actions, or steps that, when taken together, move us toward this goal. However, the seven core processes do not necessarily imply linear, sequential movement. It may be helpful to envision them as overlapping and mutually informing processes, like waves, shaping and washing over one another. It is in this sense of nonlinear movement that we can better grasp the dynamics of change produced through the ebb and flow of ideas, reflections, and actions (Tuhiwai Smith, 1999, p. 116). In the following paragraphs we outline the core processes.

Engagement. Engagement is the process through which the social worker enters the world of the participant(s) and begins to develop a working relationship. It entails entry into both context and relationship. It is a process of listening, communication, translation, and connection that seriously addresses questions of trust, power, intimacy, difference, and conflict. The social worker begins from a place of openness and curiosity and acknowledges the partiality of her knowledge. Through the engagement process the social worker anticipates the work ahead by reflecting on the participant(s) in the change process and coming to an appreciation of the other's situation. Engagement also calls for critical reflection on one's own positionality and the ways in which it may shape the relationship and the process of change.

Teaching/Learning. Teaching/learning is a participatory process of discovery and critical inquiry. In part, it entails the process of data collection, assessment, and interpretation and reframes them as collaborative activities. Teaching/learning connotes a two-way street and a relationship of interchange among participants. We teach at the same time that we are taught. We engage in mutual question posing, use various means to collaboratively collect information, identify resources and supports, discuss root causes of presenting concerns, teach and learn skills of assessment, and discover personal and collective capacities for critical practice, both our own and others'.

Action. Action is the process of carrying out plans and sustaining the momentum. Action consists of recognizing and activating, brainstorming, decision-making, planning, organizing, and putting these efforts in motion. It includes animating, facilitating, maintaining impetus, awakening the spirit and sense of possibility, advocating, and taking responsibility to speak for the values of social justice. Action is informed by reflection. It demands vigilance and a commitment to the ongoing search for one's own competence (Freire, 1990). Action calls for critical and respectful attention to resistance.

Accompaniment. Accompaniment is the actual people-to-people partnerships through which action is realized. In its simplest sense, accompaniment means to go with, to support and enhance the process. It reflects a commitment to being part of the journey over the long haul. The process entails ongoing critical dialogue regarding difference, power, and positionality among participants. It keeps us mindful of the challenges of collaboration and the need for conscious work in building alliances, mediating conflicts, and negotiating power.

Evaluation. Evaluation is an ongoing process consisting of stepping back, taking stock at different moments in the change process, and assessing the effectiveness of our efforts. Evaluation is interwoven with reflection and teaching/learning.

In evaluation, we systematically examine the process and outcomes of our efforts. Evaluation is a collaborative process done *with* rather than *to* others. It is a process of documenting, scrutinizing, and sharing the results of our efforts so that we can learn from one another and produce the changes that we have envisioned.

Critical Reflection. Critical reflection is a dialogical process of learning together from our experiences. It is a structured, analytic, and emotional process that helps us examine the ways in which we make sense of experiences and circumstances. Through critical reflection, we systematically interpret our individual and collective experiences, question taken-for-granted assumptions, and reframe our inquiry to open up new possibilities. Critical reflection enables us to challenge "common sense," make connections, and explore the patterns that connect.

Celebration. Celebration is the act of commemorating the successes, big and small, in the process of change. It consists of the activities and performances that allow us to have fun with and in the work. Celebration is a process of bringing joy to the work and honor to the workers. Celebration, as a process, is rarely examined or practiced, but it is a fundamental way in which we can give voice to the beauty and power of our work. We borrow this process from other cultural contexts where people integrate work and play and see celebration as an essential component of a just world and the struggle to achieve it.

Putting it All Together

We envision the Just Practice Framework as a guide for critical question posing throughout the change process. It enables us to structure the process of being, doing, and becoming in light of the values and principles of social justice. As we engage in each moment and facet in the praxis of social change, the Just Practice Framework keeps us critically mindful of the interplay of forces at work shaping the process. In the following matrix, we illustrate the possibilities for question posing and critical reflection that emerge as the Just Practice Framework is brought to bear in carrying out the core processes. The questions we pose here are by no means exhaustive. Rather, we offer them as a starting point for your own critical reflection and action.

FIGURE 4.1

Just Practice Matrix: Applying the Framework to the Core Processes

Framework and Processes: Critical Questions	Engagement	Teaching/ Learning	Action and Accompaniment	Evaluation, Critical Reflection and Celebration
Meaning	What is the significance of the encounter and relationship? How do the parties involved interpret the experience?	What and how do we learn from one another's interpretations? Create new meanings and understandings?	How does partiality of knowledge shape action? How do differing meanings constrain or promote differing courses of action?	How do we appreciate meaning via reflexivity? How do we validate the meaning of our work? Give meaning to social justice?
Context	How do interpersonal, organizational, social contexts shape relations and trust building? How can the context be changed in order to facilitate engagement?	How does context inhibit or facilitate possibilities for mutual learning? How does the teaching/learning process challenge the interpersonal, organizational, and social context?	How does context shape the pathways for action, access to resources, patterns of practices, social work roles, nature of partnerships? How do our actions expand contexts for social justice work?	What is context specific about the process? What can be applied to other contexts? How can reflection on the context be a catalyst for contextual change? What forms of celebration fit the context?
Power	How do differing positionalities of participants shape engagement? What forms of power need to be addressed in the engagement process? How do we use the power available to promote justice in relationship?	What can we learn from a power analysis of the situation? How can the process of teaching/learning challenge power inequalities among participants and promote social justice?	What access is there to power and resources? How do we remain mindful of power differences in the change process? How do they challenge accompaniment? How do actions contribute to empowerment of participants?	How do we evaluate redistribution of power in the change process? How do we measure individual, organizational and community empowerment? How do we both appreciate and celebrate new forms and practices of power?

FIGURE 4.1 ***(continued)***

Just Practice Matrix: Applying the Framework to the Core Processes

Framework and Processes: Critical Questions	**Engagement**	**Teaching/ Learning**	**Action and Accompaniment**	**Evaluation, Critical Reflection and Celebration**
History	How do past histories and experiences of participants shape the encounter and process of relationship building? What prior knowledge and assumptions might promote or inhibit the process?	How do we teach/ learn from and about our histories? How do our histories shape the ways that we know and experience the world? How do we learn from those who came before? How do we learn from what is historically possible?	How do histories become resources and catalysts for action? How does historical consciousness inform future action? How do we bridge differences of history and forge alliance for action? How do actions challenge inscriptions of historic injustice?	How do we evaluate change over time? How do we account for historical conditions? How does reflection on where we have been inform where we are going? How might a reclamation and celebration of our histories animate future efforts?
Possibility	What are the possible relationships that can be formed and strengthened in this change effort? What spaces of hope can be opened?	What can we learn from this other person/ group? What can we contribute? What new ways of knowing might emerge from this experience? How can this learning promote other possibilities for social justice work?	How might we expand our repertoire of roles and skills? What possible courses of action are available? How can our efforts enhance future possibilities for empowering action?	How do we select among the possibilities at hand? Assess possible courses of action? Expand the terrain of the thinkable, talkable, and do-able? Reflect on decisions made and opportunities lost? Celebrate creativity?

Chapter Summary

In this chapter we have taken a close look at the concept of theory and the making of theory. We have explored the dominant paradigms that have shaped social work practice in the U.S., particularly in the last half of the 20th century. We have drawn from a range of critical social and cultural theory to pose challenges to the dominant paradigm and suggest alternative possibilities for thought and action. Through ongoing dialogue about these ideas and reflection on our practice, we came to articulate the Just Practice Framework, which we have outlined here.

In Chapters Five through Eight we develop each of the seven core processes and address the skills needed to carry them out.

Case Study: Welfare Reform and Structural Adjustment

In this case study we briefly define what welfare reform and structural adjustment mean and then we outline the neoliberal economic logic that underlies both practices. Once you have completed reading these two vignettes, reflect upon the following questions that link to our discussion on globalization in this chapter: How do welfare reform and structural adjustment tie into globalization? What are the commonalities and differences in these two concepts? Does a difference in language mask common practices? What might be the patterns and the logic that connect these discourses and practices?

The words "welfare reform" stand for the latest in a string of federal welfare policies meant to decrease the "chronic dependency" of people, mostly women and children, from government "hand-outs" and provide "incentives" to get folks into the job market where they can achieve "self-sufficiency." The Personal Responsibility and Work Opportunity Reconciliation Act (PRWORA), signed into law by President Clinton in 1996, was a response to his campaign promise to "end welfare as we know it." And he did so with the support of Republicans and Democrats alike. Ann Withorn (1998, p. 277) refers to PRWORA as "pubic policy at its most controversial" and with these words, she sums up general public sentiment on this piece of legislation. Welfare reform has been hailed as a great success by those who measure success in terms of numbers of people off the "dole." Others, those most intimately aware of the realities of living in poverty in the U.S., call it an abysmal failure. Peter Edelman

(1997) resigned from his position as the assistant secretary for planning and evaluation at the Department of Health and Human Services in protest of the bill's passage. He argued the bill would increase rather than decrease the rates of poverty, pushing more families with children below the poverty line. Senator Edward Kennedy (as quoted in Edelman, p. 45) voted against the bill and described it as "legislative child abuse."

Welfare reform set into motion new policy directives such as mandatory work requirements; strict lifetime limits on how long someone could receive public assistance (five-year maximum); the elimination of public assistance as entitlement; punitive sanctions for policy noncompliance (e.g., missed appointments with case worker) resulting in reductions in or termination of welfare benefits; incentives for those who married or chose to stay married; and the creation of block-grant funding that, in effect, transferred responsibility for welfare reform from federal to state governments. Each state, within certain parameters, decides how to spend their welfare dollars.

Structural Adjustment Programs (SAPs) have been central to the economic policies of the International Monetary Fund (IMF) and the International Bank of Reconstruction and Development, or the World Bank, since the early 1980s. SAPs were designed to help developing countries emerge from their debt crises. They involve a set of conditions or obligations to which countries have to comply in order to have their existing loans rescheduled and to be eligible for future loans. To understand structural adjustment one must understand the economic logic of neo-liberalism. Green (1995) tells us that the word neo-liberalism is confusing. Liberal usually connotes support of human rights and community values, but in the case of neo-liberalism it has economic, not political connotations. In neo-liberalism the ideology of the free market and economic rationalism reigns. It is rooted in the belief that "unfettered free markets will promote economic growth resulting in development" (Ecumenical Coalition for Economic Justice, 2001, p. 1). The basic tenets of neo-liberalism are:

1) decrease state intervention,
2) decrease regulation of industry,
3) decrease government spending,

4) build up private sector industry, and

5) stabilize the economy by curbing inflation.

In neo-liberal eyes, the way to fight inflation is . . . "by reducing the growth in the money supply by cutting government spending and raising interest rates. Wage controls are also used to reduce demand in the economy" (Green, 1995, pp. 2-4). Green contends that structural adjustment promotes stabilization by:

> . . . getting the prices right, removing artificial distortions such as price controls or trade tariffs and allowing the unregulated market to determine the most efficient allocation of resources. Because of its role in distorting prices and generally interfering with the free operation of the market, the state is seen as part of the problem, not part of the solution, and the economy has to be restructured to reduce the state's role and unleash the private sector. (p. 4)

Critics argue that structural adjustment policies actually increase poverty. For example, the privatization of government enterprises are typically associated with layoffs and pay cuts for workers. Cuts in government spending result in reduced health, education, and welfare services available to the poor. The imposition of user fees for government services from health care to clean drinking water makes these basic services inaccessible to the poor. Measures that force countries to increase their exports are often associated with the displacement of people from land and subsistence economies. And the elimination of tariff protections for industries frequently results in massive layoffs. Ultimately, structural adjustment entails cutting the labor force to reduce labor costs. Employers achieve these ends by hiring more part-time labor and decreasing the number of full-time employees to avoid paying the costs of expensive benefit packages (Essential Action, 2001, p. 1).

Women have been especially hard hit by SAPs. When unemployment increases, women are often first to lose their jobs. Increased food prices and decreased subsistence agriculture leave women unable to meet their family's basic needs. Cuts in health and welfare services leave women in multiple jeopardy. They are expected to care for the sick, the old, and the young and are left with few resources to do so. In short, women serve as "shock absorbers" for the social impact of economic adjustment (Ecumenical Coalition for Economic Justice, 2001, p. 2).

Questions for Discussion

1. How do values shape the development of theory?
2. What does it mean to say that "theory can influence and shape racist, classist, and sexist notions of people, groups, and societies?"
3. Why is it important to think of theories as value-laden constructs?
4. What is positionality, and why is this concept important to the understanding of theory?
5. What are some of the strengths and limitations of the theoretical perspectives presented in this chapter?
6. What is the significance of the concepts of "discourse," "domination," and "globalization" for social justice work?
7. Where would you begin to build your own theory of social work? What key principles would guide your theory?
8. How do theories of practice differ from dominant theories of social work?

Suggested Readings

Agger, B. (1998). *Critical social theory: An introduction.* Boulder: Westview Press.

Freire, P. (1990). "A critical understanding of social work." *Journal of Progressive Human Services.* 1(1), 3-9.

Gutiérrez, L. & Lewis, E. (1999). *Empowering women of color.* New York: Columbia University Press.

Harvey, D. (2000). *The condition of postmodernity: An enquiry into the condition of cultural change.* Oxford: Basil Blackwell.

Hill Collins, P. (1990). *Black feminist thought: Knowledge, consciousness, and the politics of empowerment.* New York: Unwin Hyman.

Korten, D. (1995). *When corporations rule the world.* West Hartford, CT: Kumarian Press.

Leonard, P. (1997). *Postmodern welfare: Reconstructing an emancipatory project.* London: Sage.

Margolin, L. (1998). *Under the cover of kindness: The invention of social work.* Charlottesville, VA: University of Virginia Press.

Pease, B. & Fook, J. (1999). *Transforming social work practice: Postmodern critical perspectives.* New York: Routledge.

Tuhiwai Smith, L. (1999). *Decolonizing methodologies: Research and indigenous peoples.* London: Zed Books.

Chapter 5

Just Get Started: Engagement

Those Who Don't

Those who don't know any better come into our neighborhood scared. They think we're dangerous. They think we will attack them with shiny knives. They are stupid people who are lost and got here by mistake.

But we aren't afraid. We know the guy with the crooked eye is Davey the Baby's brother, and the tall one next to him in the straw brim, that's Rosa's Eddie V., and the big one that looks like a dumb grown man, he's Fat Boy, though he's not fat anymore or a boy.

All brown, all around, we are safe. But watch us drive into a neighborhood of another color and our knees go shakity-shake and our car windows get rolled up tight and our eyes look straight. Yeah. That's how it goes and goes.

Sandra Cisneros (1984), *The House on Mango Street*

Chapter Overview

In this chapter we develop the skills, activities, and issues involved in the processes of engagement and link engagement to the five themes of Just Practice. Although we will develop each process separately throughout the next three chapters, we ask that you keep the matrix presented in Chapter Four (p. 178) in mind to guide you in thinking about the framework and processes as a whole. Engagement provides the entrée to social justice work in community, organizational, and interpersonal contexts. We explore skills of communication, relationship building, and discovery, and we present principles, tools, and activities to facilitate engagement. We have devoted an entire chapter to engagement in order to do justice to its challenges and possibilities. However, we ask that you think of engagement not as a discreet process readily separable from teaching-learning or the other core processes, but as an ongoing practice integral to all aspects of social justice work. We address the concept of praxis, the interplay of action and reflection that connects engagement and teaching-learning, which we develop in Chapter Six.

Throughout this chapter we ask you to try to imagine the intertwining and mutually informing relationship between engagement and teaching-learning. One image that we have found helpful is that of a dance with partners responding to one another as they execute complex patterns and improvise new possibilities of form and expression. Through engagement, we bring both preparedness and openness to bear on the teaching-learning moment. As we learn more about one another and our social realities we reshape the nature of our relationships and the processes of engagement. The "dance" of engagement and teaching-learning may grow more intimate, confident, and creative over time. The pacing and rhythms may shift over time. Likewise, we may make mistakes and stumble and need to regroup and reflect on the limits of our engagement and learning. What might be another image that captures the dynamics of engagement and teaching-learning?

Thinking about Engagement on Multiple Levels

Engagement as Process and Commitment

Engagement is a socio-emotional, practical, and political process of coming together with others to create a space of respect and hope, pose questions, and learn from and about one another. As we engage we begin building a base of knowledge and a place of trust from which to discover, reflect, and act. Many social work texts describe engagement as the "first step" in a helping process where the social worker seeks to establish rapport with her "client" and to clarify her professional role as a representative of a social service agency and the purpose for her involvement. For example, Brill (1998, p. 111) describes engagement as "involving oneself in the situation, establishing communication, and formulating preliminary hypotheses for understanding and dealing with the problem." Landon (1999, p. 103) describes engagement as "the communicative activity characterized by mutual development of a beginning relationship between the social work response system and the client system." We argue that these depictions of engagement are useful, but limited. The Just Practice approach asks us to think of engagement as both an intentional *process* and an ongoing *commitment.* It is a process shaped by critical curiosity, humility, compassionate listening, and respectful communication. It requires a commitment of our energies to be present, open, and willing to struggle with our own preconceptions and worldviews so that we can allow space for alternative possibilities. In short, engagement is a process of being, doing, and becoming. It is about being fully present, doing the communicative and relationship-building work, and becoming more critically aware.

Engagement begins with critical reflection on one's own *positionality*. That is, where are we, as social workers, coming from? We discussed the concept of "positionality" in Chapter Four. Our positionalities are shaped by the multiple identities through which we experience the world and through which we acquire or are denied certain privileges and stakes in power. We have created opportunities throughout the text for reflection on the forces and experiences that have shaped our positionalities. In this section, as a starting point, we focus discussion on our positioning within the organizational and community contexts of practice.

Engagement and the Organizational Context of Practice

Locating Ourselves in the Organizational Context. We begin the process of engagement by reflection on our location as social workers in an organizational context. Most social work practice is carried out under the auspices of state-based human service systems, voluntary not-for-profit organizations, community- or neighborhood-based associations or cooperatives or, occasionally, for-profit corporations. Rarely are social workers engaged as "Lone Rangers" working autonomously to create change in the world. Therefore, we argue that the best place to begin engagement is with critical reflection on the organizations in which we work. What can we learn by reflecting on our positioning within organizations and the ways in which organizational context may variably constrain and enable our social justice work?

Some Basic Questions. Let's start with some very basic questions:

- What is the mission of the organization? Why does this organization exist? How does it define its meaning and purpose?
- What is the organization's history? Where does the organization fit in a larger political, social, and economic context?
- How is the organization structured? How is power distributed in the organization? How do decisions get made?
- Does the organization have the power of legal authority or sanction? If so, what sort of authority (e.g. the legal authority to remove a child from his family in order to protect the child from harm)? Does the organization have material power to provide or deny resources? Are there other forms of organizational power you can identify?
- What kinds of activities are likely to be associated with the organization's work?
- How is the organization funded? How does funding influence organizational activities?
- Where are you located within the organization?
- What is the source of your authority and scope of your responsibilities?
- What resources do you have at hand?
- How is your organization perceived by outsiders or portrayed in the media?
- Who are the people likely to be involved with your organization?
- What might be some of their perceptions of the organization?
- What might it mean to be associated with the organization as "worker," "client," "participant," "patient," "inmate," "member," or "advocate?"
- Where do you see possibilities for social justice work within this organizational context?
- What might be some of the barriers to social justice work?
- Who are the people who could support you in your efforts for social justice work?

These questions help us flesh out issues of meaning, power, history, and possibility that shape and are shaped by the organizational context of practice. They help us begin to understand the "politics of engagement." Our social work positioning is never neutral, and we need to be cognizant of our organizational location as we engage with others.

Learning from Experience. Janet Finn offers an example from her social work experience to illustrate ways that organizational context shapes the practice of engagement:

> *One of my first paid social work positions was as a "group life counselor" in a state institution for girls and young women who had been adjudicated "delinquent." I was 21 years old and fresh from college when I took the job. The institution resembled a country boarding school, with several residential cottages, a cafeteria, gymnasium, and school. Underneath its welcoming façade was a tightly controlled system of discipline, rules, and surveillance. I was a shift worker charged with overseeing cottage life in the afternoon and evening, one of the least powerful staff positions in the institution. I was barely older than many of the young women under my "supervision." In many ways, it was by not-so-simple twists of fate that I was the one with the keys. But with those keys came power and responsibility. Those keys marked my privileged position as a well-educated white woman. They symbolized a boundary of difference between me and young women who had used the resources at hand to escape violent homes and abusive parents and partners, who had survived on the streets by plying their wits and selling their bodies, and who had sought comfort or oblivion in glue and booze and dope. The keys gave me access to everything from deodorant and hairspray to cigarettes and aspirin – all securely locked away from my young charges. They symbolized my everyday power to withhold privileges and offer rewards – "Yes, you can call home this weekend... No, you cannot leave campus with your aunt on Sunday." They symbolized the power of my voice in decisions about life beyond the institution. In effect, the job was an ongoing negotiation of the nuances of power, trust, and intimacy. I worked to build trust and to be clear about my responsibilities and the limits of my authority. But the institution's policy manual did not prepare me for the everyday challenges that negotiation posed. There was so much I did not know — about myself, the young women, and the structural inequalities of justice systems. I made lots of mistakes, usually when my own lack of confidence and fear of failure pushed me to wield my authority and restrict possibilities, when what I really needed to do was listen more carefully. I felt my own sense of powerlessness as a young woman*

in a male-dominated system. And yet the young women in my cottage saw the many sources of power at my fingertips that separated me from them. I came to appreciate my privileged positioning as one with potential to advance in the system due to my degree while my co-workers often had more limited options. With time, I learned to suspend my disbelief, tether my precarious authority, and listen more carefully and respectfully to the young women's stories. Their stories of tenacity, survival, courage, and longing were their gifts to me. As I became more cognizant of both the limits and possibilities of my position, I sought ways to push the boundaries of the possible. I began to find my own voice as I learned to advocate on behalf of the young women in staff meetings and court reports where their voices were too often silenced. When I left my position after two years, I did not know enough to thank them for all they had taught me. Twenty years later, I continue to draw lessons for engagement through critical reflection on the organizational context of that profound experience.

Probing the Organizational Context of Practice

Select an organizational context of social work practice where you have worked or where you can imagine yourself working (for example, a battered women's shelter, a housing advocacy organization, a prison, a hospital, a child protective service office). Prepare a paper or class presentation based on a systematic examination of the organizational context that addresses the questions outlined above. How do you see yourself within the organizational structure? How might the organization appear from the perspective of a "client"?

Community Context of Practice

Meanings of Community. The process of engagement also calls on us to be cognizant of our personal and organizational location within a larger community. The concept of community itself has multiple meanings. Community may refer to a political entity, a circumscribed and identified social and geographic space, or a group of people with common interests or concerns. For the purposes of this discussion, we borrow Mark Homan's understanding of community:

> (A) community consists of a number of people who have something in common with one another that connects them in some way and that distinguishes them from others. This common connection could be a place where members live –

> a city or a neighborhood. It may be an activity, like a job, or perhaps something like ethnic identification could provide the connection. I do not presuppose any particular size or number of people. (Homan, 1999, p. 8)

Belonging and Difference. Communities are made, maintained, and modified through the ongoing negotiation of belonging and difference (Finn, 1998a). We may be members of multiple communities and may have varying degrees of identification with and investment in them. As social justice workers, we need to be cognizant of our own communities of connection and concern, of the communities in which our practice is based, and of the communities impacted by our work. We do not parachute in to our social justice work "from nowhere." We come from a community context and bear the markers of that context as we begin to engage with others. As we enter into relationships with individuals and groups we engage in a process of reading and interpreting one another's markers and making judgements regarding belonging and difference. The opening quote from Sandra Cisnero's *The House on Mango Street* (1984) offers a vivid image of community and the markers of belonging. Think for a moment about your own communities. What are some of the communities you belong to? What does it mean to belong? How do you know that someone belongs to your community? What might mark someone as an outsider?

Global Challenges. Questions of engagement and community are becoming increasingly complex in the face of globalizing trends and the concomitant dislocation and movement of people. Migrant and refugee "communities" are straddling precarious borders in diverse parts of the world. The 2000 Census demonstrates the growth of diverse Latino communities in the U.S. Boys and young men from Somalia and Sudan, the so-called "Lost Boys" are struggling to create some semblance of home and community in Bismarck, North Dakota, Minneapolis, Minnesota, and Burlington, Vermont (see case study in Chapter Seven, p. 316). Communities throughout Latin America and in other parts of the globe are becoming home to the very young and the very old as men and women emigrate to work and send remittances back "home" to support their families. Undocumented workers live in the shadows, fearful of encounters with "officials" and distrustful of "helpers." Language differences and differing social and cultural norms and expectations further complicate the process. Our knowledge seems to become more partial by the day as the situations we confront grow more complex.

Outside and Inside the Community Context

Imagine yourself as a social worker for an organization serving a community to which you do not belong. For example, let's say you are a program coordinator for an urban homeless shelter that serves single adults. You drive to work each day from your apartment several miles away. You spend considerable time fund raising, which means you are often well dressed for lunch meetings and presentations to potential donors. How might these markers of difference shape the process of engagement with shelter residents? How might your age, ethnicity, gender, and educational background influence the negotiation of belonging and difference? Now, imagine yourself as a social worker for an organization serving a community to which you belong. Let's say you are a single parent and you are working with other single parents in your neighborhood to organize a day care cooperative. In some ways, you are an "insider" to the community, affected by many of the same concerns as other single parents. However, there may be important markers of difference among members of this community as well. What might be some of those differences? What might be some of the challenges and possibilities for engagement through the negotiation of belonging and difference in these two scenarios? Now take a minute to reconsider each of these scenarios from the perspective of a person residing in the U.S. who speaks little or no English. Might difference of language block him or her from any form of participation? What are some of the unspoken assumptions of belonging that shape access to helping organizations and the most basic of services? Return for a moment to the opening scenario of this chapter. Imagine entering the neighborhood described by Sandra Cisneros. Imagine yourself as an outsider to the neighborhood. What might you "see?" What might you miss? What might you learn about the neighborhood and about yourself through engagement with the storyteller?

We do not want to suggest that the process of engagement is necessarily problematic when we are community "outsiders" and smooth when we are "insiders." Rather, we encourage critical reflection on one's community and organizational positionality as part of the process of engagement. As we become conscious of our own communities and their markers, we are better able to engage with others in the appreciation and negotiation of belonging and difference. And we are better prepared to recognize the power of our community and organizational positioning and to make power a talkable subject in the process of engagement.

Interpersonal Context of Practice

Centrality of Relationship. Engagement entails a process of and commitment to relationships. Person-to-person relationships provide the foundation of social justice work. Regardless of whether we work with communities, families, neighborhoods, groups, or organizations, we are called upon to build and maintain interpersonal relationships. We can think of the interpersonal context of practice as one that cross-cuts all facets of social justice work. As we noted in the Introduction, social workers have paid particular attention to the importance of building and maintaining relationships based on respect for human dignity and worth. We have claimed this as a hallmark of the profession. Bertha Reynolds (1987) has challenged us to get close to people and honor the inseparability of social work and social living. This closeness implies a relationship that respects the whole person, encourages a sense of belonging, and recognizes people as much more than "bundles of problems and needs."

In recognizing the central place of relationships in social justice work, we acknowledge that relationships have value in themselves; they are not merely means to an end. Rather, relationships are the bedrock of our humanity (Finn, 2001b, p. 193). As stated previously, we can think of the process of justice-oriented change as one of being in relationship with others, doing the work, and becoming transformed through the process. As we work to build meaningful and productive relationships we are likely to be confronted with differences in our power and positionalities and with the limits of our partial views of the world. Dynamic, change-oriented relationships create possibilities for shifting our positions and expanding our views. But this is hard work that demands humility, commitment, and reflection. In the following sections we address the essential skills that enable us to form partnerships, build trust through dialogue, and create an interpersonal context that contributes to justice-oriented practice. We begin with skills of preparation and entry and then outline basic communication skills.

Anticipatory Empathy: Getting Ready to Engage

Defining Anticipatory Empathy

Engagement calls for "anticipatory empathy" – a process of preparation through critical reflection on the possible situations, concerns, and interests of the other participants in the change effort. It is a process of readying ourselves for an encounter with others, focusing our energies and attention, and opening ourselves to new learning. In many ways it is a time of transition wherein we move away from the phone calls and email and other demands of our work and create a space for intentional reflection. We start from a place of not knowing and uncertainty and allow ourselves to wonder. What information do we have thus far? What sort of partial picture is beginning to emerge? Who has provided us with the information? How might the people we are about to encounter tell their story? How can we best open ourselves to hearing their stories and receiving them as gifts? What might the other person (people) be feeling or thinking? How might our differing histories and positionalities influence the encounter?

Anticipatory empathy may entail very concrete preparation for a specific encounter or meeting. It creates time and space to think about your understanding of the purpose of your engagement and your role in the process. It provides an opportunity to consider your expectations and those of others. Who will be present? Who else should participate? What resources are available? What may be some of the constraints? What do you hope to accomplish? What might others hope to take away from the meeting?

Rethinking the "Client"

The practice of social justice work challenges us to critically reflect on models of helping that place the social worker as expert and "client" as victim or problem. We also recognize that much of social work practice, at least in the U.S., operates on a problem-focused model and is carried out in systems that focus on one-to-one intervention with clients. Too often, our understanding of "clients" reinforces a notion of the problem being located within the person and thus limiting our cognizance of the social conditions that contribute to and exacerbate individual pain and struggle. We argue that there is space for social justice work within dominant systems, and that through the practice of social justice work we can challenge the limits of these spaces and expand their possibilities as spaces of hope. For example, part of the process of anticipatory empathy includes critical reflection on what it means to be a "client" or a recipient of service within the particular organizational context. What assumptions are embedded in the organization's construction of its clients? In the process of seeking "help"? What does it mean to be a "good client" from the organizational perspective? How might the organizational perspective conflict with those of people having to assume the role or "positionality" of client in order to receive support or gain access to resources? They may have very different understandings of what it means to be a client grounded both in beliefs and past experiences with seeking help and in assumptions and expectations of the organization. Through the process of anticipatory empathy we bring these questions to the forefront of our consciousness so that we are prepared to address them through honest dialogue.

Engaging in Self-Reflection

Anticipatory empathy is not only a time of intentional preparation for engaging with "others." It is also a time for getting in touch with one's own feelings and biases. The structural violence confronting people in poor communities, dangerous neighborhoods, and hot and crowded apartments; the human drama of a hospital emergency room; the dank air of a jail cell or nursing home – these sensory realities can tap into our histories and memories in a visceral way that is beyond words. They pummel our emotions and wrench our guts. Anticipatory empathy requires time and space to feel and to be honest with ourselves about what we feel, especially difficult feelings such as fear, anger, or revulsion. Even as we prepare to approach what we anticipate to be "comfortable" encounters, it is important that we allow space for feelings of uncertainty, anticipation, and, perhaps, excitement. Recognition of the emotional context of the work prepares us to engage with our hearts as well as heads and hands.

The practice of self-reflection in anticipation of the encounter is a crucial component of the engagement process. Unfortunately it is often neglected in practice. As the demands for "efficiency" and "productivity" and the overall businessing of social work increase, anticipatory empathy is too often construed as a luxury. We often hear social workers lament, "Who has time to sit and think. . . I have too much work to do!" We argue that reflection is a necessary part of the work, but organizational constraints are real and these impose barriers to reflection. How do we carve out spaces for contemplation in our work places?

What organizational changes might be necessary to legitimize the importance of reflection time? These are essential questions to pose, especially as we consider the linkage between reflection and anticipatory empathy.

Engaging in the Difficult Situation

Take a moment to reflect on a social work situation that you would find very difficult to engage in emotionally. Perhaps your own experiences (or lack thereof) with death and dying make it difficult for you to contemplate engaging with persons who are terminally ill. Perhaps you have experienced abuse in your own child- or adulthood and find painful memories and emotions sparked by the stories of others who have been victimized. Try to allow yourself to feel and to identify some of the feelings that are stirred. It may be very hard to come close to those feelings. Perhaps, in this moment, the most important thing you can do is honor the distance. Sometimes the distance from our own feelings is a good measure of our distance from the feelings of others. Anticipatory empathy calls on us to actively grapple with our own feelings, to appreciate the power of our feelings in shaping the possibilities of engagement, and to make a commitment to bridging the distance to the best of our abilities through honest dialogue.

Anticipating Strengths and Possibilities

Anticipatory empathy is also a time to consider the possibilities and strengths of people and communities. As we open ourselves to new learning from and with participants it is important to think not only in terms of struggles but also in terms of capacities, resilience, and creativity. We often only see that which we are conditioned to see. So part of the process may involve preparing ourselves to "see" in different ways and learning to recognize social, emotional, and material resources that may be outside of our own experience. It is helpful to ask ourselves these questions: What new knowledge and understanding might I take away from this experience? How might I be changed by my participation in this process and relationship? Too often, we assume change is about "others." In social justice work, we recognize that change is also about us.

Anticipatory empathy is essential to the *praxis* of social justice work, the interplay of reflection and action. It situates us in a mutually informing process of being, doing, and becoming. That is, by creating the time and space to be attentively present with our thoughts and feelings we can prepare ourselves to engage in co-learning and communication for action, which are the building blocks of social and personal transformation. Anticipatory empathy is not a "one-time" exercise carried out before engaging with a person or group for the first time. Rather, it is a process we engage in as we move in and out of particular contexts of communication and action. It prepares us to enter the world of the participant(s) and develop and strengthen the working relationship. Each participant in the change process approaches the encounter from the complex context of everyday life and brings the weight of history and memory to bear in crafting a new context.

Engaging through Dialogue: The Basics of Listening and Communication

Genuine Dialogue

Engagement calls for dialogue. Social workers need skills in listening and communicating in order to craft spaces where participants can build a sense of safety, trust, and hope. As Hope and Timmel (1999, V. 2) write:

> Building trust and dialogue in society cannot be done by pronouncements nor by some "magical waving of a wand." Dialogue begins at the local level, in small units and thus in groups. . . Dialogue is based on people sharing their own perceptions of a problem, offering their opinions and ideas, and having the opportunity to make decisions or recommendations. (p. 3)

Paulo Freire reminds us that dialogue "requires an intense faith in man [sic], faith in his power to make and remake, to create and recreate, faith in his vocation to be fully human, which is not the privilege of an elite, but the birthright of all people" (1974, p. 79). Freire believed that honest, genuine dialogue is founded on love, humility, and faith. It cannot exist without hope. Nor can it exist without critical thinking and the possibility of transformation. It is this understanding of dialogue that creates the possibility for social justice work. Dominant approaches to social work education tend to focus on intervention at the individual level and emphasize development of the social worker's skills in one-on-one communication. We agree with Hope and Timmel that dialogue for change often begins in groups. However, there are basic issues and skills of communication that strengthen our ability to build valuable working relationships with people both in one-to-one situations and in groups.

It is difficult to write a book without adopting a linear approach to the teaching-learning experience. The questions of context and dialogue that we are grappling with can easily become lost in a "cookbook" of strategies and techniques of practice. The skills of communication may seem like neutral "tools," but we use them in context where questions of meaning, power, history, and possibility are at stake. We ask you to think of these skills as a means for helping you to better appreciate and receive the gift of another person's story and build a base of trust and commitment that supports action for change. We begin by defining what we mean by the word "communication." Then we address basic person-to-person communication skills that are applicable in both individual and group encounters. Finally, we focus on skills of engagement with groups, which we see as the backbone of social justice work.

Communication Processes

Communication is an ongoing process of encoding, sending, receiving, decoding, and responding shaped by perception, context, and cultural knowledge (Brill, 1998, pp. 71-75). Our human capacity for meaning making has resulted in the production of multiple meaning systems, diverse languages and linguistic conventions, a rich and emergent capacity for expression, and the possibility of error and misinterpretation. In every communication process, the attitudes, feelings, and positionalities of both receiver and sender are vitally important. As Baum (1971, p. 42) writes, "we are created through ongoing communication with others." Differences in age, gender, cultural background, class positioning, and racial and ethnic identification all affect the communication process. Awareness of these differences and relations of power inherent in them is crucial to effective communication. The similarities and differences among those involved will shape the extent to which a context of common understanding can be crafted. In the following sections, we address some basic components of communication.

Observation. A fundamental communication skill is that of observation. The social work setting, whether it be a kitchen table, community hall, welfare office, or hospital room, presents both possibilities and constraints that shape the process of relationship building. It is important that we be tuned in to the immediate context of practice so that we can best appreciate and address both limits and possibilities. Our initial observations give us a very partial sense, a rough sketch of the context, but it is a beginning. In addition to taking in the physical context of our work, the communication process is also shaped by our observations of the social context. How do other participants in the change process initially respond to us, to one another, and to their surroundings? How do we interpret the mood or tone of the setting? What sorts of patterns of social interaction are in play? What unspoken rules seem to govern people's social relations and actions?

In our everyday interactions we are observers of people and social groups. We give meaning to social interactions as we take in content, "read" non-verbal expressions, and interpret feelings, attitudes, and intentions (Brill, 1998). We hone our observation skills as we become cognizant of the aspects or levels involved and systematically attend to them. Hope and Timmel (1999, V. 2, p. 54) outline a series of questions to help us become more attentive observers of group process:

1. Who talks? For how long? How often?
2. Who do people look at when they talk?
   - Other individuals, possibly potential supporters?
   - Scanning the group?
   - No one?
   - The ceiling?
3. Who talks after whom, or who interrupts whom?
4. What style of communication is used?
   - Strong statements
   - Questions
   - Gestures
   - Laughter
   - Tears, etc?

How might reflection on these observations help us better "see" relationships, patterns, and issues of trust, power, and difference in groups?

Observation is a two-way process, shaped by relations of power. We are both observers and observed in any social work relationship. Our initial and ongoing observations provide us with data from which we can engage in dialogue for co-learning. We also provide other participants with "data" regarding our comfort level and preparedness in the situation. As our impressions and understandings become more textured and detailed, we may find that interpretations based on initial observations were faulty. Careful, respectful observation is a skill that we can hone through practice.

Honing Your Observation Skills

Social workers can learn a great deal from cultural anthropologists about the power and practice of observation. Cultural anthropologists learn about cultural diversity through ethnographic fieldwork. Ethnography provides an account of particular cultural contexts or practices. One technique central to ethnography is firsthand observation of the details of everyday life. Ethnographers seek to understand the patterns and rules that shape the most taken-for-granted aspects of social life. This exercise introduces you to ethnographic observation.

Select a public setting where you can observe some aspect of everyday social interaction (a sporting event, an airport luggage claim, a restaurant, a bus terminal, the entrance to your campus Student Union). Spend one hour observing the details of social life. Record your observations. Write a brief report describing your observations, noting patterns, and probing the unspoken rules that seem to underlie these patterns. Try to suspend your pre-existing understanding of what is going on. Focus on what you observe. Did you see any patterns in people's social behavior? Did you find yourself "seeing" the setting differently over the course of the hour? How did it feel to be an observer? Did the exercise offer you any new insights or surprises regarding everyday social interactions?

Body Basics. Honest, respectful communication starts from a place of openness, curiosity, and partiality of knowledge. We need to be mentally and emotionally present and attentive. We convey that readiness through our bodies and physical presence as well as through our words. Our responses and emotions are coded on our faces and bodies and through our carriage and gestures, sounds and silences, as well as through our spoken and written words. Take a minute to think about conversations you have had when you have felt as if the other person were really listening to you. How did she convey that attentiveness? How did she position herself? How did her body indicate openness? What were the cues that indicated this person was paying attention and that what you said mattered? Take a minute to become aware of your own body and practice that physical attentiveness. How would you describe your posture? Do you feel comfortable? Try taking a deep breath in and out, relaxing and opening yourself to the person and situation as you do so. How would you describe your posture now? Do you feel ready to listen and engage?

Now take a moment to think about conversations you have had where you have felt shut out and ignored. How did that person's body convey her inattentiveness or resistance to your words? Take a minute to practice that physical inattentiveness. How would you describe your posture? Your breathing? Do you feel comfortable? Take a deep breath in and out, and then return to your posture of openness. How would you describe the difference between the two? Each of us brings particular socio-cultural knowledge and patterns of practice to the communication process. The process is a complex one of expression, reception, translation, and interpretation through screens of cultural meaning. The process is fraught with possibilities for misunderstanding. However, we can become more critically conscious participants in the process as we learn to appreciate the communicative power of our own bodies. When we are uncomfortable in the process, our bodies become physical blocks to effective communication. So, the first rule of thumb for respectful communication is to **remember to breathe!** As we remind ourselves to breathe we create the possibility of releasing the block and opening ourselves once again to respectful listening. Yes, we will make mistakes and misinterpret even when we are attending as best as we can. But as we come to better understand and value our multiple capacities for communication we can better address the mistakes and craft a space of understanding.

Mirroring Exercise

Get together with one of your classmates. Arrange your seats so that you are facing one another and a comfortable distance apart, as if you were going to engage in conversation. Sit facing one another in silence for three minutes.

Take time to observe one another without words. Be mindful of breathing. Try to mirror the rhythm of your partner's breathing, without forcing it. At the end of three minutes, talk to your partner about your response to the exercise. Did three minutes seem like a long time? Did the exercise make you feel uncomfortable? What were some of your observations? How did it feel to focus attention on breathing? If you do this exercise as a class working in pairs, you probably found it hard to maintain three minutes of silence. Most likely, bursts of laughter rippled through the class a time or two. Many of us lack experience or comfort in being present with another person without words. What reflections on communication could you draw from this exercise?

Listening. Perhaps the most important skill of communication is that of listening. It is a skill we have been developing since birth, and, as a result, we often take our listening skills for granted. For example, in various communication situations we may find ourselves tuning out what others say or busying ourselves thinking about what we would like to say next. Or we may find ourselves listening to those whose knowledge we value and failing to hear alternative views. Listening is a powerful skill, one that takes considerable discipline and a willingness to hold our own needs at bay. Listening gives voice, affirmation, and confidence to those individuals and groups who have been typically ignored, marginalized, and oppressed. It is through respectful listening that a group develops a sense of belonging and community and members see themselves as speaking subjects worthy of voice (hooks, 1994, p. 150). As bell hooks (1994) describes, teaching people how to listen is part of a pedagogy of liberation. We have to learn how to hear one another, suspend disbelief, and take what another person says seriously.

People often use the term "active listening" to describe the focused, intentional process of listening. In "active listening" we use words and gestures to show the speaker that we are attending to her words. A nod of the head may indicate that we are understanding, or perhaps encouraging the speaker to continue. We might reflect feelings we have been picking up back to the speaker or summarize the content of the story to both demonstrate that we are listening and to see if we are grasping the speaker's intended meaning (Shulman, 1992). We might ask the speaker to tell us more so that we have a better grasp of the context. However, beneath all of the tricks to demonstrate that we are "actively" listening, we need to be honestly listening. If we are busy thinking about what we will say or do next we often fail to listen deeply and fully to the other person's words.

Murphy and Dillon (1998) describe the importance of "listening intently" to what people say and how they say it. Through a practice of listening intently, "(w)e listen to our own inner process and the relationship process. We listen to what is happening in the work and what is happening in the surrounding world" (1998, p. 10). They point to the importance of listening to silence as well as speech and of listening for the "behavior, feelings, thoughts, contexts, and meanings that constitute the client's story" (p. 67). Similarly, Anderson and Jack (1991) note the importance of learning to "hear the weaker signal of thoughts and feelings that differ from conventional expectation" (p. 11). They contend that respectful listening calls on us to shed our own agendas and resist the temptation to leap to interpretation too soon. They remind us that what and how we hear is shaped by our cultural constructs and historical experience. A challenge, then, of listening intently is to try to understand another's story from his or her vantage point. This requires "listening with a third ear."

Hope and Timmel (1999, V. 2, p. 33) offer a simple list of "do's and don'ts of listening" that we have included here:

In listening we should try to do the following:

- Show interest
- Be understanding of the other person
- Express empathy
- Single out the problem if there is one
- Listen for causes of the problem
- Help the speaker associate the problem with the cause
- Encourage the speaker to develop confidence and motivation to solve his or her own problems
- Cultivate the ability to be silent when silence is needed

In listening do **not** do the following:

- Argue
- Interrupt

- Pass judgment too quickly or in advance
- Give advice unless it is requested by the other
- Jump to conclusions
- Let the speaker's emotions react too directly on your own

Based on your experience as a listener, what would you add, delete, or revise on this list?

Introductions and Openings

Social justice work is grounded in face-to-face, person-to-person relationships. We need skills in initiating these relationships. Whether we are meeting with a single individual, a family, or a group we need to address basic questions of why we are here and what each of us hopes to accomplish. The change process is structured and purposeful, and it requires that each participant have a voice in defining the purpose and creating the structure. The social worker can take responsibility for initiating the process by 1) introducing herself and her organizational position, 2) clearly stating her understanding of the reason for coming together and inviting others to do the same, 3) and asking questions and seeking clarification. It is a process of *welcoming* and *naming* ourselves, our concerns, and our hopes. Together, participants seek to establish a common understanding of purpose.

The process of getting started in face-to-face meetings is often easier said than done. It is a tentative process of feeling one another out and trying to get a sense of where others are coming from. It is important that we pay attention to the physical surroundings of the meeting and try to make the context conducive to dialogue. For example, is the seating arrangement conducive to open communication? Do others know the layout of the space and facilities available to them? If we are meeting in someone's home, how can we be sensitive to issues of space and privacy? If the meeting space poses challenges – too hot, too cold, too big, too small – can we make adjustments before the meeting gets underway? If not, how might we address the limitations of the space and be cognizant of the ways it may affect people's participation? Part of the social worker's responsibility is to set the stage and the tone and facilitate the process of opening dialogue. We can begin by acknowledging that first meetings can be difficult, especially if the participants do not share common knowledge or histories. We can encourage people to ask questions and seek clarification, and we can do the same. As facilitators of communication, we help others recognize and express their understandings, attitudes, and feelings and put them into words. We do so by encouraging elaboration of experiences, perceptions, and context. Our job is to create opportunities for participants to tell their own stories in their own words, let people know that they have been heard, and to seek clarification to build mutual understanding.

Challenges to Introductions and Openings—Resistance

Introductions and openings create challenges for workers and those with whom they work. These require clarity of role and purpose on the part of the social worker. Think for a minute about the child protection services worker sanctioned to investigate allegations of child abuse and neglect and the need to respond to stressful situations and circumstances that might entail the removal of children from their home. What must the worker know about the limits and requirements of her role, and how might these limits and requirements be communicated to set the foundation for subsequent action? How might personal values and beliefs about parenthood, the disruption of children's lives, and the sanctity of family life conflict with the prescribed functions of the child protection worker mandated by state and organizational policies? Also think about how the word "participant" fails to capture the true nature of coming together in this particular circumstance. How can the worker prepare for the resistance posed by "involuntary" contacts, those with individuals who did not seek out the contact? What ethical dilemmas and political issues might shape communication? How might these issues be addressed in introductions and openings? How does the process of coming together change given these circumstances? What preparatory work must the worker engage in to be effective?

A Short List of Interpersonal Communication Skills

- **Clarify:** Check in with the other person to make sure you are understanding what s/he is telling you. Invite the other person to seek clarification from you.
- **Paraphrase:** Restate the other person's story in your own words to make sure you are grasping the content.

- **Reflect**: Check in with the other person regarding the feelings associated with what she is telling you.
- **Encourage Elaboration:** Invite the other person to tell you more about her situation or experience.
- **Reach for Feelings**: Invite the other person to reflect on his emotional response to what he is telling you.
- **Check in:** Take a moment to reflect on the here-and-now. How is the other person doing? Does she have questions or concerns?
- **Allow for Silence:** Give the other person time and space to collect his thoughts and feel his emotions.
- **Summarize:** Take a minute to highlight both the content and feelings that have been expressed.
- **Acknowledge Mistakes and Ask for Feedback:** Remember that you are human and will make mistakes. Take responsibility and apologize. Give the other person a chance to tell you how you are doing.
- **Respect Resistance:** Remember that change is not easy, and honor ambivalence.
- **Point Out Contradictions:** If you are picking up discrepancies between what someone is telling you in words and what you are reading in non-verbal communication, respond directly and encourage reflection.

What other skills would you add to this list? What skills are needed for bridging possibilities of communication across boundaries of difference?[1]

Trust, Power, and Difference. Effective social justice work requires us to be able to acknowledge and address issues of trust, power, and difference in the relationship building process with individuals and groups. Given differing past histories and experiences, participants often have reason to be distrustful of "helpers" and processes of change. We need to start from the point of distrust and work to build trust rather than assume that it exists. For example, Gutiérrez and Lewis (1999, p. 25-26) address the troubling history of misdiagnosis and mistreatment of people of color by professional helpers. They write: "This mistrust has been exacerbated by the lack of attention to gender, ethnicity, race, economic status, and environment as variables influencing the engagement process for both service providers and service consumers" (p.26). We need to honestly and directly speak to mistrust and invite participation in the ways in which we can collectively build trust and understanding. In order to do so we need to make power, authority, and difference "talkable themes." Too often, these are taboo subjects that we shy away from even as they play out in and shape the dynamics of a meeting or relationship. We can facilitate this conversation by speaking honestly to our own power and authority and its limits in the context at hand. For example, if, in our social work capacity, we have the authority for particular types of legal or social sanction that others do not have, it is important that we speak honestly about our authority, responsibilities, and their limits, invite questions from other participants, and respond candidly to their concerns. We can also initiate a discussion of power and engage in an analysis of power as part of the process of co-learning. Finally, we need to acknowledge difference as an issue and create space for dialogue about differences that shape our meanings, interpretations, and actions.

How do we respond when our authority and assumptions are challenged? It is one thing to talk about power, trust, and difference. It is another to honestly reflect on our ability to open ourselves to challenge, especially if we come from positions of privilege where dominant views have been part of our "common sense." How do we stay open to listening and learning when faced with differences of experience and perspective that disrupt our certainties? Perhaps we respond defensively, asserting our authority in the face of challenge and attempting to discredit or dismiss the challenger. Communication across and about differences that disrupts our comfort zones is a key part of the labor of social justice work. In the following sidebar, social worker, scholar, and activist Deborah Bey draws from her own experiences to challenge her colleagues about the meaning and power of difference.

Difference is Political and Personal

The following is an excerpt from an essay by Deborah Bey, a doctoral student at the University of Michigan, reflecting on her lived experience and the politics of belonging and difference she has encountered in social work education. What challenges does she pose? What feelings does the essay provoke? How do we move beyond talk of collaboration and tackle the tough realities of difference?

After I had decided to leave my comfortable job and go back to school and earn my Ph.D. , my therapist at the time asked me what was my motivation. Getting my Ph.D. would not mean more money, and I would be dirt poor for the next five years. Besides, it would only bring prestige if I published a lot of books and became a careerist. My reply to that inquiry was that I was almost 30 and I wasn't dead or dying so I might as well make good on this promise I made to myself when I graduated from undergrad and go back to school to get my Ph.D.

By this point you might be thinking, "does she have cancer," "is she HIV positive?"

"Why would she be thinking she would be dead at age 30?" To explain that I have to go back to my childhood and my experience in the world.

When I was 12 I figured I would be dead by 30, and I might as well live my life like 30 was the ending point. Being dead by 30 made plenty of sense, most of the people in my neighborhood never saw 30 or they celebrated their 30th birthdays in prison. Or they were so cracked out that they might as well be dead. At 12 years of age I saw no prospects for the future, so I saw no reason to plan for it.

Besides all that, by age 12 I was homeless and living on my own in Detroit. You see, I was a ward of the State of Michigan, and I had liberated myself from one of the many foster homes they had shipped me to. So, at 12, I was on the streets, trying not to get caught by the police or my social workers, and sure as hell not my mother, especially not my mother, because she would have liberated my ass for bringing protective services into her life. Eventually, protective services caught me and shipped me out to another foster home in Saline, Michigan (about 50 miles from my home town), and the foster cycle would start again. They would put me in a home and either I would liberate myself or the foster parents would ask the social worker to come and get me, and then it would be off to a new placement. In between there would be stints with my mother if she were off drugs and out of her crazy relationships. But it was mostly crazy foster homes until I turned 20. With a life like that, reaching 20 seemed like a pipe dream.

Which is why I wanted to go back to school, to do research in an area, foster care, that really touched my life. The reason I chose the University of Michigan is because it was close to my family – and I was trying to re-establish ties, and it was away from the street of Detroit that I had hung out on.

Now that I am at the university, I question my decision to return to school every day. I sit in classrooms with people who want to "help" the poor, or who just want to deliver psychotherapy to middle-class suburbanites, or best yet, future community organizers who want to organize communities as long as they do not have to live in them, or have their values questioned by those people they are trying to save. Which begs the question: do the people these social workers want to work with want to be saved, helped, or patronized? Not everyone is like that – a large majority, but not everyone. There are some good Liberals (big L not little l) trying to earn their "I am sensitive to the suffering of others" Brownie Points. Of course, no one wants to talk about issues of oppression – folks will start to cry and feel uncomfortable. And, as Rodney King put it, "why can't we all just get along?"

When I buck that "can't we all get along" trend, I am constantly told that I am too judgmental, and I should cut folks slack.... I have to wonder about this. When other graduate students go home and take off their clothes for bed, do they bear scars of growing up literally on the streets? Do they have the scar from a knife wound, where some crazy girl stabbed them in the leg? Do they have the bullet wound from when they were at a party that turned ugly? When they look at their faces, do they see scars from fights, when someone cracked a beer bottle over their head, just because? Have they been thrown through plate glass windows in fights because their cousin did something to someone else's man...?

Have these students experienced what it is like to be homeless and hungry? Sleeping in cars and bushes and abandoned buildings, because you knew you were vulnerable just walking the streets? Have they had to fight their way out of gang attacks, because a group of men realized you were blossoming into a woman, and you were just a street kid anyway, so no one would care if they took some? Have these students experienced what it is like to come home and find the house empty because their mother or her boyfriend has taken everything to the pawnshop so they can get their drugs? Have they witnessed their mother getting her needle ready to shoot up because her cravings were so strong she did not realize that they were in the room? And, finally, have they experienced eleven years at the hand of the state, who said it was going to protect them, but instead screwed them more? Where they were treated more like cattle than like a person? The only thing the state helped with was to prepare you for prison or welfare once you aged out. Do they have dreams at night about living through things so horrible that they had to open their eyes just to not relive it? When they go home to their parents for the holidays, do they go to a one-bedroom apartment, shared by their mom and two siblings (when they are out of jail), with crumbling walls and floors you could fall through? To a neighborhood so rough that you keep a shotgun beneath your bed?

I don't think many of the people in social work know what this is like. So I will not cut them some slack. My job is to challenge the future social workers in the world because when they look at that and deal with me, they are dealing with their future clients. So if they can deal with my shit, they can deal with any shit...[2]

Cross-cultural Meanings and Interpretations. As we have addressed throughout the text, issues of difference and power profoundly shape our experiences and positionalities in the world and the perspectives from which we see, make sense of, and act in the world. Operating from our particular locations and partial views of the world, we give meaning to new experiences and interpret new information in differing ways. Thus each person engaged in a relationship and process for change has a somewhat different experience of the process. We "hear" things in different ways. We grant importance to some information and interactions and discount or ignore others. As a facilitator of open dialogue and effective communication, the social worker has a teaching responsibility to help other participants see that differing meanings and interpretations will emerge. Effective communication depends on helping participants seek clarification of one another's interpretations, respect differing meanings, and recognize common ground. This is a socialization process that the social worker can initiate by speaking directly to difference, acknowledging the ways difference shapes trust and dialogue, and making respect for difference and the negotiation and clarification of meaning part of the change process in which all participants are engaged.

These issues are particularly challenging in cross-cultural and multi-lingual contexts. We run quickly into barriers to understanding when attempting to bridge differing meaning and belief systems or interpret a discussion to speakers of different languages. For example, people from different cultural backgrounds may have very different assumptions regarding fundamental issues such as the meaning of family, decision-making authority, and privacy. As we discussed in Chapter Four our cultural meaning systems shape our beliefs about fundamental issues such as nature of the body and bodily integrity, causality, and health and illness. Further, our linguistic systems are rich in nuances of expression that are often not directly translatable. Readers who have had experience in multi-lingual settings know that it takes very skilled interpreters to assure that meanings, not just words, are communicated. Such is the case in professional "linguistic groups" as well. We can think of a multidisciplinary planning team as a multi-lingual context wherein representatives of different professions may require an interpreter so that they are not talking past one another as they speak in the jargon of their respective professions. Professional language is a source of power, which can exclude those who do not speak the language. Part of the challenge of social justice work is to interrupt practices of exclusion and advocate for skilled interpretation that promotes open, intelligible communication across multiple "languages" and boundaries of difference.

We argue that there are no "simple steps" to effective cross-cultural communication. Rather, it emerges through the ongoing application of critical consciousness to practice (Reed, Newman, Suarez & Lewis, 1997). We offer here some principles for cross-cultural practice presented by Reed et al. (1997, pp. 68-75) that contribute to the possibilities of effective engagement. These principles support the values, assumptions, and visions of social justice work:

- First, we must regularly interrogate the knowledge and theories that underlie our practice and strive to keep up with how theory is changing.
- Practitioners must work continuously to understand the multiple contexts of their practice and how these are shaped by differences and patterns of oppression.
- Developing and using your knowledge about your own positionality, in general and in relationship to a particular practice situation, is fundamental for a multiculturally competent practitioner.
- How might cultural and gendered assumptions be affecting our assessments?

- Are there organizational or programmatic issues that your client's reaction lead you to notice that you need to address?
- The practitioner should expand definitions of trust and safety.
- Learn about others' cultural backgrounds and learn how to learn from others and be responsive to cues from those with whom you work.
- Remember that there are many "ways of knowing" – of understanding one's world, of learning and changing. The practitioner who recognizes this develops a repertoire that uses many approaches to practice.
- The multiculturally competent practitioner recognizes that therapeutic alliances and worker-client relationships will recreate patterns of privilege and oppression unless we are actively working to recognize, challenge, and change them.
- Goals must include developing strengths, preventing problems, creating social change, and addressing the multiple ways that oppression and privilege have been incorporated and are being recreated.
- Practice must also continuously recognize and challenge the multiple dichotomies in thinking that characterize any of our social categories and behavioral options.
- Creating new words and labels can help us think and perceive differently.
- All of the above require regular and recurring scrutiny of the processes through which we work, act, and think as well as the outcomes for which we strive.
- Engage in praxis regularly with other practitioners and activists; seek feedback from those similar to and different from you on key dimensions.[3]

Engaging With and Respecting Resistance. Throughout this discussion of engagement we have emphasized that different parties in the change process bring differing meanings, positionalities, interests, and concerns to bear. We have also pointed out that people in less powerful positions and people who have experienced oppression and discrimination may have very little reason to put their trust in "helpers" and "helping systems" and have very good reason to be suspicious and guarded about becoming participants in the process. In other words, as social justice workers we need to be both mindful and respectful of resistance.

Let's think for a moment about the meanings of resistance. Webster's Dictionary (1983) defines resistance as "an opposing, a withstanding, opposition of some force, thing, etc., to another or others" (p. 1541). In systems theories resistance is described as a force that helps systems and organisms remain stable in the face of other forces. In a psychological sense resistance is viewed as a defense mechanism that we use to avoid and cope with stress and change (Wade & Travis, 1999). It is often more popularly interpreted as a deficit, a person's refusal to open up, admit to her difficulties, and engage in the work of personal change. In literature on oppression, resistance describes the many subversive, often indirect strategies through which oppressed people assert their agency in the face of dehumanizing circumstances (Scott, 1985). In literature on privilege, resistance connotes a person or group's reluctance to critically reflect on the benefits of their positionality (Fine, Weis, Powell, & Wong, 1997; McIntosh, 1995). What other meanings and images of resistance come to mind? In the practice of social justice work, it is important to consider the many facets of resistance and to consider resistance as a skill for personal and cultural survival.

In social work, a great deal has been written about "resistant clients," referring to those who are unwilling to open up in the engagement process, acknowledge particular definitions of the "problem," or participate in prescribed courses of action. "Resistance" is often the defining feature of the "involuntary client," one who is required to participate in an intervention and treatment effort as a result of legal order or other institutional sanction. Often, the person's resistance becomes defined as pathology, a symptom of her inability or unwillingness to make prescribed changes. It is possible, however, to take alternative views regarding the meaning and power of resistance. For example, Carter (1986, 1987) offers a psychological interpretation of the meaning of resistance. He argues that our capacity to resist points to our need for a balance between holding on and letting go. People need contexts of safety in order to take the risks that a change process demands. Thus, a deep sense of ambivalence often lies behind processes of change. Carter argues that while people may be consciously agreeing to participate they may be resisting change at an unconsciousness level. Change forces people to give up something of their familiar here-and-now experience and engage with uncertainty. Even if current life circumstances cause pain, there may be a degree of comfort in the familiarity and predictability of those circumstances.

Carter argues that each person has resources and potential that can be tapped into during the change process. Resistance can stem from the worker's failure to recognize and utilize a person's uniqueness.[4]

Carter's approach offers an opportunity for reframing resistance at the personal level. However, he does not address the larger social, political, and economic context or histories of oppression and discrimination that shape action and resistance. From a cultural perspective, resistance may be seen as a survival strategy invoked when powerful forces threaten to invade, invalidate, or erase one's history, knowledge, and experience. A person resisting participation in the change effort may not be demonstrating pathology but may be actively asserting her right to protect herself, lay claim to her experiences and fears, and challenge those threatening to misinterpret her experience and silence her voice. There is a rich array of cultural literature that examines the creative resistance of less powerful people and groups to the oppressive forces of dominant cultural systems (e.g., Guzman Bouvard, 1994; Ong, 1987; Scott, 1985). We have also seen evidence of resistance to social work interventions on the part of people who have very different understandings of what constitutes a problem and for whom. The policies, procedures, goals, and expectations of social service agencies are often culturally foreign and at times antagonistic to the values, beliefs, and practices of those they serve. Resistance to intervention is born of a struggle to retain one's autonomy and beliefs in the face of powerful countervailing forces.

The Just Practice Framework provides a guide for recognizing and respecting resistance through critical question posing regarding meaning, context, power, history, and possibility. Consider the following questions, for example. Are the policies, practices, goals, and language of your organization meaningful to the person with whom you are working? How do you know? What have you done to check this out? What is the context of your encounter? Under what circumstances did you come together? How do those circumstances, as well as the physical context of your meeting, contribute to or reduce resistance? What are the relations of power that impact the encounter? What forms of power do you as the social worker bring to bear? How might the other person perceive your power and his own in relation to you? Have you explored the issue of power as it affects the encounter? Are there alternatives open to you that could shift the balance of power? What prior history with the organization or with "helpers" does the other person have? How might this history, along with other experiences and feelings of powerlessness contribute to resistance? What are the non-negotiable aspects of the relationship (e.g. a person may be required to participate in a court-ordered treatment plan in order to regain custody of a child, avoid incarceration, etc)? Where are the spaces of possibility for negotiating a process that recognizes and respects the other person's values, beliefs, and interests? How might the plan not only acknowledge but also challenge and change the power differences among agency, social worker, and "clients"?

Closings and Transitions. Each meeting and encounter, whether it is a first meeting with a teenager in a youth shelter or with a newly forming advocacy group at a homeless shelter, becomes a micro-context where questions of meaning, power, history, and possibility are at play. Part of the communicative work of engagement is to value that context, acknowledge what has been accomplished in it, and prepare participants to move beyond it at its close. To do so, we need to be able to summarize both the content and process of the encounter and seek feedback from participants. What did we accomplish? Where are our points of agreement and difference? What are people thinking and feeling about the process? Where do we go from here? Who takes responsibility for what?

It is important to recognize people's participation, to thank them for their presence, to honor their silences as well as their words, and to address the challenges posed in getting started. Just as we emphasized the importance of creating time and space to prepare for engagement, it is important to give time and space to disengagement and transition. That may entail acknowledging the emotions people express and creating an opportunity for both letting go of and holding on to those feelings as participants move out of this context and into other spaces of their work and lives. It may mean giving participants the "last word." It may involve giving yourself a few minutes to absorb and reflect on the process and the responses it stirred for you. What do you take away from this "closing" that informs the next "opening"? What did you learn about yourself, others, and the possibilities for social justice work in this encounter? Thus, the basic skills of communication provide us tools for tacking back and forth between action and reflection.

Engaging with Al

Read "The Story of Al" at the end of this chapter. What responses does Al's story trigger for you? What feelings does it evoke? What questions does it raise for you regarding the engagement process? Use the matrix on the following page to record some questions that come to mind regarding engagement with Al. Does the story help you think more concretely about the process of engagement? Does the matrix help you think more holistically about the process of engagement?

	Engagement
Meaning	
Context	
Power	
History	
Possibility	

Engaging Groups

Effective social justice work is a collaborative process that calls for skills in working with groups. Breaking with the individual-focused, person-changing approaches to intervention, social justice work emphasizes the power and possibilities of collective effort to produce change. The basic communication skills outlined above apply to both one-on-one and group contexts. In this section, however, we further develop issues, skills, and possibilities for engagement with groups.

The Group Work Tradition

Social work has a lengthy history of attention to group work beginning with the settlement house movement. Early settlement house workers forged collaborative relationships with neighborhood immigrant populations through group work.

Together social workers and community members addressed child labor laws, unsafe working conditions, and health concerns. Groups were a vehicle for policy advocacy, education, and mutual aid and support. Jane Addams (1910) envisioned groups as helping people learn about democracy through participation in democratic group dynamics. She eloquently addressed the need to exchange "the music of isolated voices [for] the volume and strength of the chorus" (as cited in Schwartz, 1986, p. 12).

Schwartz (1986) reminds us of the group work tradition initially crafted by early settlement house workers: ". . . to help needy people in their own milieux, surrounded by their peers and working in an atmosphere of mutual aid" (p. 7). People came together in groups to address mutual interests and concerns, to gain support from others when they faced overwhelming personal problems, and to learn from and teach one another new skills to improve the quality of their lives. Schwartz describes some of the common features of group work and how they shape the relationship between the worker and the group members. These features include sharing information between members, instead of confidential information being held between worker and "client," and sharing leadership and supportive functions so the worker's power is diffused in what Schwartz calls "the network of relationships that goes to make up the pattern of mutual aid" (p. 8). He emphasizes how early group workers found the language of "client" distasteful and preferred to call group participants "members." Through the practice of shared control, shared power, and the shared agenda, group members create support systems whereby they empower themselves to take collective action to address personal, interpersonal, and social concerns.

Benefits of Group Work

Throughout social work's history, social workers have noted the importance of group work and the beneficial dynamics and processes groups help to support. We outline some of these dynamics and processes below:

- Groups provide the milieux in which the social worker becomes one of many helpers (Schwartz, 1986).
- Groups create opportunities for developing critical consciousness (Freire, 1974, Gutiérrez, 1990).

- Group dialogue helps to break "cultures of silence" and helps people gain confidence in themselves and find their voices (Freire, 1974).
- Groups provide people with the opportunity to become conscious of power relationships, the differing impacts of social inequalities on different social groups, and their own location therein (Gutiérrez & Lewis, 1999; Garvin & Reed, 1995).
- Groups offer spaces for mutual support and collective problem posing, action, and reflection (Shulman, 1992; Schwartz, 1971).
- Groups help us structure the time and space of co-learning and unite our change efforts (Schwartz, 1994).

Thus, as social justice workers we need to develop our own capacities as group workers and to teach skills of mutual aid and collective action to others.

Creating a Climate for Group Work

In order to engage people in a group process, we need to create a welcoming learning climate. Issues of trust and intimacy, power and authority, and difference and commonality are at the very heart of group work. We need to start by honoring feelings of distrust and ambivalence (Shulman, 1992) and recognizing that people in marginalized or vulnerable positions have good reason to be suspicious of "helpers." Reflect for a moment on your own experiences in a group context. How did you feel at the first meeting of the group? What questions and concerns did you have? What did you know about or wonder about other members of the group? Did you have a sense of common purpose? Perhaps you felt exposed or resistant. Perhaps you felt wary, not knowing what was going to be expected of you or what you could expect of others. Perhaps you had concerns about how others would respond to you and whether they would respect your contributions to the group. Reflection on our own experiences provides a helpful entry point for engaging other people in the process of working in groups. What sorts of concerns can we anticipate? How can we address those concerns honestly and openly?

We can begin building trusting relationships among participants by starting from a place of "not knowing" and acknowledging distrust. As group members share knowledge, histories, and experiences, they develop a basis for trust. Similarly, as people begin to trust that others are committed to respectful participation, they are more likely to offer more of themselves and their experiences to the process. As engaged participants, they are better able to recognize and respect differences and seek possibilities for common ground. Over time, a sense of collective wisdom and intimacy emerges. As facilitators, we also have the responsibility of engaging with questions of power and authority as they play out in the group. How does our organizational position shape our role in the group process? How do others perceive our power? If we are in the position of primary facilitator of a group process, how do we both acknowledge and share the power of that position? What forms of power do other group members bring to bear in the process and how do we acknowledge them? For example, a member may use the power of silence or silencing in ways that inhibit communication. Others may use the power of blocking, which is finding reasons to stall or stop the progress of the group. Members may draw on outside or intimate knowledge related to the group as a source of power. These various means of bringing power to bear are not inherently "wrong" or "right." Rather they are part of the group dynamics that facilitators must address openly.

A Memorable Group Experience

The following story is from Maxine Jacobson's group experience. We tell it not because it highlights the "how-tos" of group facilitation or provides the "perfect" example of the engagement principles we set forth in this section. We tell it because it makes us mindful of humanity and humility, and it highlights issues of power and gender and the ways in which these influence our engagement with a group.

> *If anyone ever asks me what I like best about social work practice, I always say "I love working with groups." This doesn't mean that every group I ever facilitated was a raving success - On the contrary. I've come up against my fair share of challenging moments in group work, most of them related to gender and power and the power of gender. Let me explain.*
>
> *When I first started out in the field of sexual assault, I worked with adolescents mandated into treatment for sexually abusing younger children. I felt comfortable with teenagers. After all, I was older and somehow my age privileged me, or so I thought, to exercise power over those younger than myself. About a year into my employment, a woman left the agency for a job in Alaska and I moved into her position. This*

meant I had to co-facilitate groups for adult men remanded into treatment for sexual assault. I thought, "No problem – I'll be co-facilitating the group with a man who was a line-backer for the University of Washington football team – I'll be perfectly safe." Now that's an interesting thought, and not one that most men doing this kind of work have to grapple with. Somehow, I felt protected by the mere thought of this man's presence.

To make a long story short, on the night of my first group, I got a message from the co-facilitator telling me he had to attend to a family emergency. I was on my own. I entered the group room scared, and my fear intensified when I felt the force of ten pairs of eyes staring at my every move. I was new to them and they were definitely new to me. I mustered up every ounce of strength and courage I could find within myself and set about the business of facilitating the group. Or so I thought. Instead of telling the group I was afraid, I did everything in my power to hide that fact. But while the brain is good at telling lies, often the body fails to comply. I barely remember one word I spoke that night but I do remember the sweat running down the back of my knees. (I think bodies do this after they've run out of sweat under the arms.) My body spoke the words I could not say.

What issues of power and gender do you see playing through this story? What observations might other members of the group have made during this session? What non-verbal cues might they have noticed? How might these cues have contradicted the spoken words of the group facilitator? How might these issues affect group practice? Given what you've read in this section on engaging with groups, what would have been the best thing to do given the circumstances?

Developing Group Ground Rules

As members of a social work practice class, you are being asked to participate in a group learning process, take risks, and develop your repertoire of skills. The experiences may leave you feeling exposed and vulnerable. What sorts of ground rules do you want to have in place that will help create a context of safety in which you can take risks? Think about the difference between "safety" and "comfort" here. The risk taking associated with new learning may create discomfort. Risk taking in a group setting may also expose challenges of difference in the classroom. By virtue of "positionality" some class members may enjoy a greater degree of taken-for-granted "safety" and "comfort" in the classroom than others. Some class members might find unacknowledged "comforts" of privilege challenged by those who have been denied those comforts. Questions of difference may play out in very personal and emotional ways. How can the classroom become a safe enough place to be uncomfortable and to learn through that discomfort? Prepare your own list of ground rules for group learning that would allow you to take risks. Get together with a small group of classmates and share your lists. See if you can come to agreement on a set of ground rules. Now get together as a class and consider each group's ground rules. Where are the points of agreement? Where are the differences? See if you can reach consensus as a full group on the ground rules for group process.

A key part of the engagement process is the socialization of group members about the dynamics of group work. By preparing people for what lies ahead, inviting candid dialogue about trust, power, and difference, and modeling openness, we help them become committed partners in the process. In order to meaningfully engage in a group process, members need to have a sense of belonging and a voice. They need to feel their experiences and perspectives are valued despite differences and disagreements among members. And they need to feel both a sense of responsibility and a sense of possibility in the process.

Chapter Summary

In this chapter we have explored the many facets and dynamics of engagement. We have considered the significance of organizational and community context in the process of engagement. We bring our histories with us to each new relationship, further shaping the possibilities and limits of engagement. We have addressed the interpersonal context of practice and the importance of preparation, observation, and respectful listening and dialogue in building mutual knowledge and trust. Social justice work calls for strong skills in interpersonal communication and the ability to engage people in teamwork. We have considered both specific skills and the larger questions of meaning, power, difference, and resistance that we need to bring to bear simultaneously in the practice of engagement. The process of and commitment to engagement prepares us for the work of teaching-learning that we address in Chapter Six.

Case Study: Remembering Al

In the following essay, "Remembering Al," Diane Byington reflects on her own struggles as a beginning social worker to engage with a challenging client and the lessons she learned in the process. We have used this essay in a number of social work classes to encourage reflection and provoke discussion about the many facets of engagement. The essay appeared in *Reflections: Narratives of Professional Helping*, 1996, 2(Spring), 21-24. It is reproduced here courtesy of the author and the journal.

> Al was my first client as a beginning social work intern. He was an alcoholic, and he taught me many things. I was sent, somewhat unwillingly, to an unfamiliar town to intern in a county-sponsored substance abuse treatment program for four months. I had never worked with substance abusers before and hadn't yet in my young life known anybody with an alcohol or other drug problem. I was ripe for a great learning experience, and Al provided it.
>
> Al was assigned to me as a client when he first entered the detoxification facility. I was a middle-class white woman in my early 20s, and he was a white man who looked ancient to me but was probably only in his late 50s. He was intoxicated when I met him that first night, but very polite nonetheless, and seemed embarrassed to be seen in his current situation. I was impressed by his courtly manners, because he wasn't what my stereotypes of an alcoholic had led me to expect.
>
> Al had a great story to tell a person such as myself who was new to taking psychosocial histories. He said he was a college graduate and had been an engineer for many years in a neighboring state. He had a family, a sister who would take him in if he could only get to where she lived. He just couldn't remember her telephone number or her married name, but

he was sure he could find her house if he was in the area. Most importantly, he had a safe deposit box containing quite a lot of money, but the box was in a bank in the town where his sister lived, and he needed cash to get there. When I naively asked why he didn't just have someone get the cash and send it to him, he patiently explained, as if to a child, that the bank wouldn't release the box to anyone but him.

He explained that his life had just somehow gone astray. He had lost his job, through no fault of his own, and his wife had kicked him out; she was a misunderstanding bitch. His kids had turned their backs on him, because they had been poisoned by their mother. He spoke eloquently of a fascinating life. He seemed to be a victim of circumstance, who had turned to alcohol completely by accident and was bewildered by where the journey had taken him.

I believed him. I believed every word the man said for nearly four months. The agency didn't have money to send him back to his family, and he had none of his own, so he stayed on with us. Al became my personal project, and I worked very hard to "save" him. I saw him every day while he was in the detoxification center. He seemed motivated to get his life back together, and I regarded myself as the agent of his return to sobriety. He played his part in this process admirably. He told me over and over how much I was helping him. It was wonderful for him to have someone understanding to talk with who believed his story, fantastic as it was. Other people hadn't seen the real person underneath the out-of-control drinker. He felt that he had a chance now to succeed, thanks to me. He laid it on thick, and I lapped it up. I had a need to be helpful, and he needed to be helped. Al and I moved together very well in our dance.

My supervisor and other agency staff warned me not to be gullible, not to believe everything a client told me. After all, these seasoned workers said, most of our clients live on the streets, and they become skilled at survival. By the time they got to us, they were pretty far down in their slide from middle-class to skid row. Because of the nature of the program as a county service center, we rarely received clients who were attached to conventional society. Mostly, the detoxification center served as a way-station for people to gather their strength, dry out before the next binge, and reconsider the idea of arresting this slide. Most of them would be dead before long, my colleagues told me, because alcoholism is a killer disease. Every now and then someone "dried out" and stayed sober, really changing, but nearly all of the clients were too far gone to do more than verbally express their desire to change. I needed to understand the reality of the situation, the staff told me, so I wouldn't be too disappointed when Al disappeared to get drunk.

I listened politely to their warnings, but privately I thought the staff to be burned out, and it was no wonder that the clients didn't recover, given their cynicism. I thought that I, with my youth and good intentions, armed with my new social work knowledge, could beat the odds. Maybe I couldn't "save" every client who came through detox, but I was convinced that I could "save" Al.

I got Al admitted into our halfway house facility following detoxification, and he was exceedingly grateful to have such a nice place to live. He was still physically weak, but he said he was determined to stay away from alcohol and to recover from this terrible disease that had claimed him for many years. He enthusiastically participated in group therapy, Alcoholics Anonymous meetings, and other program components, and he even tried to play volley-ball, although he was no natural athlete, and years of drinking had wrecked his coordination. I continued to see him daily for individual therapy. Mostly, I listened to his stories.

For a few months things appeared to be going very well with Al. Most of my other clients had joined the revolving door, entering detoxification for a few days and then leaving, only to return within a couple of weeks. They were always sheepish about seeing me again, drunk, after having only days before proclaimed their desire never to touch another drop. After a while I caught on: my part was to fill out forms and offer talk therapy, as they spent several days recovering from a seriously debilitating episode of uncontrolled drinking. The truth was, they wanted to quit but couldn't and the resources at my disposal were inadequate to help them resist the overwhelming compulsion that had them in its grip. All we could really offer then was "three hots and a cot," as well as some human caring, and hope that something someone would say or do would stop the seemingly inevitable slide.

I could accept this frustrating reality with all of my clients except Al. I wanted Al to be the exception. Together, we built elaborate plans to get him back to his money and his family, to keep him sober, and even to get him another job. Finally, after months of effort, I found an organization that would buy him a bus ticket to the neighboring state, and I dropped him off at the bus station. I thought he was gone for good, and I felt great about my ability to "save" at least one person.

My months at the substance abuse treatment program were at an end. I had evolved from thinking I could "save" all of my clients to thinking I could only "save" a few of them. I had gained an appreciation for the goodness of the souls of my clients, who seemed always ready to offer a helping hand to someone else but appeared to lack insight into their own conditions. I had attended funerals for several of them, and had watched as a couple became sober and shakily entered a new phase of life. I had learned how valuable Alcoholics Anonymous and its unconditional support can be to many people. And I better understood the allure of the dark side of alcoholism, how the bottle became the best friend of most of my clients. I had developed a few tools in working with alcoholics, but I knew I still had much to learn, and I felt optimistic about my developing skills. On my way out of town, with my car packed, I stopped at the detoxification center to say goodbye to the staff who had become my good friends during the past months. When I walked in, I was absolutely stricken to find that Al had been admitted a few hours earlier. He was drunk and overbearing. As I stared at him, aghast at seeing him again in this condition, and with such a different personality than I had experienced before, he came over to me with his hand out for a handshake.

"Hello, I'm Sam. And who are you?"

"Al, don't you remember me? I'm Diane, and I worked with you for months."

"Diane, no, I don't remember a Diane. You must have mistaken me for someone else. My name is Sam."

The other staff didn't know how to comfort me in my distress, but they confirmed that he definitely was the person I had known as Al. This new personality, Sam, had an entirely different story, not at all similar to the one told to me when he was Al. I drove away, numbed and in shock at the difference in the man and the reality of my failure, shaking my head in dismay. I never saw Al, or Sam, or whoever he was, again. I presume he is dead, because he was far into his addiction when I met him and he probably didn't have long to live even then. The few months that he stayed sober at the treatment center were probably a good respite from drinking, but were likely not enough to stop the deterioration. In talking with my supervisor, we agreed that he probably had organic brain syndrome as a result of chronic alcoholism, and it was difficult to tell which, if either, of these personalities were indicative of the real person.

I was devastated. Al's return to drinking meant that I had failed completely in my mission to "save" him, to return him to society as a productive member. What had all of my hard work meant, then, to these clients I couldn't save? Was I really cut out to be a social worker, if I couldn't even save one person?

It took years to recognize and internalize the learning from this experience, and from Al. In many ways, Al was a comfortable person for me to work with, because he was somewhat similar to me and to my family. He spoke well, and I believe that he could have been a college graduate. He might even have been an engineer at one time. His eloquent use of language and his obvious middle-class background were things I could relate to, and I clung to them as evidence that he was worthy of being "saved." I think my prejudice was that he was more worthy of efforts than many of the other clients who were of different races, with blue-collar backgrounds, were less articulate, and, most of all, didn't tell me what I wanted to hear.

I don't think I ever had the slightest idea of who Al was as a person. I doubt if even he knew. He had been on the streets for many years, I think, and he knew how to read people and tell them what they wanted to hear. This was his gift in exchange for a place to stay for a while, hot food, and safety. It seemed to be a worthy exchange, because it made me feel useful and needed.

It didn't ultimately help him, though, nor did it ultimately aid me to develop my helping skills. So our interpersonal dance, although comfortable for both of us, was at best a waste of time. The harsh reality that I finally came to understand was that I can't "save" anybody. On this essentially spiritual level, we are all responsible for saving ourselves. Other people can be there for support and guidance, but the ultimate responsibility is ours alone. Al punctured my God-complex and helped me to realize the limits of my influence.

In my ensuing years in the field, I came to believe that the clients at this detoxification center were the most challenging I would meet. My colleagues had understood better than I the value of human caring, of providing a respite from drinking, of nourishing the body with good food and rest, and of offering at least a vision of a different way of life. They were willing to settle for this contribution, and they respected the clients as unique individuals, without needing to see a change to enhance their own image as effective social workers.

I remember Al fondly, after nearly 20 years. He was a loving, caring person who was caught in the throes of a terrible disease process and who did the best he could in very difficult circumstances. He certainly had the gift of gab, entertaining me with wonderful stories, and he stayed sober for nearly four months. In the end, the addiction recalled him, but I hope that those four months helped him to last longer than he would have otherwise.

Because of Al, I learned not to take it personally when a client relapsed. Relapse isn't about me and my failure to "save." It's a reality of the disease or condition of addiction. Realizing the limits of my power helped me to accept clients wherever they were and allowed me to focus on shoring up their own sense of power to help themselves.

Al taught me a lot about myself and my blind spots. Because of him, I began to learn about humility. He helped me to distinguish boundaries, the difference between myself and somebody else. He also helped me to understand that, when somebody's story seems too good to be true, it probably is. What I should be focusing on instead is why the person feels a need to tell me such a fantastic story. I certainly don't need to reject automatically whatever a person tells me, but I don't need to accept it either. I can walk a middle road, remembering that part of the addiction process for many people involves telling other people what they want to hear. I became much more effective when I learned to confront unlikely stories while making it safe for clients to examine the truth. Working with alcoholics was a constant barometer of my own need to be needed, and it helped me to keep my priorities straight.

Eventually, I moved on to other areas of social work, although I truly enjoyed my years in the addictions field. Now that most of my work is with MSW students, I often have opportunities to remind myself of the lessons I first learned with Al, and to pass them on to other naïve students who want to "save" the world.

Al provided me with a hard but very effective learning experience, and I smile now when I think of him. I am especially grateful that I was around long enough to see more than one aspect of his addiction. Even though I was shocked and dismayed to see him drunk again after all my hard work, that was the best part of the lesson. What if I had been allowed to think that I had successfully "saved" him?

I suspect that I grew a great deal more from our experiences together than he did. Wherever he is, I thank him.[5]

Questions for Discussion

1. How could the five key concepts of meaning, context, power, history, and possibility bring understanding to the organizational context of practice?
2. Sandra Cisneros' quote from *The House on Mango Street* captures an "insider's" view of community. What creative work (novel, poem, essay, film) captures an "insider's view" of a community to which you belong? How so?
3. What is anticipatory empathy? In what situations have you made use of this skill before?
4. What are some of the cross-cultural implications of engagement, listening, and communication in general?
5. How do the concepts of power, trust, and difference affect communication? What examples illustrate your point?
6. What is resistance? How has its meaning been pathologized?
7. What example can you think of that expands the notion of resistance to include social, political, and economic contexts or histories of oppression and discrimination?
8. What are some challenges you have faced as a member or facilitator of a group? How do these experiences affect how you might approach a new group experience?

Suggested Readings

Anderson, K. & Jack, D. (1991). Learning to listen: Interview techniques and analyses. In S. Berger Gluck and D. Patai (Eds.), *Women's words: The feminist practice of oral history* (pp. 11-22). New York: Routledge.

Anderson, M., & Hill Collins, P. (Eds.). *Race, class, and gender: An anthology* (3rd ed.). Belmont, CA: Wadsworth.

Cisneros, S. (1984). *The house on Mango Street.* New York: Vintage Books

Fine, M. Weis, L. Powell, L, Wong, L.M. (Eds.), (1997). *Off white: Readings on race, power, and society.* New York: Routledge.

Homan, M. (1999). *Promoting change: Making it happen in the real world* (2nd ed.). Pacific Grove, CA: Brooks/Cole.

Hope, A. & Timmel, S. (1999). *Training for transformation: A handbook for community workers,* Volumes 1-4. London: Intermediate Technology Publications.

Schwartz, W. (1986). "The group work tradition and social work practice." *Social Work with Groups,* 8(4), 7-27.

Chapter 6

Just Understanding: Teaching-Learning

"A good teacher is not someone who puts ideas into other people's heads; he is someone who helps others build on their own ideas, to make new discoveries for themselves."

David Werner (1977), *Where There is No Doctor*

Chapter Overview

In Chapter Six we examine the teaching-learning process. We challenge the one-way flow of information that characterizes most social work approaches to data collection, assessment, and interpretation. We reframe the process as one of co-learning where the social worker and other participants in the process recognize their wisdom and the limits of their knowledge, consider the knowledge they need to inform action, identify ways to gather data, and draw on their collective wisdom in rendering the data meaningful in the context of their work. Together participants conduct listening surveys, gather data, identify resources and supports, discuss the root causes of presenting concerns, and discover their own personal and collective capacities. We consider strategies for setting the teaching-learning climate, the development of critical awareness, and the importance of teamwork in the process. We examine a variety of assessment techniques and tools, including both "classic" social work tools and alternative approaches.

Teaching-Learning

Examining the Process

In thinking and talking through the organization of this book, we struggled with ways to frame and name this collaborative process of gathering "data," learning about people and places, needs and resources, problems and possibilities. Most guides to social work practice speak of "assessment" as a key phase in the change process that follows initial engagement. Assessment refers to the collection and interpretation of information needed to inform change-oriented action. We see assessment as a central part of the teaching-learning process, but we did not feel that the word captured the sense of collaboration that is fundamental to social justice work. Moreover, assessment has often been construed as a one-way process where the "expert" gathers data, makes interpretations, and provides a "diagnosis" and course of "treatment" or "intervention" to the "client." The process has largely been problem-focused, resulting in a discourse of deficits and shortcomings. We sought a concept that disrupted a unidirectional view of "assessment" and emphasized a participatory process.

In their important work on an empowering approach to social work practice, Miley, O'Melia, and DuBois (1998) locate assessment as part of the "discovery phase" of the change process and emphasize assessment of resources and strengths rather than "problems." Similarly, Cowger (1994, p. 265) supports strengths-oriented assessments that build a base "for an examination of realizable alternatives, for the mobilization of competencies that can make things different, and for the building of self-confidence that stimulates hope." We agree with their emphases on partnership, possibilities, and strengths. However, the idea of "discovery" suggests that we "find" some truth or resource either "out there" or within. It does not speak to the social construction of knowledge, the emergence of critical consciousness, or the creation of new possibilities through dialogue and praxis. We envision this dynamic process going beyond discovery. It is a process of *learning to learn from others* through which we recognize multiple ways of knowing, challenge dichotomous thinking, question assumptions, and probe the contradictions among words, actions, and consequences. It entails systematic inquiry into questions of meaning, context, power, and history in which both problems and possibilities are embedded.

So, we frame this process as "teaching-learning," a collaborative effort of uncovering information, making it meaningful in the context of our concerns, and creating and disseminating knowledge and possibilities for action. Each party to the process brings knowledge grounded in personal experience and cultural history. Together we begin to map out what we know, consider what we need to learn more about, seek out knowledge, consider underlying forces and patterns that shape experiences, and bring our collective wisdom to bear in translating data into a meaningful guide for action. We draw inspiration from Freirian principles of popular education that contrast interactive problem-posing and search for solutions with a "banking" approach to learning (Freire, 1974).

As social justice workers, we act as animators, facilitators, and researchers in the process. We work to create a climate that promotes co-learning. We support and encourage the process of critical reflection about people's concerns and what we need to know through question posing. And we help people *systematically* examine the information at hand, *theorize* about problems and possibilities, and *strategize* courses of action. Together we can create new meanings and labels that can help us think and act differently (Reed et al., 1997). We are both learners and teachers in the process. We are learning in the context of partnership with those who possess the wisdom of lived experience. And we are teachers, helping others develop knowledge and skills in research and planning so that they can carry out their own assessments and develop action plans in the future.

On Becoming an Effective Teacher-Learner

The following are suggestions for village health workers developed by David Werner, Carol Thurman and Jane Maxwell and presented in *Where There Is No Doctor* (Werner, 1977).[1] Might these suggestions also help us in becoming effective teacher-learners? What would you add to the list?

- Be kind – a friendly word, a smile, a hand on the shoulder, or some other sign of caring often means more than anything else you do. Treat others as your equals... Often it helps to ask yourself, "What would I do if this were a member of my own family?"
- Share your knowledge... There is nothing you have learned that, if carefully explained, should be of danger to anyone.

- Respect your people's traditions and ideas... People are slow to change their attitudes and traditions, and with good reason. They are true to what they feel is right. And this we must respect. ... So go slow and always keep a deep respect for your people, their traditions, and their human dignity. Help them build on the knowledge and skills they already have.
- Know your own limits. No matter how great or small your knowledge and skills, you can do a good job as long as you know and work within your limits. Do what you know how to do... But use your judgment. Know your limits – but also use your head.
- Keep learning. Use every chance you get to learn more... Always be ready to ask questions...Never pass up a chance to take a refresher course or get additional training.
- Practice what you teach. People are more likely to pay attention to what you do than to what you say... a good leader does not tell people what to do. He sets the example.
- Work for the joy of it. If you want other people to take part in improving their village and caring for their health, you must enjoy such activity yourself. If not, who will want to follow your example? ... Try to make community work projects fun.
- Look ahead and help others to look ahead ... To correct a problem in a lasting way, you must look for and deal with the underlying causes. You must get to the root of the problem.

The Importance of Teamwork

Important learning happens in dialogue with others. Teams allow people to take risks, try out new ideas, and build a power base for change. Individuals operating alone have a more difficult time because they lack support for their efforts and have no one to challenge them and spark continued growth. Teams form a base and a place for learning about effective membership and leadership. They ensure decisions are made collectively instead of power being concentrated in the hands of an authority figure. To work effectively with and in teams, it is important to understand about group work and group dynamics (Brill, 1976).

Social work has a long history of group work as an approach to personal and social transformation. Much of the social work literature divides discussion of group work into broad categories of individual change groups (e.g. therapy, support, and self-help groups) and task groups (e.g. community, agency task, and policy groups) (Garvin & Seabury, 1997, pp. 231-32). We argue that social justice work calls for an integrated approach to teamwork that brings skills of mutual aid, analysis of power, and a commitment to the equality of participants to bear as part of the teaching-learning process. We use the concept of teamwork here to capture the integration of group dynamic and support, partnership, and collective action.

Processes of Mutual Aid

In Chapter Five, we introduced William Schwartz's concept of mutual aid as a basis for collective support and action. Let's return to the processes of mutual aid and the implications for social justice work. By conceptualizing the group as a mutual aid system, we locate all participants, including the social worker, as learners, teachers, and facilitators, or "animators." We also recognize the dialectical relationship between the individual members and the group as a whole in the process (Shulman, 1986, p. 52). As participants learn and practice the skills of mutual aid they contribute to a climate of trust and intimacy in the group that supports individuals in assuming the risks and opportunities of teaching-learning. Let's take a closer look at these processes and the elements of teaching-learning at work in carrying them out. Drawing from Lawrence Shulman (1986, 1992), we offer a description of each of the processes. As you read about the processes, reflect on the questions, "How can we as social workers facilitate the process? How does the process promote co-learning?" We offer our thoughts on these questions in our description of sharing data, the dialectical process, exploring taboo subjects, and the "all in the same boat" phenomenon. We invite you to do the same with each of the processes.

Sharing Data. Groups provide a context for members to be resources to one another by sharing ideas, data, and strategies for survival and change. We can facilitate the process by teaching groups about the value of sharing data and serving as resources to one another; giving members opportunities to share data; recognizing members for their contributions; and checking in with members to see what data they have put to use and what the results have been. The process allows each member opportunities to teach from his experience and learn from the experience of others.

The Dialectical Process. This process consists of members engaging the debate of ideas with members variably putting forth a thesis and antithesis and finally arriving at some form of synthesis. The process can help members explore contradictory forces and discourses that shape everyday life. And it can help members grapple with the pushes and pulls of ambivalent feelings. In short, as tensions and contradictions emerge and are addressed in the group, each member has an opportunity to recognize internalized contradictions. We can facilitate the process by recognizing tensions and contradictions as key parts of social experience and by naming and honoring the process when group members are engaged in it. It is especially important that facilitators be able to frame the dialectical process as a healthy part of group work and not as a "problem" between members. The process illustrates the fundamental give and take of teaching-learning.

Exploring Taboo Subjects. The group context creates a space where members can address issues that are silenced and topics whose honest discussion is avoided in other social contexts. For example, groups can be powerful places to approach questions of sexuality, terminal illness, racism, and other topics often considered taboo in dominant social discourse. Groups may experience the power of trust and intimacy as members find the courage to "speak the unspeakable." Again, we can facilitate the process by encouraging participants to approach difficult subjects and by helping members establish ground rules that help create a context of safety needed for risky discussion. The process teaches members about the possibilities in risk-taking and helps to build the trust needed for more difficult learning.

The "All in the Same Boat" Phenomenon. Realizing that one is not alone and that others share similar concerns and struggles is a powerful dimension of group work. As facilitators, we not only recognize and respect difference but also take opportunities to make connections and encourage others to critically reflect on the patterns that connect and the forces that shape both individual and group experience. We can both pose and invite questions that may help break down a sense of personal isolation or deficit and help people move to another level of questioning: "But why are we in this boat?" The process expands the critical awareness of the group beyond the teaching and learning of individual members.

Emotional Support. Group members can provide a range of immediate, direct support to individual members dealing with pain, trauma, and loss. Rather than encouraging a person to "cheer up," members can recognize and honor difficult emotions and experiences. Members can provide a gift of emotional support by sharing their own feelings and experiences and letting the other person know that his or her pain is respected, even if it may not be fully understood.

Mutual Demand. Support is only one dimension of the dynamic of group work. Members need a context of support and a base of trust in order to take the risks necessary for social and personal transformation. Thus, effective groups are also places where participants make demands on one another and hold one another accountable for responsible participation and follow-through on work. Working in a context of trust and intimacy, participants are able to confront one another on the contradictions between their words and actions.

Mutual Expectation. Hand in hand with mutual demand is mutual expectation. Individual members come to feel a commitment to one another and to the group as a whole. Trust develops as the group places expectations on its members to follow through on commitments and honor the ground rules. Likewise, members strengthen their sense of belonging as they live up to those expectations.

Helping with Specific Problems. Groups can move back and forth between general concerns of the group as a whole and the specific concerns of individual members. Members can assist one another in concrete problem solving. Successes of individual problem solving can become resources for the group as a whole.

Rehearsal. The group setting provides members with an arena for practicing alternative responses, difficult interactions, and challenging tasks. Members provide both support and critical feedback and bolster individuals' confidence in the process.

Strength in Numbers. The group experience not only breaks down isolation, it also helps members overcome feelings of powerlessness and see the possibilities of and strength in collective action.[2]

As members engage in these processes over time, they develop their knowledge of group work, skills of teaching-learning, and both individual and collective capacity for critical reflection and action. The processes support teamwork that integrates the possibilities of mutual aid and social action.

Power in the Teaching-Learning Process

The question of power is implicit in the previous discussion of mutual aid. However, it is important that we pay more explicit attention to power in the teaching-learning process. We addressed in the discussion of context and positionality in Chapter Five that, as social workers, we need to be clear about the extent and limits of our professional power and authority. By virtue of our positions we may have the power to attach labels to others, access resources, impose sanctions, and make recommendations with significant legal and social consequences. We need to be critically self-aware regarding the sources, forms, and limits of our power and to be able to communicate that honestly to others. Likewise, we need to be critically conscious of the various forms of informal power we may assume or that others might attribute to us, such as the power of credentials, titles, or access to information. People and groups who have been excluded from arenas and processes of decision-making may be very wary of both formal and informal power of the social workers. People socialized to respect the power of the expert may defer to the authority of the social worker as advice-giver and decision-maker. For social workers, an integral part of the teaching-learning process is, therefore, learning to acknowledge the power and expertise we have; learning and teaching the skills of participation so that our power and expertise is brought to bear honestly, effectively, and justly; and learning and teaching modes of leadership that challenge top-down models of authority and promote participation. We accomplish this through a power analysis.

Conducting a Power Analysis

In her development of an empowerment approach to practice with women of color, Gutiérrez (1990) describes engaging in a power analysis as a technique for empowering people in the context of a collaborative helping relationship. She writes:

> Engaging in a power analysis of the client's situation is a critical technique for empowering practice. It first involves analyzing how conditions of powerlessness are affecting the client's situation. A second crucial step is to identify sources of potential power in the client's situation. An indirect technique is

> dialogue between the worker and the client that is aimed at exploring and identifying the social structural origins of the client's current situation (Keefe, 1980; Longres, & McLeod, 1980; Resnick, 1976; Solomon, 1976). Another, more direct, technique involves focusing the client's analysis on a specific situation – either the client's own situation or a vignette developed for the intervention (Bock, 1980; Pinderhughes, 1983; Schechter et al., 1985; Solomon, 1976). Clients and workers should be encouraged to think creatively about sources of potential power, such as forgotten skills, personal qualities that could increase social influence, members of past social support networks, and organizations in their communities.

An effective power analysis requires that social workers fully comprehend the connection between the immediate situation and the distribution of power in society as a whole (Garvin, 1985; Keefe, 1980; Mathis and Richan, 1986; Pernell, 1985). The process may require consciousness-raising exercises to look beyond the specific situation to problems shared by other clients in similar situations. Also it is crucial that workers not adopt feelings of powerlessness from clients, but rather that they learn to see the potential for power and influence in every situation. (1990, p. 152)

Gutiérrez and Lewis (1999, pp. 38-51) offer suggestions for engaging in power analyses in interpersonal practice. They describe how individual practice can be transformed into an empowering process by honoring the other person's social reality, walking with rather than directing a person through the helping process, and providing mechanisms for acknowledging and responding to experiences of oppression and discrimination. They address the centrality of relationship to empowering practice, and they recognize spirituality as an empowering resource in many people's lives.

Other Ways of Thinking About Power

We also find the concepts of power presented by Townsend et al. in *Women and Power* (1999, pp. 19-45) helpful in elaborating the power analysis. As mentioned in Chapter One, they outline several dimensions of power. *Power over* is the power of oppression and domination. It may be enforced through violence and fear or through social and cultural rules and practices. "Power from within arises from a recognition that one is not helpless, not the source of all one's problems, that one is restricted in part by structures outside oneself" (Townsend et al., 1999,

p. 30). *Power with* is the capacity to achieve with others what we cannot achieve on our own. *Power to* is creative force that involves gaining access to a full range of human potential and capacities (Townsend et al., 1999, p. 33). "Power as resistance" refers to the myriad strategies of oppressed people to indirectly and directly deflect, avert, and manipulate *power over*. We can enrich the power analysis by teaching participants about dimensions of power and learning how they claim and confront power in their everyday lives. We also see the need to take the power analysis further by making the power and authority of the social worker a talkable theme in the process. How do the participants in the process variably perceive the social worker's power? How comfortable is the social worker with the power, authority, and responsibility of her position? How does her power factor into the larger power dynamics of the presenting situation and the change process? These are key questions of the teaching-learning process.

Power and Positionality

Reisch, Wenocur, and Sherman (1981) address the question of power and empowerment in terms of the worker-client relationship and the worker's organizational positionality. They note that social work clients often feel powerless to address their problems and that their sense of powerlessness is often intensified by virtue of long histories of experiences of discrimination, devaluation, and exclusion. The social worker, on the other hand, often stands between the client and sponsoring organizations that possess resources that both the client and worker need. Yet the worker's own power may be limited in terms of ability to access those resources and respond to needs. The worker may come to incorporate feelings of helplessness as well. The authors argue that workers need to understand power and empowerment both conceptually and experientially in order to help clients gain power and control over their lives. Further, workers need to be able to effectively use the power available to them and communicate their grasp of power and power dynamics to clients. The authors write: "To pursue such ends successfully, social workers have a responsibility to reverse the process of disempowerment. In this regard it is essential that workers learn to manage conflict, rather than attempt to resolve conflict permanently or ignore it altogether" (Reisch, et al., 1981, p. 111).

They argue that worker empowerment in the organizational context requires "functional non-capitulation" – a means of conflict management wherein workers position themselves as active-decision makers with both a right and responsibility to influence the organization and work to reverse the downward organizational pressure that contributes to powerlessness. The stance of functional non-capitulation "requires workers to maintain a willingness and capacity to negotiate continually the conditions of their work. In this position, workers will have to take calculated risks to achieve their goals. The worker's posture of functional non-capitulation encourages the same stance among clients, rather than shared dependency and powerlessness" (Reisch et al., 1981, p. 112). The authors argue that in order to establish this stance the worker must become aware of and comfortable with the many sources of available power, including legal power, the power of information, situational power, expert power, coalitional power, and even negative power – the power to make the agency look bad (p. 112). Thus the analysis of power is not limited to the power dynamics of the client's situation or of the particular context of the worker-client relationship. Rather it is part of the social justice worker's critical positionality in human service organizations.

Power and Powerlessness

James Barber (1995, p. 31), an Australian social worker, tells a story of the psychology of learned helplessness in an article on politically progressive casework. We summarize it here because it explains why focusing on power and its impact on people's lives is essential to justice-oriented practice. Barber discusses how in the 1960s, a group of U.S. psychologists used a conditioning procedure to "train dogs in avoidance behavior in response to a neutral tone." The dogs were placed in hammocks and suspended from the ground and "administered" painful electric shocks. Initially, as one might guess, the dogs struggled desperately in an attempt to free themselves from the situation. No matter how hard they struggled, their attempts were met with failure. Eventually, the researchers released the dogs from their constraints, placed them on the ground where they could stand, and shocked the dogs again. The dogs firmly stood their ground. What had the dogs learned? In effect, the experiment taught them that no matter how hard they tried to escape they could not avoid the pain. After repeated attempts to free themselves, the dogs had literally given up hope. Barber tells us, "This phenomenon of learned helplessness provides a useful analogy for describing what happens to all organisms, including humans, when they are denied control over their life."

Translating this analogy into practice means paying attention to how conditions of powerlessness have influenced and shaped people's lives. It guides practice by making us look for sources of potential power in participants' circumstances and using these to summon hope and possibilities for change. A power analysis must also include how you as a social worker figure into the encounter and what control, power, and status is communicated by your position in the encounter. Take a moment to reflect on a situation in which you have felt powerless. What other feelings were evoked? How did you respond? What feelings come to mind as you reflect on this experience? Now think of a situation where another person feels powerless. How might the feelings affect his ability to respond? What hopes or expectations may that person have of a social worker in a change process? What power or authority might be attributed to the social worker? As the social worker, how would you begin a power analysis of the situation?

The Practice of Systematic Inquiry

In this section we discuss the concept of *sistematización* and consider a number of approaches to systematic inquiry. We present some of the basic assessment tools that are widely used in U.S. social work. We highlight their strengths, pose questions about their limitations, and consider their fit with the teaching-learning process of social justice work. We also introduce tools from popular education, feminist practice, and international and cross-cultural contexts that can facilitate the practice of social justice work.

Sistematización

Teaching-learning involves the "systematization" of experiences. This is not a word in the English vocabulary. We borrow it from the Spanish, *sistematización.* Popular educators in Latin America, influenced by the work of Paulo Freire, describe *sistematización* as a rigorous, ordered process of taking concrete, lived experience into account, looking for generative themes, and sharing with others what we have learned from it. It is a participatory process in which people critically examine and interpret their experience and social reality in order to arrive at a more profound understanding. The process involves detailed deconstruction, examination, and reconstruction of the elements, context, and forces shaping the experience. Oscar Jara (1998) describes *sistematización* as:

> A critical interpretation of one or more experiences that, upon organization and reconstruction, enables us to find or explicate the logic of the lived experience, the factors that have intervened in the process, the relations among those factors, and why it has happened in this way. (p. 22)[3]

The key themes of Just Practice provide a foundation for *systematización,* or systematic inquiry into experiences, conditions, and possibilities for change: How do the participants in the process variably describe and give *meaning* to their experiences, interests, and concerns? What constitutes a "problem" and for whom? What is the *history* of the problem and how does it intersect with the histories of the participants? What is the *context* in which participants are coming together? How is it connected to the larger contexts of their lives? What can we learn from a *power* analysis of the situation that addresses questions of power over, power with, power within, and power to do? Where and what are the *possibilities* for transformative action? What possibilities can be realized and how? What can we learn from the process that will transform our thinking and inform future practice?

A Note on Standardized Assessment Tools

There is a wide range of standardized tools for diagnosis and assessment that are available to and used by social workers. By standardized, we refer to instruments that have been tested on large numbers of people and that provide practitioners general guidelines for problem diagnosis. Most standardized instruments used by social workers focus on the individual and not on the context of her life experience. Most are administered and interpreted by the practitioner who then uses the results to inform action. While the tools may yield useful information, we see them as fitting within the "social worker as expert" model of practice. We agree with Gutiérrez and Lewis (1999, p. 31) that social workers need to be cautious in the use of standardized instruments whose "standards" may not take into account the social reality of the person being assessed. While standardized instruments can provide valuable data, we will not be addressing them here. Instead, we focus on tools that facilitate participation, consciousness-raising, and critical action.

Generative Themes

Communities of individuals have issues that resonate for them based on the shared, contextual nature of their experience. Generative themes are those that bring strong feelings to bear on the possibilities for sustained action. Tapping into these themes and eliciting their emotional content is one way of breaking through the barriers of apathy and powerlessness that prevent people from feeling hope and keep them immobilized and incapacitated. Hopelessness is not a natural human condition (Hope & Timmel, 1999, V. 1). As we learned from the "experiment" cited by Barber recounting how dogs were rendered powerless, repeated, thwarted attempts at achieving a goal eventually create apathy. Looking for generative themes is a way to unleash this energy, break the silencing powers of oppression and stigmatization, and channel this new-found strength toward creative action. Think for a moment of generative themes that might resonate for you and the community you form with other students. Maybe you work long hours each week and have a full time course schedule at school. Perhaps some of you have families you are supporting as well. What stresses and strains do these conditions create for your well-being as a student and family member? What of tuition increases and the mounting price of textbooks? What common themes tie you together as a group? Generation, identification, and critical reflection on common themes is an important part of the teaching-learning process.

Conducting a Survey of Generative Themes

Searching for generative themes is a place to start to develop critical awareness, the kind of awareness that links personal issues with the context of lived experiences (Freire, 1974; Hope & Timmel, 1999, V. 1). This process may begin with "a non-formal listening survey." In conducting a listening survey we learn to listen for the issues that resonate with the strongest emotions in people's lives. As Hope and Timmel note: "Only on issues about which they feel strongly will people be prepared to act" (1999, V. 1, p. 53). We summarize this process below and provide guidelines for consideration. We refer you to Hope and Timmel (1999) for a more thorough explanation (see pages V. 1, 53-68).

- Whether you are working with an individual, a group, a neighborhood, or a community, the following questions should guide your inquiry. What are people worried about? Happy about? Sad about? Angry about? Fearful about? Hopeful about?

- Think of the survey as a team effort, and decide who to include in the process based on specific training and attention to gender, race, and age considerations. Be sure to include people who have insider information on the community, group, or individual level (e.g., relevant family members, local shop keepers, hairdressers, etc.).
- Remember to gather background information as well. This information could include statistics on community demographics, economic indicators, and previous studies completed that document community life.
- Conduct unstructured interviews that allow participants to tell their stories and feel relaxed in the process.
- Listen for themes that address basic needs such as housing, food. and shelter, safety and security, love and belonging, self-respect, and personal growth.
- Make sure you cover six areas of life that concern people's well-being: meeting basic physical needs; relationship between people; community decision-making processes and structures; education and socialization; recreation; and beliefs and values. Remember to approach these issues sensitively with regard to cultural differences.
- Take advantage of listening situations where you can capture the spontaneous discussion of the community. These situations could include grocery stores, sports and other recreational events, hairdressers, bars, places where people have to wait (i.e., doctor's offices, grocery store lines, movie theatre lines) and times before and after public meetings and events.
- Let people you interview know the full purpose of your questioning and what you intend to do with the information you gather.
- Gather facts as well as feelings. Remember that tapping into the emotional content of people's stories requires active listening.
- Most often, the strongest feelings will emerge in connection to the six areas of life. For example, changes in the local economy will have implications for employment and people's relationship to changing personal identities.
- Get back together with the team and identify themes that resonate most for the community or group or individual.

- Critically analyze these themes as a group, paying particular attention to basic needs, community decisions, and values and beliefs. Then decide the importance of each issue.
- You might do this by using a chart, grid or other means of graphic representation. This process helps to make connections between seemingly isolated issues and draws a more complete picture of people's situations.
- Move through each theme and then decide upon one theme and brainstorm ways in which this theme could be presented visually through a play or picture (code).
- In deciding on your "code" for this particular theme think about: the situation, the feelings involved, the difficulties, the problem, the obstacles, and the contradictions.
- Create a dramatization or drawing of the code and decide what questions you would pose for discussion.

Hope and Timmel remind us that developing critical awareness begins with connecting peoples' lived experiences to "the structures of society that keep things the way they are. . . (p. 53). The listening survey is one step in this process. They recommend that its results be combined with research already completed to provide documentation and statistics related to community life. In what particular situations might you find the listening survey useful? Are there any ways you might adapt it to better suit your needs?

"Diagnosis" and Analysis

In developing a popular education course on democratic participation and the exercise of local power in Costa Rica, Cecilia Díaz (1995) describes the "diagnostic" process that enables people to critically and systematically analyze their social reality in order to discover possible solutions and make informed collective decisions. It is a process that addresses three levels of analysis:

- **Context:** the population, economic, cultural, and natural resources, mode of production, service infrastructure, etc.

- **Practice**: what has transpired in the life of our group or community; what have been significant moments, events, achievements; how have we been transforming our reality; and
- **Values and subjectivity**: why do we act as we do, believe in working for change; why is participation important; what dreams inspire us; why do we think what we think? (p. 2)

Díaz describes a five-step process of analysis. It is a process with a wide range of applicability:

1. **Describe:** We start by recognizing things as they present themselves to us. What are the visible, exterior signs of our reality? How does our social reality present itself before our eyes? We may gather this information through interviews, group conversations, observations, review of existing data, through survey and questionnaires, and through testimonials. This is our starting point.
2. **Organize:** Then we try to classify what we have described and organize the elements into aspects of our reality, such as economic, cultural, social, and political aspects.
3. **Prioritize**: We give preference to some aspects over others as we consider those that are most significant in contributing to the situation that concerns us. The criteria by which we set priorities might include: most urgent, most serious, that which affects the most people, the most deeply felt, etc.
4. **Analyze**: We reflect on the different aspects, analyzing them separately. We seek to understand causes and consequences of each of those aspects that we have set as priorities. Then we integrate the different aspects and look for relations among them.
5. **Draw Conclusions**: We return to the basic points that emerged from the analysis – the most consistently named concerns and affirmations, the common elements across seemingly diverse problems or needs. At this point we begin to orient ourselves toward possible courses of action. (Díaz, 1995, pp. 8-11)

The process brings us to new points of arrival. They then become points of departure for further reflection and analysis.

Applying Díaz's Five-Step Process

Get together with a few classmates and select an issue relevant to social work that is currently being debated in your community – for example, housing and homelessness; access to affordable health care; disability access on campus; access to public transportation. Over a period of 2-3 weeks, gather relevant and readily accessible information on the issue (e.g. newspaper and other media reports, agency reports, etc). Identify key stakeholders in the issue and consider what their interests may be. Role play a session in which members of your group take on the roles of people struggling for improved access or services. Carry out the five steps of diagnosis and analysis outlined by Díaz. Where did you find common ground? Important differences? What difficulties did you encounter? Were you able to work through them? If so, how? What feelings did the role play evoke for you? Now, role play a session in which each member of your group takes on the role of a different stakeholder (e.g. landlord, property owner, single parent in need of decent affordable housing, housing authority director, housing advocate, director of local homeless shelter, etc). Where did you find common ground? Important differences? What difficulties did you encounter? Were you able to work through them? If so, how? What feelings did this role play evoke? Did it differ from the first? If so, how? Does this exercise challenge assumptions regarding difference and commonality?

Learning about Communities

We addressed the importance of the community context of practice in Chapter Five. How do we get to know the communities in which we live and work and understand the common and differing concerns and interests of the residents? A number of community practitioners have created useful, hands-on guides for learning about the community context of practice. We highlight some of their important work here.

Homan's Guide. Mark Homan (1999, pp. 115-123) offers a helpful guide for getting to know your community. He writes: "the information you need to know about your community can be organized into five categories:"

1. Basic community characteristics (e.g. physical features, social features, landmarks, demographics, meeting places)

2. How the community functions to meet its members' needs (physical needs, social and emotional needs, economic needs, educational and communication needs, political needs)
3. Unmet needs (e.g. for services, resources, information, action)
4. Community resources (human, material, natural, intellectual, etc.)
5. Capacity for and disposition toward purposeful change (constraints and possibilities, desire, motivation, past experience, etc.)

These five categories provide a useful outline for initiating collective inquiry into community.

Henderson and Thomas's Guide. Henderson and Thomas (1980, pp. 52-61) have developed a guide to "Getting to Know Your Community" for neighborhood workers. They write: "We suggest that the following scheme be used by workers as a guide or checklist in their data-gathering activities, and not as an analysis to straitjacket their own perceptions of the particular and unique community in which they find themselves working" (1980, p. 52). The six major categories they include are:

1. **History**: "Issues and problems of an area are connected to people, organizations and events in the past. Local people are often the best sources of historical data…" (p. 52).
2. **Environment**: Includes data on administrative and natural boundaries, population density, public space, transportation facilities, land use, etc.
3. **Residents:** Includes data on demographics, housing, employment and general welfare, as well as information on community networks, people's perceptions of the area, and values and traditions.
4. **Organizations**: Includes data on local and central government, economic activities, religious organizations, voluntary and civic associations.
5. **Communications**: Newspapers, radio, and TV, information technology, people-to-people communication via posters, leaflets, and conversations.
6. **Power and leadership**: Includes business and organized labor, elective politics, administrative politics, civic politics, community politics.

Assets-Based Approach. John L. McKnight and John Kretzmann (1990) have made important contributions to our understanding of assets-based community development. In their work on mapping community capacity they challenge "needs-oriented" approaches and focus instead on strategies for recognizing and promoting the capacities, skills, and assets of low-income people and their neighborhoods (p. 2). They frame "assessment" as a process of mapping the building blocks for community regeneration. McKnight and Kretzmann identify primary, secondary, and potential building blocks. *Primary Building Blocks* are the "assets and capacities located inside the neighborhood and under neighborhood control." These include individual assets (such as personal income, the gifts of "labeled" people, individual local businesses, and home-based enterprises) and organizational assets (such as citizen associations, business associations, financial institutions, cultural, communications, and religious organizations). *Secondary Building Blocks* are assets located within the community but largely controlled by outsiders. These include private and non-profit organizations (such as colleges and universities, hospitals, and social service agencies), public institutions, and services (schools, police, libraries, fire departments, parks), and physical resources (such as vacant land, commercial and industrial structures, housing, and energy and waste resources). *Potential Building Blocks* are resources originating outside the neighborhood and controlled by outsiders. These include welfare expenditures, public capital improvement expenditures, and public information. McKnight and Kretzmann show that it is possible to create a community assets map that contrasts sharply with an image of community framed solely around deficits and needs.

Community Health Care Guide. As mentioned earlier in this chapter, David Werner (1977) has developed guides for community health care and health workers in places where there is no doctor. He offers the following guidance to community health care workers wondering how and where to begin:

> As a village health worker, your concern is for the well-being of all the people – not just those you know well or who come to you. Go to your people. Visit their homes, fields, gathering places, and schools. Understand their joys and concerns. Examine with them their habits, the things in their daily lives that bring about good health, and those that may lead to sickness or injury.

Before you and your community attempt any project or activity, carefully think about what it will require and how likely it is to work. To do this you must consider all of the following:

1. **Felt Needs** – what people feel are their biggest problems.
2. **Real Needs** – steps people can take to meet these problems in a lasting way.
3. **Willingness** – or readiness of people to plan and take the needed steps.
4. **Resources** – the persons, skills materials, and/or money needed to carry out the activities decided upon. (Werner, 1977, p. 8)

You now have four frameworks to help you get to know a community. What do they have in common? How do they differ? How might they be used in the teaching-learning process? What steps would you take to facilitate a participatory process of community assessment? How would you decide what data to gather? Where would you look for information? What steps would you take to facilitate interpretation of the data?

Life and Death in Libby

At this end of this chapter we have included a case study entitled "Life and Death in Libby" about a rural Montana community struggling with the toxic effects of asbestos. After reading the case study, develop a plan for conducting a participatory community assessment. Which of the frameworks for getting to know a community might you use? Where and how would you look for additional information? What obstacles might you encounter? How would you involve community members in the process?

Whose Voices Count?

Rinku Sen, in her article on "Building Community Involvement in Health Care" (1994), challenges the absence of the voices of poor people of color in shaping the public health care system in the U.S.[4] Viewing the national health care debates through the lens of People United for a Better Oakland (PUEBLO), a community-based direct action and service organization, she poses critical questions: Will we ever have enough power to care for ourselves as we should? What is the role of government in providing for the basic human needs of all members of a society? How do we fight for reform that will allow greater local and cultural control over health-care options and practices? How can we build an investment in the notion of "community" and the skill level in community members themselves that will lead us to solutions to the myriad health problems that plague our communities? Sen documents the efforts of poor people of color, working collectively, to challenge and change the power relations between themselves and the health care system. PUEBLO's approach to improving health care was based on three goals: 1) building a sense of community by collectivizing problems and defining common solutions 2) challenging the institutionalized behavior and practices of health care providers and administrators, and 3) developing indigenous leaders well versed in different aspects of health care. PUEBLO members invited community residents to come together in neighborhood churches and schools, identify common and immediate problems people were experiencing in health and health care, identify concrete differences in the ways people wanted to experience their health care, and advocate for institutional change. PUEBLO won a number of local victories: parents are able to get their children immunized for free on weekends and evenings; the county hospital is providing translators for non-English speaking people to communicate with health care workers; and early diagnosis and abatement of lead poisoning is underway.

Based on her experiences with PUEBLO, Sen proposes a people's movement-based approach to envisioning and designing a new health program. The first step would be to recruit credible community organizations committed to health care issues to take on the project. Lead organizations would coordinate face-to-face visits with community members to learn about their health care needs, current access to care, their overall health, their wishes for how things could be, and the kinds of home remedies and cultural practices they and their families use to deal with health problems.

Sen writes: "As we meet people for initial purposes of the interview, we would recruit them to join the organization and help us to find out the same things from other people. We would work through whatever structures gave the most access to people's time: through door knocking, at house meetings, on long supermarket lines in poor communities (our supermarkets have the longest lines) or at the local check-cashing place. I would get children in schools to draw pictures and write essays about their families' experiences with health care. With time from students, community-health practitioners, volunteers, and whoever else I could put out in the community, this process could take anywhere from two to six months.

"When we finished the process we would tabulate the results, including anecdotes and examples of great health care and terrible health care. I would gather people locally to examine the results of those interviews and collectivize our experiences, including first-hand testimony from people willing to share. I would then hold a meeting with key leaders and staff from each of the cities to compare research experiences and data.

"The next step would be to relate our findings to a wide range of surrounding questions. What kinds of practices can we imagine to address health needs? What kinds of health practices exist locally or elsewhere that would address our problems? How do our culturally established cures compare with the practices of modern western medicine? What are the current public-health institutions doing that works and doesn't work? Which institutions are closest to the community and which are removed? How should health care in our community be funded, regionally and nationally? What kinds of changes would we make in key institutions for increased access and improvements in quality? What would it cost to test, then establish our ideas into programs, and how would we finance them? What other kinds of resources could we engage?

"I would get to these questions through a series of discussions, or study groups; each discussion informed by local and broader research conducted by members each discussion designed as a tool for simultaneous use by the lead organizations to raise consciousness, analysis and proposals for change...."

Based on her community-based experiences with PUEBLO, Sen proposes that a process which really engaged communities of color would result in a list of ideas that would include the following:

- Comprehensive programs for peer education.
- Free or low-cost food programs that provide fresh, nutritious food.
- Health-care options indigenous to cultures of color, generally ignored or blatantly dismissed by the American medical establishment.

- Open space and organized (non)competitive and individual athletics activities, particularly for girls.
- Attractive, clean, and prolific public transportation.

How does Sen approach the process of teaching-learning? What strategies for participation does she use? What elements of "systematization" and "diagnosis" can you identify here? How does her approach fit with the practice of social justice work? How does her vision of health care fit with or challenge your own?

Learning about People in Familial, Communal, and Historical Contexts

Let's turn now to approaches to learning about people's contextual experience. Considerable attention has been paid to an ecosystems approach to individuals in the context of family, with assessment focusing on two broad dimensions: family history and relationship to other systems in the environment (Garvin & Seabury, 1997, p. 216). Social workers have developed and utilized a number of assessment tools grounded in an ecosystems perspective and designed to help us learn about people's experiences in families and communities. We introduce and describe three commonly used tools here: the ecomap, genogram, and the social network map and grid.[5]

The Ecomap. This tool provides an opportunity for identifying, illustrating, and examining key aspects of a person's social context, sources of support and stress, flows of energy and resources, and patterns among them (Hartman & Laird, 1983). Generally, the tool is used in a context of dialogue between social worker and "client." With the help of prompts and questions posed by the social worker, the client maps out her current situation. Figure 6.1 illustrates the ecomap.

In the map, the "client" identifies people and social systems that are part of or that affect her current life situation. She links the systems to herself (and, possibly) to one another with lines that mark the direction of energy and resource flow in the relationship and the nature of the relationship. For example: a solid, bold line (———) indicates a strong relationship; a dotted line (- - - - -) indicates

FIGURE 6.1

Ecomap

Fill in connections where they exist.
Indicate nature of connections:
—— for strong, ----- for tenuous, +++++ for stressful
Draw arrows along lines to show flow of energy.
Identify important people and fill in empty circles as needed.

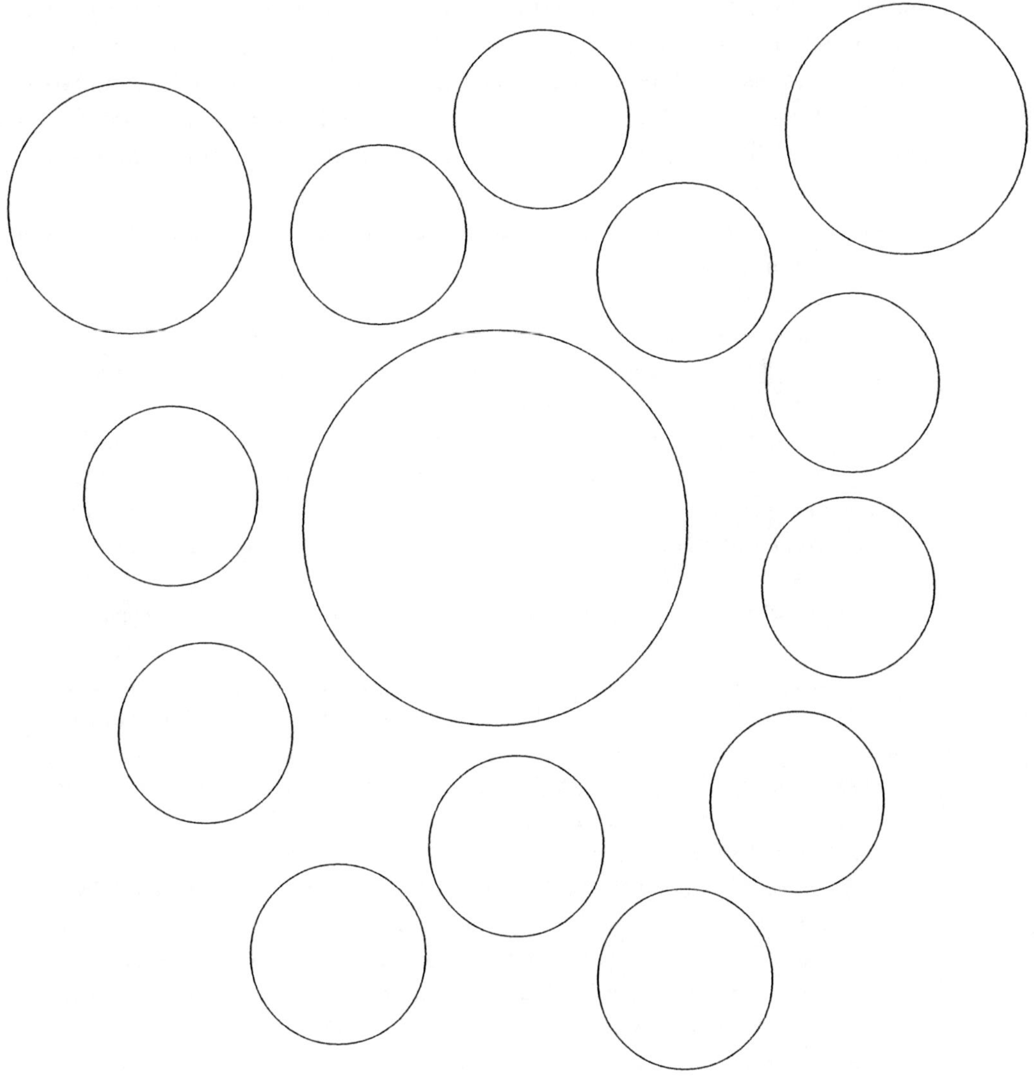

a tenuous relationship; and a slashed line (-/-/-/-/) indicates a stressful or conflicted relationship. Arrows are used to indicate the directions of energy and resource flow (toward the client, away from her, or a two-way flow). The ecomap provides a visual window into the person's current life circumstances.

The map imposes little and allows for the person drawing it to illustrate her own social relationships and consider the patterns that connect. It can create openings for teaching-learning dialogue. However, the ecomap only gives us a glimpse of a moment in time, with little sense of history or of the larger structural arrangements and practices that may have shaped the immediate context and relationships illustrated in the map. Take a moment to think about the ecomap as a resource for social justice work. Where do you see its possibilities? Its limitations? How might you modify this tool to fit particular teaching-learning situations?

Janet Finn shares a teaching-learning experience that offered a different way to envision the ecomap:

> *In my first year of teaching an undergraduate social work practice course, I spent one class period introducing and discussing the ecomap. The class members were to prepare their own ecomaps over the course of the next week. One of my students was a young woman who was blind. We had previously discussed ways to make the classroom and the learning experience more accessible. She had already taught me a great deal about being a better teacher for all students in the class, not only those with disabilities. She stopped me after class and said she would like to try her hand at reinventing the ecomap. She wanted to explore ways to make it meaningful for other people who are blind. The following week she returned with an ecomap that captured the attention and imagination of the entire class. She had created a mobile with index cards and paper plates indicating people and systems. Interlocking paper clips lent material force to conflicted relationships while rubber bands linked people and systems in flexible and reciprocal relationships. Delicate threads represented tenuous connections. Each plate and card contained information in Braille about the person or system. The student became the teacher and gave her classmates and me an opportunity to see the ecomap from a different perspective. Her creativity sparked that of others who began to wonder out loud about alternatives. For example, class members talked about the potential to engage children in creating their ecomaps in the form of mobiles or other creative designs. We not only gained knowledge about a single tool, but we also gained knowledge of the possibilities that emerge from co-learning.*

The Genogram. Another commonly cited social work tool for learning about individuals in the context of family is the genogram. The genogram borrows from anthropological kinship studies and focuses on the mapping of intergenerational family relationships (Hartman, 1978). Proponents of the genogram see it as an important complement to the ecomap. The genogram contributes a historical perspective lacking in the ecomap. It can also serve as the base for exploration and discussion of family relations, cultural practices, and traditions. The genogram focuses on the intergenerational extended family, and it is represented visually as a "family tree." The genogram is created in a collaborative teaching-learning process with social worker and "client." It includes basic information including the ages of family members, marriages, divorces, separations, and deaths. It may be elaborated to include additional information such as place of birth, employment, etc. The product represents a "client-centered" perspective on her family and her relation to family members.

Figure 6.2 gives an example of a genogram representing three generations. The following symbols are used in creating the genogram: Males are represented by squares and females by circles. A straight horizontal line connecting two people indicates a marriage (———). Cross slashes through the line indicate divorce (–/–/–/–). Some people use a dotted line to indicate cohabitation as opposed to marriage (. . . . .). The children of a particular union form the next tier of circles and squares and are listed oldest to youngest from left to right.

The genogram can provide a foundation to facilitate discussion about family relations, history, patterns, struggles, and support. Some people improvise with the genogram, adding on components of the ecomap and finding ways to visually represent additional information. According to Garvin and Seabury (1997, p. 228), the genogram is helpful in gathering the following assessment information:

- What behavioral patterns have occurred in the family that have persisted through several generations?
- What are the sources of mutual reinforcement of values in the family as well as sources of value conflict?
- What resources exist that are or could be of help to the family subsystem incorporating the client system?
- What are the kinds of issues related to the family's beliefs and common experiences that function either to limit the family's problem solving and decision making or to enhance it?

FIGURE 6.2

Genogram

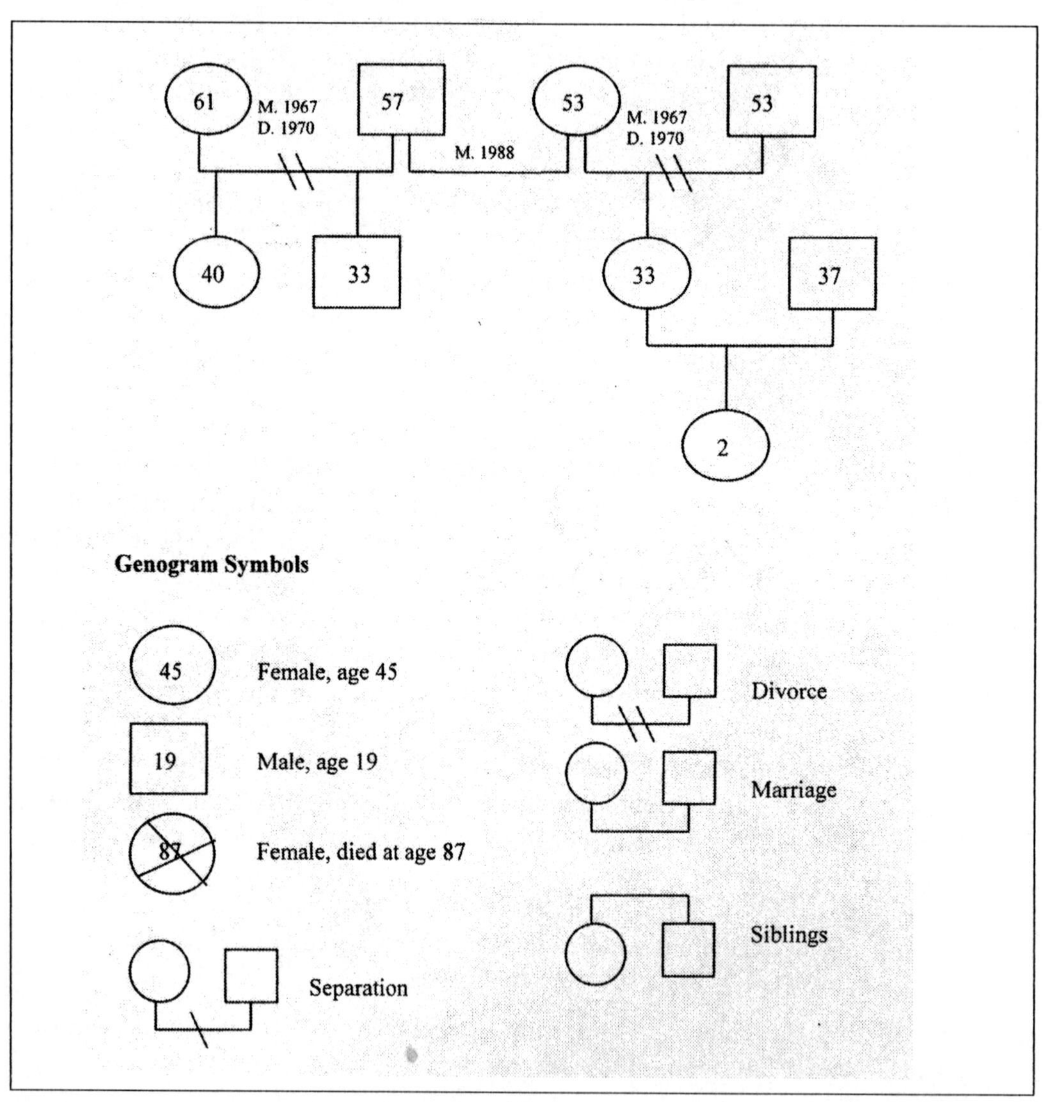

Mapping Your Family Story

Take time outside of class to prepare your own genogram. Feel free to make it as simple or elaborate as you wish, according to what best represents your concept and experience of "family." After you have completed the genogram take time to reflect on the feelings this exercise evoked for you. Are there gaps in your knowledge of family history? Do you have questions about who counts as "family" and where to draw the boundaries? Does the exercise bring back memories of loss? What have you learned from your own experience in completing the genogram that may heighten your critical awareness about using this tool with others?

Janet Finn notes: *Class discussions around the genogram have been provocative. Some have chosen to map their genogram on a 3 x 5 index card, while others have used yards of newsprint. Some people have found themselves profoundly moved by memories of a deceased loved one. Some have found the exercise to be an opening for hearing the untold stories of their ancestors. Others have found it difficult to map ties to family that have been fraught with tension. People whose experience in family has been one of numerous separations and recombinations have difficulty mapping their complex histories. They have said they would need color-coded transparencies to do justice to their "family tree." Some have chosen to include social or "fictive" kin – close friends and neighbors who have become part of family through ties of reciprocity and social support. Those with histories in adoptive and foster families have sometimes found themselves wary of a genogram – Who and what counts as "family"? To whom? Others have commented on the representations of marriage and heterosexual partnerships in the textbook illustrations of genograms that indirectly communicate a norm of what counts as a "proper" family. Take a few minutes to reflect on your genogram in light of these experiences. Which ones resonate for you? Why? What can we learn here from others' experience with the genogram about diversity and difference?*

The Social Network Map. Now let's consider the Social Network Map, a tool developed for assessing social support (Tracy & Whitakker, 1990). The developers note that while social networks play important roles in people's lives and a person-in-environment approach dominates social work, tools for assessing these networks have been lacking. Most assessment focuses on the individual and her problems rather than on the context and its possibilities. The Social Network Map was developed as part of a research and development initiative called the Family Support Project (Whitakker, Schinke, & Gilchrist, 1986). The developers argue that the Social Network Map gives more detailed attention to both structure and function of social relationships than does the ecomap. Participants complete both the map (Figure 6.3), which gathers information on the size and composition of the person's social network, and a grid (Figure 6.4), which adds specificity to network functions (Tracy & Whitakker, 1990, p. 464). The person completing the map writes in the names or initials of network members in each of seven domains: household, family/relatives, friends, people from work or school, people from clubs, organizations, or religious groups, neighbors, and agencies or formal services providers. The social worker plays the role of guide in the process, explaining the map and facilitating discussion about the process and the network.

Once the map is completed, the social worker facilitates discussion around completion of the Social Network Grid. The grid provides an opportunity for the person to consider each member of her social network, the types of support available (emotional, informational, material); the degree to which the members are supportive or critical of her; the direction of help; the closeness of the relationship; the frequency of contact, and the length of the relationships. The individuals listed on the pie chart are listed on the first column of the grid. The social worker and participant talk about the kinds of support each member of the network provides. The social worker facilitates the question posing and encourages reflection and elaboration by the person completing the map and grid.

The developers report that the Map is helpful in identifying and assessing stressors, strains, and resources in a person's social environment. The process of completing the map also helps people identify potential resources. It also may serve as a catalyst for discussion of other issues and relationships important in a person's life.[6]

Applying the Social Network Map

Work in pairs, with one person completing the Social Network Map and one serving as guide and facilitator in the process. Who is included in the network? What are the strengths and resources of the social network? Where are the gaps in support? Is there reciprocity of support? Which network members are the most supportive? The least? What are some of the barriers to using the identified and potential resources of social support? What thoughts and feelings did the Social Network Map evoke for each of the participants? What do you see as the strengths of this tool? The limitations? What values and assumptions inform this tool? Might this tool facilitate teaching-learning? How so?

FIGURE 6.3

Social Network Map

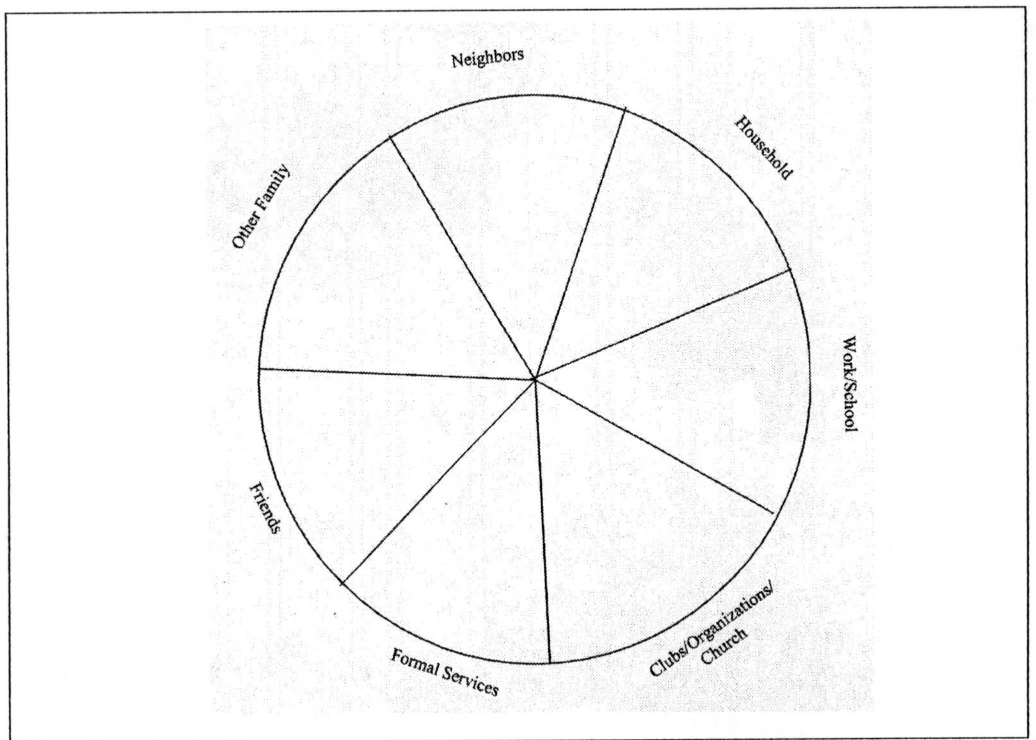

Rethinking Family

As the examples of assessment tools discussed above indicate, many social work models of the family and family dynamics have been informed by an ecological perspective and the language of systems. At times the individual is described as a part of a "subsystem" and at other times the family is referred to as a systemic whole, a single-interest unit. Critics have argued that the concept of family has

FIGURE 6.4

Social Network Grid

Respondent:____________ Name	#	**Area of Life** 1. Household 2. Other Family 3. Work/School 4. Organization 5. Other friends 6. Neighbors 7.Professionals 8. Other	**Concrete Support** 1.Hardly ever 2.Sometimes 3.Almost always	**Emotional Support** 1 Hardly ever 2.Sometimes 3.Almost always	**Information or Advice** 1.Hardly ever 2.Sometimes 3.Almost always	**Critical** 1.Hardly ever 2.Sometimes 3.Almost always	**Direction of Help** 1.Goes both ways 2.You to them 3.They to you	**Closeness** 1.Not very close 2.Sort of close 3.Very close	**How often seen** 0.Does not see 1.Few times/yr. 2.Monthly 3.Weekly 4.Daily	**How long known** 1.Less than 1yr 2.1-5 yrs. 3.More than 5yrs
	01									
	02									
	03									
	04									
	05									
	06									
	07									
	08									
	09									
	10									
	11									
	12									
	13									
	14									
	15									

often been assumed rather than defined in social work research and practice. The prototype is often the nuclear family, described as an enduring social institution established by ties of marriage and blood that link heterosexual parents and their offspring. Around that core we elaborate "alternative" forms such as single parent, stepparent, extended, and more reluctantly, gay and lesbian families. The richness of extended kinship systems, sustained among diverse cultural groups despite disruptive social and political pressures, remains largely on the margins of social work knowledge (see Baca Zinn, 1990; Cross, 1986; Stack, 1974). Social justice work challenges us to expand our thinking and practice regarding the meaning and making of family.

Meanings of Family

The contested terrain of what constitutes "family" is reflected in debates over definitions. Take a moment to think about how you would define "family"? What does family mean to you? What are the features that distinguish "family"? Do those features reflect an ideal of what family should be more than the real-life experience of family? Write your own definition of family. Get together with a small group of classmates and compare your definitions. See if you can come to consensus on a definition of family. One way of conceiving of family is as an arena of struggle where power, intimacy, conflict, and support play out in shaping gendered and generational relations. How does this conception of family fit with your group's definition?

The assessment tools addressed above offer space for considering relations beyond the nuclear family and for locating families in a larger social context. However, they offer little guidance for critical reflection on the negotiating of power and difference along gender and generational lines within families, or the ways historical, political, and economic forces differently shape the structures and practices of family life (Finn, 1998b, p. 214). Let's turn now to a few assessment tools that address questions of difference and diversity among individuals and families.

Culturagram. Elaine Congress (1994) describes the "Culturagram" as a tool developed to assess and empower culturally diverse families and challenge the impositions of a white, middle-class perspective encoded in many assessment tools. The culturagram is designed to supplement the ecomap and genogram. The assessment tool responds to the trends in immigration to the U.S. since the 1970s. The tool encourages movement beyond generalizations about difference to an appreciation of specific histories, cultural experiences, and circumstances. The concept of "culture" that informs the tool incorporates "institutions, language, religious ideals, habits of thinking, artistic expressions, and patterns of social and interpersonal relationships" (Lum, 1992: p. 62 cited in Congress, 1994, p. 533). The culturagram addresses the following topics:

- Reasons for immigration
- Length of time in the community
- Legal or undocumented status
- Age at time of immigration
- Language spoken at home and in the community
- Contact with cultural institutions
- Health beliefs
- Holidays and special events
- Impact of crisis events
- Values about family, education, and work

The culturagram provides a framework for collectively exploring a range of significant issues. It provides a guide by which the social worker can engage in co-learning about personal, cultural, political, and historical experiences with people who have immigrated to the U.S. Completion of the culturagram with individual family members or in an inclusive discussion with family members may reveal significant differences among them. The culturagram can help the social worker learn about the diversity of cultural beliefs among family members at the same time that members can learn from one another. That knowledge may be helpful in understanding differences and mediating conflicts. The culturagram can provide a platform for dialogue and participation. Congress writes: "Their involvement may empower family members by helping them see themselves and their cultural background as important…it can also be used to suggest social work interventions" (Congress, 1994, p. 537). Congress contends that the culturagram enables social workers to:

FIGURE 6.5

Culturagram (Congress, 1994)

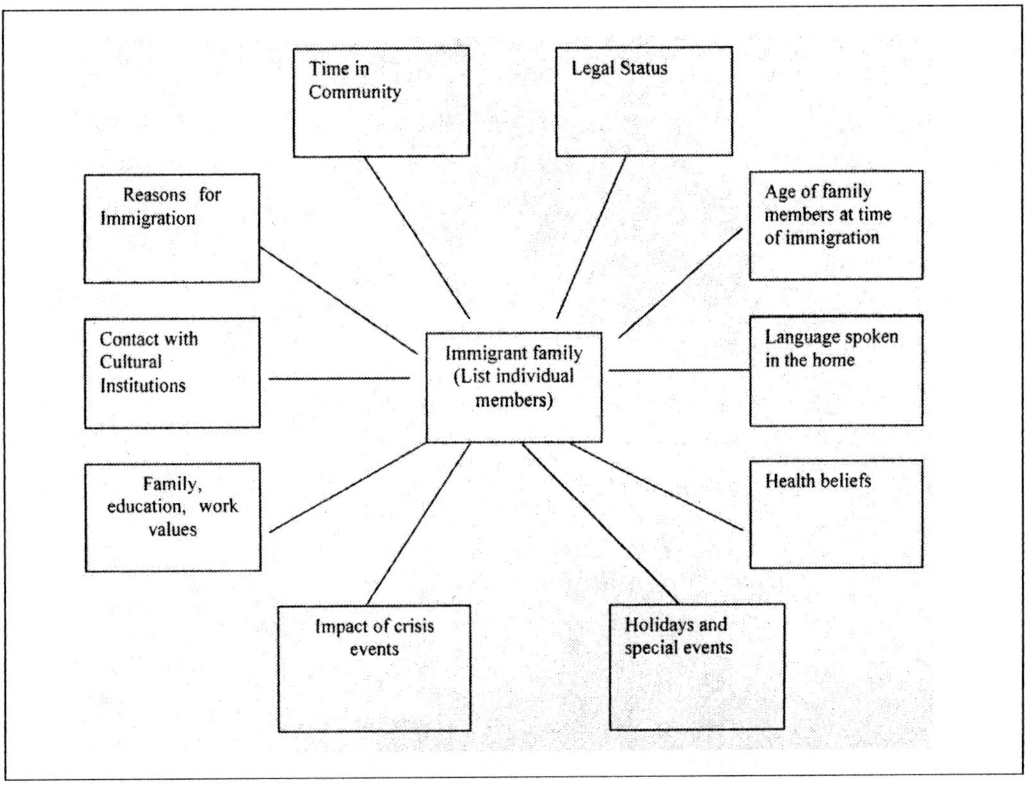

- Understand the complexities of culture as it affects families.
- Individualize families beyond cultural generalizations.
- Become sensitive to the daily experience of culturally diverse families.
- Develop differential assessments of family members.
- Involve the family in understanding its cultural background.

What do you see as the potential strengths of the culturagram? The limitations? How might it contribute to the teaching-learning process?

Gendergram. Another innovative approach to assessment that disrupts taken-for-granted notions and sparks critical dialogue is the "gendergram" developed by White and Tyson-Rawson (1995). It brings a gender lens to the process of family assessment and helps us identify significant experiences, events, and people that shaped the construction of our gendered identities in formative years. The developers write:

> The gendergram targets and separates out the influence of same and other-sex relationships on the gender role development of system members across generations and over the critical developmental transitions that highlight the characteristics of relationships over time. The focus of work with the gendergram is to make overt the assumptions about gender roles that pervade, but are typically unidentified in family systems. (White & Tyson-Rawson, 1995, p. 253)

Through a collaborative process the social worker and participant uncover and explore the learning related to gender as a result of these life events and relationships. They examine such questions as: What messages were received and internalized about what it means to be male or female? What cultural expectations were conveyed? What sorts of gendered patterns of interaction played out?

The gendergram provides a foundation for rich teaching-learning as the often unspoken assumptions and expectations of gender become a "talkable" subject. White and Tyson-Rawson (1995) note:

> Gender-related themes and issues are interwoven with many of the challenges that couples and families face, including power, control, sexuality, intimacy, money, equity, and violence. Assessing the role of gender in these issues is critical because it broadens the context of the issues and pushes members of the couple or family to examine the gender-related beliefs or stereotypes that may be contributing to the problem. (p. 257)[7]

Kinscripts. In her classic ethnography, *All Our Kin (*1974), anthropologist Carol Stack documented the networks of exchange and support through which poor African American women and men maintained extended bonds of kinship that crossed biological, generational, and household boundaries. She brought a "strengths perspective" to understanding the intersections of race, gender, and economy in the construction of family long before "strengths" was a buzz word of social work. She challenged beliefs about poverty as "pathology" and demonstrated the dynamic ways in which people crafted supportive relations and practices of kinship because and in spite of the many forces working against them. She later collaborated with Linda Burton (Stack & Burton, 1993) on development of the "kinscripts framework" as one approach to understanding the interdependence of the individual and family life course within a historical and political context.

The kinscripts framework is based on three assumptions: 1) the life courses of individuals and families are interdependent entities; 2) the life courses of families and individuals are shaped within social, cultural, and historical contexts; and 3) the life course of families involves blood and non-blood relatives who mutually share a perception of their inclusion in the family and interact accordingly (Stack & Burton, 1993, p. 160). The kinscripts framework addresses the temporal nature of the life course and the interdependence of lives. The concepts of family time and family timetables are central to the framework. Stack and Burton write: "Family timetables are representations of the shared understandings and interdependencies within kinship structures. They are, in essence, scripts that the entire family embraces about the flow of events in the life–cycle" (p. 160). The framework draws attention to family scripts, the mental representations that guide role performance of family members, and the dynamics and tensions negotiated among family members in response to these scripts.

Stack and Burton present "kinscripts" as a framework for family research. It merits consideration as a framework for teaching-learning about family experience as well. The kinscripts framework looks to the interplay of social structures, family norms and beliefs, and individual behaviors over the life course. The authors argue that a focus on both kinship and the life course "offers a more comprehensive view of the interlocking pathways of families as members influencing one another's life choices" (Stack & Burton, 1993, p. 158). The kinscripts framework builds an understanding of family drawn from multigenerational ethnographic study of low-income African-American families in the United States. Thus the understanding of family is not imposed on the basis of dominant norms, it emerges through learning about people's experiences of kinship over time. Attention to kinship in historical perspective allows insight into the impact of particular political and economic conditions on the individual and the family life course. The kinscripts framework does not translate readily into a simple "assessment tool," rather it provides another basis for posing critical questions about family that disrupt taken-for-granted assumptions and open us to engagement with issues of meaning, context, power, history, and possibility.

Learning through Difference

Throughout this chapter we have encouraged a collaborative approach to teaching-learning that appreciates different ways of knowing and being in the world. We agree with Reed et al. (1997) that social justice work demands that we move beyond "diversity" and actively engage with the meaning and power of difference. Encounters with radically different worldviews and belief systems remind us of the partiality of our knowledge and challenge us as learners. At the end of this chapter we include an example of an assessment that engages us in learning from and through difference. We hope it promotes critical reflection and discussion about the possibilities of co-learning that emerge once we break out of our assumptions and engage difference.

Difference and the Cultural Meaning of Illness. While we may verbalize an appreciation of cultural difference, the proof is in the practice, when our most deeply held and unquestioned beliefs are challenged. In this section we consider a case where fundamentally different systems regarding the meaning of health and illness collide, with tragic results. Understandings of health, illness, prevention, and treatment are embedded in cultural systems. They cannot be understood outside of an appreciation of those meaning systems. Cultural meaning systems shape how we learn to categorize "symptoms" into an illness, where we look to explain causality, and who we turn to for cures.

In her book *The Spirit Catches You and You Fall Down,* Anne Fadiman (1997) tells the poignant story of Lia Lee, a Hmong child diagnosed with "epilepsy," and the cultural collisions that occur between her family and her American doctors as they give meaning to and seek to treat her illness. Her newly arrived refugee parents understand illness as "soul loss." They seek aid from Shamans; but also, as they struggle to make a life in the U.S., they try to follow some "American" expectations regarding illness and healing. Lia's California doctors understand illness through the belief system of Western bio-medicine and intervene based on their own expertise. While both the family and the doctors want the best for the child, the lack of understanding between them has tragic consequences.

Fadiman educates readers about the culture and history of the Hmong people. She critically examines the power of medical institutions and state bureaucracies to force compliance when the dominant view of proper intervention is challenged by cultural difference. Fadiman sought out help from a medical anthropologist in trying to understand and perhaps bridge the gulf of incomprehension that separated the Lee family and the practitioners of western bio-medicine. Fadiman writes:

> Trying to understand Lia and her family by reading her medical chart (something I spent hundreds of hours doing) was like deconstructing a love sonnet by reducing it to a series of syllogisms. Yet to the residents and pediatricians who had cared for her since she was three months old, there was no guide to Lia *except* her chart. As each of them struggled to make sense of a set of problems that were not expressible in the language they knew, the chart simply grew longer and longer, until it contained more than 400,000 words. Every one of those words reflected its author's intelligence, training, and good intentions, but not one single one dealt with the Lee's perception of their daughter's illness. (p. 260)

The "Patient's Explanatory Model." Fadiman turned to the work of physician and medical anthropologist Arthur Kleinman to better understand the difference of cultural meanings and the meaning of cultural differences here. Kleinman (1980) has designed a set of eight questions to help elicit the "patient's explanatory model." The questions are simple and seemingly obvious. And yet, they are so seldom asked. Taken-for-granted assumptions about the problem and the possibilities of intervention too often get in the way. However, posing these questions can open a new terrain of teaching-learning. The answers can be rich in material to promote understanding of cultural difference and disrupt the certainties informed by a Western biomedical view. Here are Klienman's questions:

- What do you call the problem?
- What do you think has caused the problem?
- Why do you think it started when it did?
- What do you think the sickness does? How does it work?
- How severe is the sickness? Will it have a short or long course?
- What kind of treatment do you think the patient should receive? What are the most important results you hope she receives from this treatment?
- What are the chief problems the sickness has caused?
- What do you fear most from this sickness? (Kleinman (1980), in Fadiman, pp. 260-61).

Take a minute to reflect on these questions. What fundamental issues of difference do they address? What basic assumptions do they challenge? What are some implications for teaching-learning in a context of cultural difference? What sorts of questions do they suggest for use in the context of social justice work?

Assessing the Assessment Tools

This exercise gives you an opportunity to learn about the ways practitioners in your community assess problems and strengths. As a class, identify five or six areas of social work practice that you want to learn more about (e.g. child welfare, aging, mental health; school social work, etc). Break into groups, with each group focused on one of the identified practice areas. In the small group, identify several local agencies or groups that address this area and divide the list among group members. Each member takes responsibility for contacting an agency or organization, arranging a time to discuss the assessment process with an organizational representative, and requesting copies of tools, forms, or guidelines used in making an assessment. Reconvene in small groups to assess the assessment tools. The following questions serve as a guide, however, new questions may arise from the group discussions.

- What values are reflected in the tool?
- What assumptions are made about the cause of problems and directions for intervention?
- What assumptions are made about the person or group being assessed (e.g. assumptions about age, gender, ability, etc.)?
- What aspects of a person's life are addressed? What aspects are not addressed?
- Does the tool take a problem-focused approach?
- How are strengths addressed?
- What is the norm against which "deviance" is assessed?
- What sort of language does the tool use?
- Does the tool promote participation in the assessment process?
- What do you see as the possible strengths of this tool? The possible limitations?
- How would you assess the tools in terms of the criteria outlined by Rosemary Link in Chapter Three (p. 128)?

Chapter Summary

In this chapter we have developed the concept of teaching-learning – a collaborative process through which we give meaning to experience, learn about concerns, and systematically develop, share, and reflect on knowledge of those concerns. We have addressed the importance of teamwork in the teaching-learning process and outlined the foundational skills for effective group work. We have examined questions of power and power relations in the teaching-learning process and have pointed to the importance of making power a talkable theme. We have introduced a number of approaches for systematic inquiry into organizational and community contexts of social work practice and for learning about people in familial, communal, and historical context. We have challenged readers to question taken-for-granted assumptions regarding notions of family and offer possibilities for systemically learning about gender, culture, power and difference in the context of family. In Chapter Seven we consider the possibilities for translating the process and outcomes of teaching-learning into concrete action plans. As Cecilia Díaz (1995) reminds us, action and reflection will yield new understandings and bring us to new points of departure for further teaching-learning.

Case Study: Life and Death in Libby, Montana[8]

Libby, Montana, is nestled in a valley in the Northwest corner of the state, alongside the Kootenai River. For generations many of Libby's 12,000 residents have made a living in the timber and mining industries. In the past decade, the bottom dropped out of the local economy when the local saw mill closed and the W. R. Grace and Company's vermiculite mine shut down. Residents have tried to rebuild their dwindling economy around the possibilities of tourism and the hopes of selling their enticing scenery and their proximity to prime fishing and hunting spots and the famous landscape of Glacier National Park, only a couple of hours away. But a more troubling danger lurked in the shadows of Libby's history, one that was taking its toll in the lives of hundreds of residents.

For the past forty years, disease has claimed the lungs and lives of residents throughout the valley. Many miners and their family members were suffering and dying from asbestosis, a terrible disease resulting from asbestos exposure that causes a thickening of the lungs and slow death from suffocation. Others were suffering from tumors, cancers, and other respiratory illnesses. Miners at the W.R. Grace vermiculite plant would come home from work each day with their clothes and bodies covered in a fine white dust. The dust settled in their homes, on their furniture, and on the bodies of their loved ones. Their wives breathed it in even as they tried to clean it up. Their children inhaled it as they hugged their fathers and played on the living room floor. W. R. Grace told its workers the dust was merely a nuisance. What the company knew and did not reveal was that the dust was actually microscopic asbestos fibers that would settle in their lungs and eventually sentence them to death (Vollers & Barnett, 2000).

Nearly 100 asbestos related-deaths have been documented in Libby since 1960, and hundreds of other residents have been debilitated by the disease. At least one in forty residents has died from or suffers from asbestos-related illness (Vollers & Barnett, 2000, p. 54). In December 1999, after hundreds of people had been stricken with lung problems, and after a local family filed suit against W.R. Grace over their mother's death, the Environmental Protection Agency finally launched an investigation. Their evidence points to the W. R. Grace mining operation as the source of Libby's massive health crisis. While the mine and mill workers suffered the greatest exposure, the rest of the town also got daily exposure. Mine dust was dumped down the mountainside and poured into the air from the plant's ventilation stack. "By W.R. Grace's own estimates, some 5,000 pounds or more of asbestos were released each day. On still days, some of it settled back on the mine site. When the wind blew from the east, a film of white dust covered the town" (Vollers & Barnett, 2000, p. 55). Moreover, vermiculite ore packed with lethal concentrations of asbestos was packaged for export at a plant next to the town's baseball diamonds. The area was surrounded with piles of discarded ore. Libby residents, unaware of the risks, carted bags of the discarded ore home for their gardens. Vermiculate itself is harmless. It has been used in insulation and in potting soil. But the vermiculite deposit at Libby is laced with tremolite – the most toxic form of asbestos. W.R. Grace and Company knew the dangers of asbestos. They did not inform the people of Libby, and they did not offer effective safeguards to miners and residents.

For the past two years, Libby residents have been submitted to X-ray screenings to determine the state of their health. The EPA team continues to assess the extent of the damage done to people and the environment. Some political leaders have expressed their outrage that an entire community has suffered from the unconscionable acts of a single company. Other political leaders have met behind the scenes with company executives, trying to find a "quiet" solution to the toxic problem that would not hurt business interests and relations. Libby residents themselves struggle with the toxic realities of the asbestos contamination and the implications for individual, family, and community survival. Some take a fatalistic approach, and argue that mining has historically been dangerous work, and this is one more story in the tough saga of labor history. Some who have been untouched by the illness worry that the problem may be blown out of proportion. Some watch their loved ones struggling for each breath or witness the telltale signs in X-rays of their own lungs, and wonder when the inevitable symptoms will begin. Many simply want their town cleaned up and fear that the ongoing media attention to Libby's toxic troubles will further endanger an already precarious local economy.

During the summer of 2001, public debate centered around who should clean up the town. While there is nearly unanimous agreement that W.R. Grace must be held accountable, few trust the company to take charge of the clean up. The alternative is the designation of Libby as an Environmental Protection Agency (EPA) "Superfund" Cleanup site, with the EPA responsible for overseeing cleanup. Some residents have as little faith in the government's ability to do the job as they have in W.R. Grace. Some fear the mere designation of Libby as a "Superfund site" will drive away the tourist trade. Others fear that each passing day without action leaves them and their loved ones in harm's way. There is no doubt that asbestos has taken a tremendous physical, social, economic, and political toll. What is less clear is how those affected can best participate in the multiple levels of decision making that affect their health and lives. What issues of social justice work can you identify here? What questions of meaning, context, power, history, and possibility come to mind? What might be possible roles for social justice work in the community? What issues of difference might you confront?

Vollers, M. & Barnett, A. (2000) "Libby's Deadly Grace," *Mother Jones* (May/June): 53-59, 87

Questions for Discussion

1. What are the ten mutual aid group processes and how do they relate to the core process of teaching/learning?
2. What is the significance of power in relationship to the teaching/learning core process?
3. How does functional non-capitulation relate to worker empowerment? What might be some constraints and possibilities with regard to the practice of functional non-capitulation?
4. How would you proceed in developing a plan for building community involvement in health care in your community? How would you assess the situation? Who would you involve? Why?
5. Choose one of the methods of systematic inquiry discussed in the chapter and explain how you would apply this method in practice.
6. In what ways have your beliefs about health and illness been informed by a Western biomedical view? In what ways have your beliefs been informed by differing perspectives on health and illness? Think for a moment about some of the "folk" practices of medicine in your experience, such as your cure for hiccups. What beliefs inform these practices?
7. You have had the opportunity to apply Díaz's Five-Step Process to a current issue in your community. In what other contexts might you use the process? Give an example.

Suggested Readings

Barber, J. (1995). "Politically progressive casework." *Families in Society: The Journal of Contemporary Human Services*, 76(1), 30-37.

Fadiman, A. (1997). *The spirit catches you and you fall down.* New York: Farrar, Strauss, and Giroux.

Reisch, M., Wenocur, S. & Sherman, W. (1981). "Empowerment, conscientization, and animation as core social work skills." *Social Development Issues*, 5(2/3), 108-120.

Solomon, B. (1976). *Black empowerment.* New York: Columbia University Press.

Stack, C. (1974). *All our kin: Strategies for survival in a black community.* New York: Harper and Row.

Townsend, J., Zapata, E., Rowlands, J., Alberti, R., & Mercado, M. (1999). *Women and power: Fighting patriarchies and poverty.* London: Zed Books.

Werner, D. (1977). *Where there is no doctor.* Palo Alto: Hesperian Foundation.

Chapter 7

Action and Accompaniment

"It was so important. It was really a beautiful thing, women coming together to work together. We started small and we learned everything. We learned we were capable, we could do this. We talked and laughed and it was so special. It was a road to a new life of learning. It was a beautiful experience working and learning together, block by block, helping each other."

Pobladora (1999), Villa Paula Jaraquemada, Chile[1]

"Working together to build community means that we will want to plan, predict, manoeuvre, disagree, change, adapt, and strengthen or preserve what is important to us. If we did not – if we expected everyone to behave in the same way – community building would be enslavement, not liberation."

Anthony Kelly and Sandra Sewell (1988), *With Head, Heart, and Hand*[2]

Chapter Overview

In this chapter we explore the interwoven processes of action and accompaniment. Action entails the diverse activities of planning, decision-making, mobilizing resources, motivating participants, and following through in creating change. Action occurs in the company of others. A challenge of social justice work is the integration of being in relationship with others, doing the work, and becoming more critically aware and capable in the process. It is in this spirit of being, doing, and becoming that we pair action and accompaniment. We want to challenge a view of action as technical implementation and consider it instead as always carried out in the context of social relationships. So we emphasize accompaniment as part of the change process as a reminder once again that we are not "Lone Rangers." The relational aspect of social justice work demands ongoing attention and respect. We address roles of social justice workers, skills of practice, strategies for participatory planning and decision-making, creative forms of social enactment, and approaches to conflict resolution. We consider the practice of accompaniment and provide examples of accompanying the process of change. We focus on strategies and possibilities for teamwork and collective action rather than on "person-changing" interventions. We argue that the contributions of social justice workers can best be realized through concerted action with others who have a stake in the process. We emphasize here the strategies and skills for carrying out collective efforts.

Coming to Action

Social work is about change, and change means taking action. Change can provoke feelings of excitement, empowerment, and elation, but it can also churn up feelings of insecurity and fear. What does it mean to take action for the people with whom we work and ourselves? Gaining a better sense of how this works personally can help us come to a better understanding of what change and taking action might be like for those with whom we work. Consider one of the exercises below as it applies to you and your situation.

(1) Think of a time you were compelled to take action on an issue of concern. Perhaps you had a talk with an employer about getting a raise in pay. Perhaps you took the car keys away from a friend who had too much to drink. Or maybe you wrote a letter to the editor of your hometown newspaper voicing concern about welfare reform policies that pushed people into low paying jobs and did nothing to raise them out of poverty. What emotions propelled you into action? What decision-making process did you go through that got you to this point? How did others respond to your action, and how did this affect you?

(2) Certainly, many of us *think* of taking action against troubling policies, procedures, or events that have life-altering affects on peoples' lives. However, we stop ourselves short by thinking the issue is much too big to tackle or that someone else will take care of it for us. Think of a time

when you noticed something that disturbed you in your community or neighborhood. Maybe it was the litter scattered along the highway, or the need for a traffic light at a particularly dangerous intersection. What issues or concerns come to mind? What emotions kept you from taking action? What decision-making process did you go through that got you to this point? Were there any responses to your decision, and if so, how did these affect you? Discuss these exercises in class in small groups. Those who did Exercise 1 can generate a list of reasons people get involved in action, and those in who completed Exercise 2 can generate a list of reasons people use to stop themselves from taking action. Remember to catalogue both the intellectual and emotional responses to your scenarios of action and inaction. What did you learn about taking action in your discussion?

The Thinking and Skills of Action

Rethinking Social Work Roles

We start the discussion of action and accompaniment with consideration of the different parts social justice workers may play in the change process. Social workers are generally prepared to play a variety of professional "roles," shaped by both organizational mission and the worker's position and responsibilities therein. Roles are also shaped by the definition of the "problem" and determined course of action. Most likely, you have been introduced to a number of social work roles such as broker, counselor, and case manager (see for example, Sheafor, Horejsi & Horejsi, 2000, p. 55-67). We want to first reflect critically on the concept of "roles" and then outline what we see as approaches for enacting social justice work.

Discussion of roles generally addresses the workplace-related position a social worker assumes and the related expectations and activities. The role is thus viewed as separate from the particular person who fills it and carries out its "functions." It defines and delimits the activities that the worker engages in. Questions of power and meaning seldom enter into the discussion of social work roles. However, as John Coates (1992) describes, particular social work roles are associated with particular understandings of people and society, interpretations of social problems, and dynamics of power in the social work relationship. For example, Coates depicts the medical model as accepting the hierarchical nature of society and locating problem definition and intervention at the individual level. The social work relationship is top-down with a one-way flow from the social worker as "expert" and "therapist" to the passive "client." Thus, as Coates illustrates, social work roles are not neutral.

The approaches social workers take to enact their responsibilities are shaped in part by organizational expectations and job descriptions. They are also powerfully shaped by the social worker's positionality, values, and critical understanding of societal arrangements, problems, and possibilities for intervention. A role is only realized through its practice, and in that practice social workers bring their own histories, interpretations, power, and sense of possibility to bear. We outline ten roles for social justice work. We think of roles as ways of enacting our responsibilities and commitments. We argue that these roles are relevant for all contexts of social work practice. By rethinking our roles in light of the demands of social justice work, we can better address questions of power, promote meaningful participation, and expand the possibilities for transformative action.

Roles for Social Justice Work

- **Learner:** Our most fundamental and constant role is that of learner, approaching situations and relationships with openness, humility, and critical curiosity. As learners we are committed to the ongoing search for our own competence (Freire, 1990).
- **Teacher:** We not only bring our knowledge and skills to bear in the change process, we share them with others so that individuals, groups, and communities are better equipped to confront new challenges in the future. To do so we need to be effective teachers, able to engage learners and impart ideas clearly and effectively to diverse audiences.
- **Collaborator:** Co-labor is the foundation of social justice work. Our actions need to match the language of partnership. Social justice workers are not remote "advice givers." They are team members, engaging in the give and take of dialogue and action and accepting responsibilities and risks.

- **Facilitator:** With teamwork as a central tenet of practice, social justice workers require skills in facilitating group communication, decision-making, planning, and action. Whether the group in question is a family, a mutual aid group, an advisory committee, or a board of directors, skilled facilitation is key to building trust, addressing power and authority, promoting participation, and engaging in change-oriented action.
- **Animator/Activator:** We borrow the notion of animator from its French and Spanish uses as one who brings life to the change process and sparks motivation and mobilization for action. The English term activator captures some (but not all) of this spirit. The animator "stresses the individual as a shaper of his/her own destiny" (Reisch, Wenocur, & Sherman, 1981, p. 115). The animator helps sustain action through facilitative skills that recognize the power of groups coming together to create change.
- **Mediator:** Social justice work demands recognition of and respect for difference. Social justice workers will be called on to serve as mediators, working to bridge differences, craft bases of dialogue, and build critical alliances.
- **Advocate:** Social justice workers speak for the rights of those who have been historically excluded from decision-making arenas. We speak against policies, practices, and social arrangements that exacerbate, mask, or justify social injustice and inequality. This does not mean that we speak *in the place of* those living the daily realities of discrimination and oppression. Rather we stand and speak in solidarity with others.
- **Negotiator:** Critical awareness of power implies the capacity to confront conflict. As positioned actors embracing a political and ethical stance, social justice workers will face the question, "Which side are you on?" We will be called on to act as negotiators seeking the best possible outcomes for those we represent. We need to be clear about our positioning and what is at stake.
- **Researcher:** Social justice work is an integrated approach that demands ongoing critical reflection on and evaluation of our practice. The role of researcher is not something we turn over to those in the university nor something we append as an afterthought. Rather it is part of everyday practice.

- **Bricoleur:** French anthropologist Claude Levi-Strauss (1966) envisioned cultural meaning making as a process of *bricolage,* the creative process of crafting new meanings and purpose from the cultural materials at hand. People are *bricoleurs*, cultural beings with the wherewithal and imagination and sense of discovery and possibility needed to adapt and transform human and material resources in response to new challenges. We think the concept of the *bricoleur* is an apt one for social justice work. We are constantly challenged to engage with the circumstances and resources at hand, be inventive, and expand the spaces of hope.

Enacting the Roles of Social Justice Work

Take time to read the article entitled "Lost Boys of Sudan: The Newest Vermonters" by Candace Page that appears at the end of this chapter on page 318. First, consider the intersection of local and global issues and the importance of a global understanding of social work discussed in Chapter One. What challenges and opportunities for social justice work does this situation pose? What social injustices have shaped the lives of the newest Vermonters? Consider the questions of meaning, context, power, history, and possibility and their relationship to action and accompaniment that were posed in the Just Practice matrix on page 178. How would you respond to those questions regarding the situation of the "Lost Boys"? What additional questions could you pose? Now consider each of the roles addressed above. What possibilities do you see for enacting each of the roles in this context? Write down examples for each role. Get together with others, discuss your responses to the questions posed here and describe your ideas for enacting the roles of social justice work. Return for a moment to Chapter Three and the universal practice principles outlined by Rosemary Link (p. 128). What principles did you draw on in thinking through the possible roles and their enactment? How might you rethink the possibilities in light of the practice principles?

As we rethink the possibilities of social work roles we also need to rethink the skills of practice. We have addressed skills of historicizing knowledge and practice in Chapter Two; valuing in Chapter Three; theorizing and critical thinking in Chapter Four; listening, communicating, group facilitating, and consciousness raising in Chapter Five; and teaching-learning in Chapter Six. In the following sections we will address skills and practices of participatory planning and decision-making; activating and animating the change effort; promoting critical awareness and action through popular education; addressing anger and conflict; mediation and negotiation; coalition building; and policy analysis and advocacy. These become part of our repertoire as bricoleurs creating possibility from the resources at hand.

Participatory Planning

Eight Planning Moments. Social justice work calls for the participation of all of the stakeholders in planning for change. Cecilia Díaz (1997) describes participatory planning as part of the practice of democracy where people seek common interest from their individual and collective needs and work together to improve the quality of life for all. It is a process that promotes critical consciousness and self-determination. It strengthens individual and collective capacities and promotes a sense of collectivity. And it provides participants opportunities to hone and practice skills in negotiation, advocacy, and program development. Díaz (1997, pp. 15-23) describes the process of participatory planning in terms of eight "moments:"

1. **Diagnosis:** What is happening, what is the situation, who are we and what do we have? (See discussion of diagnosis in Chapter Six).
   - What is our reality? What are our needs and problems?
   - What are the causes?
   - What can we resolve ourselves? What can't we resolve ourselves?
   - What resources and capacities do we have to confront the situation?

2. **Who is involved:** Who are the various actors? What are their concerns, conditions, and interests? Where might be the common ground and important differences? This may include:
   - Residents and local social organizations
   - Local government
   - Non-governmental organizations
   - Private sector

3. **Where do we want to arrive?** What is our desired outcome? This is directly related to our hopes and values. Knowing where we want to arrive brings direction and clarity to the process of setting goals and objectives.

4. **Formulating goals and objectives:** What are our general goals for more fundamental, structural change? What do we want to accomplish in the long run? What specific objectives do we have to meet in order to get there? How viable is our general goal in light of these specific challenges? What time frame can we meet these objectives in? What will be the specific measures of our objectives? What are the concrete conditions that we need to achieve?

5. **What path are we going to take?** What is our vision of the overall journey, and what are the possible routes that we can take to get there? What route will we select and why? Who will be part of the journey? We need a vision of the parts, of the whole, and of the final goal. This involves action, tasks, responsibilities, people, and resources. For every action we need to determine what needs to be done, who is responsible for what, and what resources are needed. It involves the participation of those affected in the negotiation and decision-making process.

6. **What do we need to do in order to achieve our objectives?** What is our action plan? Díaz offers a guide for action planning:

   - **What?** Defining the action or work theme.
   - **Why?** Defining the objective. What do we want to result or where do we want to arrive?
   - **With What?** What resources (human and material) do we have, what do we need, how are we going to get them?
   - **How?** What steps and assignments have to be completed?
   - **Who?** Who are responsible?
   - **When?** What it the time frame for completion of each step and for the overall plan?

7. **Taking action:** Get to Work! In order to carry out the plans we have to engage organizational capacity and decide on a division of labor. We need to make decisions about how the implementation will be organized and overseen. Will we work in committees or task groups?

How, when, and to whom do we report? Who coordinates the overall effort? How do we maintain momentum and commitment? The action is also accompanied by ongoing analysis – are we getting the work done? What is at stake in terms of risks and opportunities? Do we need to rethink our route? This is a process of both action and reflection, wherein the information gathered along the way continually informs the action process.

8. **Evaluation, systematization, and projection of the action:** As we undertake the journey, we need to stop along the way to reflect on and learn from the experience: What gains have we made? How successfully have we fulfilled our roles and assignments? How are we confronting difficulties and conflicts? Are we meeting the goals and objectives? Díaz poses three "permanent questions" that permit us to reflect along the way: How are we doing? Are we heading where we want to go? What do we need to change? These questions may lead us to further diagnosis and systematization.

From Model to Practice. This model for participatory planning has broad applicability. It can be used in making plans with individuals and families, agency committees, advocacy groups, and community organizations. The eight "moments" follow the logic and sequencing of "top-down" approaches to planning. However, the test of a participatory model is in the practice. Is the process truly inclusive such that diverse stakeholders have a meaningful voice? Díaz presents the steps for participatory planning in inclusive, accessible language. Participatory planning efforts need to be free of jargon. Each step of the process is also a place for dialogue and teaching-learning. What does the step entail? How can its practice be illustrated with examples and images? Like most popular educators, Díaz pays close attention to these issues. She illustrates each moment with examples and figures, and she offers practical suggestions, such as the use of discussion groups, drawings, songs, newspaper murals, and socio-drama as part of the participatory process (Díaz, 1995, pp.12-14; 1997, pp. 15-23).

Participation and Difference. Now, as you may already have recognized, each step of the process may also reveal different visions, interests, and access to resources among the participants. As facilitators of and participants in the process, we can expect to encounter conflict and resistance along the way, and we need the skills and the time to identify and negotiate differences. Homan (1999, pp. 387-389) reminds us that conflict and resistance are not necessarily bad. The key is to address conflict and resistance while respecting difference. Conflict and resistance are red flags that make us pay attention to the process and may, in fact, lead to new possibilities and a more thorough analysis of the consequences of our change efforts. Homan points out that it is important to consider the sources of resistance. These can include lack of information and differing expectations and commitments and alert us to the unspoken emotional elements surrounding the work. And, as discussed in Chapter Five, resistance may stem from people's ambivalence about change and from fundamental differences in values, interests, and interpretations. Homan suggests it is best to start with the least intrusive strategies to address conflict and resistance and respond respectfully so as not to solidify and exacerbate situations and circumstances and irreparably damage existing relationships.

Who Plans?

Return to the small groups and the community issue you began to address in Chapter Six. (Or if you prefer, you may want to use the 'New Vermonters" case study at the end of this chapter or the case study of "Life and Death in Libby" at the end of Chapter Six). Go through each of the eight planning moments and consider who should participate and how you might proceed. What roles of social justice work are you likely to practice here? What might be the nature of your organizational participation as a social worker? Now, take time to assign members of your small group to play out the roles of the various participants in the process, with one of you assuming the position of social worker. Take time to think about how the reality of the situation appears from the vantage point of your particular "positionality." What are your concerns? How do you see the problem? What is at stake for you here? What do you need in this context in order to feel safe enough to speak to your concerns? How do you see your power vis a vis that of other participants? Where do you want to arrive? What path do you see to get there? The social worker has the job of facilitating initial discussion among the participants and trying to move the group through the first moment of the process. Engage in the process for 20-30 minutes and then take time to debrief. What challenges did the social worker face? What challenges did other participants face? Did issues of meaning, power, and history come to the surface in this context? How so? Were you able to identify and negotiate common ground and important differences? What sorts of decisions were you faced with? What were the possible plans? How did you do in terms of Link's universal principles of ethical practice (p. 128-129)? What feelings did the process stir for you?

Participatory Decision-Making

The change process is full of decision-making moments. Frequently, we make decisions by default as we move in a direction that "goes without saying" and fail to question our underlying assumptions. One of the most basic skills of decision-making is learning to recognize *when* and *how* we are making decisions. Social workers make seemingly mundane decisions every day, from the order in which phone calls are returned to the reports that do and don't get written, to the decision to follow up by phone or in person with a colleague or "client." Each one of these decisions is shaped by questions of meaning, context, power, and history. They, in turn, shape future possibilities. It is useful to reflect from time to time on the "micro-decisions" of our everyday practice. What can we learn about our assumptions, our practice, and ourselves?

The organizational contexts of social work practice also have histories, cultures, and protocols of decision-making. Perhaps there is a history of decision-making by decree of a director, or by default where the path of least resistance is followed. Some organizations may pride themselves on their democratic process, with decision-making by majority vote. It is important to consider what questions are put forth for a vote and the nature of the data and discussion that informs the vote. What informal relations of power might shape the voting process? Who has the right to vote, and who are affected by the outcomes? Other organizations may pride themselves on their attention to each participant's view and embrace a model of decision-making by consensus. Again, it is important to consider what questions are put forth for decision. What data and discussion inform the process? What informal relations of power might shape the consensus building process? When is silence interpreted as agreement? How is dissent addressed?

Decision-Making Processes. Groups are better prepared to make informed decisions when they have a mutual understanding of methods for decision-making and have made the initial decision regarding how group decisions will be reached. Schein (1969, p. 58 cited in Brill, 1998, p. 198) identifies six methods for decision-making, and we present them below. Schein does not suggest that there is a single "right way" to make decisions. What is important for the group process is recognition that there are multiple ways to make decisions, and that the choice of decision-making process is, in itself, a critical decision.

1. Decision-making by lack of response is one of the least desirable methods and is generally a warning signal that the team is in trouble. Lack of response indicates withdrawal, nonparticipation, and noninvolvement, and it can imply lack of commitment to the decision made. Think of an example from your own experience. How did you feel during the process? What sense of commitment did you have? What was the outcome?

2. Decision-making by authority may be appropriate in given situations, but frequently does not allow for maximum development and use of the strengths of the model. Ability to accept and work with appropriate authority is a characteristic of mature workers and is essential for good practice. Social workers in positions with powerful sanctioning authority need to be particularly mindful of the limits of their authority. What aspects of the situation are negotiable? Where is there space for other voices and views?

3. Decision-making by a minority is a process wherein a small group takes responsibility. In some instances the responsibility may be appropriately allocated, but when this is the dominant method of decision-making in a group it may indicate a misuse of power and status, a lack of involvement of other team members, and a subsequent lack of commitment to the decisions made. Think of an example from your own experience when a minority group made decisions without your participation. In what circumstances did this seem appropriate? Inappropriate? What do you see as the difference between the two?

4. Decision-making by the majority based on a vote is the most widely used method. It is effective if there is a means of considering the minority opinion. It is probably most successful when there is a general commitment to implementation of the majority decisions. Think of an instance in which you have participated in majority vote decision-making as member of the majority. How would you describe the process and outcome? Now think of a time when you were in the minority? How would you describe the process and outcome. What feelings did the first instance provoke? The second?

5. Decision-making by consensus, a natural follow-up for majority decisions, implies that team members recognize the existence of differences but agree, regardless, to act as a whole. In some consensus-based processes, a person can express disagreement, but agree to "live with" the larger consensus. A dissenting position effectively blocks the decision-making process and brings the group back to further discussion and reflection. In general, consensus-based models of decision-making work when there is already considerable common ground in terms of philosophy, values, and beliefs among the participants. Even so, the process can be very time consuming, which may be a source of frustration for participants. What has been your experience in decision-making by consensus? How were difference and dissent addressed?
6. Decision-making by unanimous consent implies a total agreement of the course of action to be taken. Here the team represents a united front and functions as a single unit. This method may by used when a group is facing opposition and wants to make its position clear and strong. What has been your experience with decision by unanimous consent? What issues were at stake? How did the decision affect the group?[3]

Building Consensus

Take time to discuss your experience in trying to reach consensus. What processes have you used? What have been the strengths and limitations of these processes? Have you had experiences with "group think" or "false consensus"? What processes have been most successful? What might be some alternative models of participatory decision-making?

Decision-Making Skills and Strategies. While it is important to consider the different ways in which decisions are made, it is equally important to learn about the skills and strategies for participatory decision-making. We have all probably had the experience of being a member of a group embroiled in a weighty decision-making process. Most of us have witnessed signs of group annoyance expressed by finger-tapping, eye-rolling, checking out, and utterances of frustration expressed through barely audible sighs and groans (Kaner, 1996). Bringing participatory decision-making processes to bear on group discussions is a way to keep people engaged in the process. At their core, these processes communicate a belief in peoples' ability to address issues of importance in their lives. These processes are based on hope, faith, and humility and they send the message that investment in the process means investment in the outcome.

Kaner reminds us that participatory decision-making strategies and skills respect opposing viewpoints and let people know their viewpoints count. They promote mutual understanding, inclusive solutions, and shared responsibility (p. 24). They stimulate new possibilities for practice as people come together to share diverse thinking and construct new solutions. In his book entitled *Facilitator's Guide to Participatory Decision-Making* (1996), Kaner outlines techniques for honoring all points of view that assist and promote movement through the decision-making process. These go beyond the scope of this text but we refer you to this work for a more in depth discussion of decision-making skills and strategies that support the underlying philosophy of social justice work.[4] These are premised on many of the skills of engagement addressed in Chapter Five.

Animating and Activating the Change Process

We want to develop further the idea of the social worker as animator and activator in the change process. The role of animator and method of animation are relatively foreign to social work practice in the U.S. The concept is more frequently associated with popular education and other liberatory social change movements. Reisch, Wenocur, and Sherman (1981), drawing from Brun (1972, pp. 60-71), describe animation as "a method of work which attempts to assist social groups seeking their own mode of expression and which promotes social programs addressed to needs defined by the group" (Reisch, et al., 1981, p. 115). It is "both a form of practice and a social movement" (p. 115). Animation involves encouragement of autonomous group development (e.g. skills of mutual aid), promotion of critical consciousness among members (conscientization), and stimulation of group action toward control over those environmental forces and resources that shape the group's development. The ultimate goal of animation is the liberation or empowerment of oppressed and marginalized people or groups. Reisch et al. argue that, for the goal of animation to be realized: "Social workers must be trained, therefore, to develop a new form of worker-client relationship based upon the establishment of trust in the motivation of others and a willingness to utilize non-traditional forms of cooperative action to produce change" (pp. 115-116). Thus, the social worker as animator acts as a catalyst, sparking consciousness that informs action and facilitating the social relations and material conditions that enable people to act. As animator, the social worker also attends to the organizational structure and infrastructure necessary to support the activation of plans. Animation and activation are at once socio-emotional, organizational-logistical, and political-ethical practices.

The animator role is grounded in genuine, caring relationships. Animators open up possibilities for meaningful participation; pose critical questions; coach participants through the risk taking, skill building, and rehearsal of new learning; and validate participants' contributions. Animators do not impose problem definitions and directions for action. Rather they encourage and nurture people's critical reflection on their own reality, validate the wisdom of lived experience, and help people envision and plan their own journeys. They remind people of their accomplishments and the importance of celebrating successes large and small. Animators attend to the orchestration of the parts and the whole, the balancing of the known and unknown, and the cultural-political questions of timing and pacing.

Drawing from the experiences of women's community-based organizing (Finn, Castellanos, McOmber & Kahan, 2000; Finn, 2001; Naples, 1998; Townsend et al., 1999), we also argue that animation involves nurturing and attention to the human spirit. *Anima*, the root word of animation, is the Latin word for soul. The stories of women community workers often contain references to the importance of healing body and soul as part of the change effort, of finding and giving inspiration, and of nurturing activism through relationships of love and support. Thus, the possibilities of animation are grounded in the meaning and power of caring human relationships.

The Possibilities of Social Enactment

Kelly and Sewell (1988) remind us that participants bring their own personalities and repertoires of interaction to bear in the practice of community building. Some people may be quick to anger and may challenge any difference of viewpoint. Others may be more conciliatory, avoiding conflict and seeking agreement. Kelly and Sewell argue that there is no one "right way" to interact in the change process. Rather, it is important to be critically aware of the range of possibilities for social enactment, the potential consequences of differing modes of enactment, and our own tendencies. With this awareness we can be more effective and aware participants and better able to appreciate and respond to the words and actions of others. They distinguish five different ways that people behave as they participate in processes of social change: by controlling, bargaining, consensus seeking, blocking, and confronting. We outline these types of social enactment below (Kelly & Sewell, 1988, pp. 74-79).

1. **Controlling** behavior tries to bring order to a situation perceived as chaotic. People may try to bring order by invoking special powers and rules. Kelly and Sewell argue that it is only possible to control from a position of strength and only when power differences exist. Sometimes people control by invoking tradition, regulations, or risk. Controlling behavior can be very damaging and disempowering to the change process. People with power will rarely let go of it. Controlling behavior can also have a positive side. In situations where there is factional conflict, confusion, and little direction, controlling behavior can offer the hope of structure. Order may be needed to assume responsibility and give leadership to the process. Kelly and Sewell write: "If we take control, we must also implement participatory processes right from the beginning, as soon as structures begin to emerge and people begin to use them" (p. 75).
2. **Blocking** behavior occurs when those unable to make their own decisions prevent others from making decisions as well. Blockers say no to all proposals and obstruct the proceedings in the process. Most likely, we have all had experience with blocking; it is often what we think of as the stereotypic bureaucratic response, "We need more information," "Put your request in writing," "We cannot consider that at this time," "Our policies don't allow for that." Blocking delays decision-making and action and saps the energy and momentum of the group. It is often a covert approach to buy time and create obstacles to the process. Blocking can also be helpful. It can provide time for more serious consideration of the issues or time to gather needed information. Blocking can force participants to develop greater clarity about their goals and objectives.
3. **Confronting** behavior occurs, in the sense used here, when people announce their decision to stand their ground. They have a firm grasp of the situation and are unwavering in their position. They are resolved to act accordingly. Confronting behavior is the process of

giving notice and drawing the proverbial "line in the sand." It can have the element of surprise and relay a clear message to other parties. It is a way of saying that we are organized, committed, and ready to defend our position. Confronting behavior can lead to a range of escalating tactics, from campaign tactics to context and conflict tactics, to violation of laws, norms and expectations, and to physical violence. A person or group engaged in confronting behavior needs to be clear about the meaning, extent and potential consequences of confrontation.

4. **Consensus** behavior sounds the most "positive." We often think of seeking consensus as an inherently good thing. Consensus is possible when there is goodwill and commonality among participants. It can promote cohesiveness of the groups. However, Kelly and Sewell note that there is a lot of confusion about consensus. People often struggle with the healthy conflict that difference and diversity require and err on the side of conformity regarding what we "should" do, which effectively limits the creative and critical possibilities of what we could do. Seeking consensus simply for the sake of conformity and avoidance of conflict degenerates into counter-productive routine. As Kelly and Sewell write, "people can invoke consensus as an ideological imperative, enshrine it in tradition, and then use it as a stick to beat dissidents into shape" (1988, p. 78).

5. **Bargaining** behavior assumes people have different goals and interests, but that they can assist or balance one another by negotiating a trade. Bargaining focuses on here and now exchanges, of goods, services, or tasks and makes no promises about future obligations. It is the classic "quid pro quo" negotiation. The parties involved, however, must have something to bargain with and have a sense of even footing in the process. In the short run, bargaining may be a way to remove immediate obstacles and unlock new energy that can "create new patterns of relationship and new situations" (p. 79). It can be a matter-of fact and concrete approach to recognizing and addressing differences.[5]

Conflict Resolution – Negotiating Difference

Social justice work calls on us to engage with conflict as part of the work. Structured inequalities and disparities of power shape and are shaped by conflicting interests. Likewise, differing histories and experiences shape divergent and at times conflicting worldviews. Conflict can be both a source of constraint and possibility. If one looks at a dictionary definition of the verb form of the word conflict one finds descriptors such as to fight, contend or do battle, clash or disagree. Its noun form relates to strife, controversy, struggle, quarrel, antagonism or opposition. Conflict carries negative connotations in our culture. Nowhere does the English language define conflict as a learning edge or an opportunity to question our own assumptions, and create better understanding of ourselves and others as intellectual and emotional human beings. The issue of conflict comes down to how we deal with it. Do we flee from controversial topics or conflictual issues? Or do we look to conflict as a battle to be won? Perhaps some of us have been rewarded for "not making waves," for keeping things "on an even keel," or for being the good child who never complained or caused any trouble. Others of us have taken pride in never conceding an issue and always having the last word in a disagreement. But somewhere in the middle of these two polarities is the notion of conflict as opportunity.

Dealing with Conflict: Fight, Flight, or Opportunity

Take a minute to think about what the word conflict means to you. Is it something you avoid at all costs? How did members of your immediate family deal with conflict? How easy is it for you to disagree with someone? Is it easier to disagree with some people and not others? How differently do you handle conflict depending upon particular situations and circumstances? Now think about conflict on a much grander scale, say between countries concerning issues of war and peace, nuclear disarmament or matters related to racial and ethnic cleansing, or the clash of religious beliefs. Recall a recent incident or event where you seriously disagreed with someone else. What was the disagreement about, and how did it feel to be engaged in a struggle? How do we create an environment where it is safe to disagree, where expressing differences is viewed as a growth-producing moment?

Conflict opens a space for learning. Conflict helps us to see different sides of an issue. It reminds us that there are different ways of defining problems and it provides the opportunity to seek alternative solutions. Conflict tells us many perspectives are being shared and that people are not agreeing just to agree. Conflict makes for better decision making in the end, but in the short run it can cause discomfort. Conflict is about learning to negotiate and value difference.

Controversial Issues

The National Coalition Building Institute (NCBI) located in Washington, DC was founded by Cherie R. Brown in 1984. Since its inception, NCBI has devoted itself to reducing prejudice and ending oppression that results from racism, sexism, and other forms of "otherism" that prevent peoples and communities from realizing their full potential. One of the primary missions of NCBI is to train people to address these issues in their communities. Maxine Jacobson completed the NCBI training and conducts NCBI training events on The University of Montana campus. One particularly powerful exercise from the NCBI training is included below.

In dealing with a controversial issue involving two parties, you may find the following six-step process developed by Brown and Mazza (1997, pp. 63-64) helpful in moving the disagreement forward. The exercise requires a third person act as facilitator to negotiate and guide the process. We quote directly from their work below:

1. Without interrupting or planning a rebuttal while the other person is speaking, listen carefully to what the person is saying.
2. Repeat back to the person who has just spoken – in the exact words, if possible – the precise reasons the other person gave for her opinion.
3. Next, ask her a question that communicates that you value her opinion and want to know more about how she sees the issue. For example, you might ask, "Please tell me more how you see this matter – is there anything from your own background that has led you to this conclusion?"
4. The parties then switch roles and repeat the first three steps.
5. Write down the concerns of both persons, checking with them to make sure that the recorded concerns accurately reflect their respective positions.
6. Review both persons' concerns, pointing out the areas of agreement. Then, propose a reframed question that takes at least one concern from each side into account. A reframed question often follows the format, "How can we do X, while at the same time doing Y?" For example, in [an] abortion dispute. . ., you might ask, "How can we guarantee that young disadvantaged women are not burdened by pregnancy and child care, while taking measures that will keep abortion from becoming a population

control policy that ultimately devalues human life?" The reframed question moves the controversy forward, inviting fresh thinking on the issue by incorporating each side's concern.

Controversies do not have to degenerate into polarization. A well-formulated, reframed question can ensure the development of policies that take into account the best thinking of all sides (Brown & Mazza, 1997).[6]

In groups of three, take some time to try out this conflict resolution model. Two people decide on an issue and the third person acts as the mediator, ensuring that the principles of the approach are followed. After completing this exercise, reflect on process and product. How difficult was it to adhere to the model? Were some topics easier to address than others? What were the challenges? What were the outcomes? What can you learn from this model about dealing with difference and conflicts that arise from difference? Develop a list of best practice principles for resolving conflict and present these to the class.

Addressing Anger

Throughout the book we have addressed questions of difference and the relations of power therein. In Chapter Six we explored the concept of resistance, and in the previous section we focused on conflict and controversy. We have not, however, considered the emotional underpinnings of these issues or the place and expression of anger associated with histories and experiences of exclusion and oppression. In much of the literature on helping, anger is addressed as an emotion to be "expressed" appropriately or somehow "managed." People, especially women and children, are acknowledged as needing permission to feel anger. Men are often the targets of "anger management" programs. The high incarceration rates of young men of color in the U.S. perhaps speak to the power of racially coded images of rage that can only be "contained" through imprisonment.

Anger and Cultural Expression. Certain social, cultural, and psychological parameters are often laid out regarding the proper expression of anger. Discussions of anger and emotions in general often assume that human emotions are universal, instinctual, if you will, and that their modes of expression are modulated through screens of cultural meaning. Cultural anthropologists have questioned assumptions about the universality of core human emotions and have helped us to see the production of emotion – the experience and its interpretation, the modes of expression, the range of identification of emotion and the rules of positionality, context, and expression - as culturally constructed (Briggs, 1970; Rosaldo, 1989). Neither anger nor other emotions necessarily fit into the neat scripts for expression and management that have been constructed in the helping professions.

We draw attention to anger here in the context of social justice work. People and groups with longstanding histories of oppression, exploitation, and discrimination may also have deep individual and collective experiences of anger, frustration, and distrust. The emotions and lived experience connected to histories of exclusion, abuse, and marginality and to the everyday indignities of "otherness" are not readily contained in individual models of emotional capacity, expression, and management. To strip powerful feelings from their larger context and locate them within the bodies of individuals is to distort the depth and complexity of their meanings, power, and histories. Social justice work calls for the expression and honoring of anger and frustration, rather than their containment. Working effectively with difference means allowing for anger and engaging with conflict as a valid and valued part of the work.

Skills for Defusing Anger. Let's take a look at one approach to dealing with anger developed by Charles Confer in his book *Managing Anger: Yours and Mine* (1987). Confer writes about five "defusing skills:"

1. **Listen**: The other person is angry for a reason: he is trying to get his needs met. It is important to listen not only to his words but also to the message behind his words. Respect his point of view even if you do not agree.
2. **Acknowledge the anger**: Acknowledge the person's anger by paraphrasing and summarizing what he is telling you. Acknowledge the anger without communicating blame and criticism.
3. **Apologize**: One way to reduce anger is to honestly and genuinely apologize for the pain and suffering the person may be experiencing.
4. **Agree with the Angry Person**: There is some truth behind most people's anger. Listen for that truth and agree with it. Perhaps you can agree with the facts of the situation, or the principles at stake, or with the other person's right to his opinion and feelings.
5. **Invite the Angry Person's Criticism**: By inviting criticism you are communicating that you want to understand the person's point of view and identify what he would like to have happen.[7]

Let's reflect for a moment on Confer's approach to anger. Confer presents interpersonal skills that parallel a number of skills addressed in Chapter Five. For example, he focuses on respectful engagement with the angry person. But what seems to be missing here? What is the history behind this interaction? What are the positionalities of those involved, and how do they shape the power dynamics of the encounter? Whose "truth" counts? How might an approach aimed at "defusing" anger also depoliticize it? By seeking to defuse the emotional energy might we, in effect, be deactivating a possible catalyst for change? Perhaps, for the practice of social justice work, we could draw inspiration from the Spanish term *coraje*, which translates as both "rage" and "courage." How might we conceive of anger as a resource for social action rather than a time bomb to be defused? What possibilities for individual and collective action may open up as we reframe the meaning and power of anger?

The Meaning and Power of Anger

Here is an account by a young woman that speaks to the meaning and power of anger (and other feelings). What responses does her story evoke in you? What more do you want to learn about her history and experience? How might critical reflection on her story inform action?

"Not My Alma Mater," from *Pretty in Punk: Girls Gender Resistance in a Boys' Subculture,* Lauraine Leblanc (1999).

Montreal, May 1984

I got kicked out of high school today. I can't fucking believe it. I have an A average and I've never gotten a detention or even so much as a demerit point and those fuckers go and kick me out, fucking assholes.

It's not like I was doing anything that I don't usually do. I was hanging out at my locker wearing my spray painted "Eat Dirt and Die" shirt that I made and the vice principal walks by and tells me not to wear That Shirt anymore. Totally out of the blue. I've been wearing this shirt two, maybe three times a week for the past six months, and today he decides I can't wear it anymore. Dickwad.

Then later I'm in technical drawing and he comes back and takes me out of class. He makes me go to the principal's office and they tell me not to come to school anymore looking like this. I tell them to call my mom and she shows up and totally supports them. I mean, I know she hates the way I look, but this has BULLSHIT written all over it in mile-high letters and everyone's acting like this is totally my fault.

The v. p. tells me that I'm distracting the other students. Sure, when I got my mohawk, the lady who runs the cosmetology department asked me not to hang around there because I scare the old ladies who come in to get the hair dyed blue (now, that's a joke) by the girly-girls. So I try, but it's kind of hard to do with my locker right down the hall and my technical drawing class right across from cosmetology. Still. I sit in the back of the class all of the time, so there's no reason why they should say I'm distracting everybody. Besides which, my hair's been like this for six, seven months now. Get over it already.

Then the v.p. says that I'm just trying to be like this girl whose picture's in my locker. What the fuck? The only reason Ms. Wendy O Williams of the Plasmatics graces my locker door is because she looks like me, not the other way around. I had a big blonde fin way before I'd ever seen one on anybody else. And when's the last time they saw me standing on a tank wearing nothing but leather underwear? Please. "Besides" I tell them, "if anyone's going to be like anybody else, you should want your other students to be like me. I'm the one who gets straight A's and has never got detention." Right assholes?

Okay. That didn't go over so well. The principal says that the way I dress is indecent. Like the first time I came to school in ripped-up fishnets, spike heels, thigh-high red mini, spiked belt, ripped-up T shirt (no skin, though), lace gloves, full geisha make-up and full-up fin, I brought a pair of jeans. I knew I was pushing it. Did they say anything then? No. But everyone else did. For some reason, these little peckerhead boys in this school thought I was trying to be sexy, just like these asswipes are thinking now. Guess again. I'm just taking what they and their society thinks is sexy and I'm making it ugly, because that's what it is. Get it? Guess not.

So, I'm outta here. I got one year of high school left and they've just kicked their smartest student out of their ugly dumb-ass building. They just don't get it. Well, fuck, 'em if they can't take a joke" (Leblanc, 1999, pp. 1-2).

Lauraine Leblanc has written a powerful, eloquent ethnographic account of girls' participation in the heavily gendered world of punk. She wrote this passage when she was expelled from high school as a teen. Her own experiences were the motive force for her work in documenting the voices and lives of girls and young women in punk culture.

Popular Education: A Strategy for Change

Understanding Popular Education. Popular education "aims to create change by raising critical consciousness of common concerns" (Checkoway, 1990, p. 20). It is a form of education in which people reflect critically on objective reality and act on that reflection to "transform the world" (p. 20). Its aim is to educate about injustice and inequality. Through practices of popular education, people come together to confront oppression in institutional systems that wield power over their lives. In this sense popular education is a form of resistance. It can be a way of channeling anger into productive social action to address issues of social justice and inequality. Popular education seeks to raise consciousness by helping people challenge misinformation, examine the history of a social problem to deepen understanding of current realities, and develop alternative perspectives. It connects personal issues to their root causes through critical question posing and mobilizing people for action to rectify these concerns. Knowledge development in popular education is from the ground up. For example, Cecilia Díaz (1995, 1997) is committed to popular education. The tenets of popular education underlie her approach to participatory diagnosis and planning outlined in Chapters Six and Seven.

The method of popular education as developed by Paulo Freire has played a central role in poor peoples' struggles and movements throughout Latin American and beyond. Freire brought together small groups of illiterate peasants, living in squatter communities in Brazil, to reflect on the conditions of their daily lives. He found that, in learning to read and write, they also came to a new awareness of selfhood, looked critically at their life circumstances, and often took bold initiatives for transforming their worlds (Shaull, 1970, p. 9). Freire held the conviction that "every human being, no matter how 'ignorant' or submerged in the 'culture of silence' he may be, is capable of looking critically at his world in a dialogical encounter with others" (Shaull, 1970, p. 13). Through this method, poor and marginalized people have transformed "ignorance," frustration, and anger into powerful collective action.

Key Features and Methods. Poertner (1994) discusses three distinguishing features of popular education: 1) locus of action, 2) cultural specificity, and 3) political intention. People who have been alienated from their culture due to globalization of markets, patriarchy, or racial discrimination, are the locus of action in popular education. Popular education sets into motion a process by which people can come to understand themselves and the root causes of their alienation. Through this process, people create and validate their own cultural knowledge, rather than having an interpretation of their reality imposed from the outside. Political intention speaks to the issue of social change. Once groups identify the sources of their alienation and critically reflect on their cultural context, the stage is set to explore alternative practices to address concerns.

Popular education makes use of a variety of tools to help people gain deeper understanding of cultural, economic, and political influences on their lives. Methods include skits and dramatizations, where boundaries between actor and audience are challenged. The linkages of performance, education, and change have been developed through the work of noted Brazilian director, activist, and educator Augusto Boal. He has translated principles of popular education into a theatrical philosophy and practice of personal and social change known as Theatre of the Oppressed (1982). The use of theater and performance has come to play an important role in popular education. For example, Andrew Boyd, author of *The Activist Cookbook: Creative Actions for a Fair Economy* (1999), catalogues a rich collection of "recipes" for social action based on the principles of popular education. These highlight the importance of art and culture "[at] the heart of any movement, any moving of people. . ." (p. 2). Boyd provides a number of sample recipes for popular theater performances and playfully teases the reader to "Help yourself. Spice to taste. Play with your food" (p. 28). We include a sample here to whet your appetite for popular theater and to stimulate your creative juices. Boyd calls this popular theater performance *War of the Worlds, Part II*:

> A skit based on Orson Welles' famous 1930's-era radio play – but instead of Martians, trans-national corporations take over the Earth. Samples: "They're hideous to behold; cold and calculating, their tentacles reaching out everywhere…can nothing stop them…?" " Their dark ships hovering over government buildings, their deadly lasers striking out without warning, aaaarrrrggg, oh my God! They've burned a Mickey Mouse symbol into the White House lawn…" (p. 28)

Boyd and his colleagues at United for a Fair Economy (formerly Share the Wealth) organize themselves and others to draw ". . . public attention to the dangerous consequences of growing income and wealth inequality . . ." (p. 93). How might you use or adapt the *War of the Worlds, Part II* "recipe?" In what context might this particular brand of acting out your message be helpful? What might be the constraints or the fall-out? Are there similar situations of economic disparity in your own community that might be addressed through this kind of public message?

Creative Acting Out

Did the reenactment of Welles' radio show give you any ideas for a popular education performance of your own? Here are some other ideas borrowed from *The Activist Cookbook* (Boyd, 1999) to get the creative juices flowing:

In the early 80s, to help sell the idea of "trickle-down" economics to the public, the American Conservative Union held a gala dinner featuring the world's largest pie. Over 17 feet across, the pie was to be sliced and distributed to all in attendance as a way of demonstrating that "everyone will get a piece of the pie." Five members of the Community for Creative Non-Violence, wearing oversize business suits and name tags of Reagan's wealthy friends, walked into the party and jumped into the pie. With the TV cameras rolling, they slopped around in the pie goop, slinging it around at each other, screaming, "It's all for me! It's all for me!" To get them out, security guards had to wade into the pie themselves. The event was ruined, and that night an incredible image of greed run amok was beamed out to living rooms across America.

****

In the early 90's, labor activists in Baltimore were outraged at the huge government subsidies that downtown corporations had received. Activists organized a "sightseeing tour" of the worst offenders and invited the community and media along. At each stop, with the target site in the background, folks held up huge dollar signs and numbers on placards, making it very clear who was getting welfare and exactly how much. The media loved it. These snap shots of forms of popular education illustrate that activism can be serious business with a sense of humor and playfulness (Boyd, 1999, pp. 1-2). Meet with other students in small groups and see if you can come up with some imaginative ways to get a message across. What areas of concern could be well demonstrated using these methods? How might you feel about educating others and yourself by acting out? What might be the constraints or drawbacks?

Coalition Building for Change

Defining Coalitions. Coalitions are forged when the power base of a small group of people acting to create change is much too small to accomplish the task on its own, especially when resources are insufficient (Homan, 1999, p. 306). You can think of coalitions as organizations of organizations. There are different kinds of coalitions, and each serves a different purpose and outcome. For example, many coalitions are *ad hoc*, which means they emerge over expressed need, and once the task is accomplished they disband. Other coalitions are more permanent. They emerge and become instituted around a specific problem area such as homelessness, hunger, or poverty. Homan points out the benefits of forming coalitions to a change effort. He tells us we can think of the organizations that compose a coalition as arms that spread out to capture necessary resources to get the job done. Many arms can gather more resources than one alone. When people are gathered together in coalitions, resources are more abundant. They consist of credibility, funding, people power, volunteers, support staff, office equipment, and different ways of thinking about and perceiving situations. Increased resources enlarge the power base of a change effort.

Guidelines for Building a Coalition. Homan (1999) outlines a number of guidelines for assembling a coalition and building alliances across organizations and groups (pp. 307-308). We summarize from his work below and add some of our own thoughts regarding coalitions:

1. Determine whom you would like to have involved in the coalition. Think first about organizations and groups with whom you already have existing relationships and then ask the critical questions, "Who is most likely to join?" Which organizations are most affected by the issues we intend to address? What talents, skills, and competencies are important to the work we hope to accomplish? Who has what we need? Besides the obvious resources such as money, expertise, and sheer numbers, who can relate best to the different publics you want to influence?

2. Contact these individuals and emphasize how the issue affects their self-interest. This is best accomplished face-to-face. This allows you the opportunity to clarify, answer questions, and explain the benefits of collaboration.

3. Secure a commitment to the coalition, preferably through a written contract that spells out obligations and clarifies roles and procedures. As an alternative to a written contract, you could get a letter of support written on the organization's stationary. Securing a commitment allows you to list this organization's name as part of your group.
4. Involve the new members in organizing an initial meeting and use this as an opportunity to build further support and enthusiasm for your work.
5. Don't expect that all members will attend each meeting, but keep members on board by appraising them of the group's progress. However, don't be afraid to personally ask specific members to be involved in the accomplishment of certain tasks.
6. Effective communication among coalition members is crucial to the effort. Never forget the importance of appreciating people's work.

Montana Income Support Collaboration. An example of a coalition is the Montana Income Support Collaboration (MISC). This coalition formed early in 2000 to address concerns regarding Montana's welfare reform policy, Families Achieving Independence in Montana (FAIM). MISC brought together three organizations whose work focused on addressing the needs of people living in poverty and the working poor in Montana (Working for Equality and Economic Liberation (WEEL), Women's Opportunity and Resource Development, Inc. (WORD) and Montana People's Action (MPA)). Representatives from the three organizations identified the following goals: 1) to work to create a more united economic-justice voice throughout the legislative session, 2) to more effectively use the areas of expertise from the participating organizations to address the reduction of poverty in Montana, and 3) to highlight strengths and support the efforts of the other organizations in the collaboration. MISC's long-term goal is to create a stable community for progressive organizations in Montana and to document the collaborative process to serve as a potential resource for future efforts in Montana.[8] Recently, MISC hosted a policy roundtable that brought together other individuals in Montana concerned about the reauthorization of welfare reform policies in 2002. Through the concerted and united efforts of MISC, Montana policymakers are better educated and prepared to address the issue of welfare reform and to assess its success based on the reduction of poverty rather than on the previous rhetoric of decreasing welfare recipient caseloads.

Bridging Difference: Skills of Multicultural Practice

Effective social justice work requires the ability to recognize, honor, and bridge differences. As we have just discussed, coalition building is a sensitive and strategic process of finding common interest, creating common ground, recognizing differences, mobilizing alliances, and valuing participants. Social justice work also requires the capacity to build and sustain organizations where people with different histories, experiences, and interests can come together, pool knowledge and resources, and make a commitment to work together over the long haul. John Anner (2000) offers the following thoughts on building successful multicultural social justice organizations:

- Build personal relationships among members from different backgrounds.
- Actively engage in solidarity campaigns, actions, and activities with social justice organizations in other communities.
- Challenge bigoted statements and attitudes when they arise.
- Hold regular discussions, forums, "educationals," and workshops to enhance people's understandings of other communities and individuals.
- Work to change the culture of the organization so that members see themselves as "members of the community" first instead of members of a particular part of the community.
- Develop issues, tactics, and campaigns that are relevant to different communities and that reveal fundamental areas of common interests.
- Conduct antiracism training to get people to confront and deal with their biases.
- Examine and change the organization's practices in order to hire, promote, and develop people of color.
- Confront white privilege and nationalism.
- Hire, recruit, and train more people of color for leadership positions.

What examples of putting these tactics to practice can you draw from your own experience? How successful were they? Where were the sources of support and resistance? What would you add to the list?

Policy Practice: Analysis and Advocacy

Linking Policy and Practice. Josefina Figueira-McDonough (1993) reminds us that social policy has long been a neglected side of social work practice. She poses the question that perhaps professional identity precludes social workers' engagement in policy activities. Others concur with Figueira-McDonough's claim and note that the profession favors "direct intervention" work over policy practice and separates out policy work as "indirect" service (Chapin, 1995; Jansson, 1999). However, this bifurcation of practice into categories of "direct" and "indirect" ignores the fact that initiating new policies requires the same skills of relationship building, communication, and negotiation as does traditional work with individuals, families, and communities. The importance of policy practice to social work is difficult to overlook. The nature and direction of social work practice and the structure and activities of social welfare organizations are shaped by social policy. In turn individuals, groups, and organizations "make" social policy as they interpret, respond to, resist, and translate policies into practice. Thus social policy issues are at the heart of social work practice. Social justice work calls for the critical integration of policy and practice and recognition of the ways in which policy and practice are mutually constituted.

At their most basic level, policies are rules, guiding principles established to maintain order in the social sphere. Policies are generally thought of as statements about how we, as a culture, define social problems. Implicitly, they represent beliefs and values about a given social condition (Tropman, 1984). Chapin (1995, p. 506) asks us to rethink the notion of policy built on "careful problem definition." She critically examines the emphasis on personal deficits and pathology written into social policy and advocates policy development and analysis that address problems in terms of environmental barriers and inadequacy of resources. Chapin contends:

> . . . this problem-centered approach to policy formulation with its intense focus on definition and assessment has not been coupled with similar attention to assessment of the strengths of the people and environment that the policy targets. (p. 506)

While this approach may sound good in theory, Chapin cautions us that bringing a strengths perspective to policy development, analysis, and advocacy requires addressing the social construction of knowledge and how a problem-centered approach may meet the needs of people in power. Rappaport, Davidson,

Wilson, and Mitchell (1975, as cited in Chapin, p. 508) suggest that, in order to provide alternative approaches, we need to look to people who know their communities and who are ultimately affected by policy decisions and see them as partners in the policy development and analysis process. Integrating a strengths perspective into the policymaking process starts by redefining our ideas about policy. A new definition of policy would view it as a tool to help people meet their basic needs for food, shelter, health care, and protection.

Deficit- versus Strengths-Based Approaches to Policy. Chapin (1995, p. 510) presents an informative comparison between deficits and strengths-based approaches to policy. We include her model here and ask you to think about the potential of the strengths perspective as an alternative to a problem-centered, deficits-focused approach to policy development. What differences do you see between these two approaches? What challenges does a strengths approach to policy development pose? How does this model attend to the key themes of meaning, context, power, history and possibility? Are there any areas you might expand on to make the strengths approach outlined by Chapin more congruent with the Just Practice Framework?

FIGURE 7.1

Comparison of Policy Formation Process Based on the Problem-Centered Approach and the Strengths Approach

Problem-Centered Approach	**Strengths Approach**
Problem definition	Identification of basic needs and barriers to meeting needs Definition negotiation
Problem analysis – causes and consequences	Identification of the ways that barriers are currently overcome by clients and through programs (best practice)
Informing the public	[Direct participation in the policy process by those affected][9]
Development of policy goals	Identification of opportunities and resources necessary for people to meet their needs Policy formulation
Consensus building	Negotiating consensus on policy goals
Program design	Program design
Implementation	Implementation
Evaluation and assessment	Evaluation and assessment of client outcomes

Four Methods of Policy Practice

Social policy shapes and is shaped by the practice of social work. For example, Figueira-McDonough (1993) contends that taking the profession's core value of social justice seriously means making a commitment to "policy practice." She outlines four methods of policy practice: 1) legislative advocacy; 2) reform through litigation; 3) social action; and 4) social policy analysis. We summarize these methods here, provide examples from practice, and refer you to Figueira-McDonough's article (see pp. 181-186) for an expanded description of each.

Legislative advocacy. The task of legislative advocacy is to gain access to needed resources and social goods. Figueira-McDonough points out that legislative advocacy usually takes the form of lobbying in traditional U.S. social work. Lobbying is the act of trying to influence legislators and other government officials to support particular perspectives to their colleagues. Lobbyists can wield considerable power and influence, especially if they are backed by interest groups with large sums of money and connections to other sources of support. For example, representatives of NASW and CSWE join forces and collaborate to amass strength in numbers and lobby for particular causes and concerns relevant to the profession and those individuals it serves. However, these efforts are generally top-down approaches initiated by organization officials, and they often fail to include those most affected by policy decisions. Legislative advocacy efforts can also include the voices of the citizenry. The Skipping School in Montana Project discussed in Chapter Eight used participatory research and legislative advocacy methods to reach its goal of influencing the state legislature to change welfare reform policy and count school hours as part of the work requirement for welfare recipients enrolled in post-secondary education. The Project included the voices of welfare recipients and enlisted their participation in the process.

Reform through litigation. This form of policy practice receives the least attention in the social work literature perhaps because it requires a certain amount of legal shrewdness and is a slow way of achieving social reform (Figueira-McDonough, 1993, p. 182). Anyone who has dealt with the judicial system knows it has its own time clock, and cases can drag out for months and even years. Yet reform through litigation has some inherent characteristics that make it exceptionally well-suited for addressing issues of minority groups:

> (1) the process is initiated by the interested party, not the court, and (2) the decision is made exclusively on the basis of legal antecedents and evidence – both brought to the court by the involved parties. Openness of access and equal chance in defining the issue put the parties on a level playing field (Figueira-McDonough, 1993, p. 183).

Social action. Figueira-McDonough calls our attention to the civil rights movement of the 1950s and 1960s as an example of social action and its potential to promote social change. Checkoway (1990) describes social action as a way to "create change by building powerful organizations at the community level" (p. 12). When compared with other methods of policy practice addressed in this section, social action is by far the most participatory. Social change is forged from the ground up and relies, almost entirely, on the involvement of ordinary people in addressing their concerns. It seeks to create structural change in society's institutions and addresses issues of inequality and injustice.

Social policy analysis. Figueira-McDonough outlines an analytic framework for policy analysis that attends to questions of values, knowledge, and effectiveness. To achieve these ends one focuses on the fit between the stated goals of the policy and the proposals for its implementation, the accuracy and reliability of the knowledge informing the policy development and the means of implementation, and the costs of the proposal, both in human and financial terms. Sarri (1988, as cited in Figueira-McDonough, p. 186) provides an example of policy analysis that focuses on these particular areas of concern: "Before leaving office in 1989, President Reagan supported a policy requiring mothers on welfare to work for their benefits. Because no guaranteed provision of child care was included and the benefits these mothers receive are not sufficient to pay for child care, the anticipated result is deterioration in the supervision of their children." This policy analysis illustrates how policy can fail to consider the consequences of its implementation and that cost-saving initiatives may actually be more expensive (both monetarily and socially) in the end.

Think for a moment of the methods of policy practice summarized here. How realistic is it to envision social workers as policy practitioners? What do you see as some of the constraints and challenges of policy practice in community and organizational contexts? What do you see as some of the possibilities? What values and beliefs do these methods support? How do these methods fit with the key concepts of the Just Practice Framework? Where are the gaps?

The Thinking and Skills of Accompaniment

Defining Accompaniment

Accompaniment is the actual people-to-people partnerships through which action is realized. It represents another facet of practice where we are once again reminded of the commitment to collaboration and dialogue over the long haul and to the interplay of power and possibility that shapes practice. Traditional approaches to the change process in social work often refer to the activity that coincides with implementation of an action plan as "monitoring." The notion of monitoring positions the social worker outside the process and in the role of overseer. It places the burden for action on others and suggests that the worker retains the power of scrutiny. The language of monitoring disconnects the worker from her relationship to the participants in the process. We find the notion of accompaniment more conducive to the values and assumptions of social justice work.

In its simplest terms, accompaniment means to go with, to support and enhance the process. We often hear this word used in reference to music. The dictionary defines accompaniment as "a musical part supporting and enhancing the principal part" (Merriam-Webster's Collegiate Dictionary, 1971). While this definition alludes to accompaniment as secondary or "taking a back seat," the principal part would not be the principal without support and enhancement. Each part complements the other and together produce a richer and more complex whole.

Principles of Accompaniment

We develop our notion of accompaniment from the work of Elizabeth Whitmore and Maureen Wilson, who we discuss in Chapter One in connection with their research in Nicaragua. They were inspired by the work of their Latin American colleagues in collaborative efforts of community change (Whitmore & Wilson, 1997, p. 57-58). Whitmore and Wilson describe the relationship of social justice workers to the communities, groups, and individuals with whom they are engaged as one of "*acompañamiento,*" a Spanish term that best translates as accompanying the process. Whitmore and Wilson, describing their work as North American social worker/scholars working in collaboration with colleagues in Nicaragua, write: "We are attracted to this way of expressing such a relationship precisely because of its inherent clarity about who owns and controls the process: our partners do; it is *we* who accompany *their* process" (p. 58). They have identified a set of principles of accompaniment, which have applicability to a variety of settings. These include:

1) non-intrusive collaboration;
2) mutual trust and respect;
3) a common analysis of what the problem is;
4) a commitment to solidarity;
5) equality in the relationship;
6) an explicit focus on process; and
7) the importance of language (Wilson & Whitmore, 1995).

Wilson and Whitmore argue that these principles parallel both feminist principles and the attributes of a good social worker as well. They advocate an approach to accompaniment that combines both "structural and conjunctural analysis with the interpersonal skills so essential to effective collaboration" (Whitmore & Wilson, 1997, p. 58). They contend that a true partnership of equals calls for the democratization of information flow, collaborative knowledge development and dissemination, and action networking. Participation cannot be confined to "local" arenas but must also engage political activity in broader arenas. Accompaniment calls for a deep appreciation of process and a sense of dignity and hope. It is a process of "participatory alignment" that attends to the ways in which marginalized people become critical agents of transformation, going beyond personal troubles to public issues (p. 61). Accompaniment demands ongoing critical attention to questions of power and the power differences among the participants in the change process. Accompaniment is a process of joining across diverse borders to build mutual trust, explore possibilities for cooperative work and division of labor, and create a two-way movement of people, knowledge, and power.

Lessons Learned Through Accompaniment

Wilson and Whitmore learned important lessons in accompaniment through their participation in a five-year, collaborative social development project funded by the Canadian International Development Agency and involving the Schools of

Social Work at Managua's Universidad Centroamericana and the University of Calgary, Canada. The goals of the project were to strengthen the capacities of social work teachers in the Universidad Centroamericana and to develop a social action documentation center. The experience taught them about *how* one engages in the process of accompaniment. It requires the skills and attitudes of good social work: empathy, respect, a non-judgmental approach, openness, tolerance for ambiguity, and ability to facilitate interaction. Further, they argue that meaningful structural change comes through collaborative action in coalitions and networks where people join to challenge forms and practices of domination. Accompaniment includes the ability to be an active, supportive member of coalitions and networks and to understand one's stake and positionality therein.

As Canadians working in Nicaragua, Wilson and Whitmore needed to be constantly mindful of North-South power imbalances and the implication for their work. Issues and pressures of time shaped the process. While Whitmore and Wilson had a block of time to be present and work with their colleagues, their Nicaraguan counterparts were juggling the many time and resource demands of their everyday lives. The Nicaraguans had also had previous experience with well-intentioned foreigners presenting ideas and proposals that never materialized. Wilson and Whitmore had to guard against taking over the process by virtue of their access to resources and by the nuances of language. For example, many of the conceptual frameworks that shaped their assumptions were developed in English and reflected a "long ideological history and way of life" that were not readily translatable to the Nicaraguan context (1997, pp. 66-67). They found a participatory research methodology most conducive to collaborative knowledge development in this context. Based on their experiences they conclude: ". . .sympathetic listening, engaged questioning, nondirective suggesting, and solidarity in the face of setback are the stuff of accompaniment" (p. 68).

Accompaniment and Alliance

Effective accompaniment demands reflection on what it means to be an ally and how we build alliances. For example, in documenting the contributions and possibilities of young people as competent community builders, Finn and Checkoway (1998) found that a common theme among many thriving community-based youth initiatives was the role of adults as allies. Successful, sustained, youth-directed initiatives often have strong intergenerational ties and longstanding relationships with adults who offer counsel and mentoring, support their efforts without usurping them, and help facilitate access to other networks and resources. Effective allies are engaged in ongoing critical reflection on the balance of power and the importance of autonomy as well as connection.

Gloria Anzaldúa speaks powerfully about allies from her perspective as a Chicana lesbian feminist. She writes:

> Becoming allies means helping each other heal. It can be hard to expose yourself and your wounds to a stranger who could be an ally or an enemy. But if you and I were to do good alliance work together, be good allies to each other, I would have to expose my wounds to you and you would have to expose your wounds to me and then we could start from a place of openness. During our alliance work, doors will close and we'll have to open them again. People who engage in alliances and are working toward certain goals want to keep their personal feelings out of it, but you can't. You have to work out your personal problems while you are working out the problems of this particular community or the particular culture. (Anzaldúa, 1994, in Adams et al., 2000, p. 495)

Anzaldúa challenges those who mask practices of tokenism in the language of alliance. She asks those in positions of relative privilege to critically reflect on their motives for building alliances. Are they looking to assimilate the "other" voice? Are they trying to avoid charges of elitism and racism? She warns that the biggest risk in forming alliances is betrayal:

> When you are betrayed you feel shitty… And betrayal makes you feel like less of a person – you feel shame, it reduces your self-esteem. It is politically deadening and dangerous; it's disempowering. (1994, in Adams et al., 2000, p. 496)

Margaret Ledwith and Paula Asgill (2000) propose the concept of *critical alliance*, which they argue is vital to the future of community work and collective action for social justice. They draw from their identities and collaborative work experiences as an African-Caribbean woman and a white British woman in attempting to articulate the crafting of alliance across difference. They begin with acknowledgement of their differences and critical reflection on the socio-political context in which they are coming together. They take seriously questions regarding the unspoken privileges of whiteness and questions of "'black rage,' which is silenced within this whiteness" (hooks, 1995, p. 11 cited in Ledwith & Asgill, 2000, p. 291). They argue that effective alliances need to address the complexity of identities as "emergent histories which are located at the critical intersection of our lived experience within the social, cultural, and economic relations of our time, shifting, not fixed" (Ledwith & Asgill, 2000, p. 293). They contend that effective community work calls for honest engagement with these knotty issues. They write:

> Our position is one of locating community work at the heart of liberation by defining and contextualizing its critical potential. The feminist challenge is that, by a process of democratisation based on mutual accountability and collective action, alliances of difference can transform those social institutions that entrench prejudice, discrimination and exploitation as legitimate. (p. 294)

Ledwith and Asgill speak to the challenge of dialogue across difference, and the need to explore the anger, the silences, and the misunderstandings between them through ongoing, honest conversation. They echo Anzaldúa's contention that developing alliances is a painful process, but that the naming and exposing of pain is essential to transformative action.

Personalizing Accompaniment

This exercise can be done individually, in pairs, in small groups, or with your entire class. Find a comfortable position, take a few deep breathes, and let yourself relax. Now imagine you have embarked on a journey with a potential partner or partners. Allow yourself to create a detailed picture of your partner(s). Where do you go on your journey? The possibilities are infinite. Perhaps a hike in the woods, a canoe trip down the river, or off to a country you have never explored before. How do you make this decision collectively and what do you do to form an alliance with your partner(s)? Do you do this through dialogue or nonverbal signs? Given your choice of partner(s), what feelings does accompaniment evoke? Comfort? Constraint? Anticipation? How do you negotiate these feelings? Now take a minute to investigate your surroundings. Where does your journey take you and what happens along the way? Do obstacles surface that slow you down, or is it smooth sailing? How do you illustrate through your actions the key themes of accompaniment? Once you have arrived at your destination, you meet someone there who gives you and your partner(s) a "gift" that embodies the key principles of accompaniment. You bring this gift with you on the return trip home. Who is this gift-giver? Does the exchange happen nonverbally or through dialogue? What does the gift look like? What lessons does the gift teach you about accompaniment? You and your partner(s) make your way back to where you began. Take time to process this imagery.

Chapter Summary

Throughout this chapter we have examined ways in which the knowledge and values of social justice work are translated into concrete actions for change. The practice of social justice work calls for a reconceptualization of social work roles in order to address questions of power and positionality, the partial and emergent nature of knowledge and knowledge development, a commitment to critical curiosity, the challenges of collaboration, and the possibilities of creative intervention. We have emphasized the significance of the social worker as animator, engaging people in meaningful action and weaving the connections of head, heart, and hand. We recognized that the "proof" of social justice work is in the meaningful participation of those affected in challenging and changing the conditions of their lives. To that end we addressed skills and strategies for participatory planning, decision-making, and enactment. We have probed the linkage of policy and practice and argued that social justice workers need to grasp and engage with their integration. People-to-people partnerships that respect difference pose both challenges and possibilities. Conflict is part of the process. As social justice workers we need to be able to confront strong feelings, both our own and others, and give time, space, and value to the recognition and expression of feelings. The process of accompaniment can never be taken for granted. Partnerships need to be nurtured, respected, and energized. We invite you to return to the questions regarding action and accompaniment that we outlined in the Just Practice matrix at the end of Chapter Four (p. 178). How might these questions guide you in developing action plans and building critical alliances and supportive partnerships? What questions would you add to the matrix? As we noted in Chapter One, action and reflection are dialectical, mutually informing processes. As we take time to evaluate and reflect on our practice and celebrate our achievements, we open up new possibilities for action. In Chapter Eight we explore the processes of evaluation, critical reflection, and celebration.

Case Study

The Lost Boys: Linking the Global and the Local

Following are two news articles regarding the resettlement of the "Lost Boys" of Sudan. The first is from a media site for the United Nations Office for the Coordination of Humanitarian Affairs. The second is an account of these young men's efforts to make a life in a new and very foreign place: Burlington, Vermont. Consider this situation in light of the Just Practice Framework. What questions of meaning, context, power, history, and possibility does this account speak to? What challenges and opportunities for social justice work does this situation pose?

Sudan: American resettlement of "lost boys" continues

NAIROBI 12 June [2001] (IRIN). – The US State Department expects to complete by September of this year a programme of resettling approximately 3,800 Sudanese children and young adults from Kakuma Refugee Camp in northwestern Kenya, which it began in November 2000. These refugees, predominantly boys and young men, known as the "lost boys" of Sudan, are among an estimated 17,000 who were separated from their parents and fled on foot to Ethiopia – walking more that 1,000 km on the four-month journey, a State Department press release noted on Monday.

Management of the refugee camps to which the boys went was delegated to the rebel Sudan People's Liberation Army (SPLA), which subjected the youths to military training and viewed them as a recruitment pool for the rebel army, according to the NGO Refugees International. Some joined the army voluntarily with the promise of education; others were taken forcibly by the SPLA, who had organised their original flight from Sudan, it said.

In 1991, the Ethiopian government closed the refugee camps, and the boys were sent back to Sudan. Many were enslaved by armed tribesmen; others succumbed to starvation or bombings by government planes, but, remarkably, thousands survived, according to Refugees International. By May 1992, 10,500 of the "lost boys" had reached Kakuma camp in Turkana district, where they were classified as unaccompanied minors (UACs) and placed in special sections of the camp.

Most of the estimated 10,000 "lost boys" left the camp over the years before the US resettlement scheme started, and were therefore not eligible for it, [United Nations High Commissioner on Refugees] UNHCR spokesman Paul Stromberg told IRIN on Tuesday. That left some 4,000 in Kakuma to be considered, of whom some had married and others had left the camp and later returned – rendering them ineligible for the US programmes, he said.

"UNHCR undertook a careful and rigorous "best-interest" survey of a couple of hundred Sudanese youths under 18 years of age, and found that US resettlement was not in the best interests of all, either because their families had been traced or for other reasons," Stromberg said. "This explained the US resettlement figure of 3,800," he added.

"Despite years of family tracing efforts by humanitarian organizations, many of the children (in the American resettlement programme) have little hope that they will ever see their parents again," the US State Department said on Monday. "With war in Sudan continuing, return to a homeland for these children and young adults could mean forced military conscription and/or other danger to their lives," it added.

These minors' education in camp schools (rather than training as traditional cattle herders) and the segregation imposed on them as UACs in Kakuma put them out of step with Dinka and Nuer tribal concepts of a young man's place in society, according to Refugees International.

Many refused to undergo scarification of their foreheads – the Dinka and Nuer rite of passage to adulthood, it said. And without money to pay the traditional wedding dowry, they were barred from marriage – the other avenue of reintegration into society. Their communities had effectively stigmatised the youths as unruly outcasts, though they remained vulnerable to conscription by the SPLA, the NGO reported in 1998.

In 1999 the UN High Commission for Refugees (UNHCR), working in collaboration with the US State Department, referred about 3,800 of these young adults and children to the US for refugee resettlement. Last year, the US began formally processing them for placement in the US, and arrivals are scheduled to continue into September.

About 500 children, mostly boys and a small number of girls, have already entered the United States and been placed in refugee foster care programmes in 10 states. In all, the Kakuma refugees will be resettled in 28 states by 10 resettlement agencies that work with the US government.

The resettlement agencies will provide them with basic necessities and assist them in connecting to social services, high school and other education/ training, and job services for up to 90 days after arrival in the US, according to the State Department. In addition, a number of social services programmes funded by the Office of Refugee Resettlement are available to refugees for longer periods, it added.

(The material contained in this report comes via IRIN, a UN humanitarian information unit, but may not necessarily reflect the views of the United Nations or its agencies. Text copyright © UN Office for the Coordination of Humanitarian Affairs.[10])

Lost Boys of Sudan: The Newest Vermonters[11]

Candace Page, *The Burlington Free Press*

Burlington, Vermont, 12 May 2001

The Lost Boys of Sudan watched their parents get killed and their villages burned. Boys as young as 6 walked a thousand miles in search of safety. The survivors of that epic journey are now young men; 24 of them are making a new life in Vermont.

Ben Yak Bol, 21, shares a Burlington apartment with five other young refugees from Sudan. "This place is quite advanced," he says. He had not seen an electric stove, a traffic light or a computer.

Deng Kuot Kuot wants to ask a question about America. It's about girls, a subject important to any 21-year old. Deng has lived here 22 days, long enough to master the toothbrush, the flush toilet, the electric stove and a dinner table set with enough food to fill one's stomach. "Please, can you tell me," he asks, as his friends Ben Yak Bol and Gabriel Malwal lean forward to listen, "in America, if you wish to marry a girl, what is the dowry to be paid? How many cattle must be promised?"

One April night, Deng, Ben, and Gabriel flew into Burlington, though they might as well have landed on the moon. Eight hours earlier, they had never heard the word "Vermont." Two days earlier, they would not have recognized anything in the airport terminal; not carpet, TV monitor, nor overhead lights that turned night into day. Outside, the throngs of cars reminded Ben of herds of cattle.

They had arrived in an unimaginably distant place, carried by the power of their story to move hearts around the world, the tale of the Lost Boys of Sudan. The name, borrowed from the children's story, "Peter Pan," describes a generation of Sudanese boys driven from their tribal villages by a devastating civil war between north and south Sudan. Ben, Deng, and Gabriel fled their burning villages in the late 1980s. Ben had watched as his father was shot to death. They joined a city of wandering boys, at least 17,000 strong.

The boys walked anywhere from 700 to 1,000 miles, first to Ethiopia, then back to Sudan, then south to Kenya, looking for safety. They survived death by starvation and thirst, death by crocodile and lion, death by dysentery and cholera, death by bullet and bomb.

Seven- and 8-year olds became each other's parents, binding one another's wounds, sharing sips of muddy water, burying their dead. No one knows how many thousands died. In 1992, about 12,000 boys stumbled into Kenya. Their ribs stuck out, and their eyes were huge with hunger. At a refugee camp called Kakuma they found thin rations, a makeshift school and precarious safety.

The Lost Boys' story spread to Europe and America. Even governments were moved. Last year the United States agreed to resettle about 3,800 Lost Boys and a few dozen girls in places like Burlington, Seattle, Grand Rapids, Mich., and Fargo, ND (Few girls were among the fleeing children because they were more likely to have escaped or died, with their parents.)

Since January, 24 Lost Boys – now young men of 18-26 – have arrived in Vermont from a world lit only by fire and lantern. Their only preparation was three days of "cultural orientation." In the 100-degree heat of Kakuma, Ben touched his first piece of ice to understand "cold." Pain shot up his arm.

They stepped from the airplane owning nothing but thin plastic bags of immigration documents. They do not even know their birth dates. Without parents, they can only guess their ages, so officials at Kakuma assigned them all the same birthday, January 1.

"This place is the backbone of the world," says 21-year-old Isaac Luek with wonder. "There is no fighting... This is a good place for me." Isaac, Deng, Ben, and the rest have been placed in apartments in Winsooki and Burlington by the Vermont Refugee Resettlement Program. They will receive a government grant of $456 a month for up to eight months. The center will arrange English and high school equivalency classes. Most have never held a job, ridden a bus, operated a machine, worn a coat. As adult refugees, they are expected to find work and move toward self-sufficiency within 90 days. As boys newborn to this world, they are excited and terrified.

One moment they laugh uproariously at the improvidence of American fathers for failing to collect dowries. "But he has had all of the expenses of raising this girl. How is he to be compensated?" Ben asks in his careful English. His friends chuckle, shaking their heads. Their fathers paid 50, 100, even 200 cows for a wife. The next moment the young men are depressed and anxious. They know almost no one. They are fearful of walking even the mile to Church Street, unsure of what is allowed, scared of the speeding traffic, unconvinced that Burlington is friendly territory.

But, as when they fled across Sudan, they know there is no turning back. "If you go back to Sudan, you will be killed," says round-faced Gabriel. "Here I am now, wearing good clothes with a mattress to sleep on and I have a light. It is a very wonderful thing to me."

Ben, Deng and some friends lope through the Burlington airport parking garage, eager to meet groups of new Sudanese arrivals. As they pass a set of automatic doors, the doors slide open and shut, open and shut. They gaze a second in amazement, then collapse in laughter and a chatter of Dinka. One backs up a step, just to watch the doors obey this invisible command. One way or another, the Lost Boys have spent their lives adapting. Once, their world was bounded by small villages of mud-and-grass huts, the home of the Dinka tribe on the high, hot grasslands of southern Sudan. Dinka are tall men with skin the color of Lake Champlain slate. Their lives center on their herds of milk-giving, long-horned cattle. Men name each cow, sing songs to them, use them for barter. Boys dig clay and make their own toy cows. "You cannot say 'I am Dinka' if you are not having cattle," says Bior Kuer, the 19-year-old son of a Dinka chief.

War destroyed this world. Sudan's government is controlled by Muslim northerners who have waged relentless war on the Christian and animist tribes of the south, slaughtering their cattle, burning their homes. Women and children have paid the price. Deng was 8, a little boy caring for his family's herds of goats, when government soldiers attacked. He ran into the forest and lost his mother in the confusion. He followed other children and elders of his village as began walking east, away from the fighting. He learned to drink water instead of milk, to go to sleep hungry and to walk when his legs felt too tired to move. Even when he reached Kakuma refugee camp, life was comfortless and primitive. The boys lived on wheat flour and dried corn, slept on plastic sheets on the ground.

They seemed to have no future. Their numbers dwindled from 12,000 to about 4,000. Some died, many more ran away to Kenya's cities. To the north, war and famine had turned southern Sudan into a nation of displaced persons – 4 million people have been forced from their villages, according to the U.S. Committee for Refugees. They lived in Dinka limbo, too old to be boys, but – without any cattle wealth, without the facial scarification and other rituals of manhood – too young to be Dinka men. "Those ones who have the signs of manhood, they can call you a boy," says Ben. He loved a Dinka girl, Mary, at Kakuma but had no chance of marriage. He had no cattle, even to promise for the future.

Simon Jok, just four days in America, drains a glass of ordinary, made-from-concentrate Hood orange juice and closes his eyes a moment. "I thought, unless you go to heaven, you cannot get juice like this," he says reverently. "Perhaps not even in heaven." Compared to surviving civil war, adjusting to the surface of American life – to telephones, pizza, and traffic lights – has left Deng, Ben, Gabriel and the others more amused than bewildered. "They are the smartest guys," says Rachel Hutchins of Charlotte, a volunteer who spends hours each day with them. "You never have to explain anything twice." Some who arrived in February had never made a telephone call. Now the phone list on the wall is 11 inches long, with numbers in Seattle, Phoenix, New York City, Nairobi, and Khartoum.

Ben saunters along the dairy case at Shaw's supermarket, loading juice carton after juice carton into his cart and fussily searching along the shelf for the pineapple-orange juice he now prefers after two weeks in America. In the vegetable section, he turns a head of broccoli over and over. "What is this?" he starts to ask, then tosses it into the cart, deciding to try it, whatever it is. Later, he zips a debit card into a computer terminal to pay the bill. His only questions about the transaction: "But, from where is the money coming?" Some lessons have been easy. Don't put the lettuce in the freezer. Pull the paper cover off to find the tea bag. Turn the handle to open the screen door. "This stove is quite advanced," Ben says, looking at the aging four-burner model in the kitchen of his chase Street apartment. "I was quite confused by these controls. I thought, 'will it explode?'" Other concepts remain bewildering. Ben, Deng, and their four apartment mates – all of them giraffe-thin and recovering from semi-starvation – pull big bottles of Coke out of the refrigerator at dinnertime. Diet Coke.

Deng Kuot, clad in a tank top, jeans, hightops and a Chicago Bulls wool hat, sits amid the after-dinner chaos of nine large men in a small kitchen. He props the book in front of him and tries to study it. The title reads: "The Declaration of Independence and the U.S. Constitution." Abraham Awolich, 22, spent his refugee camp days attending school for six hours, then walking a four-mile round trip to a Kenyan library. He sometimes sold part of his 15-day food allotment to acquire a 20-shilling library card. "That is difficult, to give up food, but I can do it because my interest is to read," he says. He made himself a study timetable and began to learn cell physiology and the "chemicals of life" (organic chemistry, he means) from books in the library. Now he works the second shift as a custodian at the University of Vermont. That work was exhausting at first. Abraham stands 6-feet 2-inches and weighed 120 pounds when he arrived in Vermont in February. He's put on 30 pounds but still tires too easily. From Marsh Life Sciences, where he cleans the floors, he can see Bailey/Howe Library 50 yards away, a building with thousands of books. "But I fear to go in," he says, "Perhaps it is not allowed? Perhaps a ticket is needed?"

A week ago a dozen of the young men sat along the wall at a dance party at Memorial Auditorium and watched the American couples. They remembered the girlfriends they were allowed to see, by appointment, at Kakuma. "Everybody at that dance had a friend but us," says Abraham Makur Malual sadly. "Now we have another invitation to a party. Are we permitted not to go?" The evening's cook, Deng Deng, divides rice into small bowls. He puts a pot of chicken cooked with onions and cabbage on the table of the Chase Street kitchen and each young man dips out a small piece and some sauce. They eat what would amount to a snack for most Americans, but otherwise joke and jostle like any group of college pals –though few American roommates have saved each others' lives.

Ben, whose Dinka name Yak means "drought," and Deng Kuot, whose name means "rain," fled together across Sudan. Deng was 8, Ben was 7. Many children died on that trip. "If I had water, I shared with Deng," Ben says simply. "We cared for each other."

A visitor slowly begins to sort out the roommates – Ben, the self-assured high school graduate; Deng Denge, the joking clown; Jakob Nyinger, grave, mature and dreaming of becoming a bishop; Deng Kuot, offhand and graceful as a pro basketball player; nearly silent Marthona Malual; and Gabriel Malwal, wide-eyed and earnest. But they resist singling out, finishing each other's sentences, sharing the kitchen work as smoothly as long-married couples. They come from a tribe with an intricate clan structure, in which a man's responsibilities include all his distant relatives. They have formed their own new family in this strange land. It's the first thing that struck Charles Shipman, head of Vermont Refugee Resettlement, who has watched hundreds of refugees fit themselves into Vermont. "There is tremendous cohesiveness in the group," Shipman said, speaking of all 24 Sudanese men. "There is no hierarchy; they all have to consult one another." Hutchins, who has spent the most time with them, says, "This is the greatest thing that has happened to me in my life. They are a joy."

Abraham Malual awakes each day at 4 a.m., his body still set to Kakuma time. He has nothing to do but study the Vermont Drivers Manual, memorizing the insurance rules and puzzling through the shapes of road signs. The day holds a few appointments at government offices, but nothing else. Vermont Refugee Resettlement and the Vermont Adult Learning Program are still struggling to set up classes for the youths. "What is my work?" cries Abraham. "I like to work and here I have nothing. I feel tired and dizzy." Together, they worry – about finding work, about paying the bills. They worry about the friends they left behind in Kakuma. They worry about Sudan, and wish America would bring peace there. Most of all, they worry that they will not get the college education most believed was part of the American bargain. Some finished the Kenyan equivalent of high school, but many have not. Their education is uneven, though all speak some degree of heavily-accented British English.

Though they describe life in Kakuma as "horrible," they attended school there six hours a day. Now they have a 75-minute English class three nights a week, a pace that leaves some of them impatient and wanting more. "They may have very good math skills and never have heard of World War II," says Mary McQuillen, education coordinator at the refugee program. She hopes to start GED, or high school equivalency, classes for them soon. Gabriel sometimes listens to a tape cassette of advice sent with him by Dinka elders. "They say, 'Go to college. Learn to help your people. Don't forget Sudan.'" They are not forgetting, Gabriel wants to be a computer engineer. Deng Kuot, an agriculture minister; Ben, "A social scientist and peacemaker, to help my people." But even three weeks in America has taught them the price of an education. For eight years, whatever meager food and learning they received was given to them. Now they will have to learn self-sufficiency. "To go to college costs much money in America," Deng says. "From where will we obtain this money?" Other youths chime in. Gabriel won't hear of this pessimism. "In Africa, I lived in the darkness," he says, "Now I live in the light."

Questions for Discussion

1. What are the roles for social justice work and how do these roles address the power dynamics inherent in the social work relationship?
2. What roles of social justice work are likely to be practiced using Díaz's process of participatory planning (i.e., eight moments)? Who would be important participants in the process?
3. From your own experience, what specific participatory decision-making strategies and skills respect opposing viewpoints and let people know their viewpoints count?
4. In your own words, how would you describe the role of animator and methods of animation?
5. What are the strengths and challenges of Kelly & Sewell's types of social enactment? How does an understanding of types of social enactment inform practice?
6. How would you define popular education, and what role do you see it playing in social justice work?
7. Where might you need to use the guidelines for building a coalition and forming alliances across organizations and groups? Give an example.
8. How would you describe policy practice? What factors do you think have made it difficult for social workers to realize Figueira-McDonough's meaning of the policy practitioner?
9. What are Figueira-McDonough's four methods of policy practice, and how do these fit with your understanding of social justice work?

Suggested Readings

Anner, J. (Ed.) (1996). *Beyond identity politics.* Boston: South End Press.

Boal, A. (1982). *Theatre of the oppressed.* New York: Routledge.

Boyd, A. (1999). *The activist cookbook. Creative actions for a fair economy.* Boston, MA: United for a Fair Economy.

Brown, C. & Mazza, G. (1997). *Healing into action: A leadership guide for creating diverse communities.* Washington, DC: National Coalition Building Institute.

Figueira-McDonough, J. (1993). "Policy practice: The neglected side of social work intervention." *Social Work,* 43(4), 335-345.

hooks, b. (1995). *Killing rage: Ending racism.* New York: Henry Holt.

Jansson, B. (1999). *Becoming an effective policy advocate: From policy practice to social justice.* Pacific Grove, CA: Brooks/Cole Publishing Co.

Kaner, S. (1996). *Facilitator's guide to participatory decision-making.* Gabriola Island, BC: New Society.

Leblanc, L. (1999). *Pretty in punk: Girls' resistance in a boys' subculture.* New Brunswick, NJ: Rutger's University Press.

Chapter 8

Evaluating, Reflecting On, and Celebrating Our Efforts

"Knowledge emerges only through invention and re-invention, through the restless, impatient, continuing, hopeful inquiry men [sic] pursue in the world, with the world, and with each other."

Paulo Freire (1970), *Pedagogy of the Oppressed*[1]

"This project was unforgettable for what it left behind. Both the houses and our capacity to have done this. Now you walk down the street and see what we have accomplished. I see things that are, in truth, so beautiful, and that we had the knowledge and skill to create it. It is something that doesn't happen everywhere. Here is a humble group of folks like us and we've achieved such a valiant effort... We'd gone through all of these problems with lights, sanitation, and water, and now we have left behind something important."

Pobladora (1999), Villa Paula Jaraquemada, Chile[2]

Chapter Overview

In Chapter Eight we elaborate on the Just Practice core processes of evaluation, critical reflection, and celebration. We begin by looking at different approaches to evaluation and highlighting participatory evaluation and its importance for social justice work. We discuss the strengths and challenges of participatory evaluation. We present the concept of catalytic validity as a way to assess the effectiveness of research efforts and their capacity to promote social justice-oriented action. Guidelines are presented for the participatory design of evaluation tools and processes. We explore the time and resource constraints that can often hamper such efforts. Drawing from practice examples, we show how participatory evaluation can contribute to personal, organizational, community, and sociopolitical empowerment, and how the processes and outcomes contribute to critical theory and practice knowledge.

In Chapter Eight we also identify characteristics of the reflective thinker and explore ways to build capacity for critical reflection. Critical reflection is both a tool of inquiry and a constant companion of evaluation practice. We discuss problem posing as a way to initiate, sustain, and enrich critical reflection. We consider the kinds of questions that the Just Practice Framework asks us to reflect upon in order to make meaningful connections between personal struggles and larger social, political, economic, and cultural forces. Critical reflection guides us in questioning the structures and relations of power embedded in the definitions of personal and societal concerns. Critical reflection demands vigilance on the part of the social worker to look for potential pitfalls and barriers to our actions. We expand on the core process of celebration and argue the importance of recognizing successes, appreciating contributions, and relishing in the learning that happens at rough spots along the way. We introduce notions of ritual and play as essential elements of social justice work. We draw attention to the aesthetics of practice and the importance of finding joy and beauty in the work we do.

Evaluation

Defining Evaluation

We define evaluation as the act of taking stock and determining the significance, effectiveness, or quality of a change effort. It is also about asking questions that appraise the effort and assess whether actions were consistent with the values of social justice work. Striving toward congruence in values and action is of critical importance here. Evaluation is an integral and ongoing part of social justice work that shapes and is shaped by teaching-learning, action, and accompaniment. One can think of evaluation in a number of ways:

1. **Evaluation as research.** Evaluation is a form of research that follows a systematic process. The process consists of planning, implementing the plan, collecting information, making sense of the information, and disseminating the results. Evaluation has three major thrusts: a) assessing process, the ways and means of meeting goals and objectives; b) assessing outcomes or the impacts of particular change strategies; and c) assessing the strengths, skills, and challenges of workers and others involved in the change effort.
2. **Evaluation as a benchmark.** Evaluation needs to be continuous. It should happen at various checkpoints in the change process, not only at the end. Checkpoints create stopping off places where participants can reflect on cumulative change, make comparisons to other checkpoints, and appreciate the distance covered in understanding and altering attitudes and events. As Díaz (1997) notes in Chapter Seven, evaluation is a point on our journey where we step back and consider the place we want to reach and the path we are taking. It is a point where we ask: Are we moving in the direction that we want to go?
3. **Evaluation as an individual and group memory process.** Evaluation is the act of recording lessons learned, thus enabling history to become a basis for ongoing learning. Lappe and Dubois (1994) describe this as a process of creating individual and group memory. Having a sense of history helps us learn from experience. And, through the sharing of experiences among participants in the change process, we develop critical consciousness and collective memory of our histories, struggles, hopes, and actions that can both inform the process and motivate the participants.
4. **Evaluation as a statement of assumptions and values.** Behind every evaluation method or strategy is a set of assumptions about people, human nature, power, and the nature of reality. It is important to think about these assumptions and how they influence and shape evaluation practice. Just as we spoke of valuing as an ethical and political practice in Chapter Three, we can think of evaluation as the systematization of valuing.
5. **Evaluation as private and participatory processes.** Evaluation is a private, personal, reflective act. Paulo Freire (1990) describes the

progressive social worker as someone who is on a life-long search for competence. Self-evaluation is key to this search. Evaluation is also a participatory process, not something *done on* others, but *with* others. Thinking of evaluation as a joint project is a way to value the contributions of others and open up possibilities for new solutions to old problems. We elaborate on evaluation as a participatory process later on in this chapter.

6. **Evaluation as accountability.** Evaluation is a process of demonstrating accountability to participants in the change process, to those affected, to our organizations, and to funding sources. Participatory approaches to change and to evaluation of change efforts are demanding and time consuming. They require dedication and commitment from all parties involved. Evaluation gives us pause to consider whether people's time has been well spent with results to show for their work. Has the process enhanced their skills and capacities? Has the process made the most of available resources? Has it strengthened our organizational capacity and sparked the imagination of funders? Has it challenged or silenced critics?

Different Approaches to Evaluation

Positivist Assumptions. Evaluation principles and methods derive from two very different ways of thinking about research. Each approach is a value statement that shapes and guides different practice possibilities. As we discussed in Chapter Four, *positivism* has been the dominant philosophy and ideology guiding research and evaluation in social work and the social sciences in general. Although there are many versions of positivism, it is generally described as rooted in assumptions of objectivity – the idea that there is indeed a single, stable, and ultimately "knowable" reality outside ourselves that we can break into controllable parts called variables and subject them to inquiry. In the interest of objectivity, the researcher maintains distance from the subject of the research to prevent contamination and bias. In effect, the researcher is separated from the researched – the object of inquiry (Maguire, 1987). Positivism seeks to make generalizations about reality that are truth claims, free from context and time, and therefore applicable to other times and places. Positivism attempts to control and isolate reality to uncover causes and effects in linear fashion. If one's methods are thought to be objective, then it follows that these methods control for the personal values and assumptions of the researcher. Inquiry based on a positivist perspective is thus considered to be value free (Denzin & Lincoln, 1994; Lincoln & Guba, 1985; Maguire, 1987; Neuman, 1997; Rubin & Babbie, 2001).[3]

Participatory Assumptions. Participatory approaches to research question positivist assumptions. They challenge notions of objectivity and value-free inquiry and practices that separate the researcher from the researched. They are more interpretive in nature, recognizing the importance of local knowledge and experience in developing a grounded understanding of social reality. As reported by Finn (1994, p. 26), the basic tenets of participatory research include "the meaningful involvement of people in addressing the concerns that affect their lives; recognition of knowledge as power; and commitment to a process of critical action and reflection (Brown, 1985; Fernandes, 1989; Gaventa, 1988; Maguire, 1987)."

Participatory approaches hold that meaningful research is only possible through cooperation and involvement with those from whom one seeks to gain information (Finn, 1994; Hall, 1975, 1981; Park, 1993, 1997). Time and place are viewed as shapers of knowledge and, therefore, inextricable from the process of meaningful research. Participatory approaches see reality as mutually constituted and mutually shaping, thereby making it impossible to separate cause from effect. All inquiry is embedded in values and assumptions that underlie each step of the research process from conception through implementation and interpretation. Participatory researchers make values explicit, expose personal assumptions and perspectives, and openly contend with how these influence their choice of methods and modes of analysis. They strive for critical awareness of their own subjectivity in the research situation and process, and in their effects upon it. Evaluation is viewed as a social process and the participants have a role and impact in the process. It is, nonetheless, a systematic and rigorous process that attempts to account for the ways in which values, positioning, and perspective may shape the process (Lather, 1986, 1991; Maguire, 1987; Park, 1993, 1997).

Proponents of participatory approaches to research understand that research produces knowledge and that knowledge is power. For this reason, "Research can never be neutral. It is always supporting or questioning social forces, both by its content and by its method. It has effects and side-effects, and these benefit or harm people" (Reason & Rowan, 1981, p. 489, quoted in Maguire, 1987, p. 24). In sum, participatory research is about people, power, and praxis. As Finn (1994) writes:

> [P]articipatory research is grounded in an explicit political stance and clearly articulated value base. It challenges positivist notions of scientific objectivity and value neutrality. Participatory researchers support a process of inquiry in which private problems become public questions (As, 1988). Participatory research links personal experience to political contexts through critical reflection and action. In this process, theory is emergent, not imposed. Ideally, participatory research generates knowledge for action, contributes to organization building, and supports sustained efforts for social change. (p. 27)

Qualitative versus Quantitative Approaches? Participatory approaches value both qualitative and quantitative methods of inquiry. In social work, as well as the social sciences, there has been ongoing debate about the relative merits of *qualitative* research, that is, research that emphasizes "... processes and meaning that are not rigourously examined, or measured (if measured at all), in terms of quantity, amount, intensity, or frequency" (Denzin & Lincoln, 1994, p. 4). On the other hand, *quantitative* research is said to "...emphasize the measurement and analysis of causal relationships between variables, not processes" (Denzin & Lincoln, 1994, p. 4). When we explored the history of social work in Chapter Two, we discussed the dichotomies that have, at times, served to polarize the profession into two distinct camps (i.e. distinctions between casework and community-based practice). We prefer to move beyond these dichotomies in our discussion here and remind the reader that qualitative and quantitative research approaches can be quite complementary (Firestone, 1986). Each method brings its own strengths to the process, and they can be effectively combined. In fact, part of a participatory process may involve decisions to gather very specific quantitative information or use existing quantitative measures in order to evaluate ways in which particular programs, policies, or practices affect particular groups. Using multiple methods provides the opportunity to "triangulate," that is, to make comparisons of the data across methods. As Jicks (1979) contends, triangulation "can improve the accuracy of [researchers'] judgments by collecting different kinds of data bearing on the same phenomenon" (p. 602). Triangulation also adds to the richness and depth of the inquiry by providing a means in which to accommodate multiple perspectives.

Questions of Reliability and Validity

Claims against participatory modes of inquiry call it undisciplined and too subjective to count as "real" research. Critics contend that "legitimate" research must be reliable and valid. These terms may be familiar to you if you have already taken a research methods course. Reliability and validity relate to the trustworthiness of the research knowledge and its results (Lincoln & Guba, 1985). Williams, Unrau, and Grinnell (1998) contend that the test of reliability is whether an evaluation tool measures the same variable repeatedly, with consistency, and produces the same results. The concept of validity relates to:

> . . . the ways in which the research design ensures that the introduction of the independent variable (if any) can be identified as the sole cause of change in the dependent variable. . . and the extent to which the research design allows for generalization of the findings of the study to other groups and other situations. (p. 194)

For example, in studying whether drug abuse causes domestic violence, the independent variable is drug abuse and the dependent variable is domestic violence. Internal validity asks how we know that changes in domestic violence (dependent variable) are a result of drug abuse (independent variable) and not a result of other factors. External validity asks how can we be sure that the information we have gathered reflects only respondents' information and not the researcher's biases or judgments (Marlow, 2001). Can we generalize our information to other circumstances and situations? The ideal study is thought to be one where the research design attempts to control both internal and external threats to validity.[4]

These notions of what is right and true in research are under question today. In an effort to bridge schools of thought, some have referred to research inquiry as "objectively subjective" (Lincoln & Guba, 1985). For example, Lincoln and Guba argue for rigor in qualitative approaches to research and present a set of techniques to ensure validity and to establish the reliability or trustworthiness of the results. One of these techniques is member checks (pp. 314-316).[5] Individual research team members appraise and analyze information alone before discussing their findings with the entire research team. Agreement and working out disagreements assure some measure of truth in the data. These are areas of ongoing debate and dialogue.

Lather (1986,1991) takes on the controversial subject of reliability and validity and looks at particular criteria that best serve research with a participatory approach and a social justice aim. She argues that researchers who blend theory and justice-oriented action (praxis) may want to consider the less well-known notion of *catalytic validity* as a guiding light. Lather defines catalytic validity as "the degree to which the research process re-orients, focuses and energizes participants toward knowing reality in order to transform it . . ." (Lather, 1991, p. 68).[6] She ties this in with the Freirean concept of conscientization, meaning that all involved in the knowledge generation process (research) and changed through this process, "gain self-understanding and, ultimately, self-determination through research participation" (p. 68). Lather emphasizes that participatory inquiry can stand up to the test of rigor and relevance in research and must do so to promote the emanicipatory possibilities of participatory research and evaluation.

Bricoleur – The Role of the Researcher

Recall from our discussion in Chapter Seven of social worker roles how we highlighted the role of researcher in social justice work. Our definition stressed the importance of ongoing critical reflection on and evaluation of one's practice. We also emphasized incorporating this idea of research into our daily practice rather than excluding those we work with and ourselves from a process that lends itself readily to teaching-learning. We also introduced you to the notion of the *bricoleur*, a role never mentioned in social work texts. It is one that we borrow from the field of anthropology. Levi-Strauss defined a *bricoleur* as a "Jack of all trades or a kind of professional do-it-yourself person" (Levi-Strauss, 1966, p. 17 as cited in Denzin & Lincoln, 1994, p. 2). We revisit this notion of the *bricoleur* to make some important linkages between this role and doing research (Denzin & Lincoln, 1994, pp. 2-3). Imagine someone who improvises, makes use of the material and expertise at hand, combines multiple methods in which to achieve solutions, and adds to her repertoire of skills and techniques as the situation demands:

> If new tools have to be invented, or pieced together, then the researcher will do this. The choice of which tools to use, which research practices to employ, is not set in advance. The 'choice of research practices depends upon the questions that are asked, and the questions depend on their context' (Nelson et al., 1992, p. 2), what is available in the context, and what the researcher can do in the setting. . . The *bricoleur* is adept at performing a large number of diverse tasks, ranging from interviewing to observing, to interpreting personal and historical documents, to intensive self-reflection and introspection. (Denzin & Lincoln, p. 2)

The *bricoleur* is also mindful of the subjective nature of inquiry (Denzin and Lincoln, p. 3). Denzin and Lincoln remind us that all facets of the research process, from planning to analysis, are influenced by the positionality of the researcher and in the case of participatory approaches to inquiry, the positionality of others involved in the process. Issues concerning personal history, race, social class, and gender shape the ways in which those involved in the process arrive at questions to pose, the means and methods through which these questions will be addressed, and the strategies for analyzing the information collected. The process and end product of the *bricoleur's* work is what Denzin and Lincoln call the bricolage – "a collage-like creation that represents the researcher's images, understandings, and interpretation of the world or phenomenon under analysis" (p. 3). Think for a moment of how the results could be represented based on the intended impact you wish to make. Who could be influenced or changed by the results? Through what means (codes, graphics, skits, etc.) might you realize your intentions?

Participatory Approaches to Evaluation

Positivist-oriented evaluation practices generally do not include the involvement of participants in a change effort or project. Instead, evaluation tends to be a top/down approach, conceived by program administrators and conducted by outside experts. Workers and those they work with are the researched. Evaluation is something done *to* them, not *with* them. We imagine evaluation differently. We see it as a participatory process whereby all participants are afforded opportunities to reflect on programs, projects, and policies, the mission and aims of the organization, and their own and others' involvement in change efforts. Evaluation is something done *with* people, not *on* people.

Origination and Intent of Participatory Approaches

Participatory approaches to research are reported to have originated in Latin America, India, and Africa where understandings of power and domination forged resistance to knowledge development and research methods based on the positivist paradigm. Yet, early settlement house workers also engaged in community-based research methods where they enlisted neighborhood residents as research team members. For example, they gathered information about the disparities between women's and men's wages, investigated the working conditions of female-dominated employment settings and designed and implemented survey research to assess community needs and conditions (Van Kleeck, 1913, 1917; Zimbalist, 1977). Their methodology was shaped by the historical, political, and economic context at the turn of the 20th century, a context similar to conditions that shaped similar research methods in Latin America, India, and Africa beginning in the 1960s.

Generally, survey research is constructed with researcher-predetermined, forced-choice questions. Often this type of research fails to consider the racist and class biases built into the structuring of questions. They are languaged for the educated, white, middle-class respondent and allow no room for the richness and depth of understanding that ordinary people might bring to the issues that shape their daily lives. To address these omissions, early participatory researchers developed alternative strategies for information gathering and analysis that valued and included peoples' lived experience in every stage of the research process (Hall, 1993). Research by the people and for the people is a powerful tool for addressing power imbalances and other forms of inequality that shape people's lives.

Survey Research for Social Change: The Appalachian Land Ownership Study

Billy D. Horton's (1993, pp. 85-102) work provides an example of survey research for social change and how the participation of "ordinary" people in the research process addresses inequality in the generation of knowledge. He tells the story of a coalition of individuals and organizations who formed the Appalachian Alliance to address problems related to the ownership and control of the region's natural resources by absentee corporations with little investment in the community or its people. This loss of control over land ownership and land-use patterns had forged feelings of hopelessness among residents who had little power to influence social and economic development in their communities. After the flood of 1977, when many communities were devastated by rising floodwaters, citizens began to connect the severity of the damage to unregulated strip-mining in the watersheds. The Appalachian Alliance formed a task group to document the extent and effects of absentee ownership and control. The group arrived at a set of goals for their project which consisted of providing a model for citizen-conducted research; training local citizens and groups in obtaining the necessary information; developing a network of people concerned with land-related issues; and using the research results to mobilize and educate a broader constituency of people to impact change at federal and state policy levels.

The task force conducted a participatory study that took two years to complete. The results supported popular knowledge and confirmed that 1% of the population owned 53% of the land holdings. Mineral and land resources were absentee-owned with large corporations dominating the land ownership picture. Taxation of corporations for mineral rights was minimal, thereby adding little to the revenues supporting local government and the needs of its citizens. Horton explains that although the results of the study were impressive, the measure of the study's success is in the continued use of information to forge social change and the networks established through the research. These networks built a power base for sustained action.

Take a moment to reflect on what Horton's story teaches about how research can be a tool used to affect change in the lives of ordinary people. What does Horton's story tell you about knowledge and research as power? Think of some issues you may have wanted to take action on in your life but needed more information before you could act. How could Horton's story inform your process?

Summary of Participatory Principles

Participatory evaluation has some distinct features and assumptions when compared to traditional forms of evaluation. It brings individuals most affected by an issue together with administrators and researchers to pose questions and arrive at solutions. As we have seen in the preceding chapters, the conduit of knowledge is *dialogue*. Everyone learns from each other through collective interaction. In addition, program or project participants also learn the skills of collecting, analyzing, and disseminating evaluation knowledge. Action plans and strategies implemented collectively feed into the evaluation process and initiate change in research methods and strategies and in the participants themselves. Patricia Maguire (1987) states:

> Collective investigation, education, and action are important to the re-humanizing goal of participatory research. By treating people as objects to be counted, surveyed, predicted, and controlled, traditional research mirrors oppressive social conditions which cause ordinary people to relinquish their capacity to

> make real choices and to be cut out of meaningful decision making. The collective processes of participatory research help rebuild people's capacity to be creative actors on the world. (p. 30)

Participatory research challenges the lack of attention to *power* in traditional research. It assumes that everything we do is embedded within a political context, and this context shapes the questions we ask and the kinds of research we conduct. Participatory evaluation disrupts the idea of expert knowledge and research as a tool solely of the "educated." It holds that all people have the capacity to better understand their lives and shape their own reality. Theoretically, participatory evaluation shares common ground with social work's empowerment perspective. Both seek to promote social justice and equality through full participation in society. Both seek to build human capacity.

The Skipping School in Montana Project

Maxine Jacobson tells the story of a community-based, participatory research project that involved welfare activist organizations, legislators, policy advocates, program administrators, students, and welfare recipients. As you read through this narrative see if you can identify some of the elements of participatory research discussed so far in this chapter. What participatory principles emerge from this work? What issues of importance might you address through a similar process?

> The objectives of the Skipping School Project responded to some alarming local statistics indicating a substantial decrease in the number of welfare recipients enrolled in post-secondary education in the first four years of Families Achieving Independence In Montana (FAIM), Montana's response to federal welfare reform policies enacted in 1996 during the Clinton Administration. In Missoula County alone, during the first three years of FAIM welfare recipient enrollments plummeted from 178 to 33. Nationally, similar patterns emerged to add credibility to this local trend. For example, City University of New York reported a precipitous decline in welfare recipients' enrollment from 27,000 to 17,000 over a three-year period (Pierre, 1997; Schmidt, 1998). Local research studies completed in the first few years of FAIM overwhelmingly indicated a plethora of other problems connected to the poorly thought out welfare reform policies of

the Clinton Administration. These policies threatened to change the face of welfare "as we know it" and they did. The impacts of welfare reform in Montana were rapid and far reaching. They reverberated through the system, influencing nonprofit community agencies working with low-income families and state agencies mandated to enforce the new policies (Finn & Underwood, 2000; Miller, 1998).

Overwhelmingly, the research literature indicates that post-secondary education has always been women's most promising pathway out of poverty (Abramovitz, 1996; Dujon & Withorn, 1996; Jimenez, 1999; Kates, 1996). Current federal and state welfare policies and practices fly in the face of empirical evidence and in effect, narrow the pathway out of poverty by posing substantial barriers to post-secondary education for low income families receiving public assistance. Barriers include strict assistance time limits preventing completion of school; mandatory workfare programs that trap people into low-paying jobs; lack of child care benefits and failure on the part of child care services to accommodate to the school and work schedules of families; and school quotas limiting the number of welfare recipients enrolled in post-secondary education at any one point in time (Cholewa & Smith, 1999; Sklar, 1995; Spatz, 1997).

The Skipping School Project addressed the declining numbers of welfare recipients enrolled in post-secondary education by incorporating service learning and feminist pedagogy with community-based participatory research. It brought together students from a University of Montana course on Gender and the Politics of Welfare, a Missoula-based feminist organization called Women's Opportunity and Resource Development, Inc. (WORD), a welfare rights advocacy organization called Working for Equality and Economic Liberation (WEEL), and the Montana's Women's Lobby with welfare program administrators and workers, welfare recipients, child care providers and Montana State legislators. I co-facilitated the class with the director of WORD. She brought her expertise on Montana politics and I brought mine on participatory research. Students played a major role in the project. They compiled secondary data on welfare reform, arranged and developed questions for and facilitated meetings with key players, taped and transcribed the meetings, analyzed the results, and presented these to legislators at Montana's state capitol in

Helena in February of 2001. One of the biggest achievements of the project was that Montana legislators voted to have school count as work to satisfy the work requirements of FAIM. This objective was achieved through the collaborative efforts of all involved.

Students found their experience enlivening and inspiring but also frustrating and challenging. They identified the emotional content of their learning and brought their awareness to bear on class discussion. They learned about partializing problems to avoid feeling overwhelmed and hopeless. They came to understand how power plays through their assumptions of welfare recipients and welfare reform, and they began to appreciate the political implications of these assumptions and their impact on policy decisions and definitions of social problems. They learned about research and themselves by engaging in research. They began to understand the research process as a way to collectively take action and as a means to build their own and others' political engagement and empowerment.

The Participatory Process

Some Examples. Participatory research follows a process quite similar to processes we employ to solve problems and find solutions. Peter Park (1993) outlines the research process and recounts how all participatory research begins with a problem. He illustrates this point by using examples of participatory projects from around the world and the problems they addressed: peasants struggles for land in the Philippines and India; women's efforts to achieve equality around the issues of economic exploitation, sexual harassment, and domestic violence in India and the United States; immigrants' need to organize themselves for cultural solidarity in Canada and the U.S.; the health conditions of the poor in Brazil; and popular participation in the sociocultural transformation accompanying the revolution in Nicaragua (see Park, 1993, p. 8).

Ted Jackson (1993) reports on the use of participatory research methods by Canada's Aboriginal movement. This interest coincided with the politicization of Aboriginal organizations following a governmental move toward assimilation in 1969. This push stimulated Aboriginal organizations to insist on claiming their traditional land. Jackson states that "Aboriginal leaders began to see that research activities could assist in the movement toward political strength and, ultimately, political self-determination" (p. 49). The research project consisted of oral histories, documenting traditional land use for hunting, fishing, and trapping and accessing maps of the territory. Research results fed into legislative processes to influence land use policies. As these examples illustrate, participatory research has been used around the world to forge change and win people a voice in the issues that have importance to their lives.

People and Participation. Ideally, participatory projects originate from the people whose lives are most affected by particular concerns. Pragmatically speaking, given the powerlessness that keeps many people from organizing, participatory projects most often originate through an external agent such as a community agency, a university, or a church group. Getting people involved is the next step. People's participation starts with the formulation of the research questions. The research team makes decisions collaboratively. They decide what information needs to be gathered and then they divide research tasks among participants. Social workers facilitate this process by gathering people together, conducting small and large group discussions, and helping to formulate the problem in such a way that it can be researched. Participants play active research roles, instead of merely being the providers of information as is typical in most evaluation efforts. Participants help to decide the research design and method used to carry out the evaluation. People learn about research by actively participating in research. This process demystifies research and puts it in the hands of ordinary people. Through these methods, participatory research projects build human capacity. They teach the skills of conducting research while simultaneously promoting critical consciousness.

Grassroots Research with Homeless People

Susan Yeich (1996) describes the principles and processes of participatory research by using the case example of the Homeless Union project. The project's goal was to empower participants in Lansing, Michigan in the struggle to fight homelessness in their community. The outcome of the research process was the formation of a union for and of homeless people, which, after three years, grew to include 350 people.

In her role as an organizer, Yeich approached homeless people and got them interested in forming a union. The union's activities included fundraising, presenting information at conferences to legislators, city council members, educators, and concerned citizen groups, organizing public demonstrations, and recruiting new members. Yeich offered to serve initially as the group's advisor, and other advisors came on board along the way. Eventually, the union gained non-profit status, and it continues to be a vital organization sustained solely by its membership.

In describing how the union formed, Yeich breaks down the research process into three components commonly discussed in reference to participatory research approaches - research, education, and action (Hall, 1981; Maguire, 1987):

- **Research Component**: The union started their work by accessing previous studies that had been completed on the topic of homelessness. Some of these studies were completed locally and others were accessed via the library. There was no need for the group to complete yet another study with so much relevant material at hand.
- **Education Component**: This component consists of three subparts: "creation of common knowledge, transfer of knowledge to the people, and development of critical awareness" (Yeich, 1996, p. 117). The formation of the union brought people together to share their experiences of homelessness and poverty's influence on their lives. Yeich, in her role as advisor, shared her knowledge about unions and their formation. Participants took up the task and developed one of their own. Developing critical awareness, in this case, means linking structural forces with causations of poverty. Yeich discusses how the development of critical awareness was a natural byproduct of other activities undertaken by the group.
- **Social Action Component:** Yeich describes how gradually this component of the participatory research process evolved. The union and its membership took action to address the cutting of social programs by a new governor. Union members demonstrated, networked with other groups to form a more powerful base for change, and educated other citizens about the need to come to action.

  Yeich maps out the progression of activities and events and how these unfold in her participatory research on homelessness. Think for a moment of the components she outlines and their usefulness as a framework for thinking about and structuring participatory research. How might you use this framework? What issues, problems, or concerns might you address? How might the role of bricoleur be helpful to you here?

Why Evaluate, What to Evaluate, and How?

The Wisdom of Evaluation

The old saying, "The only way forward is to take one step back," illustrates well the wisdom of evaluation. Evaluation allows time for rethinking and reorganizing change efforts and strategies based on reflection, interpretation, and analysis. Evaluation calls on participants to see gains, growth, and successes in organized efforts and to use these as a springboard into subsequent action. Evaluation also calls attention to the challenges of our change efforts and provides a process to address these challenges and build new knowledge to forge subsequent efforts. There is also subsidiary knowledge gained from a participatory evaluation process that has little to do with programs or policy but everything to do with people. Involving people in a partnership to investigate social reality is an empowering and transformative process.

Taking Evaluation Seriously

Social work texts address other reasons why we should take evaluation seriously (Kirst-Ashman & Hull, 2002, pp. 256-260). Political and economic forces call on program administrators to measure their contributions. Social work programs, services, and projects are fund-driven enterprises, and governmental and foundation funders demand results to illustrate their money is well spent. Social workers are accountable to these funding streams. A move toward increased accountability in a context of a diminishing social contract influences the landscape of social work practice and can constrain efforts at individual, group, and community change or forge new possibilities for action. Community organizations that typically conduct evaluations that only indicate the number of "client hours," or cases administered over a year's time are being called upon to evaluate the outcomes of their interventions to assess their effectiveness. At the same time, consumers of services want to know if they are receiving a tried- and-true product, one that will assist them in meeting their needs. Kirst-Ashman and Hull (2002, pp. 256-260) also stress the importance of social workers knowing the outcomes of their efforts. They argue that this point is less attended to than other factors advocating the need for evaluation for the following reasons:

1). Evaluation opens social workers up for scrutiny, leaving them vulnerable.

2). Most service work is crisis-driven, stressful work. Caseloads are high and time for conducting evaluations is at a premium.

3). Many organizations fail to emphasize the importance of evaluation. Evaluation is often an add-on, poorly thought out, and rarely integrated into the structuring of many community organizations.

Evaluation and Constraints

As you can see from this discussion, evaluation is very important to social work but there are also personal, organizational, and external constraints. While Kirst-Ashman and Hull illustrate some of the systemic reasons for the devaluation of evaluation, we argue that social work education must also assume part of the responsibility for the lack of attention given to evaluation in social work practice. Evaluation is often taught in schools of social work as an add-on, poorly integrated into the curriculum, and quarantined to classes in research. Research methods are heavily weighted toward quantitative designs that separate the researcher from the researched. The principles of social justice work support collaborative methods in research design, implementation, and analysis, thus requiring social workers to use the skills they learn in practice courses to conduct research. Participatory approaches to research demand knowledge of relationship and trust building, require skills of leadership and effective communication, and promote the creation of knowledge useful to the worker and the community. It is interesting to note, given this discussion, that Lindsey and Kirk's (1992) study assessing research utilization by NASW members found that only 5% read journal articles to inform their practice. What do you make of this disconnection between social workers and research? Why might these social workers place little value on research? Or should we be asking another question entirely? How does time, or the lack thereof, devoted to reflection on practice within agencies affect attitudes about research? What kinds of research would be the most relevant to practitioners? What reasons can you think of that address why so few NASW members use research to inform their practice?

What Do We Need to Evaluate?

Think for a moment of the varied work situations social workers find themselves in and the multiple functions of social work within particular settings. What should we evaluate and why? What would be important for the child protection services worker to evaluate, for example? Or what might be an important question for a school social worker to pose of a school program that seeks to facilitate parents' increased involvement with their children's education? Hope and Timmel (1999, V. 2, p. 124) suggest we need to evaluate the following areas, although not necessarily at the same time. We pose questions for you to think about as they relate to each area:

- **Aims.** Given the original mission and purpose of the organization or the goals laid out by participants, where are we now? Are we far adrift from these aims or right on the mark?
- **Ethics.** Are practices and procedures ethical and by whose standards? Who is included and who is left out and why? Are we adhering to the principles of social justice work? Do practices and procedures reflect a commitment to social justice?
- **Participation.** Who is involved in the organization's decision making? Are the voices of those the program was meant to benefit valued? Who participates and how?
- **Methods.** Are methods employed consistent with the values of social justice work? Do procedures, policies, and practices allow for the contributions of those most directly concerned with the issues we wish to address? How do these methods deal with or address the issue of difference? Do any methods discriminate based on race, gender, sexual orientation, class, and age?
- **Content.** Does the program or project address participants' expectations? Does the program or project address the root causes of concerns?
- **Animators and Administrators.** What are the leadership skills of the project facilitators or program administrators? What are their strengths and challenges?
- **Follow-up.** How is the program or the project assessed when the work is completed? At checkpoints down the road? Is there a mechanism in place to conduct follow-up?

- **Time and Money.** How much time and money goes into this program or project? Has the time and money produced visible, sustainable results? Is sufficient time and money put toward the effort? Would a different allocation of time and money produce better results?
- **Planning, Coordination, and Administration.** What is the quality of program or project planning? How would you rate the level of coordination among participants, projects, programs, and other community groups and organizations? How are programs and projects administered? What are the strengths and challenges of planning, coordination, and administration?
- **Decision Making.** How does the project or program make decisions? Are these top/down, bottom/up, or a little bit of both? What process is used to make decisions? Is this process collaborative? Whose voices contribute to the decision-making process?

Evaluating Methods of Course Evaluation

Think about the evaluation tool you are administered to assess the college courses you take. Write a list of the types of questions and the kinds of information this tool attempts to elicit. In small groups, brainstorm with other students ways in which you might reconfigure the tool to get at what you feel are the essential components of your teaching/learning experience. Course evaluation tools generally attempt to assess the "teacher." For example, you might be asked whether your teacher came to class prepared or if instructions were clear and easy to understand. Rarely do these tools ask you to assess yourself as a learner/teacher or to make comments about your participation in the learning process. Develop a tool with your classmates that you feel gets at gaps in these evaluation tools. Now, think about how your learning is evaluated. Most teachers assess your learning by administering tests or quizzes, or writing assignments. Brainstorm alternative ways in which your learning could be assessed and evaluated. Present your list to the class for discussion. What did you learn about the meaning of evaluation through this exercise? How does evaluation link to questions of power? What changes would you recommend? What resistance might you meet and why?

Methods of Participatory Evaluation

Participatory evaluation can take many different shapes and forms. It borrows its methods from a variety of social science tools used to conduct other types of research. However, some methods are modified to allow increased interaction between those administering the methods and those providing information. For example, participatory evaluation questionnaires are not mailed out but used instead as a "vehicle of dialogue" (Park, 1993, p. 12). Dialogue is the distinguishing feature of participatory research. Through dialogue, we come to know our communities and ourselves. Park comments on dialogue as a tool of research:

> ". . .dialogue produces not just factual knowledge but also interpersonal and critical knowledge, which defines humans as autonomous social beings. This is an essential reason for the people's participation in research. It is not just so they can reveal private facts that are hidden from others but really so they may know themselves better as individuals and as a community." (pp. 12-13).

Participatory methods must be tailored to the particular context and include consideration of available resources and the assets participants bring with them to the effort. It is important to assess each method for its strengths and limitations. We encourage you to consider the five key concepts of meaning, context, power, history, and possibility as you undertake this assessment. For example:

- Does this method allow for the expression of multiple meanings of objects, events, and situations?
- Does this method help connect personal problems and their larger political, economic, and sociocultural contexts?
- Does this method consider power as it affects relationships among participants? Is this method empowering?
- Does this method allow for points of comparison so history can be a source of learning?
- What creative uses can this method be put to and what possible approaches to evaluation does it bring to mind?

Below we outline some evaluation methods. Can you think of specific situations where different methods might be helpful or where they might be counterproductive?

Written Questionnaires. Questionnaires are the most common method used for participatory evaluation because of their versatility. They can be used when evaluating efforts with individuals, groups, neighborhoods, and entire communities. Through a collaborative process, participants tailor questionnaires to the investigation at hand by prioritizing questions and making sure the wording is clear and easy to understand. Questionnaires generally include both closed- and open-ended questions, which value information respondents choose to give. However, each type of question has its advantages and disadvantages (Neuman, 1997). Questionnaires can be used as a tool to stimulate dialogue. Making the decision to mail out questionnaires or administer them directly depends upon the particular aims of the research and the context of the particular situation. For example, administering questionnaires face-to-face provides you the opportunity to get to know a community or specific population affected by a particular issue. Face-to-face administration also increases the response rate. Mailed questionnaires might be more expedient and cost-effective given the resources you have at hand. However, the response rates are generally lower (Neuman, 1997; Reinhartz, 1992; Rubin & Babbie, 2001).[7]

Informal/Oral Interviews. Conducting informal interviews is another useful way to gather information. They are especially handy at the beginning of an evaluation project when there is a need to gather preliminary information. Perhaps the research team is not quite sure what they need to evaluate or what strategies might be best, or what questions to ask. Conducting informal interviews can be a good way to begin (Neuman, 1997; Reinhartz, 1992; Rubin & Babbie, 2001).

Structured/Semi-structured Interviews. As the group becomes more familiar with the issues and concerns, more focused interviewing can take place. With structured and semi-structured interviews, the interviewer asks questions moving from the general to the specific and from the less personal to the more personal. The research team plans the questions beforehand. Structured and semi-structured interviews are appropriate for repeat interviews, once rapport and trust are developed and once the focus of the evaluation is narrowed down (Neuman, 1997; Reinhartz, 1992; Rubin & Babbie, 2001). The interview process itself may be a catalyst for change (Brown & Tandon, 1978).

Small and Large Group Discussion. Discussion groups are the *sine qua non* of participatory evaluation. Group discussion allows for maximum participation. Groups fulfill other purposes as well. They can be a source of support as well as a venue for addressing differences and conflict. Focus groups are a good example of small group discussion as an evaluation research method (Krueger, 1994; Krueger & King, 1998; Morgan, 1988). Krueger defines the focus group as a special kind of group that values participants' experiences, attitudes, and opinions. The open, semi-directed format allows participants a voice in the issues that concern their lives and creates a space where responses to questions can be open rather than constrained by a yes or no reply. Moreover, when people are gathered together in a group context they learn from and can be further stimulated in their thinking from the responses of other participants. This allows the discussion to reach greater depth than would be possible in a structured or semi-structured one-to-one interview. Typically, focus groups consist of no more than 6 to 10 people. They can be conducted in a series to allow for richer discussion and a more thorough purview of the issue at hand. Community members familiar with the focus-group participants can be trained to facilitate the meeting, thereby maximizing the potential for trust to develop more rapidly. For example, Richard Krueger and Jean King (1998) elaborate on the virtues of using focus groups for participatory research, and they discuss ways in which to involve volunteers in the facilitation process and the advantages therein.

Surveys. Although surveys typically conjure up images of telephone interviews, survey methods can be rethought to include participatory components. For example, Carr-Hill (1984) argues that survey research can be "radicalized" and transformed into a process where the inquiry creates a catalyst for participation and change. Hope and Timmel (1999, V. 1, p. 24) describe the use of the listening survey, which we discussed in Chapter Six. This approach is quite different from typical survey work where questions are decided beforehand by a group of "experts." They use the listening survey to develop a program based on the issues most salient to the community. However, this approach can be modified to fit the needs of program or project evaluation. We present our version of a listening survey adapted for the participatory evaluation later in The Evaluator's Tool Kit section of this chapter.

Case Studies. Case studies are becoming more common in evaluation research (Yin, 1994). These best address the "how" and "why" research questions, making them well suited to evaluation. "How does the program or project deal with difference? Why does the program or project work so well?" Cases can be programs, projects, processes, neighborhoods, whole communities, and organizations. While case studies zero in on a specific entity, such as a program or project, they view this entity within its context (Stake, 1995; Yin, 1994). They also attend to history as a shaper of present day structures and practices. Case study methodology considers the multiple systems at play that affect organizations and projects thereby enriching evaluation information and making it contextually relevant. Case studies use multiple methods such as interviewing, participant observation, focus groups, and questionnaires to achieve these ends.

Illustrated Presentations. Slides, photos, or drawings help to catalogue the history of a program, a project or an individual change effort. They can evoke a historical perspective, aid in the recall of significant memories, signify points of comparison, and serve as a jumping off place for critical reflection. Posing questions about the effort brings successes and challenges to bear upon future efforts. For example, community researchers have invited participants in collective change processes to illustrate the impacts of their participation through "before" and "after" pictures. How did they see their life situations before becoming involved? How do they envision themselves and their social realities after becoming active contributors to a community change effort? Participants are then invited to tell their stories of participation and describe the meanings of their before and after images.

Skits and Dramatizations. Enacting the change effort using prepared scripts or impromptu dramatizations is an exciting and energizing way to get body and spirit into the evaluation process. Visual representations of efforts create pictures or images of the work accomplished, its surprises, successes, and challenges. When captured on video or camera, these representations provide the means for instant replay. Ongoing learning occurs through repeat performances.

Testimonials. Individual and/or group testimonials are yet another way to bring the voices of those involved in the process to bear on analyzing efforts, support and appreciate the work, and create a memorable moment for all participants. When getting the research message out is of timely and critical importance, testimonials are a way to put a human face and a human voice to the message.

As this discussion suggests, there are multiple ways in which to engage in the development of knowledge. Each strategy for collecting information has its strengths and limitations. Consideration must be given to how a certain strategy will fit, given a particular context, and the resources in terms of time, money and expertise needed to carry them out. It is also important to consider that each strategy by itself gathers a partial picture of the phenomenon under study. We suggest that you think of ways in which you can incorporate different strategies to enrich and deepen the quality of information you collect. Recall from our earlier discussion, a mixed methods approach also provides an opportunity where participants can triangulate the data, thereby increasing the reliability or trustworthiness of the information. We present these strategies here as possibilities for further exploration and ask you to add to this list and think of ways to combine approaches with ideas of your own.

Making it Participatory

Interview an administrator or supervisor of a local community social work organization. Your task is to find out what evaluation means to this organization and what methods the organization uses to evaluate its programs, projects, and personnel. In small groups of three, draw up a tentative list of interview questions. Then present these back to the whole class. What questions might you ask and why? After you have conducted your interview, bring the results with you to class for discussion. What sort of methods does the organization use to evaluate itself? What does it evaluate? People? Policies? Practices? How often? By whom? How are the results used? What is the degree of participation in the process? Use the Just Practice Framework and the five key concepts of meaning, context, power, history, and possibility as a framework for critique. What *meaning* does evaluation have for the organization? What is the *context*(s) in which it occurs? Who has the *power* to make decisions regarding what to evaluate and which methods to choose? How has *history* affected these decisions and methods? What other evaluation *possibilities* exist? Now think about how you might transform this organization's evaluation strategy to be empowering and participatory. What would you do differently? How would you do it? How does your transformation incorporate the key concepts and what role do they each play in building your evaluation process? How do the values of Just Practice translate into a working model of evaluation when you bring the concept of collaboration to bear on your reflections? What might be some of the challenges and constraints of implementing your model in an organization? What might be some of its successes?

Cautions, Considerations, and Challenges

Participatory evaluation is not without its challenges. Evaluation tools and the ways in which we structure the process of evaluation carry assumptions, values, and standards for how we presume to operate. It is important to consider these assumptions in order to assess whether a particular tool or method is appropriate in another context. In other words, is participation always the best way to go? While the rewards are great, participatory evaluation takes time, and a considerable proportion of this time must be spent in reflection. As we learned early in this chapter, evaluation falls low on the priority list for many organizational administrators and workers. Given the context and culture of most social work organizations, the primary mode of operation is one of reactivity, not reflection. Social workers respond to long-neglected societal problems, but they often do so through programs established to pick up the pieces instead of addressing the root cause of problems and intervening before problems get out of control. In these situations, workers find themselves with little time for reflection.

Participatory evaluation demands responsibility and commitment to the process. The three major aims of participatory research — to investigate, to educate, and to take action — require versatile, risk-taking participants who are comfortable playing the roles of researcher, educator, activist, and bricoleur. For example, think about the amount of time it would take you to get to know, more than superficially, your community, the key power players, and those excluded from meaningful participation in the decisions that concern their lives. Also, consider how difficult it might be to get the most oppressed people to participate, people who spend most of their time and energy meeting their basic survival needs. Given the intensive time requirements of participatory research, how might you get these people involved? And what would it take to keep you committed and involved? Further, consider as well, the lack of access you and your group might have to support from financial and institutional resources, all of which are necessary to push a project forward and keep up the momentum. Given these challenges the default solution is often to return to more top/down models of evaluation. Here is a place where social justice workers can exercise "functional non-capitulation" that we discussed in Chapter Five. The social worker may not have control over the decision making regarding the evaluation process. She can, however, raise questions regarding who participates, what is being measured, and whose voices are or are not being heard in the process.

Involving Children in Evaluating Change: The Experience of ACTIONAID Nepal.

ACTIONAID Nepal's mission is the eradication of absolute poverty through empowerment of women, men, and children. In 1993-95 they carried out participatory research enabling children to share their experiences and opinions. Their work showed that children need to be integral in the process, their voices and views heard, and their rights and needs considered in order to assure that interventions truly address and improve their quality of life. The researchers began by bringing groups of children ages 11-15 together to analyze their social reality and to serve as ongoing consultants to AAN's planning process. Children were also involved in an evaluation of AAN's efforts in two sectors where projects have been underway for four years. Boys and girls from the children's groups participated. The techniques used included focus group discussions about changes, diaries to record children's daily activities, and social maps to show how children went to school. Children's thematic drawings presented graphic images of their life circumstances, and they also provided a base for evaluating changes in those circumstances. Rapport between children and facilitators was key to meaningful participation.

The researchers write: "By forming groups the right of children to have a space to discuss their issues has been formally acknowledged. Adults in the community and AAN are beginning to listen to these groups, and participation in these groups has allowed children to develop skills, knowledge, experience and confidence.... A key problem identified by the groups was children being sent for wage labor, which prevented them from attending school. Their groups have raised awareness, for example through street drama, about girls' rights to education. They have directly persuaded male household heads to send girls and women to school..." (p. 93)

Participants in one of the children's groups write: "In the past we were innocent and no one would listen to us, and the adults sometimes used to scold and dominate us. Now the situation has changed. We are able to read, write, and speak ... we are able to solve our problems ourselves" (Hill, 1998, p. 92-94).

What situations or programs can you think of that could be improved if children's voices were represented? How does the idea of children evaluating change challenge or confirm your own assumptions about children and their capabilities?

The Universal Declaration of Human Rights in Your Community

Recall from Chapter Three how we suggested using The Universal Declaration of Human Rights (UDHR) as a foundation for ethical practice. In this exercise, you will be using the UDHR as an evaluation tool. Divide your class into small groups and have each group pick articles from The Universal Declaration of Human Rights included in the appendix of this text. You can omit articles 29 and 30 for this exercise. You will be evaluating the human rights climate in your community. Each group completes three tasks:

1). Read the articles you chose together, discuss their meaning, and be prepared to explain their meaning to the main group when you report in on your discussion.

2). Decide to what extent people in your community enjoy these human rights: Everyone, Most People, Some People, A Few People, No One?

3). If everyone does not enjoy a particular right, write down who is excluded.

Share your small group evaluations with the larger group and discuss how you might go about developing an evaluation instrument to assess the human rights climate in your community. How might your evaluation steer social justice-oriented practice? How could you use your results to stimulate action in your community? How would you disseminate your findings?[8]

Critical Reflection

What is Critical Reflection?

Evaluation goes hand-in-hand with reflection. We begin this section by looking at the meaning of reflection and then compare the differences when we add the word "critical." Mezirow (1998, pp. 185-186) defines reflection as a "turning back" on experience, but he contends it can mean many things. It includes simple awareness of objects or events or states of being. It can also mean the act of considering something, letting our thoughts wander, and contemplating alternatives. As humans, we have the capacity to reflect on ourselves reflecting. Reflection, however, does not imply *assessing* the object of contemplation, and herein lies the crucial difference between reflection and critical reflection. Mezirow argues that critical reflection "may be either implicit, as when we mindlessly choose between good and evil because of our assimilated values, or explicit, as when we bring the process of choice into awareness to examine and assess the reasons for making choice" (p. 186).

Critical reflection includes questioning taken-for-granted beliefs that relate to different aspects of our experiences. These beliefs may be about how the world works economically, politically, philosophically, psychologically, and culturally. Think for a minute of a belief that you once held firm but no longer believe in its truth-value. Perhaps you assumed, "a woman's place was in the home," or "real men don't eat quiche" or "children should be seen and not heard." Think of the reasons you employed to bolster your faith in this belief. Now recall the process or event that occurred that made you question this long-held assumption.

Critical reflection is a structured, analytic and emotional process that helps us examine the ways in which we make meaning of circumstances, events, and situations. Critical reflection pushes us to interpret experience, question our taken-for-granted assumptions of how things ought to work and reframe our inquiry to open up new possibilities for thought and action. Posing critical questions is key to critical reflection.

Critical Reflection and Social Justice Work

There are a number of reasons why we include critical reflection as a core process of justice-oriented social work practice. Our list below is far from inclusive, so think of other reasons you might add:

- **Critical Reflection Promotes Continuous Self-Assessment.** Posing questions of our own performance is key to social work practice that takes social justice seriously. Assessing personal, emotional, and intellectual challenges and successes and addressing these through augmenting or changing the ways in which we work increases personal and professional competence and integrity (Freire, 1990).
- **Critical Reflection Fosters Connections and Linkages Between Personal and Social Concerns:** As we discussed in Chapter Three, the dominant mode of thought in U.S. culture is based on individualism. The tendency is to look only within ourselves for causes of our concerns. Critical reflection demands we look at the linkages between personal issues and the ways in which these are influenced and shaped by systems much larger than ourselves.

- **Critical Reflection Legitimizes Challenging Dominant Explanations and Observations.** Engaging with issues in a critical way means questioning the power structures and the structuring of power embedded in the definitions attributed to social problems and concerns. Think of some unquestioned myths you adhered to and later discovered you simply lacked sufficient information for an informed opinion. How were these myths perpetuated?
- **Critical Reflection Opens Up and Strengthens Spaces of Possibility.** As discussed earlier, binary logic or the logic of "either/or" is the dominant social logic in U.S. culture (Kelly & Sewell, 1988). The primary limitation of this particular mode of thinking is that it narrows choices. For example, something is either right or wrong – there are no shades of gray. Kelly and Sewell remind us that a "trialectic" logic or the logic of wholeness provides a space to "grasp the wholeness which emerges" (p. 22-23) when we consider relationship among factors in terms of threes instead of twos.
- **Critical Reflection Links to Problem Posing:** At the heart of critical reflection is problem-posing. Certain types of questions promote critical inquiry. Posing the subject matter as a problem or what Freire called "problematizing the ordinary" connects us to the work of evaluation and systematization. We are engaged in an ongoing process of examining the conditions of our lives, identifying concerns, asking the "but why?" questions and looking for themes and patterns that connect. These become the foundations for developing action plans.

The Critically Reflective Thinker

John Dewey (1910, 1933), early 20th century educator and philosopher, emphasized the importance of reflection and understood it as both an intellectual and an emotional endeavor:

> Given a genuine difficulty and a reasonable amount of analogous experience to draw upon, the difference, *par excellence*, between good and bad thinking is found at this point. The easiest way is to accept any suggestion that seems plausible and thereby bring to an end the condition of mental uneasiness. Reflective thinking is always more or less troublesome because it involves overcoming the inertia that inclines one to accept suggestions at their face value; it involves

> willingness to endure a condition of mental unrest and disturbance. Reflective thinking, in short, means judgment suspended during further inquiry; and suspense is likely to be somewhat painful . . . To maintain the state of doubt and to carry on systematic and protracted inquiry – these are the essentials of thinking. (Dewey, 1910, p. 13)

The goal then of critical reflection is to promote tension and uncertainty. As Dewey suggests above, we must be prepared to deal with the uncomfortableness that comes from having one's long held assumptions open for question. Dewey (1933) identified three characteristics of the reflective thinker that negotiate the "mental unrest and disturbance" resulting from the contradictions between old and new ways of thinking. He called these *open-mindedness*, *responsibility*, and *wholeheartedness*. *Open-mindedness* is the desire to hear more than one side of an issue, to listen to alternative perspectives, and to recognize that even the most engrained beliefs are open to question. *Responsibility* connotes the desire to seek out the truth and apply new information learned to troublesome situations. *Wholeheartedness* encompasses the emotional aspect of reflective thinking. It implies that, through commitment, one can overcome fear and uncertainty to make meaningful change and marshal the capacity to critically evaluate self, others, and society.

Building Critical Reflection Capacity

Dewey's characteristics of the reflective thinker are not innate, inborn attributes bestowed on some of us and not on others. In fact, these characteristics and the skills of critical reflection can be developed. Here are some suggestions for fine-tuning your critical reflection skills.

1. **Dialogue.** As we addressed earlier, engaging in participatory learning is the primary way we develop critical reflection capacity. Discussing our ideas, thoughts, and feelings with others externalizes our thinking and helps us engage with others and work on open-mindedness. It is also one of the most viable ways we learn. True dialogue occurs when we open ourselves to new learning and challenge ourselves and change in the process.
2. **Critical Friends Dyads.** Hatton and Smith (1995) describe the use of critical friends dyads and how these critical relationships help to develop higher levels of thinking. A critical friend is someone who is

not afraid to disagree, who will challenge your viewpoint and question your assumptions about reality. Think for a moment what it might be like if the expectation of the "critical friend" was part of your work in a community organization. How might the notion of critical friend change the ways in which we think about our work and how might this notion of continual critique provide permission for altering structures towards more just and equitable arrangements?

3. **Research.** As we have addressed earlier in this chapter, research nurtures reflective practice and critical reflection skills. The research process itself mirrors the critical reflection process. First, one formulates a hypothesis or a point of inquiry to investigate. Then one uncovers the literature that addresses the issue. Next, one makes decisions on how to collect and analyze the information. Finally, conclusions are drawn and decisions made regarding how to disseminate the results of the research.

4. **Writing Experiences.** Journaling and other forms of reflective writing are ways in which to keep a record of personal growth and changing perceptions. There are a number of approaches to journal writing that range from unstructured narrative to focused writing on specific topics with specific intent. Journals can be used to catalogue and reflect upon critical, perplexing incidents or to examine in-depth, particular case studies. Journals can also provide the means for linking theory and practice.

5. **Artistic Reflection.** Photos, artwork, and theater can be used to stimulate critical thinking in their production and presentation. For example, students in Maxine Jacobson's class on Women and Social Action in the Americas engaged in an assignment where each student proposed and completed a special project that spoke to students' individual interests regarding women and social action. One student captured her experience at the World Trade Organization protest in Seattle through photographs depicting the human elements of protestors' struggles. When presented to the class, these powerful black and white images of personal and collective anguish, elation, intimidation, and solidarity evoked critical discussion on the more intimate elements of social injustice and struggles for social change.

Learning Letters Home

Think of a close friend or a relative with whom you can share your most intimate thoughts. Compose a letter to this person that addresses the following questions: (1) What are you thinking and how are you feeling at this point in your course work about choosing social work as a career? (2) What are you learning that challenges your thinking about social work and yourself as a potential social worker? (3) What have been some key areas of personal, emotional, and intellectual growth? This letter need not be shared with others. In class, discuss with others what the process of reflection was like for you and how you brought the key themes of critical reflection to bear on the completion of this exercise.

Celebration

Why Celebration As a Core Process?

Scour the social work literature and you will find hardly a mention of celebration as a core process of social work practice. How do you make sense of this – a mere oversight or is this a concept incongruent with the practice of social work? While our inclusion of celebration as a core process in the Just Practice Framework may make us appear too idealistic or out of touch with the "real" world of practice, we believe it fits well in a model of justice-oriented practice. We hope to challenge traditional meanings and practices of social work and nurture idealism in others and ourselves. We see celebration as a key component of practice that insists we look beyond the present and keep our sights on a vision of a just world. Typically, traditional meanings of social work highlight the drudgery of practice and emphasize social workers' proclivity for "burn-out." Even the media's attention to social work through television programs such as "Judging Amy," paint a picture of the social worker (Amy's mother) as a brittle and at times, emotionally confused woman, who knows what is right for everyone else but is somehow continually thwarted by bureaucratic rules - the perpetual mother, the perpetual martyr.

Celebration As an Integral Part of Practice

What would it mean to bring the notion of celebration into our work as social justice workers? How might celebration reconfigure the ways in which we envision practice? Lappe and Dubois (1994) remind us that the most effective organizations see celebration and appreciation as integral to their work. Celebration and appreciation breathe new life into the work and recharge the batteries; at the same time they build loyalty and strengthen relationships. Lappe and Dubois provide a list of suggestions or "how-to's" to brush up on our celebration and appreciation skills. We share some of their wisdom below:

- **Celebrate the Learning, Not Just the Winning.** "We don't always get what we want. But out of every effort comes learning to be appreciated. After one citizen group's legislative campaign failed, we noticed that their newsletter celebrated how much their members had learned about both the issue and the citizen lobbying process. So by "celebration" we don't necessarily mean throwing a party. We also mean acknowledging and expressing satisfaction in what has been accomplished, even when an intended target is not met."
- **Create a Celebratory Spirit.** "Colored balloons. Noisemakers. Streamers. Amusing props. Live music. All these features create a mood of celebration, even in a public gathering dealing with deadly serious problems. Each time we've attended public meetings held by the Sonoma County Faith-Based Organizing Project, for example, our moods are lifted as soon as we enter the auditorium. These techniques infuse their meetings with a spirit of celebration, despite the fact that this group faces such difficult issues as affordable housing and school reform."
- **Show Appreciation of Your Adversaries as Well as Your Allies.** "The most successful groups that we know acknowledge their volunteers at events in which the particular contribution of each individual is described. As members hear what others do, appreciation becomes a means of building a sense of interdependence within the group . . .letters and calls of thanks (even when you disagree with the person), do not signal weakness. You'll establish your credibility as a person or group with strength, who knows you'll be around for the long haul." (Lappe & DuBois, 1994, pp. 278-279)

Now we add a few of our own:

- **Animation.** Think of the animator role (discussed in Chapter Seven) in part as one that sparks the celebratory spirit and brings joy to life. It may be through gestures such as remembering participants' birthdays, celebrating organizational anniversaries and milestones, and recognizing the many successes along the way – the first time a participant speaks in public about an issue she cares about, or a child's first month in a new school. It may be taking time to recognize events and transitions that shape personal and collective history and memory, such as the naming of a group, move to a new home, etc.
- **Celebration as Resistance.** Celebrating rights is a way of claiming voices, time, and space, and resisting forces trying to silence and threaten - Celebration of social holidays and religious feast days to mark the right to practice and to honor histories. For example, during the 1980s the people of La Victoria, a poor *población* - or community - in Santiago, Chile, publicly celebrated International Women's Day as a form of resistance to the military dictatorship. The celebration was a way of enabling residents to move beyond the fear and into the streets. It was both a celebration and a strategy for community mobilization (Finn, Rodriguez & Núñez, 2000).
- **Celebration Also Means Finding Joy in the Work.** Townsend et al. (1999), in writing about women and power in Mexico, acknowledge the importance of enjoyment in women's discovery of power from within. Women take and express pleasure in their achievements, in "getting out of the house" and coming together with others. Likewise, the women of Villa Paula Jaraquemada who joined together to build community from the ground up through a housing auto-construction project express a sense of joy in both the process and products of their work: "I love it, that's why I do it. As you learn something new you get more enthused about learning. I love it. I love the learning. I love seeing results. That's what keeps me coming back" (Finn, 2001, p. 191). They speak often of the "beauty" of the experience of participation, and they celebrate the beauty of their successes large and small. They talk of the positive outlook they now have and their faith in their own capacity to create change.

Celebrating Small Steps

Brainstorm what the word celebration means to the members of your group. How do you celebrate birthdays, holidays, and rites of passage such as moving from adolescence to adulthood or the end of a long week in school? Brainstorm another list of successes and challenges you have experienced individually and as a class that spring from your involvement in class this term. Decide as a group how you might celebrate your work together.

Chapter Summary

In this chapter we have developed the Just Practice core processes of Evaluation, Critical Reflection, and Celebration. We have defined evaluation and explored different approaches to evaluation, and we have highlighted participatory approaches for their congruence with social justice-oriented social work practice. We have examined questions of reliability, validity, and trustworthiness as they relate to current debates about what is right and true in research. We have provided examples of participatory research and explored participatory processes, and we have asked the reader to examine these examples and processes for the key principles that underlie social-justice oriented practice. We have emphasized the role of bricoleur for its fit with the principles and goals of participatory approaches to research. We have outlined what we need to evaluate and a set of strategies or methods that can be used alone or in combination to promote critical inquiry into the problems of everyday life, and examples of traditional and alternative tools for research practice. We have defined critical reflection and its importance to social justice work and addressed methods for developing one's critical reflection capacity. Finally, we have introduced and defined celebration as a core process, and we have presented strategies that draw attention to the need to see the beauty in our work and help us sustain the momentum necessary for Just Practice. In Chapter Nine we close the circle on our journey through the principles and practices of social justice work. We reflect on the future of social work, and we revisit and expand on the challenges facing the profession as we move into the 21st century. Finally, we summarize key principles we have discussed throughout this text.

Teaching-Learning Resource: The Evaluator's Tool Kit

In this section, we put together a beginning tool kit for evaluators. We include examples of both traditional and participatory approaches to evaluation. (See if you can tell them apart.) As you read through these think of how these tools translate into social justice-oriented practice. What contradictions do you find and how might you alter these tools so they reflect the values of social justice work?

Getting Started

In their description of evaluation and its applicability to participatory democracy, Hope and Timmel (1999, V. 2, pp. 121-133), suggest how workers might enlist people's participation in reflecting critically on their own projects, programs, aims, and leadership. They start by conducting a workshop with potential participants where they define evaluation, discuss potential pitfalls, and learn when to conduct evaluations, why these should be conducted, and various evaluation methods and strategies. The final step is to develop a plan for how the group will implement the participatory evaluation process. Hope and Timmel use the following questions to initiate this process:

1. What aspects of your program do you aim to evaluate?
2. What methods will you use for each of the aims you have mentioned? What indicators and what questions are important to include?
3. Who will do what, when, and where? Make out a time, place, and person chart to indicate your plan.

The final step is when all plans are shared with the whole group. (p. 130)

Simply simple

Lappe and DuBois (1994) outline some simple questions they believe are powerful tools for change when applied to small and large group evaluation processes:

1). How do you feel about what happened? (Answers can be in one-word descriptions of emotions: upset, happy, relieved, angry, energized. No intellectualizing allowed.)

2). What worked?

3). What didn't work?

4). What could we do better? (p. 281)

Elegant in their simplicity, these questions provide a framework for group discussion. Responses can be tape recorded, or written out on flip chart paper. This preserves the discussion for later reflection so history can become a basis for continued learning.

Listening Survey for Program Evaluation

Earlier in this chapter we addressed the listening survey as a way to conduct participatory evaluation. We use the model presented by Hope and Timmel (1999, V. 1) and adapt it for program or project evaluation. A listening survey for program evaluation might look something like this:

1) First, the research team listens to unstructured conversations with program or project participants, board members or other key players with information relevant to an evaluation.

2) Next, the research team takes information from the survey, looks at it critically and analyzes it for themes. Pertinent questions might include: What are people speaking about with strong feeling? Are project or program issues mainly dealing with problems of exclusion, difficulties with accessing resources, or contradictions between the stated mission and modes of doing practice?

3) Next, the research team prepares problem-posing materials, based on the survey information, to stimulate discussion in learning groups. These could be bulleted points typed on handouts, or graphic or pictorial representations of themes or problematic issues. Hope and Timmel (1999, V.1, p. 24) call these codes and contend that the better the code, the more people in a learning group will learn for themselves.

4) Next, the learning environment must be conducive to learning. Simultaneously, people must be supported and people must be challenged to allow for critical reflection. Establishing guidelines for participants assists with the development of group safety and trust. The group leader's role is to facilitate discussion, summarize when necessary, and build on the contributions of participants.

5) Lastly, the research team decides on ways in which they want to present their codifications.

Building Community Capacity through Empowering Evaluation

Steven Mayer (1996) runs a nonprofit organization called Rainbow Research. The purpose of Rainbow Research is "to assist socially concerned communities and organizations in responding more effectively to social problems" (p. 332). The organization's primary task is to disseminate valuable information about what works to build leadership capacity. Mayer suggests three key features of empowering evaluations that assist programs and projects in building capacity. We summarize these as follows:

1) *Help Create a Constructive Environment for the Evaluation* – a constructive environment is one conducive to action that helps the community use the evaluation process to develop its commitment, resources, and skills.
   a. Minimize the distance between evaluator (as expert) and program participants (as ignorant).
   b. Recommend a policy where negative evaluation findings do not lead directly to punishment by program funders or directors.
   c. The intention of an evaluation should be to strengthen community responses, not punish. Move away from fault finding to identify opportunities for improvement.
2) *Actively Include the Voices of Intended Beneficiaries* – Capacity-building projects should lead to improvements in the systems for service communities. It stands to reason, then, that the voice of community members should be included in the evaluation process.
   a. Intended beneficiaries should have a voice in deciding not only the methods of evaluation, but also the sources of information and the interpretation of the findings.
   b. Include their experience, wisdom, and standards of excellence. They should be thought of as the ultimate source for assessing the merits of a program or project.
   c. Include those not normally included. Bridge the divide between the helpers and the helped.

3) *Help Communities Use Evaluation Findings to Strengthen Community Responses* – Evaluators and others wanting to help communities build capacity can help make sure that community voices are heard, not just in designing and conducting the evaluation but in helping communities and other audiences (such as policymakers) move forward with the findings.

   a. Help spread the lessons learned. Evaluation findings that stay on the shelf are worthless. Consider spreading the word through the media in some form or fashion.

   b. Help create links among people who can use the information. All too often community work is compartmentalized, segregated into departments, regions, agencies and professional groups. Evaluation may have implications across boundaries and borders. Consider your audience broadly.

   c. Help communities and their organizations build on gains. Recommendations should be written that allow community organizations to mobilize and strengthen the commitment they bring to their work, increase the financial and other resources usable for strengthening their work, and further develop the skills needed to make their work effective. (pp. 335-337)

How Burn-Out Prone is My Organization

This tool was developed to help evaluate the sustainability of social justice organizations (Shields, 1994, p. 146-147). Think of how it might be adapted to fit any human services or health organization.

- **Planning and project management**

  How clear are your group's goals and priorities? (Scale: Very Unclear to Well Planned/Clear)

- **Expectations**

  How clear is it to each worker (including volunteers) what is expected of her/him? (Scale: Very clear to Well Planned/Clear)

- **Evaluation**

  How often does your group evaluate what it has achieved? (Scale: Never to Very Often)

- **Celebrating and acknowledging achievements**

  How often does your group celebrate successes and achievements? (Scale: Never to Frequently)

- **Individual needs**

  How much value does you group put on individual needs and opportunities for development? (Scale: None to High Priority)

- **Pressure, tension and urgency**

  What is the overall pace and intensity like? (Scale: Unrelentingly Urgent and Intense to Relaxed, Steady Pace)

- **Work conditions**

  In general, what are the resources (work space, wages, equipment) like for your group? (Scale: Poor to Very Good)

- **General working atmosphere**

  In general, what is the atmosphere in your workplace? (Scale: Chaotic/ Disorganized to Centered/Organized)

- **Autonomy**

  How satisfied are you with your level of autonomy in your work? (Scale: Very Dissatisfied to Very Satisfied)

- **Supervision**

  How satisfied are you with the quality of supervision you receive? (Scale: Very Dissatisfied to Very Satisfied)

- **Dealing with conflict**

  How effective is your group at resolving conflict constructively? (Scale: Totally Ineffective to Highly Effective)[9]

What questions and scales might you add to this list that get at the forces and structures that impose themselves on the functioning of organization? How could this tool be adapted to consider the larger context of social justice work? (i.e., working against the grain, dealing with contradictory forces and expectations, conflicting discourses and patterns of practice.)

Fireproofing My Organization

This is another exercise we borrow from *In the Tiger's Eye: An Empowerment Guide for Social Action* by Katrina Shields (1994, p. 145-146). The purpose of this tool is to formulate strategies to prevent group burnout. Because it is likely to highlight a number of issues that will need attention, first outline the symptoms of burnout and recognize that there are usually individual and organizational factors that contribute to it. This tool draws attention to the potential organizational factors for your group.

First, generate ideas by doing three short brainstorms of five minutes each on the following three questions. There should be no discussion, comments, or censure at this stage. Just put down all the phases and ideas as people offer them.

- How might the way this group operates be contributing towards burnout among our workers?
- What needs to be included in our group's anti-burnout strategy?
- What can we do (as individuals or as a group) when we perceive that a co-worker is on the path to burnout?

After the three topics have been brainstormed, spend up to ten minutes discussing the ideas for each one and formulate concise summaries and recommendations. There may be suggestions that not everyone agrees with – note the controversial ones on a separate list. A spokesperson should then read these summaries back to the larger group. Spend the next thirty minutes to one hour deciding on any policy decisions, planning, and changes that will put your strategy into effect. Keep discussing the controversial items until either you reach a solution, or you make some plan to deal with them at another time.

Questions for Discussion

1. Describe three ways of thinking about evaluation. How do they relate to social justice work?
2. What are some points of comparison between qualitative and quantitative approaches to inquiry?

3. What is catalytic validity, and how does this notion of validity fit with social justice work?
4. We have described one of the roles of social justice work as that of the "bricoleur." What is the significance of this role for the process of research and evaluation?
5. What are the common linkages between participatory approaches to research and social work's theory base discussed in Chapter Four?
6. In addition to the reasons listed in the chapter, why is evaluation not well attended to in social work practice?
7. What further suggestions regarding what we need to evaluate could you add to the list on pages 345-346?
8. What are some cautions and challenges associated with participatory approaches to evaluation?
9. Given the principles of Just Practice, how might you construct an evaluation tool to assess your practice? How does this instrument compare to traditional self-evaluative tools?
10. Are there other suggestions you might have for building critical reflection skills beyond those discussed in the chapter?

Suggested Readings

Fetterman, S., Kaftarian, J., & Wandersman, A. (Eds.). (1996). *Empowerment evaluation: Knowledge and tools for self-assessment and accountability.* Thousand Oaks, CA: Sage Publications.

Finn, J. (1994). "The promise of participatory research." *Journal of Progressive Human Services,* 5(2), 25-42.

Flowers, N. Bernbaum, M., Rudelius-Palmer, K., & Tolman, J. (2000). *The human rights education handbook: Effective practices for learning, action, and change.* Minneapolis, MN: Human Rights Resource Center, University of Minnesota.

Johnson, V., Ivan-Smith, E., Gordon, G., Pridmore, P., & Scott, P. (1998). *Stepping forward: Children and young people's participation in the development process.* London: Intermediate Technology Publications.

Lappe, F. M. & DuBois, P.M. (1994). *The quickening of America: Rebuilding our nation, remaking our lives.* San Francisco, CA: Jossey-Bass, Inc.

Lather, P. (1991). *Getting smart: Feminist research and pedagogy with/in the postmodern.* New York: Routledge.

Maguire, P. (1987). *Doing participatory research: A feminist approach.* Amherst, MA: The Center for International Education, University of Massachusetts.

Park, P., Brydon-Miller, B., Hall, B., & Jackson, T. (Eds.). (1993). *Voices of change: Participatory research in the United States and Canada.* Westport, CT: Bergin & Garvey.

Zimbalist, S. (1977). *Historic themes and landmarks in social welfare research.* New York: Harper & Row.

Chapter 9

Just Futures: Social Justice-Oriented Practice in the 21st Century

"Hope, as it happens, is so important for our existence, individual and social, that we must take every care not to experience it in a mistaken form, and thereby allow it to slip toward hopelessness and despair. Hopelessness and despair are both the consequence and the cause of inaction and immobilism.

Paulo Freire (1999), *Pedagogy of Hope*[1]

"If, as most of us believe, we have the power to shape the world according to our visions and desires then how come we have collectively made such a mess of it? Our social and physical world can and must be made, re-made, and, if that goes awry, re-made again. Where to begin and what is to be done are the key questions."

David Harvey (2000), *Spaces of Hope*[2]

Chapter Overview

In this chapter we reflect on the future of social work and the challenges facing the field in the coming years. We return to some of the issues confronting social work in the 21st century that we identified at the beginning of the book. In Chapter One we gave the example of the emergence of social work in Russia over the past decade. We asked, "how will social work configure itself against this newly forming landscape?" Perhaps that is a question to be posed to social workers in the U.S. and internationally as we confront the lived realities and growing uncertainties of the "new global order" (Caufield, 1996; Mayadas & Elliott, 1992). We argue that the Just Practice Framework provides an approach to critical thought and action as we build future paths for social work while walking them.

We summarize a number of principles for social justice-oriented practice, drawing from themes highlighted throughout the text. We invite readers to join us in articulating principles of social justice work and putting them into practice. We close with examples of the possibilities of social justice work in action. We hope this ending marks a transition to many new beginnings.

The Future of Social Work

The coming of the millennium brought forth myriad predictions of hope and doom regarding humanity's future. Social work was certainly not immune to millennial musings. In fact, over the past few years, a diverse range of social work academics and practitioners have engaged in serious reflection on social work's past, present, and future. They have considered the emergence, movement, and maturation of social work over the past century and probed its possible futures. Let's take a brief look at some of their predictions for the state of social work practice and social welfare systems in the 21st century.

Children Are Our Future??

A number of U.S. writers have addressed the acceleration and businessing of everyday life and the implications for social work of rapid changes in work, family, and community. Ozawa (1997) points to the challenges posed by demographic changes that include a burgeoning elderly population and a nonwhite majority of children by 2050. She predicts that children of color will be worse off by mid-century than they are today. Similarly, Hochman (1997) predicts continued increases in the percentage of children living in poverty in the U.S. She argues that disparities between the rich and poor will continue to be exacerbated in education. As federal and state dollars and tax bases for public education erode, poor children will attend poorer schools, and the poor will continue to be blamed for their inability to "get ahead."

Race Matters

Stern (1997) voices concern regarding the solidification of physical, socioeconomic, and ideological barriers between low-income Americans, disproportionately people of color, and the white middle and upper classes. He is hopeful, however, that growing multiracial demographics may challenge the bipolar view of race that has dominated in the U.S. Midgley (1997, p. 61), on the other hand, argues, that "problems such as the exploitation of women migrants (particularly in domestic service), the harsh treatment of illegal migrants, and the growing attachment of racist sentiment to social policy issues affecting migrants" are ones that social work needs to directly address. Hochman (1997, p. 267) sees growing racism as a trend that accompanies reduced funding and increasing poverty as key issues in schools. A number of observers have also critically addressed growing incidents of xenophobia in response to immigration and movements of people across diverse borders (Karger & Stoesz, 1998; Mayadas & Elliott, 1992).

"Global Graying"

George (1997) draws attention to what she terms "global graying," referring to the growing aging population. As Lyons (1999, pp. 69-70) indicates, researchers are seeing a universal increase in the number of individuals over the age of 65. In fact, predictions say that by 2025, 1.2 billion people will be 65 and older. Moreover, the fastest growing age group is that of individuals 85 and above. The effects of global graying will be felt in business, politics, education, and pension and health care systems. However, while much of the world is aging, some of the poorest sectors face a shortened life expectancy as the deadly impact of the AIDS epidemic continues. It is predicted that children born today in the 29 countries of sub-Saharan Africa hardest hit by AIDS will have an average life expectancy of only 47 years, compared to 54 years before the epidemic (Bureau of the Census, 1999; Lyons, 1999; UNAIDS, 1999).

The Businessing of Human Services

Franklin (2000) contends that the devolution of federal and state responsibilities to local communities and the private sector will continue. The effects of privatization will be increasingly felt in health and mental health service systems, where "managed care" will dominate and service providers will find themselves in ever increasing competition for scarce resources. The infiltration of managerial "oversight" and market principles on health and mental health work demands increased efficiency and cost containment and calls upon workers to practice brief, solution-based modes of treatment in an effort to cut work short.

Growing Disparities

Rose (1997) and Korten (1995) argue that we will see a widening income gap as a result of corporate restructuring, economic globalization, increasing un- and underemployment, and a growing propensity toward elitism in social and economic policies. Keigher and Lowry (1998) address the "sickening implications" of these global disparities as manifest in infant mortality, AIDS, and other epidemics, environmental disasters, and the growing numbers of refugee populations. For example, 1.6 billion people in the Global South now live without potable water (Danaher, 1994). The negative consequences of Structural Adjustment Programs are likely to contribute to even more dire conditions for people living in extreme poverty.

Death of Social Work?

Kreuger (1997) envisions a grim scenario for the future of social work. He predicts the profession's demise in the next century, arguing that "hypertechnologies" and the genetic-chemical revolution will make social work intervention obsolete. Kreuger also predicts the collapse of the "grand narratives" upon which social work has premised its knowledge base. Notions of modernity, progress, and the role of the state that informed 20th century social welfare projects will be replaced by the logic and practice of privatization. In short, his prediction is one of social implosion: radical economic dislocations accompanied by the breakdown of traditional political boundaries and the geo-social space of neighborhood and community. By 2100, argues Kreuger, social work will no longer be.

Meeting the Challenges Ahead

Most writers do not share Kreuger's vision of the end of social work. However, they do agree that the challenges ahead call for fundamental rethinking of the nature and direction of practice as we come to grips with the rapidly changing environment in which we do our work. Let's consider some of those directions for practice and the knowledge and skills they demand for social workers in the 21st century.

Critical Community Practice

Schorr (1997) reminds us that the most successful programs never forget that the individuals and families they work with are part of a much larger community context. These programs teach the difficult, and often-ignored lessons that solutions imposed from outside local structures fail to grasp. They value the importance of local *meanings* and the immediate *context* of practice and of people's lived experience. They recognize *power* as both a constraining and enabling force for community change. They appreciate *history* in shaping current patterns of living. And they are open to the *possibility* of new ways of looking at and addressing both human needs and human rights given varying levels of and access to social supports and resources. In short, they advocate an integrated approach to practice in which social workers are equipped with facilitation, animation, mediation, advocacy, and coalition-building skills. Social workers must also be experts at engagement and collaboration and willing to learn from neighborhoods and the community and to understand and reconfigure community practice skills for a devolution environment.

Internationalism

In light of the challenges of globalization, a number of social workers are calling for a greater emphasis on internationalism (George, 1997; Hokenstad & Midgley, 1997; Lyons, 1999; Ramanathan & Link, 1999; Sarri, 1997). Transnational institutions and global actors, such as the World Bank, International Monetary Fund, and World Trade Organization, exert increasingly powerful influence on domestic social policies (Hokenstad & Midgley, 1997). Practice in the 21st century needs to understand and attend to these influences. Taking internationalism seriously pushes social workers to move away from simplistic and often paternalistic solutions to global problems such as "giving aid," to considering the strengths and capacities that can be drawn on through "mutual aid" and meaningful accompaniment. Thinking of social work in international terms also provides a wealth of new theoretical possibilities to support alternative forms of practice and the exchange of creative and innovative ways of thinking and acting with social workers around the globe.

The Political Dimensions of Practice

Reisch (1997) contends that, in order to speak to possible futures of social work, we first need to examine trends that have been shaping the field. He addresses three interlocking political trends: changes in ideological context of politics, changes in the distribution of political power, and changes in popular attitudes about politics and the role of government. Reisch argues that a "mythology of simplicity" has shaped both public policy debates and analysis of those debates, thus obscuring a much more ambiguous and complex reality. Social workers, Reisch contends, need to incorporate a political dimension into their practice and to serve as *interpreters* of environments to both policy makers and the public, as advocates for those who lack power, and as mediators between communities and institutions in the public, non-profit, and for-profit sector. Reisch (1997, p. 81) writes:

> In the 21st century the survival of the social services, the well-being of clients and communities, and the ability of social workers to derive satisfaction from our careers depend on the integration of political action into a broader pro-social welfare strategy. Political knowledge and skills should become as much a part of every social worker's repertoire as skills in assessment and intervention with individuals and families. (Abramovitz, 1993; Fisher, 1995)

Theorizing for Transformation

Pease and Fook (1999) argue for serious engagement with postmodern critical theory (see Chapter Four) as a prerequisite for addressing the complexities of 21st century practice. They envision social work as an emancipatory project that legitimizes personal and political struggles against oppressive structures and practices. They argue that to achieve these ends, social work needs to transform itself by moving beyond dualisms; challenging notions of objective truth and value-free knowledge; building theory from the grounded realities of practice; deconstructing the truth claims of traditional social work; demonstrating commitment to political struggles; engaging with questions of difference, power, and oppression; and creating an alternative social work discourse.

People, Partnership, and Participation

Ashley and Gaventa (1997) argue that a commitment to social justice demands the democratization of processes of knowledge development, and they call for new forms of partnership and participation to realize this. Korten (1995) echoes this claim, arguing that meaningful, justice-oriented change comes through promotion of the right and possibility for people to control their own resources, economies, and means of livelihood. Sarri (1997, p. 394) challenges social workers to ask ourselves: How genuinely are we committed to the principle of people's participation? A challenge to social justice workers, then, is to advocate and open spaces for people's meaningful and empowering participation in the decisions and decision-making arenas that affect their lives.

Just Practice: A Guide for the Future?

Revisiting the Framework

We contend that the Just Practice Framework makes a significant contribution to reconfiguring social work thinking and practice so that we are better equipped to meet these challenges. The five key themes of *meaning, context, power, history,* and *possibility* bring together many of the concerns addressed above regarding the future of social work and the challenges therein. The framework provides a means for appreciating and reflecting on the complexities of 21st century social work practice as we hold these themes in relationship and consider the dynamics of their intersection. The core processes of *engagement, teaching-learning, action, accompaniment, evaluation, critical reflection,* and *celebration* presented in Chapters Five through Eight invite participation, reflection, nonlinear movement, collaborative knowledge development, and attention to the mutual interplay of the personal, historical, cultural, and political. The Just Practice matrix (see

Chapter Four and below) offers a guide to question posing and critical inquiry that engages with contextual complexity, provides a means for mapping constraints and possibilities, and creates space for dialogue to inform action grounded in the concrete circumstances at hand.

Crafting a Flexible Frame

In developing the Just Practice Framework, we have attempted to speak to the concerns and challenges of 21st century social work. The Just Practice Framework begins with the assumptions that our knowledge of the world is partial and shaped by our perspectives and positionalities. Social work knowledge development is an emergent, dialogue-based process gained through engagement with changing contexts and the forces that shape them. We have tried to craft a "flexible" frame that helps us structure inquiry and action and remain open to challenge and possibility. This question-posing approach serves to disrupt our "certainties" and keep us engaged as humble and curious learners.

Fundamental Issues for the 21st Century

Many of the concerns addressed above regarding social work in the 21st century speak to fundamental issues of economic and political power and inequality. By recognizing power as a key theme in social justice work, we have attempted to bring questions of power and inequality to bear in every context of social work practice and to challenge social workers to seriously and honestly address the many micropractices of power in play in every change process. We concur with Michael Reisch (1997) that social workers need to incorporate a political dimension into their practice, not as an "appendage" but at the heart of our work. The Just Practice Framework does not stand without questions of power at its foundation.

Disrupting Nationalism

We have also attempted to disrupt the bounded nationalism of U.S. social work and engage with a greater internationalism here. The critical thinking and practice of social workers and other theorists and activists beyond our borders have challenged and informed our thinking over the past several years as the seeds of ideas for this book were being planted. The Just Practice Framework is, in many aspects, a product of concrete engagement with context, histories, knowledge, and practices beyond the U.S. We have tried to incorporate these influences into the model and craft an approach that better enables us to think outside the box and beyond the borders of familiar experience. Fundamentally, social justice work calls on us to ask " social justice for whom?" and to constantly question the ways in which we circumscribe the boundaries of justice in our practice.

Strengthening Democratic Participation

In line with the directions advocated by Pease and Fook (1999), we have attempted to move beyond dualisms, craft an alternative discourse, and encourage new forms of partnership and participation. We concur with Ashley and Gaventa (1997) that collaborative partnerships which strengthen democratic participation offer "lessons of humility, care, and equity… lessons, at least in part, that return us to the importance of social capital… "(p. 51). Ashley and Gaventa encourage us to see social capital:

> . . . less as a substance than as a network. We see social capital as consisting of connections between and among groups and individuals – connections built incrementally through shared histories of activity and interchange; more like a circulatory system than like the liquid flowing through it. (p. 51)

We find the Just Practice Framework and processes to be a helpful guide for making and strengthening these connections. However, our own view is at best partial. We encourage readers to challenge us, help us see the limits, and suggest directions for enhancing and transforming the knowledge and practice of social justice work.

The "Attack on America": Thinking About It Using the Just Practice Framework.

September 11, 2001: Shaken in the wake of the violence and heavy with the weight of tragedy, people are trying to make sense of the attack on the World Trade Center and the Pentagon. The shock waves reverberate through the media, classrooms, community halls, and dinner tables across the country. The violence touched each of us in some way. U.S. residents, their sympathizers, and their critics alike turn to questions of power and history in order to give meanings to the devastating event and the context in which it occurred. In the immediate aftermath, the space of possibility is crowded with military options on the U.S. front as the space of critical questioning diminishes. The notion of "globalization" and the concepts of borders and difference have acquired a heightened salience. We face pressing questions of social justice at home and abroad. Will the Just Practice Framework serve as our guide?

Joy Akin, one of our students in an introductory social work practice course put the five key concepts of meaning, context, power, history, and possibility to use in her struggle to make sense of the events of September 11th. She writes,

How does a social "justice" worker interpret the events of September 11th? If I were a social worker in New York, would I be preoccupied only with the individuals, families, and communities that were directly impacted? What are the implications of this event on a national and global level?

Meaning: For many of us in America, the attack on two power symbols, economic and political, was an act that calls for retaliation and vengeance: "An eye for an eye." It was a blow that rattled our sense of security and invincibility. But for others of us, perhaps, especially those who have not experienced the "American Dream" of security and prosperity in this country, the attack may seem justified. Native Americans, for example, felt the might of the American military turned against them, killing men, women and children. And how many African Americans or women worked in the top floors of the World Trade Center towers?

Context: America prides itself on its democratic government, humanitarianism, and high standard of living. But how many people in this country live in poverty, experience some form of racism, sexism, ethnocentrism, classism, or ageism, and feel that they have no voice? From a global perspective, America may appear a greedy giant, consuming far more than its share of world resources, building its fat bank accounts and military might on the backs of workers in Third World countries who struggle to obtain even the most basic human needs, and forcing its culture and values on those who are weaker. What about the innocent civilians we have killed in the name of world peace and democracy? What are the motivations and grievances of terrorists like Osama bin Ladin? What injustices could have inspired those people to sacrifice their lives?

Power: The media over the last few days, has made it clear who has the power to have their interpretations of this situation valued as "true": conservatives, big business, and those who stand to profit the most by waging war. The media has played and replayed the horrifying images ad nauseum. They have played and preyed on every patriotic person's sensibilities, working to fan the fires of vengeance using inflammatory rhetoric. There have been endless references to God and praying, "one nation under God." People of Arabic descent in this country are being hounded, harassed, and even imprisoned for no reason but their nationality. The U.S. is using its economic and military clout to coerce countries such as Pakistan into cooperating with our agenda. Nobody seems to know exactly who, where, or how, but somebody must and will be punished: "We will hunt them down..."

History: History, if anyone can tune out the media long enough to hear it, might have much to teach us, about past U.S. relations with countries in the Middle East, about how other "private" wars have mushroomed into world wars, about how violence always breeds more violence.

Possibility: What alternatives can we find to war? What about an international peace conference, where dialogue between world leaders might illuminate other perspectives, alternative solutions and possibilities, cooperation in eliminating terrorism by seeking out its sources, both contextually and individually? Why did those people cheer when they heard about the attack? Do we want the answer?

As a social "justice" work student, I think it is my responsibility to take a stand for world peace and universal human rights. How? By organizing with other students in a peace march, writing my Congressmen, engaging in critical dialogues where I live, work, and study. How can I walk the talk?

Principles of Social Justice Work

Throughout this text, we have been bridging social work and social justice and seeking ways to translate our visions of social justice work into concrete principles and practices. In this section we summarize fifteen principles for social justice work that we have highlighted throughout the text. These principles are interrelated and mutually informing. We see this set of principles as a work in progress that will be shaped over time through dialogue about our diverse efforts to engage in social justice work. We invite readers to add to the list.

1. **Take a Global Perspective**. Social justice work challenges us to look both to and beyond the immediate context of our work and consider the larger structures and forces that bear on the situation. By taking a global perspective, we challenge our assumptions about borders and boundaries in their many forms. In taking a global perspective seriously, we are challenged to address questions of human rights and consider the ripple effects of our actions. A global perspective also serves as a reminder of the partiality of our knowledge and of the many ways of seeing and knowing refracted through the lenses of cultural and historical experience. Even in our most "micro" or "local" practice of social work it is possible to think and act from a global perspective.
2. **Appreciate Interconnectedness.** Social justice work challenges us to explore the patterns that connect, often across seemingly disparate contexts and experiences. In order to meet the complex challenges of 21st century social work, we cannot limit our efforts to the safety of narrow specialization. We need to grapple with the relationships between individual, family, and community struggles and broader political, social, and economic arrangements. Likewise, we need to maintain the connectedness of head, heart, and hand in our work such that our actions are guided by both grounded knowledge and by a felt connection and commitment to human dignity and relationships. As we explore and appreciate the patterns that connect, we may discover opportunities for new partnerships and networks to support social justice work.
3. **Take History Seriously.** People, problems, and ideas have histories. Throughout the book, we have stressed the importance of a historical perspective both in understanding contemporary concerns and in appreciating a sense of the possible. People are historical beings, conscious of time, and at once makers and products of history. It is through attention to the histories of people, problems, and ideas that we come to question certainties of the moment and inevitabilities of the future. Too often, our engagement with history in social work is limited to a class on the history of social welfare. Social justice work calls for critical reflection on our own histories and that of our policies, practices, and certainties as part of the work.

4. **Challenge Our Certainties:** Social justice work demands that we be willing to constantly question our assumptions, especially those that we hold most dear. We cannot effectively open ourselves to new ways of hearing, seeing, and thinking without ongoing reflection on what and how we know. Moreover, social justice work calls on us to let go of our certainties and be willing to embrace ambiguities and engage with contradictions. In so doing, we open ourselves to learning about the ways in which others attempt to negotiate the conflicting and often contradictory expectations of everyday life and make sense of their experiences in the process. It is often in the slippery spaces of ambiguity and contradiction that the possibilities for transformational change emerge.

5. **Learn through Dialogue.** In contrast to approaches that value the "expert" role, social justice work asks us to begin from a place of uncertainty, of not knowing. We enter into each new relationship and change process as learners, with humility and openness, cognizant of the partiality of our knowledge and the limits of our worldview. It is through dialogue that we come to appreciate new meanings and interpretations and alternative ways of seeing, being, and acting in the world. This does not imply that we necessarily come to accept or adopt others' interpretations of social reality as our own. Rather, it is through respectful dialogue that we probe, question, and disagree as well. Social justice work involves the art of diplomacy, wherein we help bring to light diverse views and interests, identify important differences as well as common ground, examine the power relations at stake, and seek courses of action that value human dignity and rights.

6. **Confront Questions of Power.** Social justice work recognizes the importance of thinking and talking about power in its many forms. Possibilities for meaningful change emerge when people come to recognize and analyze the forms and relations of power that constrain their lives and realize personal and collective forms of power – power to be, to act, and to join together. We have pointed to the power of discourse in the construction of both problems and interventions. We have examined the power of labels to define and, in effect, stand for the person and the power of the expert to diagnose and treat. We have also demonstrated the power of people to create change as they join together, question their life circumstances, develop critical awareness, build personal and group capacity, and utilize collective knowledge and capacity to challenge

and change the conditions of their lives. Social justice workers exert their own power to question, resist, and act in ways that open spaces of hope and possibility.

7. **Recognize and Embrace the Political Nature of Social Work.** As Paulo Freire reminds us, social justice workers are not neutral agents. We are positioned and acting in contexts of power and inequality. In so doing we need not only acknowledge but also embrace the political nature of the work and prepare ourselves to carry out our work with integrity. The commitment to social justice work is both an ethical and a political commitment. Exercising this commitment demands knowledge of the power relations in which our practice is situated, an understanding of strategies and tactics that enable us to effectively engage as players, and the will and skills to enable others to participate in the work of justice-oriented change.

8. **Value Difference and Address the Production of Difference.** A critical understanding of difference is central to social justice work. The production of difference – different ways of interpreting, organizing, and acting in the world – is part of our capacities as meaning-making, cultural beings. Encounters with difference can challenge our most deeply held truths about the world and our place in it and our abilities to remain open to alternative ways of thinking, feeling, being, and acting. Moreover, social justice work challenges us to grapple with the politics of difference. By this we mean the processes, mechanisms, and relations of power through which particular forms of difference and inequality are produced, maintained, and justified. We need to both value the meaning and power of difference and question the construction and representation of differences and the multiple meanings and values attached to them. For example, the American Anthropological Statement on Race presented at the end of Chapter One helps us to understand the historical and political context in which ideas of race and difference in America were produced and reproduced. Social justice work calls on us to ask, "what differences make a difference here and to whom?"

9. **Be Cognizant of Positionality.** The social work profession has always recognized the significance of self-awareness for social workers. Self-awareness most often takes on the meaning of reflecting on the "baggage" the worker brings to the work, that is,

thinking about personal attitudes and beliefs and how these might get in the way of working with particular clients or specific situations. Positionality, however, encapsulates this notion of knowledge of the self and expands it to include awareness of the powerful shaping influences of gender, class, sexual identity, and race, how these shape attitudes and beliefs, and how these locate the worker differently in reference to differently positioned clients. Fully comprehending this idea of positionality is a humbling endeavor. It serves as a constant reminder of one's social/political location, the challenges and strengths inherent in one's location, and the partiality of one's worldview. It keeps us from making broad generalizations about the way things work and calls on us to see each situation as unique.

10. **Promote Participation**. We contend that there is no such thing as empowerment without participation. We must be vigilant in our search for ways to encourage the participation of people in the full range of change endeavors, from the interpersonal to the social. When in doubt, we must ask ourselves who is included, who is excluded and why? We must also begin the process of evaluating programs and projects based on the criteria of participation, and for social justice work, this means giving people a voice in the issues that most directly concern their lives and their well-being.

11. **Keep the Social in Social Work**. As we have tried to illustrate throughout the book, social justice work is a collective endeavor. We cannot readily "go it alone." We have pointed to the importance of raising critical consciousness through dialogue and building team work for change-oriented action as central components of social justice work. This holds true not only for our actions with individuals, families, and communities, but also for building support, solidarity, and quite literally, a movement of social justice workers. It can be very intimidating to pose critical questions in the context of our everyday practice. If we are attempting to engage in "functional noncapitulation" in isolation from others, we can become frustrated and overwhelmed. As social justice workers, we need to build relationships with one another, through intra-and interorganizational networks, with local, national, and international social justice organizations, and with the "rank and file" activists and advocates in our own communities. Together we can nurture our relationships and ourselves and fuel our sense of possibility and commitment to praxis.

12. **Build and Share Leadership.** Social justice work is about building capacity and sharing leadership. Reaching back to the participatory democracy exemplified in the work of Jane Addams and other social reformers at the turn of the 20th century, a pattern emerges and weaves its way through social work history. This pattern is one of having faith in the capacity of humans, even under the most severe conditions, to challenge the conditions of their lives and participate in its transformation. Thinking of our practice, at least in part, as a way to create opportunities for participation and leadership development, provides us with a clear goal upon which to set our sights. It forces us to pose the following questions: How do I do my work in such a way that I build and support new forms of leadership? What forms and shapes might practice take should I strive to build the leadership capacity of those with whom I work?

13. **Be Willing to Take "Bold and Courageous Action"** (Roby, 1998). Homan (1999) reminds us that, "It is the lack of will to confront the barriers, real and imagined, that preserves conditions that should be changed" (p. 321). Confronting barriers mean confronting unfair policies and practices in welfare agencies that prevent some people from moving out of poverty through post-secondary education and training. It means organizing a rally for laborers overlooked in recent legislation passed by Congress that provides funding and tax relief for corporations hurt by economic recession but ignores the plight of common laborers who have far fewer resources at their disposal. It means getting angry and sustaining anger as a motivating force, choosing your battles well, and taking bold moves with others as a base of power and support.

14. **Create a Spirit of Hope and Spaces of Possibility.** A major theme of social justice work is attention to creating spaces of hope and possibility through visions of a more just tomorrow. Throughout history, others have shared and acted on similar visions and sought to carve out the possible from seemingly impossible situations and circumstances. These individuals and groups understood that without hope there is no purpose and in some cases, lose of hope meant lose of life itself. While for some, this notion of the possible spurred on dreams of a better world, for others it meant contemplating and acting upon alternative ways of being and doing in the world at that very moment. We must continually challenge ourselves to ask how

we can infuse our work with this same sense of purpose and recognize the dialectical relationship of hope and possibility – hope brings possibility and possibility brings hope.

15. **Find and Create Joy in the Work.** In Chapter Eight, we discussed how social workers in the U.S. rarely think about or take the time to celebrate the joy and beauty of their work. We continue to question why the concept of celebration is foreign to our work on U.S. soil and probe the possibility of reconfiguring programs, policies, practices, and projects, and our relationships with others and ourselves should we take celebration seriously. We (the authors) learn from our students who teach us that the core process of celebration is one they embrace to combat societal stereotypes of social work as drudgery and "the burn-out profession" and social workers as society's "street sweepers" and "garbage collectors." They appreciate the permission that celebration gives to carve out space for patting themselves on the back, supporting each other in the hard work that they do, and giving new meaning to social work that elicits pride and renewed commitment.

Revisiting Voices from Just Practice

Let us take some time to revisit some of the voices we have learned from throughout the text: For example, John Brown Childs, the "Newest Vermonters" and Al. What more can we learn from their stories? What can we take from their stories that strengthen our commitment to social justice work? What principles of social justice work do these voices exemplify?

Chapter Summary: Social Justice Work in the Real World

We opened this chapter with a snapshot of the challenges facing social workers in the 21st century. Some readers may argue that, in the face of these overwhelming demands and increasingly scarce resources, our vision of social justice work is simply too idealistic. Some might argue that the idea of social justice is all well and good but the realities of everyday practice demand attention to more immediate and pragmatic concerns, such as responding to crises, getting clients access to benefits, and keeping our jobs in the era of downsizing. We do not underestimate the daily stresses and struggles of social work practice in a context of increasing complexity of problems and scarcity of resources. We take them quite seriously. In fact, we contend that, given these pressures, the need for social justice work is all the more urgent, and that possibilities await us in every practice setting. The Just Practice Framework offers an alternative way of thinking about our practice settings, relationships, possible courses of actions, and, fundamentally, ourselves. Many social workers in hospitals, prison settings, schools, refugee camps, child welfare offices, and other settings are realizing their own possibilities for social justice work in ways large and small everyday. We have offered here a framework with which to embrace that energy and creativity, build on the possibilities, and, hopefully, bring together the knowledge, power, and commitment for a new collective vision and practice of social work that is grounded in the best of our history and up to the task of 21st century challenges.

Revisiting the Just Practice Matrix

This final reflection exercise calls forth the Just Practice Matrix we included at the end of Chapter Four. Now that you have finished reading the entire Just Practice text, find an example, perhaps from your own experience, of Just Practice in action. Are there programs or practices in your own community where you see Just Practice in action? Have you read about or discussed in your other classes, examples of social work practice that take social justice seriously?

FIGURE 9.1

Just Practice Matrix: Applying the Framework to the Core Processes

Framework and Processes: Critical Questions	Engagement	Teaching/ Learning	Action and Accompaniment	Evaluation, Reflection and Celebration
Meaning	What is the significance of the encounter and relationship? How do the parties involved interpret the experience?	What and how do we learn from one another's interpretations? Create new meanings and understandings?	How does partiality of knowledge shape action? How do differing meanings constrain or promote differing courses of action?	How do we appreciate meaning via reflexivity? How do we validate the meaning of our work? Give meaning to social justice?
Context	How do interpersonal, organizational, social contexts shape relations and trust building? How can the context be changed in order to facilitate engagement?	How does context inhibit or facilitate possibilities for mutual learning? How does the teaching/learning process challenge the interpersonal, organizational, and social context?	How does context shape the pathways for action, access to resources, patterns of practices, social work roles, nature of partnerships? How do our actions expand contexts for social justice work?	What is context specific about the process? What can be applied to other contexts? How can reflection on the context be a catalyst for contextual change? What forms of celebration fit the context?
Power	How do differing positionalities of participants shape engagement? What forms of power need to be addressed in the engagement process? How do we use the power available to promote justice in relationship?	What can we learn from a power analysis of the situation? How can the process of teaching/learning challenge power inequalities among participants and promote social justice?	What access is there to power and resources? How do we remain mindful of power differences in the change process? How do they challenge accompaniment? How do actions contribute to empowerment of participants?	How do we evaluate redistribution of power in the change process? How do we measure individual, organizational and community empowerment? How do we both appreciate and celebrate new forms and practices of power?

FIGURE 9.1 *(Concluded)*

Just Practice Matrix: Applying the Framework to the Core Processes

Framework and Processes: Critical Questions	**Engagement**	**Teaching/ Learning**	**Action and Accompaniment**	**Evaluation, Reflection and Celebration**
History	How do past histories and experiences of participants shape the encounter and process of relationship building? What prior knowledge and assumptions might promote or inhibit the process?	How do we teach/ learn from and about our histories? How do our histories shape the ways that we know and experience the world? How do we learn from those who came before? How do we learn from what is historically possible?	How do histories become resources and catalysts for action? How does historical consciousness inform future action? How do we bridge differences of history and forge alliance for action? How do actions challenge inscriptions of historic injustice?	How do we evaluate change over time? How do we account for historical conditions? How does reflection on where we have been inform where we are going? How might a reclamation and celebration of our histories animate future efforts?
Possibility	What are the possible relationships that can be formed and strengthened in this change effort? What spaces of hope can be opened?	What can we learn from this other person/ group? What can we contribute? What new ways of knowing might emerge from this experience? How can this learning promote other possibilities for social justice work?	How might we expand own repertoire of roles and skills? What possible courses of action are available? How can our efforts enhance future possibilities for empowering action?	How do we select among the possibilities at hand? Assess possible courses of action? Expand the terrain of the thinkable, talkable, and do-able? Reflect on decisions made and opportunities lost? Celebrate creativity?

Final Collaborative Project - Scenarios of Possibility:

The stories and examples we have used throughout this text illustrate how questioning taken for granted assumptions leads to refreshing, creative new ways of conceptualizing social work practice. Divide into groups with students in your class and brainstorm areas of interest in social work. In your groups, begin the process of revising social work practice in this area of interest based on the Just Practice key concepts and practice principles. Areas of interest could include juvenile delinquency, child and families, elderly, child abuse, community organizing, social policy, etc. How do the key concepts and practice principles lead you to conceptualize new methods and forms of practice? Which practice principles helped you most? What new possibilities did you envision? What might be some of the constraints and points of resistance? How might you mitigate these?

Case Study: Social Justice Work in Practice

Let's look at an example of social justice work in practice. In writing this book, we have gained a deeper appreciation for the many ways in which people practice social justice work. We have also had the opportunity to learn from social work students as they apply the Just Practice Framework as a guide to their thinking and action. We hope the example will encourage readers to reflect on the ways in which you might engage in social justice work and imagine new practice possibilities. We invite you to continue the dialogue and share your ideas with us at justpractice@selway.umt.edu.

The Story of Working for Equality and Economic Liberation (WEEL)

WEEL is an education, advocacy, and action organization dedicated to promoting welfare rights in Montana. The organization is grounded in principles of popular education and concerns about the intersections of sexism, racism, and classism. WEEL's mission statement reflects these principles: "WEEL is a grassroots organization committed to securing justice for people living in poverty. We envision a world with equal access to quality shelter, food, health care, education, and economic opportunity. We are dedicated to changing the beliefs and policy systems that keep people oppressed. Through action and education, we are working on a future of equality and economic liberation for all."

Launched in 1996, WEEL currently has chapters in Missoula and Helena, Montana and on the campus of the University of Montana. WEEL has more than 1000 members and supporters statewide and an active core membership of forty. WEEL organizers write: "By educating, organizing, speaking out, rallying, and testifying on many of the issues concerning low income Montanans, WEEL plays an integral part in Montana's welfare rights battle." WEEL has also gained national attention for its advocacy work on behalf of people living in poverty. In 2001, five years after President Clinton's authorization of the Personal Responsibility and Work Opportunity Act, WEEL members have built a credible organization and claimed a place at the table in negotiating the future direction of welfare and its reform.

This bold organization had modest beginnings in the conversations between two women employed in a Montana welfare-to-work program. In the anti-welfare climate of the 1990s, the state of Montana followed the national trend and introduced "Families Achieving Independence in Montana (FAIM), a time-limited, welfare-to-work program. FAIM seeks to replace "welfare dependency" with "self sufficiency" through mandatory work requirements and strict time limits. Welfare workers are encouraged to "divert" their clients from benefits and programs. Further, the policy specifically discourages out of wedlock births and promotes marriage as a "better choice" than welfare.

The two women felt the contradictory effects of this policy in the *context* of their everyday work and lives. Their program was committed to the education and empowerment of poor women. But these new policies undermined that commitment. At the same time, program funding was contingent upon implementation of state policy. The women and their clients were caught in a no-win situation. The women began to question the *meaning* of "self-sufficiency" and "dependency" and the *power* of the state to impose particular moral codes and sanctions on its more vulnerable citizens. They began to question the *power* of gendered images and discourses in shaping the life chances of poor women. They began meeting after work each day to share their frustrations and analyze what they were experiencing.

The two invited other women to come together to reflect on their experiences and talk about the *possibilities* for action. At first, seven or eight women came together to share their stories, reflect on their own *histories* and experiences, and learn through dialogue. They began to ask questions of *history* as a guide for future action: How did "ending welfare as we know it" rather than "ending poverty as we know it" become an issue of national priority? How have others challenged the limits of public policy and won?

Drawing on their many community ties, this core group formed an advisory board of low-income women who had an interest in welfare activism. They began to build a grassroots organization run by and for people living in poverty. They took a two-pronged approach: 1) focus on mitigating the *immediate* harm to low-income people as a result of the punitive welfare policies and 2) collective action to challenge and change the punitive direction of "welfare reform." The fledgling group did not "go it alone." They turned to other women activists and community organizations to learn lessons of *history* and *possibility* from their experiences.

WEEL's founding board of directors was made up of nine low-income women, all single mothers. Some were working in low-paying jobs, some were trying to complete their college education, and others had found themselves unemployed or homeless after a family or health crisis. Members crafted spaces of support for women to come together, validate their experiences, and build the personal and collective capacities for action. They recognized that a *context* of affection and mutual support was key to their activism, and they made caring relations the foundation for their collective action. Being together and caring for one another is not something apart from activism, but central to its success. As one WEEL member describes:

My WEEL sisters have always accepted me for just who I am. They never tried to change me or alter the way I think or feel, and I have always loved and accepted them just the way they are. I don't know where I would be, or who, if they had not come into my life... There is no way I could ever put into words the love and acceptance I have felt and feel for these brave and incredible women.

WEEL members advocate for and with people on welfare and educate the community regarding welfare reform. Members know and use the *power* of communication for popular education. From its inception, WEEL has combined organization building with direct action. Members have utilized the *possibilities* at hand - popular theater, community forums, newsletters, radio shows, letter-writing campaigns, and encampments at the State Capitol - to communicate their messages. WEEL's annual "Momma Jam" is a celebration of children and motherhood and a reminder of the hard work that parenting entails. WEEL has received national recognition for its advocacy work, and members are now mentoring other budding activists and organizations in order to share the *meaning* of their work and keep the *history* and *possibilities* of activism alive.

WEEL works in collaboration with other progressive groups to build coalitions for social justice throughout the Western U.S. WEEL has also joined with other welfare rights groups across the country in National Days of Action. WEEL connects local and global concerns by engaging in International Human Rights Day actions that address economic and social well being as fundamental human rights. WEEL members have become effective advocates and lobbyists. They have taken leadership in campaigns for children's health insurance, and they have lobbied hard for the rights of people on welfare to pursue a college education. They have claimed a voice and demanded a place at the welfare reform policy table.

WEEL has demonstrated its capacity to blend nurture and activism, use the media and create media events, and renew itself with expanding membership, changing leadership, and ongoing reflection on its action. WEEL has met with some resistance from those who did not appreciate their feminist-informed approach and has weathered some internal struggles as well. Through these struggles WEEL members have come to clarify and value their positions as women and organizers. Reflecting collectively on their experiences, members offered these lessons for success which may benefit other women's efforts: 1) Value relationships; 2) Keep the process heart-centered because the head is going to fail sometimes; 3) Don't be afraid to think that your intuition matters; 4) Take time to reflect and question; 5) Think and act holistically; 6) Recognize and respect your limits; 7) Collaborate with others and help build bridges; 8) Keep your creative spark; 9) Take pride in and celebrate your accomplishments; 10) Have fun together. WEEL members speak a language of love and justice and recognize the inseparability of the two. "WEEL moves ahead by remaining respectful of the partiality of its knowledge, hopeful of the possibilities for social transformation, and ever mindful of the delicate interplay of head, heart, and hand" (Finn et al, 2000, p. 308). What aspects of the Just Practice Framework play out here? What principles of Just Practice does WEEL draw on in its work? Where do you see similar efforts underway in your community?

Questions for Discussion

1. What additional issues do you believe will have an important effect on the practice of social work in years to come?
2. What principles of social justice work might you add to our list? Are there any that you would eliminate and why?
3. What is your vision of a more just world? What steps might you take locally to begin to realize that vision?
4. If you were to give a guest lecture on social justice work to a beginning class of social work students how would you proceed? What would be the key components of your presentation? How might you involve the students in the learning process?
5. If you were to write a letter to the editor of your local newspaper with a number of concrete suggestions for promoting social justice in your community, what would you include?
6. If you were a member of the curriculum committee in your social work program, what suggestions would you make for strengthening attention to issues of diversity and social justice in the curriculum?

Suggested Readings

Abramovitz, M. (1993). "Should all social workers be educated for social change? Pro." *Journal of Social Work Education*, 29, 6-11.

Franklin, C. (2000). "Predicting the future of school social work practice in the new millennium." *Journal of Social Work in Education*, 22(1), 3-5.

Harvey, D. (2000). *Spaces of hope*. Berkeley: University of California Press.

Korten, D. (1995). *When corporations rule the world.* West Hartford, CT: Kumarian Press.

Lyons, K. (1999). *International social work: Themes and perspectives*. Brookfield, VT: Ashgate Publishing.

Pease, B. & Fook, J. (1999). *Transforming social work practice: Postmodern critical perspectives*. New York: Routledge.

Ramanathan, C. & Link, R. (Eds.). (1999). *All our futures: Social work practice in a global era*. Belmont, CA: Wadsworth.

Reisch, M. & Gambrill, E. (Eds.). (1997). *Social work in the 21st century*. Thousand Oaks, CA: Pine Forge Press.

Appendix

Universal Declaration of Human Rights

Preamble

Whereas recognition of the inherent dignity and of the equal and inalienable rights of all members of the human family is the foundation of freedom, justice and peace in the world,

Whereas disregard and contempt for human rights have resulted in barbarous acts which have outraged the conscience of mankind, and the advent of a world in which human beings shall enjoy freedom of speech and belief and freedom from fear and want has been proclaimed as the highest aspiration of the common people,

Whereas it is essential, if a man is not to be compelled to have recourse, as a last resort, to rebellion against tyranny and oppression, that human rights should be protected by the rule of the law,

Whereas it is essential to promote the development of friendly relations between nations,

Whereas the peoples of the United Nations have in the Charter reaffirmed their faith in fundamental human rights, in the dignity and worth of the human person and in the equal rights of men and women and have determined to promote social progress and better standards of life in larger freedom,

Whereas Member States have pledged themselves to achieve, in co-operation with the United Nations, the promotion of universal respect for and observance of human rights and fundamental freedoms,

Whereas a common understanding of these rights and freedoms is of the greatest importance for the full realization of this pledge,

Now Therefore,
The General Assembly
proclaims
This Universal Declaration of Human Rights

as a common standard of achievement for all peoples and all nations, to the end that every individual and every organ of society, keeping this Declaration constantly in mind, shall strive by teaching and education to promote respect for these rights and freedoms and by progressive measures, national and international, to secure their universal and effective recognition and observance, both among the people of Member States themselves and among peoples of territories under their jurisdiction.

Article 1
All human beings are born free and equal in dignity and rights. They are endowed with reason and conscience and should act toward one another in a spirit of brotherhood.

Article 2
Everyone is entitled to all the rights and freedoms set forth in this Declaration, without distinction of any kind, such as race, color, sex, language, religion, political or other opinion, national or social origin, property, birth or other status.

Furthermore, no distinction shall be made on the basis of the political, jurisdictional or international status of the country or territory to which a person belongs, whether it be independent, trust, non-self governing or under any other limitation of sovereignty.

Article 3
Everyone has the right to life, liberty and security of person.

Article 4
No one shall be held in slavery or servitude; slavery and the slave trade shall be prohibited in all their forms.

Article 5
No one shall be subjected to torture or to cruel, inhuman or degrading treatment or punishment.

Article 6
Everyone has the right to recognition everywhere as a person before the law.

Article 7
All are equal before the law and are entitled without any discrimination to equal protection of the law. All are entitled to equal protection against any discrimination in violation of this Declaration and against any incitement to such discrimination.

Article 8
Everyone has the right to an effective remedy by the competent national tribunals for acts violating the fundamental rights granted him by the constitution or by law.

Article 9
No one shall be subjected to arbitrary arrest, detention or exile.

Article 10
Everyone is entitled in full equality to a fair and public hearing by an independent and impartial tribunal, in the determination of his rights and obligations and of any criminal charge against him.

Article 11
(1) Everyone charged with a penal offence has the right to be presumed innocent until proved guilty according to law in a public trial at which he has had all the guarantees necessary for his defense.

(2) No one shall be held guilty of any penal offense on account of any act or omission which did not constitute a penal offense, under national or international law, at the time when it was committed. Nor shall a heavier penalty be imposed than the one that was applicable at the time the penal offence was committed.

Article 12
No one shall be subjected to arbitrary interference with his privacy, family, home or correspondence, nor to attacks upon his honor and reputation. Everyone has the right to the protection of the law against such interference or attacks.

Article 13
(1) Everyone has the right to freedom of movement and residence within the borders of each State.
(2) Everyone has the right to leave any country, including his own, and to return to his country.

Article 14
(1) Everyone has the right to seek and to enjoy in other countries asylum from persecution.
(2) This right may not be invoked in the case of prosecutions genuinely arising from non-political crimes or from acts contrary to the purposes and principles of the United Nations.

Article 15
(1) Everyone has the right to a nationality.
(2) No one shall be arbitrarily deprived of his nationality nor denied the right to change his nationality.

Article 16
(1) Men and women of full age, without any limitation due to race, nationality or religion, have the right to marry and found a family. They are entitled to equal rights as to marriage, during marriage and at its dissolution.
(2) Marriage shall be entered into only with the free and full consent of the intending spouses.
(3) The family is the natural and fundamental group unit of society and is entitled to protection by society and the State.

Article 17

(1) Everyone has the right to own property alone as well as in association with others.

(2) No one shall be arbitrarily deprived of his property.

Article 18

Everyone has the right to freedom of thought, conscience and religion; this right includes freedom to change his religion or belief, and freedom, either alone or in community with others and in public and private, to manifest his religion or belief in teaching, practice, worship and observance.

Article 19

Everyone has the right to freedom of opinion and expression; this right includes freedom to hold opinions without interference and to seek, receive and impart information and ideas through any media and regardless of frontiers.

Article 20

(1) Everyone has the right to freedom of peaceful assembly and association.

(2) No one may be compelled to belong to an association.

Article 21

(1) Everyone has the right to take part in the government of his country, directly or through freely chosen representatives.

(2) Everyone has the right of equal access to public service in his country.

(3) The will of the people shall be the basis of the authority of government; this will shall be expressed in periodic and genuine elections which shall be by universal and equal suffrage and shall be held by secret vote or by equivalent free voting procedures.

Article 22

Everyone, as a member of society, has the right to social security and is entitled to realization, through national effort and international cooperation and in accordance with the organization and resources of each State, of the economic, social and cultural rights indispensable for his dignity and the free development of his personality.

Article 23

(1) Everyone has the right to work, to free choice of employment, to just and favorable conditions of work and to protection against unemployment.
(2) Everyone, without any discrimination, has the right to equal pay for equal work.
(3) Everyone who works has the right to just and favorable remuneration ensuring for himself and his family an existence worthy of human dignity, and supplemented, if necessary, by other means of social protection.
(4) Everyone has the right to form and to join trade unions for the protection of his interests.

Article 24

Everyone has the right to rest and leisure, including reasonable limitations of working hours and periodic holidays with pay.

Article 25

(1) Everyone has the right to a standard of living adequate for the health and well-being of himself and of his family, including food, clothing, housing and medical care and necessary social services, and the right to security in the event of unemployment, sickness, disability, widowhood, old age or other lack of livelihood in circumstances beyond his control.
(2) Motherhood and childhood are entitled to special care and assistance. All children, whether born in or out of wedlock, shall enjoy the same social protection.

Article 26

(1) Everyone has the right to education. Education shall be free, at least in the elementary and fundamental stages. Elementary education shall be compulsory. Technical and professional education shall be made generally available and higher education shall be equally accessible to all on his basis of merit.
(2) Education shall be directed to the full development of the human personality and to the strengthening of respect for human rights and fundamental freedoms. It shall promote understanding, tolerance and friendship among all nations, racial or religious groups, and shall further the activities of the United Nations for the maintenance of peace.
(3) Parents have a prior right to choose the kind of education that shall be given to their children.

Article 27

(1) Everyone has the right freely to participate in the cultural life of the community, to enjoy the arts and to share in scientific advancement and its benefits.

(2) Everyone has the right to the protection of the moral and material interests resulting from any scientific, literary or artistic production of which he is the author.

Article 28

Everyone is entitled to a social and international order in which the rights and freedoms set for them in this Declaration can be fully realized.

Article 29

(1) Everyone has duties to the community in which alone the free and full development of his personality is possible.

(2) In the exercise of his rights and freedoms, everyone shall be subject only to such limitations as are determined by law solely for the purpose of securing due recognition and respect for the rights and freedoms of others and of meeting the just requirements of morality, public order and the general welfare in a democratic society.

(3) These rights and freedoms may in no case be exercised contrary to the purposes and principles of the United Nations.

Article 30

Nothing in this Declaration may be interpreted as implying for any State, group or person any right to engage in any activity or to perform any act aimed at the destruction of any of the rights and freedoms set forth herein.[1]

[1] For a summary history of the United Nations Declaration of Human Rights see www.un.org/Depts/dhl/resguide/hrdec.htm. For further information regarding links to The United Nations Committee on Human Rights, Committee against Torture, Committee on Economic, Social and Cultural Rights, Committee on Elimination of Discrimination against Women; Committee on Elimination of Racial Discrimination, and Committee on the Rights of the Child see www.un.org/Depts/dhl/resguide/spechr.htm. For materials relating to the Universal Declaration of Human Rights and a small pocket size pamphlet of the Declaration we distribute in our classes, contact: Human Rights USA Resource Center, 229-19th Avenue South, Room 439, Minneapolis, MN 55455, Phone: 612-626-0041 or the toll free number: 1-888-HREDUC8. Web Site: www.hrusa.org or email: hrusa@tc.umn.edu

Notes

Chapter 1

1. From Ramsey Clark (1988) "Social justice and issues of human rights in the international context." In D. S. Sanders & J. Fischer (Eds.), *Visions for the future: Social work and the Pacific Asian perspective*. Honolulu: University of Hawaii Press, pp. 3-10.
2. According to the IFSW website (www.ifsw.org): "This international definition of the social work profession replaces the IFSW definition adopted in 1982. It is understood that social work in the 21st century is dynamic and evolving, and therefore no definition should be regarded as exhaustive." The definition was adopted by the General Meeting of the International Federation of Social Workers, Montreal, Canada, July, 2000.
3. Key for countries (Canada, Russia, Sweden, Japan, and Chile)
4. These points are drawn from U.S. Catholic Bishops (1986) "Economic Justice for All," Pastoral letter on Catholic Social Teaching and the U.S. Economy. The numbers in the excerpts quoted here correspond to numbered points in the letter.
5. For a more thorough discussion of Rawls' concept of distributive justice and its relation to social work see Jerome Carl Wakefield's important articles "Psychotherapy, distributive justice, and social work," Parts I and II, *Social Service Review*, 62(2/3), 1988.
6. Permission to reprint this essay courtesy of John Brown Childs.
7. Such confederacies were fluid, and their composition could change over time.
8. This statement revised in 2001, appears in the website of The American Anthropological Association (AAA). It is reprinted here with permission from AAA.

Chapter 2

1. From Horton, M. (1998). *The long haul: An autobiography* (with Judith Kohl and Herbert Kohl). New York: Teachers College Press, p. 51. Permission to quote courtesy of Teachers College Press.
2. See *The Nation,* February 5, 2001 – entire issue devoted to "The Tainted Presidency." The full report on the investigation was to appear in mid-September but the events of September 11th intervened.

3. Karl DeSchweinitz's quotation comes originally from correspondence to Fedele Fauri, September 9, 1955, Council of Social Work Education Manuscripts, Box 7, Folder 24, Social Welfare History Archives, University of Minnesota, Minneapolis, MN.
4. See Ana Maria Garcia's 1982 *La Operación* that addresses the sterilization of women in Puerto Rico.
5. Scientific management principles were promoted by Fredrick Taylor during the early 1900s. See J. Schriver, *Human behavior and the social environment,* pp. 427-428 for a thorough explanation of Taylor's organizational theory and its main principles.
6. We borrow from Ann Withorn's (1984) seminal work, *Serving the people: Social service and social change.* New York: Columbia University Press.
7. See David Wagner (2000) *What's love got to do with it: A critical look at American charity.* New York: The New Press.
8. These scripts are based on excerpts from Jane Addams, *Twenty years at Hull House* (1910), *Democracy and social ethics* (1902) and *A centennial reader* (1960) and Bertha Capen Reynolds, *Social work and social living* (1975) and *Between client and community* (1934). Sally Brown, a graduate of the University of Montana Social Work Program, lives and works in Missoula, Montana. Sally, the mother of four, returned to school and finished her degree at age 50. She encourages other women to take the risk and do the same.
9. Adapted from Mary Van Kleeck (1934/1991) *Our illusions regarding government.* Reprinted in *Journal of Progressive Human Services.* 2(1), 75-86.
10. Based on the Jeannette Rankin Commemorative Booklet, (no date) by Joan Hoff-Wilson, Executive Secretary, Organization of American Historians. For more information contact OAH at www.oah.org. For further background on Jeannette Rankin see also Mary Barmeyer O'Brien (1995) *Bright star in the big sky, Jeannette Rankin, 1880-1973.*
11. Adapted from Myles Horton (1998). *The long haul: An autobiography.*
12. Based on Jones, M. and Kerr, C. (1996). *The autobiography of Mother Jones.* Ashley Atkinson, MSW student, University of Michigan, researched and wrote the biographical sketch on Mother Jones.
13. Adapted from W. E. B. DuBois (1968). *A soliloquy on viewing my life from the last decade of the first century*, and (1903/1996) *The souls of black folk.* New York: Random House. Ashley Atkinson, MSW student, University of Michigan, researched and wrote the biographical sketch on W.E.B. Dubois.

Chapter 3

1. The following quotes are taken from George Seldes (1985) (Ed.) *The great thoughts.* New York: Balantine Books. Confucius (p. 92), from *The doctrine of the mean*, Ch. XX, 8; Diderot (p. 108) from "On man, a refutation of Helvetius'

work, 1774"; Nietzsche (p. 311) from *Ecco homo*, 1908, Pt. I, 1; Arendt (p.16) from *The life of the mind*, unfinished trilogy, no date; Einstein (p. 119) from *My world picture, 1934*; Schweitzer (p. 376) from *The philosophy of civilization,* 1923, Pt. II.

2 This side bar is based on excerpts from J. Finn (1998) "Gender and Families," Chapter Six in Josefina Figueira-McDonough, F. Ellen Netting, and Ann Nichols-Casebolt (Eds.) *The role of gender in practice knowledge: Claiming half the human experience*, pp. 207-208.

3. See Nakanishi and Rittner (1992) for a discussion of the "Inclusionary cultural model" and exercises that enable students to work through a process of cultural self-definition. The authors address the role of family and childhood lessons in values and valuing as part of the process of cultural self-definition.
4. This exercise on values and valuing is informed by White and Tyson-Rawson's (1995) work on the "gendergram," a tool for assessing gender role socialization.
5. From John H. Oberly, Annual Report of the Commissioner of Indian Affairs, 1888, in Washburn (1973, p. 422).
6. From T. J. Morgan, Annual Report of the Commissioner of Indian Affairs, 1889, in Washburn (1973, p. 433).
7. From Brill (1976) *Teamwork: Working together in the human services*, cited in Day (2000) *A new history of social welfare*, p. 2.
8. From the Preamble to the NASW Code of Ethics, approved by the Delegate Assembly in 1996 and revised by the delegate assembly in 1999.
9. This section summarizes Day's carefully developed discussion of American social values and their relations to social work. See Day (2000, p. 4-12) for a fuller treatment of these values.
10. For the full text of the Case Con Manifesto please see the Barefoot Social Worker: The Voice of Radical Social Work in Britain website at: http://homepage.dtn.ntl.com/terence.p/barefoot/casecon
11. This chart was developed based on Levy's discussion of preferred conceptions of people, outcomes for people, and instrumentalities for dealing with people (Levy, 1973, pp. 38-42).
12. Permission to reproduce excerpt from the Code of Ethics of NABSW courtesy of NABSW, Detroit, Michigan.
13. From Canadian Association of Social Workers website, www.casw-acts.ca, 2001.
14. From the International Federation of Social Workers website, www.ifsw.org, 2001.
15. See the website of the School of Social Work, University of Costa Rica, San Jose, Costa Rica, at www.ts.ucr.ac.cr/decla, for an archive of declarations and debates regarding the definition of social work.
16. The Southern Cone is made of up Argentina, Bolivia, Brazil, Chile, Paraguay, and Uruguay.
17. From the First Regional Seminar on Ethics and Social Work organized by the Comité MERCOSUR de Organizaciones Profesionales de Trabajo Social y

Servicio Social en Montevideo, Uruguay, June 1-3, 2000. See the full text of principles at the website of the School of Social Work, University of Costa Rica, San Jose, Costa Rica: www.ts.ucr.ac.cr/decla-002.

18. For more information on Human Rights and links to documents and archives see the Office of the High Commissioner for Human Rights website at http://www.unhchr.ch.
19. The social class questionnaire is reproduced here courtesy of *Radical Teacher* where it was published in Spring, 1995.

Chapter 4

1. Quotation taken from bell hooks (1994). *Teaching to transgress* (p. 59). New York: Routledge.
2. Thanks to Holly Peters-Golden, medical anthropologist at The University of Michigan, and her daughter Becca for permission to use this story.
3. While Carol Stack did find more similarity than difference in moral reasoning among African American women and men returning to the rural South, she did find striking difference in ways of acting. She notes: "Men and women in these rural southern communities differ in their assumptions of the work of kinship, in the roles they perceive as wage-earners, and in their political actions" (Stack, 1990, p. 25). We recommend this essay to readers, and also invite you to explore other works in Faye Ginsberg and Anna Lowenhaupt Tsing's important collection, *Uncertain terms: Negotiating gender in American culture* (Boston: Beacon, 1990).
4. Nancy Naples (1998) offers a helpful distinction regarding the broad tradition of feminist standpoint epistemologies. She writes:

   > Those writing within this broad tradition of feminist standpoint epistemologies draw on three different definitions of standpoint: standpoint viewed 1) as embodied in particular knowers who possess certain racial, ethnic, class and gender identities as in certain aspects of [Patricia Hill] Collins' approach; 2) through communal or relational processes through which a standpoint is achieved, as in [Donna] Haraway's approach; and 3) as an axis point of investigation as in [Dorothy] Smith's "everyday world" perspective. (p. 224)

5. Lincoln and Guba (1985, p. 15) state that paradigms represent what we think about the world (but cannot prove). Historically and contextually embedded in fundamental belief systems about how the world works, approaches to inquiry shift with time. Paradigms therefore have the power to enable and constrain:

   > The power of a paradigm is that it shapes, in nearly unconscious and thus unquestioned ways, perceptions and practice within disciplines. It shapes what we look at, how we look at things, what we label as problems, what problems we consider worth investigating and

solving, and what methods are preferred for investigation and action. Likewise, a paradigm influences what we choose not to attend to; what we do not see. (Maguire, 1987, p.11)

6. For further discussion of the concept of "dependency" see Nancy Fraser and Linda Gordon's important article "A genealogy of *dependency*: Tracing a keyword of the U.S. welfare state," in *Signs: Journal of Women in Culture and Society,* 1994, 19(21), 309-336.
7. This quote comes from the Critical Resistance website: www.criticalresistance.org
8. Our idea of practice is informed by a range of contemporary anthropological and sociological inquiry (Bourdieu, 1977; Giddens, 1979; Ortner, 1989, 1996; Sahlins, 1981; Sewell, 1992).
9. The term praxis refers to the ongoing systematic process of action and critical reflection.

Chapter 5

1. This list of communication skills draws from the work of Shulman (1992), Brill (1998) and Miley et al. (1998).
2. Excerpt from "When the academic becomes personal and the personal is academic," text of presentation by Deborah Bey, University of Michigan, 2000.
3. Reed et al. (1997, pp. 68-75) develop each of these points. We refer the reader to their text for further discussion of the application of critical consciousness to practice.
4. This discussion of resistance is taken from the work of Paul Carter as presented in his "Parts Work" workshops in Nelson, British Columbia and Edmonton, Alberta, Canada in 1987.
5. Diane Byington's essay (1996), "Remembering Al," *Reflections: Narratives of professional helping,* 2 (Spring), 21-24 is reprinted here courtesy of the author and the journal.

Chapter 6

1. Permission to draw from David Werner, Carol Thuman, and Jane Maxwell, "Words to the village health worker," in David Werner (1977) *Where there is no doctor*, courtesy of the Hesperian Foundation, Berkeley, California.
2. Permission to present skills of mutual aid, based on excerpts from Lawrence Shulman (1999) *The skills of helping individuals, groups, and families*. (3rd Ed.) Courtesy of F.E. Peacock Publishers, Itasca, IL.
3. Original text by Jara is in Spanish. English translation of quote by J. Finn.
4. Permission to reprint excerpts from Rinku Sen, "Building community

involvement in health care," *Social Policy*, 1994 24(3), 32-43, courtesy of *Social Policy*. Copyright by Social Policy Corporation.

5. Permission to utilize adaptation of ecomap courtesy of Ann Hartman and Joan Laird. This is a very brief introduction to the ecomap. We refer readers to Ann Hartman and Joan Laird (1983) *Family-centered social work practice,* New York: Free Press. For a concise guide to a range of frequently used social work tools see also Kim Strom-Gottfried (1999) *Social work practice: cases, activities, and exercises*. Thousand Oaks, CA: Pine Forge Press.
6. Permission to print Social Network Map and Grid courtesy of *Families in Society.* We have presented a summary review of the Social Network Map here. For more detailed discussion of the Social Network Map and Grid and their use in practice see Tracy and Whitaker (1990).
7. We refer the reader to White and Tyson-Rawson's article, "Assessing the dynamics of gender in couples and families" (1995) for a full account of the theoretical underpinnings and use of the gendergram.
8. This case study is based on Maryanne Vollers and Andrea Barnett (2000) "Libby's Deadly Grace," *Mother Jones* (May/June): 53-59, 87, and various Montana news reports during June-August, 2001. For further reading on the situation in Libby see the series of special reports, entitled "Uncivil action: Asbestos mining leaves a deadly legacy in Libby, MT – and nation wide," published by the *Seattle Post-Intelligencer* at: http://seattlep-i.nwsource.com/uncivilaction. See also David Kotelchuck, "The sad tale of Libby, Montana," *UE NEWS (Bulletin of the United Electrical, Radio and Machine Workers of America)*, May, 2000 at http://www.ranknfile-ue.org/hts0500.html.

Chapter 7

1. From Janet Finn (2001). "The women of Villa Paula Jaraquemada: Building community in Chile's transition to democracy." *Community Development Journal,* 36(3), p. 183.
2. From Kelly & Sewell (1988). *With head, heart and hand: Dimensions of community building.* (p. 80). Brisbane, Qld: Boolarong Press.
3. Adapted from excerpts of Schein (1969), cited in Brill (1998, p. 198).
4. See Kaner, S. (1996). *Facilitator's guide to participatory decision-making.* Gabriola Island, BC: New Society Publishers, pp. 42-54. The author addresses skills for honoring all points of view in the participatory decision-making process. Specifically, Kaner addresses the ways in which to value the input of group members with diverse modes of communication and to engage all participants in the process.
5. The discussion of social enactment is drawn from Anthony Kelly and Sandra Sewell (1988) *With head, heart, and hand: Dimensions of community building.* Chapter Six, pp. 70-81.

6. Permission to print excerpt on dealing with controversial issues from *Healing into action: A leadership guide for creating diverse communities*, (pp. 63-64), courtesy of National Coalition Building Institute, Washington, DC.
7. Permission to print summary discussion of "Defusing Skills" from Charles E. Confer (1986), *Managing anger: Yours and mine.* Courtesy of American Foster Care Resources, Inc. King George, VA.
8. We want to acknowledge the work of MISC and their key representatives (Kate Kahan, WEEL; Judy Smith, WORD, and Derek Birney, MPA) for giving us permission to discuss their work.
9. We add this missing element of direct participation to Chapin's chart. Otherwise, the chart is taken verbatim from text.
10. Permission to reprint this report in its entirety courtesy of IRIN.
11. Permission to reprint "Lost Boy of Sudan: The Newest Vermonters" courtesy of The Burlington Free Press.

Chapter 8

1. Permission to reproduce quotation from Paulo Freire (1970) *Pedagogy of the oppressed* courtesy of Continuum Publishing, New York.
2. From J. Finn (2001) "The women of Villa Paula Jaraquemada: Building community in Chile's transition to democracy." *Community Development Journal,* 36(3), p. 192.
3. For a more thorough description of positivism we refer you to the following sources for additional information – Denzin, N. & Lincoln, Y. (1994). (Eds.). *Handbook of qualitative research* (pp. 5-6). Thousand Oaks, CA: Sage Publications; Lincoln, Y. & Guba, E. (1985). *Naturalistic inquiry* (pp. 19-28). Newbury Park, CA: Sage Publications; Neuman, W. (1997). *Social research methods: Qualitative and quantitative approaches* (pp. 63-66). Needham Heights, MA: Allyn & Bacon; Rubin, A. & Babbie, E. (2001). *Research methods for social work* (pp. 33-34). Belmont, CA: Wadsworth/Thompson Learning.
4. There are numerous threats to internal and external validity. Articulating these goes beyond the scope of this text but we refer you to the following sources for additional information (Marlow, 2001; Neuman, 1997; Rubin & Babbie, 2001; Williams, Unrau, & Grinnell, 1998).
5. For further techniques that address the reliability and validity of qualitative data, see Yvonna Lincoln and Egon Guba's comprehensive volume entitled *Naturalistic Inquiry* (1985). They expand on techniques such as peer debriefing and negative case analysis that also help to ensure the credibility of research findings (see Chapter Eleven "Establishing Trustworthiness"- pp. 289-331).
6. See Reason and Rowan (1981, p. 240) and Brown and Tandon (1978) for additional information on catalytic validity.

7. For additional information we refer you to two exceptional sources on constructing and administering questionnaires: see W. Neuman, (1997). *Social research methods*, Chapter 10 – Survey Research, Needham Heights, MA: Allyn and Bacon. and see Allen Rubin and Earl Babbie (2001). *Research methods for social work*, Chapter 8 – Constructing Measurement Instruments, Belmont, CA: Brooks/Cole.
8. This exercise has been adapted and modified from page 96 of *The human rights education handbook*, (2000), Nancy Flowers et al., publication of the Human Rights Resource Center, Minneapolis, MN: University of Minnesota and The Stanley Foundation.
9. This exercise is from *In the tiger's mouth* by Katrinia Shields. New Society Publishers, PO Box 189, Gabriola Island, BC, Canada, VOR 1XO, email: info@newsociety.com, http:// www. newsociety.com).

Chapter 9

1. From Paulo Freire (1999), *Pedagogy of hope*: *Reliving pedagogy of the oppressed.* New York Continuum, (p. 9). Permission to quote courtesy of Continuum Press.
2. From David Harvey (2000). *Spaces of hope*. Berkeley: University of California Press, (p. 281). Permission to quote courtesy of Board of Regents of the University of California.

Bibliography

Introduction Bibliography

Abramovitz, M. (1998). "Social work and social reform: An arena of struggle." *Social Work,* 43(6), 512-526.

Barker, R. (1995). *The social work dictionary.* (3rd ed.). Washington, DC: NASW Press.

Bartlett, H. (1970). *The common base of social work practice.* New York: NASW.

Biestek, F. (1957). *The casework relationship.* Chicago: Loyola University Press.

Johnson, L. (1998). *Social work practice: A generalist approach.* (6th ed.). Needham Heights, MA: Allyn & Bacon.

Hamilton, G. (1940). *The theory and practice of social casework.* New York: Columbia University Press.

Landon, P. (1999). *Generalist social work practice.* Dubuque, IA: Eddie Bowers Publishing, Inc.

Lee. P. (1930). "Cause and function," in *Proceedings of the National Conference of Social Work, 1929* (pp. 3-20). Chicago: University of Chicago Press.

Miley, K., O'Melia, M. & DuBois, B. (1998). *Generalist social work practice: An empowering perspective.* (2nd ed.) Needham Heights, MA: Allyn & Bacon.

National Association of Social Work (1977). *Encyclopedia of Social Work.* New York: NASW.

Perlman, H. (1957). *Social casework – A problem-solving process.* Chicago: University of Chicago Press.

Pincus, A. & Minahan, A. (1973). *Social work practice: Model and method.* Itasca, IL: F. E. Peacock.

Reisch, M. & Andrews, J. (2001). *The road not taken: A history of radical social work in the United States.* New York: Brunner/Routledge.

Richmond, M. (1917). *Social diagnosis.* New York: Russell Sage Foundation.

Specht, H. & Courtney, M. (1994). *Unfaithful angels: How social work has abandoned its mission.* New York: Free Press.

Todd, A. J. (1920). *The scientific spirit and social work.* New York: Macmillan.

Wenocur, S. & Reisch, M. (1989). *From charity to enterprise: The development of American social work in a market economy.* Chicago: University of Chicago Press.

Withorn, A. (1984). *Serving the people: Social services and social change.* New York: Columbia University Press.

Witkin, S. (1998). "Human rights and social work," *Social Work, 43(3), 197-201.*

General Bibliography

Abramovitz, M. (1993). "Should all social workers be educated for social change? Pro." *Journal of Social Work Education,* 29, 6-11.

________. (1996). *Under attack, fighting back: Women and welfare in the United States.* New York: Monthly Review Press.

________. (1998). "Social work and social reform: an arena of struggle." *Social Work,* 43(6), 512-526.

Adams, M., Blumenfeld, W., Castañeda, R., Hackman, H., Peters, M., & Zuñiga, X. (2000). *Readings for diversity and social justice.* New York: Routledge.

Addams, J. (1902). *Democracy and social ethics.* New York: Macmillan.

________. (1910). *Twenty years at Hull House.* New York: Crowell/Macmillan.

________. (1930). *The second twenty years at Hull House.* New York: Macmillan.

________. (1960). *A centennial reader.* New York: Macmillan.

Agger, B. (1998). *Critical social theories: An introduction.* Boulder: Westview Press.

Albee, G. (1986). "Toward a just society: Lessons on observation of primary prevention of psychopathology." *American Psychologist,* 41(8), 891-898.

Albelda, R. & Tilly, C. (1997). *Glass ceilings and bottomless pits: Women's work, women's poverty.* Boston: South End Press.

Allen, F. (1957). *Only yesterday.* New York: Harper.

Alvarez, S., Dagnino, E. & Escobar, A. (Eds.). (1998). *Cultures of politics and politics of cultures: Revisioning Latin American social movements.* Boulder: Westview Press.

American Anthropological Association Executive Board. (2001). "Statement on race."Alexandria, VA: American Anthropological Association.

Anderson, C. & Jack, D. (1991). "Learning to listen: Interview techniques and analyses." In S. Gluck & D. Patai (Eds.), *Women's words: The feminist practice of our history* (pp. 11-26). New York: Routledge.

Anderson, R. & Carter, I. (1990). *Human behavior in the social environment: A social systems approach.* (4th ed.). New York: Aldine de Gruyter.

Andrews, J. & Reisch, M. (1997). "Social work and anti-communism: A historical analysis of the McCarthy era." *Journal of Progressive Human Services,* 8(2), 29-49.

Anner, J. (1996). "Having the tools at hand: Building successful multicultural social justice organizations." In J. Anner (Ed.), *Beyond identity politics.* Boston: South End Press.

Anzaldúa, G. (2000). "Allies." In M. Adams, W. Blumfeld, R. Castañeda, H. Hackman, M. Peters, & X. Zuñiga (Eds.), *Readings for diversity and social justice* (pp. 475-477). New York: Routledge. (Reprinted from Sinister Wisdom, 52, Spring/Summer, 1994, pp. 47-52.)

Apple, M. (1982). *Education and power*. London: Routledge and Kegan Paul.

Arendt, H. (1973). *The origins of totalitarianism.* New York: Harcourt, Brace, Jovanovich.

Armstrong, L. (1995). *Of 'sluts' and 'bastards:' A feminist decodes the child welfare debate.* Monroe, ME: Common Courage Press.

Aronowitz, S. & Giroux, H. (1985). *Education under siege: The conservative, liberal and radical debate over schooling.* South Hadley, MA: Bergin & Garvey.

Ashley, F. & Gaventa, J. (1997). "Researching for democracy and democratizing research." *Change,* 29(10), 46-54.

Axinn, J. & Levin, H. (1997). *Social welfare: A history of the American response to need* (4th ed.). New York: Longman Publishers.

Baber, K. & Allen, K. (1992). *Women and families: Feminist reconstructions*. New York: Guilford.

Baca Zinn, M. (1990). "Family, feminism, and race in America." *Gender and Society,* 4, 68-82.

Bailey, R. & Brake, M. (1976). *Radical social work.* New York: Random House.

Barber, J. G. (1995). "Politically progressive casework." *Families in Society: The Journal of Contemporary Human Services,* 76(1), 30-37.

Barker, R. (1995). *The social work dictionary* (3rd ed.). Washington, D.C: NASW Press.

Bartlett, H. (1970). *The common base of social work practice.* New York: NASW.

Baum, G. (1971). *Man becoming*. New York: Herder and Herder.

Berger, P. & Luckman, T. (1966). *The social construction of knowledge: A treatise in the sociology of knowledge.* New York: Anchor Books.

Biestek, F. (1957). *The casework relationship*. Chicago: Loyola University Press.

Boal, A. (1982). *Theatre of the oppressed.* New York: Routledge (Originally published in 1979).

Bock, S. (1980). "Conscientization: Paulo Freire and class-based practice." *Catalyst,* 2, 5-25.

Bourdieu, P. (1977). *Outline of a theory of practice* (Trans. R. Nice). Cambridge: Cambridge University Press.

________. (1984). *Distinction: A social critique of the judgment of taste* (Trans. R. Nice). Cambridge: Harvard University Press. (Originally published in 1979).

Boyd, A. (1999). *The activist cookbook: Creative actions for a fair economy*. Boston, MA: United for a Fair Economy.

Brace, C.L. (1872). *The dangerous classes of New York and my twenty years' work among them*. New York: Wynkoop & Hallenbeck.

Briggs, J. (1970). *Never in anger: Portrait of an Eskimo family.* Cambridge, MA: Harvard University Press.

Brill, N. (1976). *Teamwork: Working together in the human services.* New York: J. B. Lippincott.

________. (1998). *Working with people: The helping process* (6th ed.) New York: Longman.

Brown C. & Mazza, G. (1997). *Healing into action: A leadership guide for creating diverse communities.* Washington, DC: National Coalition Building Institute.

Brown, L.D. & Tandon, R. (1978). "Interviews as catalysts." *Journal of Applied Psychology*, 63(2), 197-205.

Brun, M. (1972). "Animation and social work." *New themes in social work education: Proceedings of the XVI international congress of schools of social work* (pp. 60-71). The Hague, Netherlands, August, 1972. New York: International Association of Schools of Social Work.

Bureau of the Census (1999). "World population at a glance: 1998 and beyond." Washington, DC: U.S. Department of Commerce.

Byington, D. (1996). "The story of Al." *Reflections: Narrative of Professional Helping*, 2 (Spring), 21-24.

Canadian Association of Social Work (1994). Code of ethics. Ottowa, Canada: Canadian Association of Social Work.

Cante, D. (1973). *The fellow travelers: A post-script to the Enlightenment.* New York: Macmillan.

Carr, E. (1961). *What is history?* New York: St. Martin's Press.

Carr-Hill, R. (1994). "Radicalizing survey methodology." *Quality and Quantity,* 18, 275-292.

Carter, P. (1986/1987). "Parts work," Seminars on trance work and mind/body healing, Nelson, British Columbia, 1986: Edmonton, Alberta, 1987.

Caufield, C. (1996). *Masters of illusion: The World Bank and poverty nations.* New York: Henry Holt.

Chambers, C. (1963). *Seedtime of reform: American social service and social action – 1918-1933.* Minneapolis, MN: University of Minnesota.

Chambon, A. (1999). "Foucault's approach: Making the familiar visible." In A. Chambon, A. Irving, & L. Epstein (Eds.), *Reading Foucault for social work* (pp. 51-82). New York: Columbia University Press.

Chapin, R. (1995). "Social policy development: The strengths perspective." *Social Work*, 40(4), 506-514.

Checkoway, B. (1990). "Six strategies of community change." Arnulf Pins Memorial Lecture, Hebrew University, Jerusalem.

Cholewa K. & Smith, J. (1999). *Montana welfare reform today: Shifting alliances, dropping caseloads, and lost opportunity.* Coping with Block Grants Project, Missoula, MT: Women's Opportunity and Resource Development.

Cisneros, S. (1984). *The house on Mango Street.* New York: Vintage Books.

Coates, J. (1992). "Ideology and education for social work practice." *Journal of Progressive Human Services*, 3(2), 15-30.

Coates, J. & McKay, M. (1995). "Toward a new pedagogy for social transformation." *Journal of Progressive Human Services,* 6(1), 27-43.

Confer, C. (1987). *Managing anger: Yours and mine.* King George, Virginia: American Foster Care Resources, Inc.

Congress, E. (1994). "The use of culturagrams to assess and empower culturally diverse families." *Families in Society: The Journal of Contemporary Human Services,* 75(9), 531-539.

Council on Social Work Education (1994). *Handbook of accreditation standards and procedures.* Alexandria, VA: Author.

Cowger, C. (1994). "Assessing client strengths: Clinical assessment for client empowerment." *Social Work,* 39(2), 262-268.

Critical Resistance (2001). "Mission Statement." Critical Resistance Website: www.criticalresistance.org/mission. Oakland, CA: Authors.

Cross, T. (1986). "Drawing on cultural tradition in Indian child welfare practice." *Social Casework,* 67, 283-289.

Danaher, K. (Ed.). (1994). *Fifty years is enough: The case against the World Bank and the International Monetary Fund.* Boston: South End Press.

Day. P. (2000). *A new history of social welfare* (3rd ed.). Boston: Allyn and Bacon.

Denzin, N. & Lincoln, Y. (Eds.). (1994). *Handbook of qualitative research.* Thousand Oaks, CA: Sage Publications.

Derrida, J. (1976). *Of grammatology* (Trans. G. Spivak). Baltimore: John Hopkins. (Originally published in 1967).

Desai, A. (1987). "Development of social work education." In *Encyclopedia of social work of India.* New Delhi: Government of India, Ministry of Social Welfare.

DeSchweinitz, K. (1955). Correspondence to Fedele Fauri, 8 September, Council of Social Work Education Manuscripts, Box 7, Folder, 24, Social Welfare History Archives, University of Minnesota, Minneapolis, MN.

Dewey, J. (1910). *How we think.* Boston: D.C. Heath & Co.

________. (1933). *How we think: A restatement of the relations of reflective thinking to the educative process.* Boston: D. C. Heath & Co.

Díaz, C. (1995). *El diagnóstico para la participación.* San Jose, Costa Rica: Alforja.

________. (1997). *Planificación participativa.* San Jose, Costa Rica: Alforja.

DiLeonardo, M. (1984). *The varieties of ethnic experience: Kinship, class and gender among California Italian-Americans.* Ithaca, NY: Cornell University Press.

________. (1987). "The female world of cards and holidays: Women, families and the work of kinship." *Signs,* 12, 440-453.

Dirks, N., Eley, G. & Ortner, S. (1994). "Introduction." In N. Dirks, G. Eley, & S. Ortner (Eds.), *Culture/power/history: A reader in contemporary social theory* (pp. 3-45). Princeton: Princeton University Press.

Dobelstein, A. (1999). *Moral authority, ideology and the future of American social welfare.* Boulder: Westview Press.

Driedger, O. (1995). "Russia and the republics." In T. Watts, D. Elliott, & N. Mayadas (Eds.), *International handbook on social work education.* Westport, CT: Greenwood Publishing.

Dubois, B. & Miley, K. (1999). *Social work: An empowering profession.* Needham Heights, MA: Allyn & Bacon.

DuBois, W.E.B. (1968). *The autobiography of W. E. B. DuBois: A soliloquy on viewing my life from the last decade of its first century.* (Apthekeer, Ed.). New York: International Publishers.

________. (1985). *Against racism: Unpublished essays, papers and addresses,* 1887-1961. Amherst, MA: University of Massachussetts Press.

________. (1989). *The souls of black folk.* New York: Bantam. (Originally published in 1903).

Dujon, D. & Withorn, A. (Eds.). (1996). *For crying out loud: Women's poverty in the United States.* Boston: South End Press.

Ecumenical Coalition for Economic Justice (2001). "Structural adjustment programs." Ecumenical Coalition for Economic Justice website: www.ecej.org. Toronto: Canada: Author.

Edelman, P. (1997). "The worst thing that Bill Clinton has done." *Atlantic Monthly,* 279(3), 43-58.

Ehrenreich, J. H. (1985). *The altruistic imagination: A history of social work and social policy in the United States.* Ithaca, NY: Cornell University Press.

Epstein, L. (1999). "The culture of social work." In A. Chambon, A. Irving, & L. Epstein (Eds.), *Reading Foucault for social work* (pp. 3-26). New York: Columbia University Press.

Erikson, E. (1963). *Childhood and society.* New York: Norton. (Originally published in 1950).

Escuela de Trabajo Social (ETS) (1984). "Modelo del professional del trabajo social." Managua, Nicaragua: Universidad Centroamericana Escuela de Trabajo Social.

Essential Action (2001). "How structural adjustments worsens poverty." www.essentialaction.org.

Fadiman, A. (1997). *The spirit catches you and you fall down.* New York: Farrar, Strauss, Giroux.

Fernandes, W. (1989). "Participatory research and action in India today." *Social Action,* 39, 1-21.

Ferree, M. (1990). "Beyond separate spheres: Feminism and family research." *Journal of Marriage and the Family,* 52, 866-884.

Figueira-McDonough, J. (1993). "Policy practice: The neglected side of social work intervention." *Social Work,* 38(2), 179-188.

Figueira-McDonough, J., Netting, F. E., & Nichols-Casebolt, A. (Eds.). (1998). *The role of gender in practice knowledge: Claiming half the human experience.* New York: Garland.

Fine, M., Weis, L., Powell, L., Wong, L.M., (Eds.). (1997). *Off white: Readings on race, power, and society.* New York: Routledge.

Finn, J. (1994a). "The promise of participatory research." *Journal of Progressive Human Services.* 5, 25-42.

________.(1994b). "Contested caring: women's roles in foster family care." *Affilia,* 9, 382-400.

________. (1998a). *Tracing the veins: Of copper, culture, and community from Butte to Chuquicamata.* Berkeley: University of California Press.

________. (1998b). "Gender and families." In J. Figuiera-McDonough, F. Netting, & A. Nichols-Casebolt (Eds.), *The role of gender in practice knowledge* (pp. 205-239). New York: Garland.

________. (2001a). "Text and turbulence: Representing adolescence as pathology in the human services." *Childhood,* 8(2), 167-191.

________. (2001b)."The women of Villa Paula Jaraquemada: Building community in Chile's transition to democracy." *Community Development Journal,* 36(3), 183-197.

Finn, J. & Checkoway, B. (1998). "Young people as competent community builders: A challenge to social work." *Social Work,* 43(4), 335-345.

Finn, J. & Underwood, L. (2000). "The state the clock and the struggle: An inquiry into the discipline for welfare reform in Montana." *Social Text,* 18(1), 109-134.

Finn, J., Castellanos, R., McOmber, T., & Kahan, K. (2000). "Working for equality and economic liberation: Advocacy and education for welfare reform." *Affilia: Journal of Women and Social Work,* 15(2), 294-310.

Finn, J., Rodriguez, G. Nuñez, N. (2000). *La Victoria: Rescatando la Historia.* Community History Project Document. La Victoria, Santiago, Chile.

Firestone, W. (1986). "Meaning in method: The rhetoric of quantitative and qualitative research." *Educational Researcher,* 16(7), 16-21.

Fisher, J. (1990). "The rank and file movement – 1930-1936." *Journal of Progressive Human Services,* 1(1), 95-99. (Originally published in 1936).

Fisher, R. (1995). "Political social work." *Journal of Social Work Education,* 31(2), 194-203.

________. (1999). "Speaking for the contribution of history: Context and the origins of the Social Welfare History Group." *Social Service Review,* 73(2), 191-217.

Flowers, N., Bernbaum, M., Rudelius-Palmer, K., & Tolman, J. (2000). *The human rights education handbook: Effective practices for learning, action, and change.* Minneapolis, MN: Human Rights Resource Center, University of Minnesota.

Forgacs, D. (Ed.). (1988). *An Antonio Gramsci reader: Selected writings, 1919-1935.* New York: Schocken Books.

Foucault, M. (1977). *Discipline and punish.* London: Allen Lane.

________. (1978). *The history of sexuality: An introduction, Vol. 1.* (Trans. R. Hurley). New York: Random House. (Originally published in English in 1976).

________. (1979). "Truth and power." In M. Morris & P. Patton (Eds.), *Michel Foucault: Power, truth, and strategy* (pp. 29-48). Sydney: Feral Publications.

________. (1980). *Power/knowledge: Selected interviews and others writings, 1972-77.* (Ed. and Trans. C. Gordon). New York: Pantheon.

Franklin, C. (2000). "Predicting the future of school social work practice in the new millennium." *Journal of Social Work Education,* 22(1), 3-5.

Fraser, N. & Gordon, L. (1994). "A genealogy of dependency: Tracing a keyword of the U.S. welfare state." *Signs,* 19(2), 309-336.

Freire, P. (1974). *Pedagogy of the oppressed.* New York: Seabury/Continuum. (Originally published in English in 1970).

________. (1990). "A critical understanding of social work." *Journal of Progressive Human Services*, 1(1), 3-9.

________. (1999). *Pedagogy of hope: Reliving pedagogy of the oppressed.* New York: Continuum.

Frick, W. (1995). "Sweden." In T. Watts, D. Elliot, & N. Mayadas (Eds.), *International handbook on social work education* (p. 149-160). Westport, CT: Greenwood Publishing Co.

Galper, J. (1975). *The politics of social services.* Englewood Cliffs, NJ: Prentice-Hall.

Garcia, A. M. (1982) *La operación* (Film). New York: Cinema Guild.

Garreton, M. (1996). "Human rights in democratization processes." In E. Jelin & E. Hershberg (Eds.), *Constructing democracy: Human rights, citizenship and society in Latin America* (pp. 39-56). Boulder: Westview Press.

Garvin, C. (1985). "Work with disadvantaged and oppressed groups." In M. Sundel, P. Glasser, R. Sarri, & R. Vinter (Eds.), *Individual change through small groups* (2nd ed.), (pp. 461-472). New York: Free Press.

Garvin, C. & Reed, B. (1995). "Sources and visions for feminist group work: Reflective processes, social justice, diversity, and connection." In N. Van Den Bergh (Ed.), *Feminist social work practice in the 21st century.* Washington, DC: NASW.

Garvin, C. & Seabury, B. (1997). *Interpersonal practice in social work: Promoting competence and social justice.* (2nd ed.), Boston: Allyn and Bacon.

Gates, L. & West, C. (1996). *The future of the race.* New York: Knopf.

Gaventa, J. (1988). "Participatory research in North America." *Convergence*, 21(1), 19-29.

George, J. (1997). "Global graying: What role for social work?" In M. Hokenstad & J. Midgley (Eds.), *Issues in international social work: Global challenges for a new century.* Washington, D.C: NASW Press.

________. (1999). "Conceptual muddle, practical dilemma: Human rights, social development, and social work education." *International Social Work,* 42(1), 15-26.

Gergen, K. (1999). *An invitation to social construction.* London: Sage Publications.

Germain, C. (1979). "Ecology and social work." In C. B. Germain (Ed.), *Social work practice: People and environments* (pp. 1-22). New York: Columbia University Press.

________. (1983). "Using social and physical environments." In A. Rosenblatt & D. Waldfogel (Eds.), *Handbook of clinical social work* (pp. 110-133). San Francisco: Jossey Bass.

________. (1994a) "Human behavior in the social environment." In F. Reamer (Ed.),

The foundations of social work knowledge (pp. 88-121). New York: Columbia University Press.

________. (1994b). "Emerging conceptions of family development over the life course." *Families in Society*, 75(5), 259-268.

Germain, C. & Gitterman, A. (1980). *The life model of social work practice.* New York: Columbia University Press.

________. (1995). "Ecological perspective." In R. L. Edwards (Ed.), *Encyclopedia of social work, Vol. I* (19th ed.), (pp. 816-824). Washington, DC: NASW Press.

Giddens, A. (1979). *Central problems in social theory: Action, structure and contradiction in social analysis.* Berkeley: University of California Press.

________. (1991). *The consequences of modernity.* Cambridge: Polity Press.

Gil, D. (1994). "Confronting injustice and oppression." In F. Reamer (Ed.), *The foundations of social work knowledge.* New York: Columbia University Press.

________. (1998). *Confronting injustice and oppression: Concepts and strategies for social workers.* New York: Columbia University Press.

Gilligan, C. (1982). *In a different voice: Psychological theory and women's development.* Cambridge: Harvard University Press.

Gilman, S. (1985). *Difference and pathology: Stereotypes of sexuality, race, and madness.* Ithaca, NY: Cornell University Press.

Ginsberg, F. & Tsing, A. (Eds.). (1990). *Uncertain terms: Negotiating gender in American culture.* Boston: Beacon.

Goodman, E. (1998). "The hidden suffering of women in Afghanistan." *The Boston Globe*, 6 December.

Gordon, L. (1988). *Heroes of their own lives: The politics and history of family violence.* New York: Viking Penguin, Inc.

________. (Ed.). (1990). *Women, the state, and welfare.* Madison: University of Wisconsin Press.

Gould, S. (1981). *The mismeasure of man.* New York: W.W. Norton and Co.

Gramsci, A. (1987). *The modern prince and other stories.* New York: International Publishers. (Originally published in 1957).

Green, D. (1995). *Silent revolution: The rise of market economics in Latin America.* London: Cassell/Latin American Bureau.

Greenwood, E. (1957). "Attributes of a profession." *Social Work,* 2(3), 45-55.

Gutiérrez, L. (1990). "Working with women of color: An empowerment perspective." *Social Work,* 35(2), 149-153.

Gutiérrez, L. & Lewis, E. (1999). *Empowering women of color.* Columbia University Press.

Guzman Bouvard, M. (1994). *Revolutionizing motherhood: The mothers of the Plaza de Mayo.* Wilmington, DE: Scholarly Resources, Inc.

Hall, B. (1975). "Participatory research: An approach for change." *Convergence,* 8(2), 24-32.

________. (1981). "Participatory research, popular knowledge, and power. A personal reflection." *Convergence*, 14(3), 6-19.

________. (1993). "Introduction." In P. Park, M. Brydon-Miller, B. Hall, & T. Jackson (Eds.), *Voices of change: Participatory research in the United States and Canada* (pp. xiii-xxii). Westport, CN: Bergin & Garvey.

Hamilton, G. (1940). *The theory and practice of social casework.* New York: Columbia University Press.

Hartman, A. (1978). "Diagrammatic assessment of family relationships." *Social Casework,* 59(8), 465-476.

Hartman, A. & Laird, J. (1983). *Family-centered social work practice.* New York: Free Press.

Hartmann, H. (1981). "The family as locus of gender, class and political struggle: The example of housework." *Signs,* 6, 366-394.

Harvey, D. (1989). *The condition of postmodernity: An enquiry into the origins of cultural change.* Oxford, UK: Basil Blackwell, Ltd.

________. (2000). *Spaces of hope.* Berkeley: University of California Press.

Hatton, N. & Smith, D. (1995). "Reflection in teacher education: Towards definition and implementation." *Teaching and Teacher Education*, 11(1), 33-39.

Henderson, P. & Thomas, D. (1980). "Getting to know the community." In *Skills in neighbourhood work* (pp. 49-83). London: George Allen and Unwin.

Herman, J. (1992). *Trauma and recovery.* New York: Basic Books.

Hill Collins, P. (1990) *Black feminist thought: Knowledge, consciousness, and the politics of empowerment.* New York: Unwin Hyman.

________. (1991). "Learning from the outsider within: The sociological significance of black feminist thought." In M. Fonow & J. Cook (Eds.), *Beyond methodology: Feminist scholarship as lived research* (pp. 35-59). Bloomington, IN: Indiana University Press.

Hill, J. (1998). "Toward louder voices: ActionAid Nepal's experience of working with children." In V. Johnson, E. Ivan-Smith, G. Gordon, P. Pridmore, & P. Scott (Eds.), *Stepping forward: Children and young people's participation in the development process* (pp. 92-95). London: Intermediate Technology Publications.

Hochman, S. (1997). "School-community collaboratives: The missing links." In M. Reisch & E. Gambrill (Eds.), *Social work in the 21st century* (pp. 260-270).Thousand Oaks, CA: Pine Forge Press.

Hoff-Wilson, J. (n.d.). *The Jeannette Rankin Commemorative Booklet.* Bloomington, IN: Organization of American Historians. (www.oag.org).

Hokenstad, M. & Midgley, J. (Eds.). (1997). *Issues in international social work: Global challenges for a new century.* Washington, D.C.: NASW Press.

Homan, M. (1999). *Promoting community change: Making it happen in the real world* (2nd ed.). Pacific Grove, CA: Brooks/Cole.

hooks, b. (1984). *Feminist theory from margin to center.* Boston: South End Press.

________. (1994). Teaching to transgress. New York: Routledge.

________. (1995). *Killing rage: Ending racism.* New York: Henry Holt.

Hope, A. & Timmel, S. (1999). *Training for transformation: A handbook for community workers – Books 1-4.* London, UK: Intermediate Technology Publications. (Originally published in 1984).

Hopmeyer, E., Kimberly, M. & Hawkins, F. (1995). "Canada." In T. Watts, D. Elliott, & N. Mayadas (Eds.), *Instructional handbook of social work education* (pp. 23-29). Westport, CT: Greenwood Publishing Co.

Horejsi, C. (1999). "Social and economic justice: Concepts and principles for social work practice." Unpublished document. University of Montana, Department of Social Work.

Horton, B. (1993). "The Appalachian land ownership study: Research and citizen action in Appalachia." In P. Park, M. Brydon-Miller, B. Hall, & T. Jackson (Eds.), *Voices of change: Participatory research in the United States and Canada* (pp. 85-102). Westport, CT: Bergin & Garvey.

Horton, M. (1998). *The long haul: An autobiography* (with Judith Kohl and Herbert Kohl). New York: Teachers College Press.

Howe, D. (1994). "Modernity, postmodernity, and social work." *British Journal of Social Work,* 24, 513-532.

Husock, H. (1993). "Bringing back the settlement house." *Public Welfare*, 51(4), 16-25.

Hutchinson, E. & Charlesworth, L. (1998). "Human behavior in the social environment: The role of gender in the expansion of practice knowledge." In J. Figuiera-McDonough, F. Netting & A. Nichols-Casebolt (Eds.), *The role of gender in practice knowledge: Claiming half the human experience* (pp. 41-92). New York: Garland.

International Federation of Social Workers (1994). *The ethics of social work: Principles and standards.* Berne, Switzerland: IFSW. (See website: www.ifsw.org for text).

________. (1997). *Policy paper: Human rights*. Oslo: IFSW.

________. (2001). "IFSW General Information." IFSW website, www.ifsw.org.

International Labour Organization (ILO) (1998). *Annual Report.* Geneva, Switzerland: 1994.

Jackson, T. (1993). "A way of working: Participatory research and the aboriginal movement in Canada." In P. Park, M. Brydon-Miller, B. Hall, & T. Jackson (Eds.), *Voices of change: Participatory research in the United States and Canada* (pp. 47-64). Westport, CN: Bergin & Garvey.

Jacobson, M. (1997). *Child sexual abuse and the multidisciplinary team approach in Montana: A mixed methods, participatory study*. Unpublished doctoral dissertation, University of Utah, Salt Lake City.

________. (2001). "Child sexual abuse and the multidisciplinary team approach: Contradictions in practice." *Childhood*, 8(2), 231-250.

Jaggar, A. (1983). *Feminist politics and human nature.* Totowa, NJ: Rowman & Littlefield Publishers, Inc.

Jansson, B. (1999). *Becoming an effective policy advocate: From policy practice to social justice.* Pacific Grove, CA: Brooks/Cole Publishing Co.

Jara, O. (1998). *Para sistematizar experiencias.* San Jose, Costa Rica: Alforja.

Jelin, E. (1996). "Citizenship revisited: Solidarity, responsibility, and rights." In E. Jelin & E. Hershberg (Eds.), *Constructing democracy: Human rights, citizenship and society in Latin America* (pp. 101-120). Boulder: Westview Press.

Jenkins, K. (1995). *On 'What is history?' From Carr and Elton to Rorty and White.* London: Routledge.

Jicks, T. (1979). "Mixing qualitative and quantitative methods: Triangulation in action." *Administrative Science Quarterly*, 24, 602-611.

Jimenez, M. (1999). "A feminist analysis of welfare reform: The Personal Responsibility Act of 1996." *Affilia: Journal of Women and Social Work,* 14(3), 278-293.

Jimenez, M. & Aylwin, N. (1992). "Social work in Chile: Support for the struggle for justice in Latin America." In M. C. Hokenstad, S. K. Khinduka, & J. Midgley (Eds.), *Profiles in International Social Work.* Washington, DC: NASW.

Johnson, L. (1998). *Social work practice: A generalist approach* (6th ed.) Needham Heights, MA: Allyn & Bacon.

Jones, D. (1991). "Professional and clinical challenges to protection of children." *Child Abuse and Neglect,* 15, 57-66.

Jones, J. (1984). *Labor of love, labor of sorrow: Black women, work and family from slavery to the present.* New York: Basic Books.

Jones, M. & Kerr, C. (1996). *The autobiography of Mother Jones.* Chicago: Charles H. Kerr Publishing Co.

Kaner, S. (1996). *Facilitator's guide to participatory decision-making.* Gabriola Island, BC: New Society.

Karger, H. (1987). "Minneapolis settlement houses in the 'not so roaring 20s:' Americanization, morality, and the revolt against popular culture." *Journal of Sociology and Social Welfare*, 14(2), 89-110.

Karger, H. & Stoesz, D. (1998). *American social welfare policy: A pluralist approach.* Whie Plains, NY: Longman.

Karston-Larson, J. (1977). "And then there were none: IHA sterilization practice." *Christian Century,* 94 (26 January), 61-63.

Kates, E. (1996). "Colleges can help women in poverty." In D. Dujon & A. Withorn (Eds.), *For crying out loud: Women's poverty in the United States* (pp. 341-348). Boston: South End Press.

Keefe, T. (1980). "Empathy and critical consciousness." *Social Casework,* 61, 387-393.

Keigher, S. & Lowry, K. (1998). "The sickening implications of globalization." *Health and Social Work*, 23(2), 153-160.

Kelly, A. & Sewell, S. (1988). *With head, heart, and hand: Dimensions of community building* (4th ed.). Brisbane, Qld: Boolarong Press.

Kirst-Ashman, K. & Hull, G. (2002). *Understanding generalist practice* (3rd ed.).

Pacific Grove, CA: Brooks/Cole.
Kleinman, A. (1980). *Patients and healers in the context of culture: An exploration of the borderland between anthropology, medicine, and psychiatry.* Berkeley: University of California Press.
Korten, D. (1995). *When corporations rule the world.* West Hartford, CN: Kumarian Press.
Kotlowitz, A. (1991). *There are no children here.* New York: Doubleday.
Kozol, J. (1991). *Savage inequalities: Children in America's schools.* New York: Crown.
Kreuger, L. (1997). "The end of social work." *Journal of Social Work Education,* 33(1), 19-27.
Krueger, R. (1994). *Focus groups: A practical guide for applied research.* Thousand Oaks, CA: Sage Publications.
Krueger, R. & King, J. (1998). *Involving community members in focus groups.* Thousand Oaks, CA: Sage Publications.
Kubler-Ross, E. (1970). *On death and dying.* New York: MacMillan.
Laird, J. (Ed.). (1993). *Revisioning social work education: A social constructivist approach.* New York: Haworth.
Landon, P. (1999). *Generalist social work practice.* Dubuque, IA: Eddie Bowers Publishing.
Lappe, F.M. & DuBois, P.M. (1994). *The quickening of America: Rebuilding our nation, remaking our lives.* San Francisco, CA: Jossey-Bass, Inc. Publishers.
Lather, P. (1986). "Research as praxis." *Harvard Educational Review*, 56(3), 257-277.
________. (1991). *Getting smart: Feminist research and pedagogy with/in the postmodern.* New York: Routledge.
Leblanc, L. (1999). *Pretty in punk: Girls' resistance in a boys' subculture.* New Brunswick, NJ: Rutgers University Press.
Ledwith, M. and Asgill, P. (2000). "Critical alliance: Black and white women working together for social justice." *Community Development Journal*, 35(3), 290-299.
Lee, J. (1992). "Jane Addams in Boston: Intersecting time and space." *Social Work with Groups*, 15(2/3), 7-21.
Lemert, C. (1993/1999). *Social theory: Multicultural and classical readings.* Boulder: Westview Press.
Lengermann, P. & Niebrugge-Brantly, J. (1998). *The women founders: Sociology and social theory, 1830-1930.* Boston: McGraw-Hill.
Leonard, P. (1997). *Postmodern welfare: Reconstructing an emancipatory project.* London: Sage.
Levi-Strauss, C. (1966). *The savage mind* (2nd ed.). Chicago: University of Chicago Press.
Levy, C.S. (1973). "The value base of social work." *Journal of Education for Social Work,* 9(1), 34-42.
________. (1976). *Social work ethics.* New York: Human Sciences Press.

Lincoln, Y. & Guba, E. (1985). *Naturalistic inquiry*. Newbury Park, CA: Sage Publications.

Lindsey, D. & Kirk, S. (1992). "The role of social work journals in the development of a knowledge base for the profession." *Social Service Review*, 66(2), 295-310.

Link, R. (1999). "Infusing global perspectives into social work values and ethics." In C. Ramanathan & R. Link (Eds.), *All our futures: Social work practice in a global era* (pp. 69-93). Belmont, CA: Wadsworth.

Link, R. Ramanathan, C., & Asamoah, Y. (1999). "Understanding the human condition and human behavior in a global era." In C. Ramanathan & R. Link (Eds.), *All our futures: Social work practice in a global era*. Belmont: CA: Wadsworth Publishing.

Longres, J. & McLeod, E. (1980). "Consciousness raising and social work practice." *Social Casework,* 61, 267-277.

Lowe, L. & Lloyd, D. (1997). *The politics of culture in the shadow of capital.* Durham, NC: Duke University Press.

Lum, D. (1992). *Social work with people of color: A process stage approach* (2nd ed.). Pacific Grove, CA: Brooks Cole.

Lyons, K. (1999). *International social work: Themes and perspectives.* Brookfield, VT: Ashgate Publishing.

Maguire, P. (1987). *Doing participatory research: A feminist approach*. Amherst, MA: The Center for International Education, University of Massachusetts.

Marable, M. (1997). *Speaking truth to power: Essays on race, resistance and radicalism.* Boulder: Westview Press.

________. (1999). *How capitalism underdeveloped Black America.* Boston: South End Press.

Margolin, L. (1998). *Under the cover of kindness: The invention of social work.* Richmond: University of Virginia Press.

Marion, M. (1996). "Living in an era of multiple loss and trauma: Understanding global loss in the gay community." In C. Alexander (Ed.), *Gay and lesbian mental health: A sourcebook for practitioners.* Binghamton, NY: Harrington Park Press.

Marlow, C. (2001). *Research methods for generalist social work* (3rd ed.). Belmont, CA: Brooks/Cole

Mathis, T. & Richan, D. (1986). "Empowerment: Practice in search of a theory." Paper presented at the Annual Program Meeting of the Council on Social Work Education, Miami, FL.

Matsubara, N. (1992). "Social work in Japan: Responding to demographic dilemmas." In M. C. Hokenstad, S. K. Khinduka, & J. Midgley (Eds.), *Profiles in international social work* (pp. 85-90). Washington, DC: NASW Press.

Mayadas, N. & Elliott, D. (1992). "Integration and xenophobia: An inherent conflict in international migration." *Journal of Multicultural Social Work*, 2(1), 47-62.

Mayer, S. (1996). "Building community capacity with evaluation activities that empower." In D.M. Fetterman, S. J. Faftarian, & A. Wandersman (Eds.*),*

Empowerment evaluation: Knowledge and tools for self-assessment and accountability (pp. 332-375). Thousand Oaks, CA: Sage Publications.

McIntosh, P. (1988). "White privilege and male privilege: A personal account of coming to see correspondence through work in women's studies." In M. Anderson & P. Hill Collins (Eds.), *Race, class, and gender: An anthology* (2nd ed.), (pp. 7-82). Belmont, CA: Wadsworth.

McKnight, J. & Kretzmann, J. (1990). "Mapping community capacity." Report of the Neighborhood Innovations Network. Evanston, Ill.: Northwestern University Institute for Policy Research.

Merriam-Webster Collegiate Dictionary (1971). (18th ed.). Springfield, MA: Merriam-Webster.

Mezirow, J. (1998). "On critical reflection." *Adult Education Quarterly*, 48(3), 185-198.

Midgley, J. (1997). "Social work in international context: Challenges and opportunities for the 21st century." In M. Reisch & E. Gambrill (Eds.), *Social work in the 21st century* (pp. 59-67). Thousand Oaks, CA.: Pine Forge Press.

Miley, K., O'Melia, M. & DuBois, B. (1998). *Generalist social work practice: An empowering perspective* (2nd ed.). Boston: Allyn and Bacon.

Miller, D. (1976). *Social justice*. Oxford: Clarendon Press.

Miller, P. (1998). *Hunger, welfare reform, and non-profits: Food banks and churches.* Missoula: University of Montana Department of Sociology.

Mohanty, C. (1991). "Under western eyes: Feminist scholarship and colonial discourses." In C. Mohanty, A. Russo, & L. Torres (Eds.), *Third world women and the politics of feminism* (pp. 1-47). Bloomington, IN: University of Indiana Press.

Mohanty, C., Russo, A, & Torres, L. (Eds.). (1991). *Third world women and the politics of feminism.* Bloomington, IN: University of Indiana Press.

Moore, M. (1996). *Downsize this.* New York: Crown Publishers.

Moraga, C. & Anzaldúa, G. (Eds.). (1981). *This bridge called my back. Writings by radical women of color.* New York: Kitchen Table/Women of Color Press.

Morgan, D. L. (1988). *Focus groups as qualitative research.* Newbury Park, CA: Sage Publications.

Morales, & Sheafor, B. (1998). *Social work: A profession of many faces* (8th ed.). Needham Heights, MA: Allyn & Bacon.

Morgan, D. L. (1988). *Focus groups as qualitative research*. Newbury Park, CA: Sage Publications.

Mullaly, R. (1998). *Structural social work: Ideology, theory and practice* (2nded.). Oxford: Oxford University Press.

Murphy, B. & Dillon, C. (1998). *Interviewing in action: Process and practice.* Pacific Grove, CA: Brooks/Cole.

Nagenast, C. & Turner, T. (1997). "Introduction: Universal human rights versus cultural relativity." *Journal of Anthropological Research,* 53(3), 269-272.

Nakanishi, M. & Ritter, B. (1992). "The inclusionary cultural model." *Journal of Social Work Education.* 28(1), 27-35.

Naples, N. (1998). *Grassroots warriors: Activist mothering, community work, and the war on poverty.* New York: Routledge.

National Association of Black Social Workers. (1971). *Code of ethics of the National Association of Black Social Workers.* Detroit, MI: Author.

National Association of Social Workers. (1977). *Encyclopedia of social work.* New York: Author.

_________. (1979, rev. 1990, 1993). *Code of ethics of the National Association of Social Workers.* Washington, DC: Author.

________. (1996). *Code of Ethics of the National Association of Social Workers.* Washington, DC: Author.

Nelson, B. (1984). *Making an issue of child abuse.* Chicago: University of Chicago Press.

Nelson, C. Treichler, P., & Grossberg, L. (1992). "Cultural studies." In L. Grossberg, C. Nelson, & P. Treichler (Eds.), *Cultural studies* (pp. 1-16). New York: Routledge.

Neuman, W. (1997). *Social research methods: Qualitative and quantitative approaches.* Needham Heights, MA: Allyn and Bacon.

Nicholson, L. (1986). *Gender and history: The limits of social theory in the age of the family.* New York: Columbia University Press.

O'Brien, M. (1995*). Jeannette Rankin, 1880-1973: Bright star in the big sky.* Helena, Montana: Falcon Press.

Ong, A. (1987). *Spirits of resistance and capitalist discipline: Factory women in Malaysia.* Albany: SUNY Press.

Ortner, S. (1984). "Theory in anthropology since the sixties." *Comparative Studies in Society and History,* 26(19), 126-166.

________. (1989) *High Religion.* Princeton, NJ: Princeton University Press.

________. (1996). *Making gender: The politics and erotics of culture.* Boston: Beacon Press.

Ortner, S. & Whitehead, H. (Eds.). (1981). *Sexual meanings.* Cambridge, MA: Cambridge University Press.

Ozawa, M. (1997). "Demographic changes and their implications." In M. Reisch & E. Gambrill (Eds.), *Social work in the 21st century* (pp. 8-27). Thousand Oaks, CA: Pine Forge Press.

Page, C. (2001). "The Lost Boys of Sudan: The newest Vermonters." *Burlington Free Press* (Burlington, Vermont), May 13.

Park, P. (1993). "What is participatory research: A theoretical and methodological perspective." In P. Park, M. Brydon-Miller, B. Hall, & T. Jackson (Eds.), *Voices of change: Participatory research in the United States and Canada* (pp. 1-19). Westport, CT: Bergin & Garvey.

________. (1997)."Participatory research, democracy and community." *Practicing Anthropology*, 19(3). 8-13.

Parton, N. (Ed.). (1996). *Social theory, social change, and social work.* London: Routledge.

Patton, M. (1975). *Alternative evaluation research paradigm.* Grand Forks, ND: University of North Dakota.

Payne, M. (1997). *Modern social work theory.* Chicago: Lyceum Books.

Pease, B. & Fook, J. (Eds.). (1999). *Transforming social work practice: Postmodern critical perspectives.* New York: Routledge.

Peebles-Wilkins, W. & Francis, E. (1990). "Two outstanding black women in social welfare history: Mary Church Terrell and Ida B. Wells-Barnett." *Affilia: Journal of Women and Social Work,* 5(4), 87-100.

Perlman, H. (1957). *Social casework – A problem-solving process.* Chicago: University of Chicago Press.

Pernell, R. (1985). "Empowerment and social group work." In M. Parenes (Ed.), *Innovations in social group work: Feedback from practice to theory* (pp. 107-117). New York: Hawthorn.

Pfohl, S. (1977). "The discovery of child abuse." *Social Problems*, 24, 310-323.

Pierre, R. (1997). "Trading textbooks for jobs: Welfare changes force many to leave college." *Washington Post.* December 29.

Pincus, A. & Minahan, A. (1973). *Social work practice: Model and method.* Itasca, IL: F. E. Peacock Publishers.

________. (1977). "A conceptual framework for social work practice." *Social Work,* 22(5). 347-352.

Pinderhughes, E. (1980). "Empowerment for our clients and for ourselves." *Social Casework,* 64(6): 331-338.

Piven, F. F. & Cloward, R. (1997). *The breaking of the American social compact.* New York: Free Press.

Poertner, J. (1994). "Popular education in Latin America: A technology for the North?" *International Social Work*, 37(3), 265-275.

Ramanathan, C. & Link, R. (Eds.). (1999). *All our futures: Principles and resources for social work practice in a global era.* Belmont: CA: Wadsworth.

Rappaport, J., Davidson, W., Wilson, M., & Mitchell, A. (1975). "Alternatives to blaming the victim or the environment: Our places to stand have not moved the earth." *American Psychologist*, 30, 525-528.

Rawls, J. (1995). *A theory of justice.* (1st & 2nd eds.). Cambridge, MA: Harvard University Press. (Originally published in 1971).

Reamer, F. (1994). "Social work values and ethics." In F. Reamer (Ed.). *The foundations of social work knowledge* (pp. 195-230). New York: Columbia University Press.

________. (1995). *Social work values and ethics.* New York: Columbia University.

Reason, P. & Rowan, J. (Eds). (1981). *Human inquiry: A sourcebook of new paradigm research.* New York: John Wiley and Sons.

Reed, B. G., Newman, P., Suarez, Z., & Lewis, E. (1997). "Interpersonal practice beyond diversity and toward social justice: The importance of critical consciousness." In C. Garvin and B. Seabury (Eds.), *Interpersonal practice in social work: Promoting competence and social justice* (2nd ed.), (pp. 44-78).

Boston: Allyn and Bacon.
Reese, W. (1980). *Dictionary of philosophy and religion.* Atlantic Highlands, NJ: Humanities Press.
Reinhartz, S. (1992). *Feminist methods in social research.* New York: Oxford University Press.
Reisch, M. (1988). "The uses of history in teaching social work." *Journal of Teaching in Social Work,* 2(1), 3-16.
________. (1997). "The political context of social work." In M. Reisch & E. Gambrill (Eds.), *Social work in the 21st century* (pp. 80-92).Thousand Oaks, CA: Pine Forge Press.
________. (1998a). "Economic globalization and the future of the welfare state." Welfare Reform and Social Justice Visiting Scholars Program. Ann Arbor: The University of Michigan School of Social Work.
________. (1998b). "The sociopolitical context and social work method, 1890-1950." *Social Service Review,* 72(2), 163-181.
Reisch, M. & Andrews, J. (2001). *The road not taken: A history of radical social work in the United States.* New York: Brunner/Routledge.
Reisch, M. & Wenocur, S. (1986). "The future of community organization in social work: Social activism and the politics of profession building." *Social Service Review,* 60(1), 70-91.
Reisch, M., Wenocur, S., and Sherman, W. (1981). "Empowerment, conscientization, and animation as core social work skills." *Social Development Issues,* 5(2/3), 108-120.
Resnick, R. (1976). "Conscientization: An indigenous approach to international social work." *International Social Work,* 19, 21-29.
Reynolds, B. C. (1934). "Between client and community." *Smith College Studies in Social Work,* 5(1).
________. (1942). *Learning and teaching in the practice of social work.* New York: Farrar & Rinehart, Inc.
________. (1963). *An uncharted journey.* Washington, DC: NASW Press.
________. (1987). *Social work and social living.* Silver Spring, MD: NASW Press. (Originally published in 1951).
________. (1992). "Rethinking social case work." *Journal of Progressive Human Services,* 3(1), 73-84. (Originally published in 1932).
Richmond, M. (1917). *Social diagnosis.* New York: Russell Sage Foundation.
________. (1922). *What is social case work? An introductory description.* New York: Russell Sage Foundation.
Riis, J. (1890). *How the other half lives.* New York: Charles Scribner and Sons.
Robbins, S. P., Chatterjee, P. & Canda, E. R. (1998). *Contemporary human behavior theory: A critical perspective for social work.* Needham Heights, MA: Allyn & Bacon.
________. (1999). "Ideology, scientific theory, and social work practice." *Families in Society,* 80(4), 374-384.

Roby, P. (1998). "Creating a just world: Leadership for the twenty-first century." *Social Problems*, 45(1), 1-20.

Rosaldo, M. & Lamphere, L. (Eds). (1974). *Women, culture, and society.* Stanford, CA: Stanford University Press.

Rosaldo, R. (1989). *Culture and truth: The remaking of social analysis*. Boston: Beacon Press.

Rose, N. (1997). "The future economic landscape: Implications for social work practice and education." In M. Reisch & E. Gambrill (Eds.), *Social work in the 21st century* (pp. 28-38). Thousand Oaks, CA: Pine Forge Press.

Rossiter, A. (1996). "A perspective on critical social work." *Journal of Progressive Human Services*, 7(2), 23-441.

Rouse, R. (1995). "Thinking through transnationalism: Notes on the cultural politics of class relations in the contemporary United States." *Public Culture*, 7, 353-402.

Rubin, A. & Babbie, E. (2001). *Research methods for social work* (4th ed.). Belmont, CA: Wadsworth/Thompson Learning.

Sahlins, M. (1981). *Historical metaphors and mythical realities: Structure in the early history of the Sandwich Island Kingdom.* Ann Arbor: University of Michigan Press.

Saleebey, D. (1990). "Philosophical disputes in social work: Social justice denied." *Journal of Sociology and Social Welfare*, 17(2), 29-40.

________. (1992). *The strengths perspective in social work practice.* New York: Longman.

________. (1993). "Theory and the generation and subversion of knowledge." *Journal of Sociology and Social Welfare*, 20(1), 5-25.

________. (1994). "Culture, theory, and narrative: The intersection of meanings in practice." *Social Work*, 39(4), 351-359.

________. (1997). *The strengths perspective in social work practice*, (2nd ed.). New York: Longman Press. (Originally published in 1992).

Sarri, R. (1988). "The impact of federal policy change on the well-being of poor women and children." In P. Voydanoff & L. Majka (Eds.), *Families and economic distress* (pp. 209-232). Newbury Park, CA: Sage Publication.

________. (1997). "International social work at the millennium." In M. Reisch & E. Gambrill (Eds.), *Social work in the 21st century* (pp. 387-395). Thousand Oaks, CA.: Pine Forge Press.

Schechter, S. Szymanski, S. & Cahill, M. (1985). *Violence against women: A curriculum for empowerment*. (Facilitator's Manual). New York: Women's Education Institute.

Schein, E. (1969). *Process consultation*. Reading, MA: Addison Wesley.

Schmidt, P. (1998). "State discourages welfare recipients from pursuing a higher education." *The Chronicle of Higher Education*. January 23.

Schorr, L. (1997). *Common purpose: Strengthening families and neighborhoods to rebuild America.* New York: Anchor Books.

Schreiber, M. (1995). "Labeling a social worker a national security risk: A memoir." *Social Work*, 40 (5), 656-660.

Schriver, J. (1998). *Human behavior in the social environment* (2nd ed.). Needham Heights, MA: Allyn & Bacon.

Schwartz, W. (1971). "Social group work: The interactional approach." *Encyclopedia of Social Work*, V. II (p. 1255). New York: NASW.

________. (1986). "The group work tradition and social work practice." *Social Work with Groups*, 8(4), 7-27.

________. (1994). "The social worker in the group." In T. Berman-Rossi (Ed.), *Social work: The collected writings of William Schwartz* (pp. 263-264). Ithasca, IL: F. E. Peacock. (Originally published in 1961).

Scott, J. (1985). *Weapons of the weak: Everyday forms of resistance.* New Haven: Yale University Press.

Segura, D. & Pearce, J. (1993). "Chicano/a family structure and gender personality: Chodorow, familism, and psychoanalytic sociology revisited." *Signs*, 19, 62-91.

Seldes, G. (Ed.). (1985). *The great thoughts.* New York: Balantine Books.

Sen, R. (1994). "Building community involvement in health care." *Social Policy*, 24(3), 32-43.

Sewell, W. (1992). "A theory of structure: Duality, agency, and transformation." *American Journal of Sociology*, 98(1), 1-29.

Shaull, R. (1974). "Foreword." In P. Freire, *Pedagogy of the oppressed.* New York: Seabury Press/Continuum. (Originally published in 1970).

Sheafor, B., Horejsi, C. & Horejsi, G. (2000). *Techniques and guidelines for social work practice* (5th ed.). Boston: Allyn and Bacon.

Shields, K. (1994). *In the tiger's mouth: An empowerment guide for social action.* Philadelphia: PA: New Society.

Shor, I. (1980). *Critical teaching and everyday life.* Boston: South End Press.

Shulman, L. (1986). "The dynamics of mutual aid." In A. Gitterman & L. Shulman (Eds.) *The Legacy of William Schwartz* (pp. 51-60). Binghamton, NY: Haworth.

________. (1992). *The skills of helping individuals, families and groups* (3rd ed.). Itasca, IL: F. E. Peacock Publishers.

Sklar, H. (1995). *Chaos or community: Seeking solutions, not scapegoats for bad economics.* Boston: South End Press.

Smith, B. (1985). "Business, politics, and Indian land settlement in Montana, 1881-1904," *Canadian Journal of History*, 20(1), 45-64.

Smith, D. (1987). *The everyday world as problematic: A feminist sociology.* Toronto: University of Toronto Press.

________. (1990). *The conceptual practices of power: A feminist sociology of knowledge.* Boston: Northeastern University Press.

Solomon, B. (1976). *Black empowerment.* New York: Columbia University Press.

Spatz, D. (1997). "Welfare reform skips school" (pp. 15-18). *The Nation*, June 2.

Specht, H. & Courtney. M. (1994). *Unfaithful angels: How social work has abandoned its mission.* New York: Free Press.

Stack, C. (1974). *All our kin: Strategies for survival in a black community.* New York: Harper and Row.

________. (1990). "Different visions: Gender, culture, and moral reasoning." In F. Ginsberg & A. Lowenhaupt Tsing (Eds.), *Uncertain terms: Negotiating gender in American culture.* Boston: Beacon.

Stack, C. and Burton, L. (1993). "Kinscripts." *Journal of Comparative Family Studies,* 24, 157-170.

Stake, R.E. (1995). *The art of case study research.* Thousand Oaks, CA: Sage Publications.

Stern, M. (1997). "Poverty and postmodernity." In M. Reisch & E. Gambrill (Eds.), *Social work in the 21st century* (pp. 48-58). Thousand Oaks, CA: Pine Forge Press.

Strauss, A. & Corbin, J. (1990). *Basics of qualitative research: Grounded theory procedures and techniques.* Newbury Park, CA: Sage Publications, Inc.

Strom-Gottfried, K. (1999) *Social work practice: Cases, activities, and exercises.* Thousand Oaks, CA: Pine Forge Press.

Swigonski, M. (1994). "The logic of feminist standpoint theory for social work research." *Social Work,* 39 (4). 387-393.

Takaki, R. (1979). *Iron cages: Race and culture in nineteenth century America.* New York: Knopf.

________. (1993). *A different mirror: A history of multicultural America.* Boston: Little, Brown.

Thompson, E. P. (1966). *The making of the English working class.* New York: Vintage.

Thompson, L. (1992). "Feminist methodology for family studies." *Journal of Marriage and the Family,* 54, 3-18.

Thorne, B. & Yalom, M. (1982). *Rethinking the family: Some feminist questions.* New York: Longman.

Tice, K. (1998). *Tales of wayward girls and immoral women.* Chicago: University of Illinois Press.

Todd, A. J. (1920). *The scientific spirit and social work.* NY: Macmillan.

Tonn, M. (1996). "Militant motherhood: Labor's Mary Harris "Mother" Jones." *Quarterly Journal of Free Speech,* 82(10), 1-21.

Townsend, J., Zapata, E., Rowlands, J., Alberti, P. & Mercado, M. (1999). *Women and power: Fighting patriarchies and poverty.* London: Zed Books.

Tracy, E. and Whitakker, J. (1990). "The social support network map: Assessing social support in clinical practice." *Families in Society,* 71, 461-470.

Tropman, J. (1984). *Policy management in the human services.* New York: Columbia University Press.

Tuhiwai Smith, L. (1999). *Decolonizing methodologies: research and indigenous peoples.* London: Zed.

Turner, T. (1997). "Human rights, human difference: Anthropology's contribution to an emancipatory cultural politics." *Journal of Anthropological Research*, 53(3), 273-291.

UNAIDS (1999). "HIV/AIDS in Africa: A socioeconomic response." Geneva/New York: Joint UN Programme on HIV/AIDS.

United States Catholic Bishops (1986). "Economic justice for all: Pastoral letter on Catholic social teaching and the U.S. economy." Washington, DC: National Conference of Catholic Bishops.

Valenstein, E. (1986). *Great and desperate cures: The rise and decline of psychosurgery and other radical treatments for mental illness.* New York: Basic Books, Inc.

Van Kleeck, M. (1913). *Artificial flower makers*. New York: Russell Sage Foundation

________ (1917). *A seasonal industry: A study of the millinery trade in New York.* New York: Russell Sage Foundation.

________. (1991). "Our illusions regarding government." *Journal of Progressive Human Services,* 2(1), 75-86. (Originally published in 1934).

Vollers, M. & Barnett, A. (2000). "Libby's deadly Grace." *Mother Jones* (May/June), 53-59, 87.

Wade, C. & Travis, C. (1999) *Invitation to psychology.* New York: Longman.

Wagner, D. (2000). *What's love got to do with it? A critical look at American charity.* New York: The New Press.

Wakefield, J. (1988a). "Psychotherapy, distributive justice, and social work: Part I – Distributive justice as a conceptual framework for social work." *Social Service Review*, 62(2), 187-210.

________. (1988b). "Psychotherapy, distributive justice, and social work: Part II – Psychotherapy and the pursuit of justice." *Social Service Review,* 62(3), 353-382.

Washburn, W. (Ed.). (1973). *The American Indian and the United States: A documentary history, V. I* and *II.* New York: Random House.

Watzalawick, P., Bavelas, J. & Jackson, D. (1967). *Pragmatics of human communication.* New York: W. W. Norton

Webster's New Universal Unabridged Dictionary (1983). (2nd ed.). New York: New World Dictionaries/ Simon and Schuster.

Weedon, C. (1997). *Feminist practice and poststructuralist theory.* Oxford: Basil Blackwell.

Weiler, K. (1988). *Women teaching for change: Gender, class and power*. New York: Bergin & Garvey.

Wells, H. G. (1911). *The country of the blind and other stories.* New York: T. Nelson and Sons.

Wenocur, S. and Reisch, M. (1989). *From charity to enterprise: The development of American social work in a market economy.* Chicago: University of Illinois Press.

Werner, D. (1977). *Where there is no doctor: A village health care handbook.* Palo Alto, CA: The Hesperian Foundation.

West, C. (1993). *Race matters.* New York: Vintage.

Whitakker, J. Schinke, S., & Gilchrist, L. (1986). "The ecological paradigm in child, youth, and family services: Implications for policy and practice." *Social Service Review,* 60, 483-503.

White, M. & Tyson-Rawson, K. (1995). "Assessing the dynamics of gender in couples and families." *Family Relations,* 11, 253-259.

Whitmore, E. & Wilson, M. (1997). "Accompanying the process: Social work and international development practice." *International Social Work,* 40 (1), 57-74.

Williams, M., Unrau, Y., & Grinnell, R. (1998). *Introduction to social work research.* Itasca, IL: F.E. Peacock Publishers.

Williams, R. (1997). *Marxism and literature.* Oxford: Oxford University Press.

________. (1980). *Problems in Marxism and culture.* Oxford: Oxford University Press.

Willis, P. (1981). *Learning to labor: How working class kids get working class jobs.* New York: Columbia. (Originally published in 1977).

Wilson, M. & Whitmore, E. (1995). "Accompanying the process: Principles for international development practice." *International Social Work*, 40(1), 57-74.

Withorn, A. (1984). *Serving the people: Social services and social change.* New York: Columbia University Press.

________. (1998). "No win... facing the ethical perils of welfare reform." *Families in Society*, 79, 277-287.

Witkin, S. (1998). "Human rights and social work." *Social Work,* 43(3), 197-201.

Wrong, D. (1995). *Power: Its forms, bases and uses*. New Brunswick, NJ: Transaction.

Yeich, S. (1996). "Grassroots organizing with homeless people: A participatory research approach." *Journal of Social Issues*, 52(1), 111-121.

Yin, R. (1994). *Case study research: Design and methods*. Thousand Oaks, CA: Sage Publications.

Zavella, P. (1987). *Women's work and Chicano families.* Ithaca: Cornell University Press.

Zimbalist, S. (1977). *Historic themes and landmarks in social welfare research.* New York: Harper & Row.

Zinn, H. (1970). *The politics of history*. Boston: Beacon Press.

________ . (1995). *A peoples' history of the United States.* New York: Harper Perennial. (Originally published in 1980).

Permissions and Credits

Global Income Distribution (Figure 1.1) reprinted from *The Human Development Report, 1992,* (c. 1992 by United Nations Development Programme) by permission of Oxford University Press, Inc.

American Anthropological Association Statement on Race reprinted with permission of the American Anthropological Association, Arlington, VA.

The essay "Red Clay, Blue Hills," by John Brown Childs is reprinted here with permission of the author.

Quotation from Myles Horton (c. 1998) *The Long Haul*, New York: Teachers College Press, Columbia University, p. 51, reprinted with permission of the Publishers. All rights reserved.

Permission to reprint excerpt from *Jeannette Rankin Commemorative Booklet*, Bloomington, IN: Organization of American Historians, courtesy of the Organization of American Historians.

The National Association of Black Social Workers Code of Ethics is reproduced here with the permission of the National Association of Black Social Workers. Detroit, MI.

Permission to reprint "The Ethics of Social Work: Principles and Standards," of the International Federation of Social Workers (IFSW) courtesy of IFSW, Berne Switzerland.

The "Social Class Questionnaire" was used in an undergraduate course in American Civilization entitled "Basic Issues in American Culture," taught at Brown University by Professor Susan Smulyan. It is reproduced here courtesy of *Radical Teacher*, where it was originally published in Spring, 1995.

Summary discussion from Phyllis J. Day (c. 2000). *A New History of Social Welfare*, 3rd ed., pp. 4-12, adapted and printed by permission of Allyn & Bacon, Boston, MA.

Permission to print principles adapted from Dennis Saleebey (c. 1990), "Philosophical disputes in social work: Social justice denied," *Journal of Sociology and Social Welfare* 17(2), p. 37, courtesy of *Journal of Sociology and Social Welfare.*

Permission to reproduce quotation from b. hooks (c.1994). *Teaching to Trangress* New York: Routledge, p. 59, courtesy of Routledge, Inc., part of the Taylor & Francis Group.

Permission to reproduce S. Cisneros (c.1984 by Sandra Cisneros) "Those Who Don't" from *The House on Mango Street* courtesy of Susan Bergholz Literary Services, New York. All rights reserved. Published by Vintage Books, a division of Random House, Inc., and in hardcover by Alfred A. Knopf in 1994.

Permission to print summary discussion and accompanying figure of the "Genogram" based on A. Hartman (c. 1978). "Diagrammatic assessment of family relationships," *Social Casework,* 59(8), 465-476 courtesy of Sage Publications, Inc.

Permission to print summary discussion and adaptation of the "Ecomap" courtesy of Ann Hartman and Joan Laird.

Permission to print summary discussion and reproduce chart of the culturagram from E. Congress (c. 1994), "The use of culturagrams to assess and empower culturally diverse families," *Families in Society: The Journal of Contemporary Human Services* 75(9), 531-539, courtesy of *Families in Society.*

Permission to reproduce adaptation from J. Barber (c. 1995) "Politically progressive casework, " *Families in Society: The Journal of Contemporary Human Services* 76(1), pp. 31-32, courtesy of *Families in Society.*

Permission to reproduce summary discussion of the Social Network Map and Grid along with figures of the map and grid from E. Tracy and J. Whitakker (c. 1990). "The social network map: assessing social support in clinical practice," *Families in Society.* 71(8), pp. 461-470, courtesy of *Families in Society.*

Permission to draw from Carol Thuman, Jane Maxwell and David Werner (c. 1977), "Words to the Village Health Worker" in *Where There Is No Doctor* courtesy of the Hesperian Foundation, Berkeley, California.

Excerpt from Jane Addams, *Twenty Years at Hull House* (c 1960 by The Saturday Review) used by permission of Signet, a division of Penguin Putnam, Inc.

Permission to reprint excerpts from Rinku Sen (c. 1994), "Building community involvement in health care, " *Social Policy* 24(3), pp. 32-43, courtesy of *Social Policy.* Copyright by Social Policy Corporation.

Excerpts from Lawrence Shulman (c. 1992), "The Processes of Mutual Aid" in *The Skills of Helping Individuals and Families* (3rd Ed.) reproduced by permission of the publisher, F. E. Peacock Publishers, Inc, Itasca, IL.

Adaptation from Naomi Brill *Working with People: The Helping Process* (6th ed., c. 1998 by Allyn & Bacon) pp. 96-102, printed by permission of Allyn & Bacon, Boston, MA.

Permission to reprint new article by Candace Page, "The Lost Boys of Sudan: The Newest Vermonters"(13 May 2001), in its entirety, courtesy of *The Burlington Free Press,* Burlington, VT.

Permission to print summary discussion of policy practice based on Josefina Figueira-McDonough (c. 1993), "Policy practice: The neglected side of social work intervention," *Social Work* 38(2), pp. 179-188 courtesy of the National Association of Social Workers, Washington, DC.

Excerpts from S. Mayer (c. 1996) "Building community capacity with evaluation activities that empower" in D.M. Fetterman, S.J. Faftarian & A. Wandersman (Eds.) *Empowerment Evaluation: Knowledge and Tools for Self-Assessment and Accountability*, pp. 335-337 reproduced by permission of Sage Publications, Inc.

The Universal Declaration of Human Rights is a public document. The text printed here is from the Human Rights Center, University of Minnesota, Minneapolis, MN. Please see the Center's website at www.hrusa.org for further information.

Permission to reprint Table 1: "Comparison of policy formulation process based on the problem-centered approach and the strengths approach" from R. K. Chapin (c. 1995) "Social policy development: The strengths perspective." *Social Work*, 40(4), p. 510 courtesy of the National Association of Social Workers, Washington, DC.

Excerpts from F. M. Lappe and P. M. DuBois (c.1994). *The Quickening of America: Rebuilding our Nation, Remaking our Lives*, used by permission of John Wiley & Sons, Inc, New York.

Permission to print summary discussion based on D. Saleebey (c. 1994), "Culture, theory and narrative: The intersection of meaning and practice," *Social Work* 39(4), p. 355, courtesy of the National Association of Social Workers.

Permission to reproduce quote from B. C. Reynolds (c. 1963), *An Uncharted Journey: Fifty Years in Social Work by One of Its Great Teachers*, p. 173-174 courtesy of the National Association of Social Workers, Washington, DC..

Permission to reprint excerpt from L. Leblanc (c. 1999 by Lauraine Leblanc). *Pretty in Punk: Girls' Gender Resistance in a Boys' Subculture* courtesy of Rutgers University Press.

Permission to print summary discussion and excerpts from A. Boyd (c. 1999). *The Activist Cookbook: Creative Action for a Fair Economy*, pp 1-2, 28, courtesy of United for a Fair Economy, Boston, MA.

Permission to reproduce excerpts from C. Brown and G. Mazza (c. 1997) *Healing into Action*, pp. 63-64 courtesy of the National Coalition Building Institute, Washington, D.C.

Permission to reproduce adaptations and excerpts from A. Hope and S. Timmell (c.1984, Rev. 1995, from 1999 reprint) *Training for Transformation: A Handbook for Community Workers, Books 1-4* courtesy of Intermediate Technology Development Group Publishing, London.

Permission to print summary discussion of "Defusing Skills" from C. Confer (c.1987) *Managing Anger: Yours and Mine* courtesy of American Foster Care Resources, Inc.

Summary discussion from Billy D. Horton (1993), "The Appalachian land ownership study: Research and citizen action in Appalachia. In Peter Park, Mary Brydon-Miller, Budd Hall, and Ted Jackson (Eds.). *Voices of Changes: Participatory Research in the United States and Canada.* Westport, CT: Bergin & Gavery, pp. 85-102, printed with permission of Greenwoods Publishing Group, Westport, CT.

Permission to print excerpts from K. Shields (c. 1994), "How Burnout Prone is my organization" and "Fireproofing my organization" in *In the Tiger's Mouth: An Empowerment Guide for Social Action*, courtesy of New Society Publishers, Philadelphia, PA.

Permission to reprint quotation from M. Horton (c. 1998). *The Long Haul: An Autobiography*, New York: Teachers College Press, p. 51, courtesy of Teachers College Press, Columbia University.

Permission to reproduce quotation from D. Harvey (c. 2000 David Harvey). *Spaces of Hope*, Berkeley: The University of California Press, p. 281, as chapter epigraph courtesy of The University of California Press.

Permission to reproduce quotation from P. Freire (c. 1999). *Pedagogy of Hope*, New York, Continuum, p. 9, courtesy of The Continuum International Publishing Group.

Index